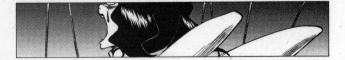

Endlessly adorned
Knowing it will be cut off,

Endlessly polished
Knowing they will be cut off,

They are terrifying, terrifying
In their fall.

The hair flutters to the ground
A lifeless husk.

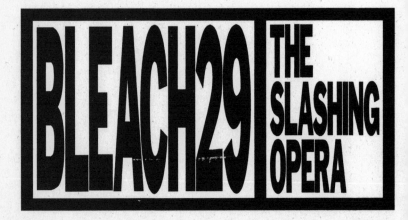

BLEACH 29 THE SLASHING OPERA

Hair and fingernails
Are beautiful ornaments.
So why do they seem so baleful
When removed?
The answer is simple.
They are
Previews of what is to come, of death.

STARS AND

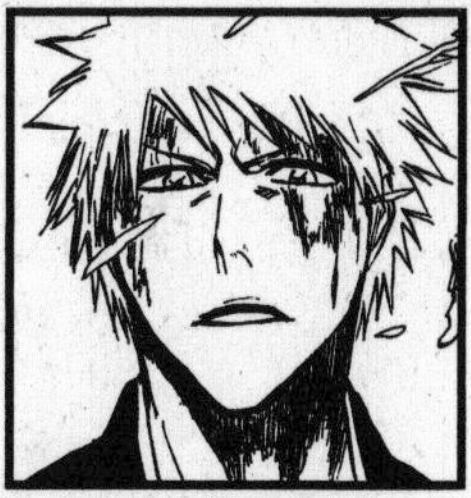

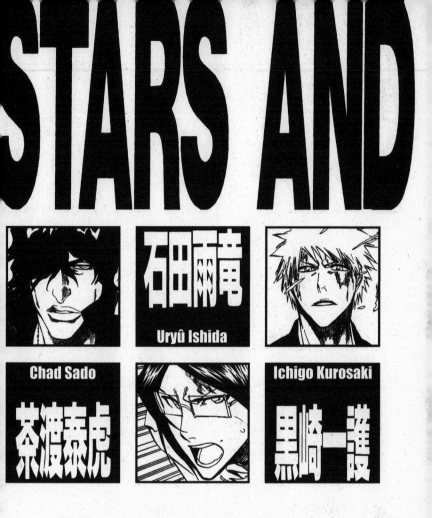

石田雨竜
Uryû Ishida

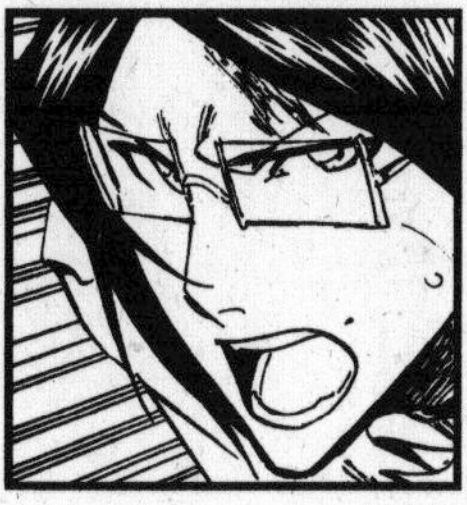

Ichigo Kurosaki
黒崎一護

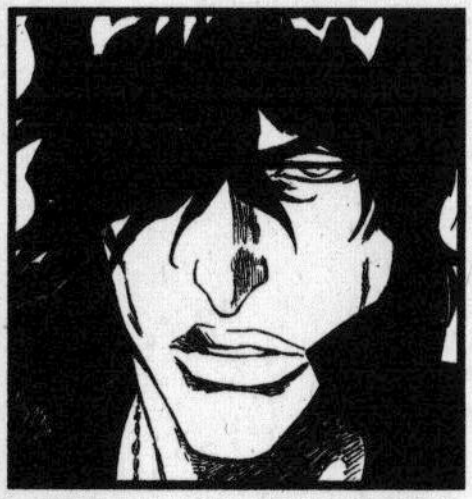

Chad Sado
茶渡泰虎

plot

When high school student Ichigo Kurosaki meets Soul Reaper Rukia Kuchiki his life is changed forever. Soon Ichigo is a soul-cleansing Soul Reaper too, and he finds himself having adventures–and problems–he never could have imagined. Now Ichigo and his friends face their greatest challenge yet in the form of the renegade Soul Reaper Aizen and his army of Arrancars, who are bent on killing the king of the Soul Society and wiping out Karakura in the process.

As the war with Aizen's forces looms, Orihime is abducted to Hueco Mundo and Ichigo and his friends defy orders to go after her. They are soon befriended by a little Arrancar named Nel and learn the location of Aizen's stronghold, Las Noches. Now, separated from his comrades, Ichigo finds himself locked in battle with a Privaron Espada named Dordoni, who demands to see Ichigo's Bankai!

BLEACH ALL STORIES

ネル

Nel

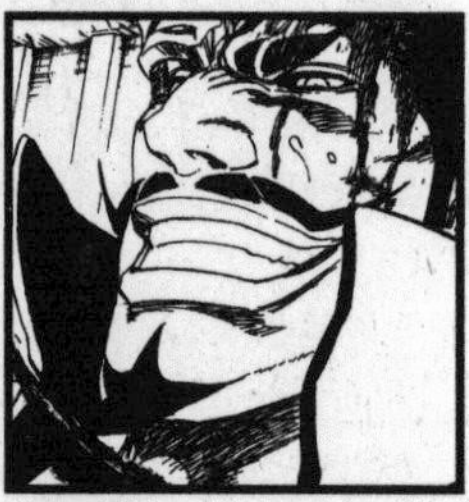

チルッチ

Cirucci

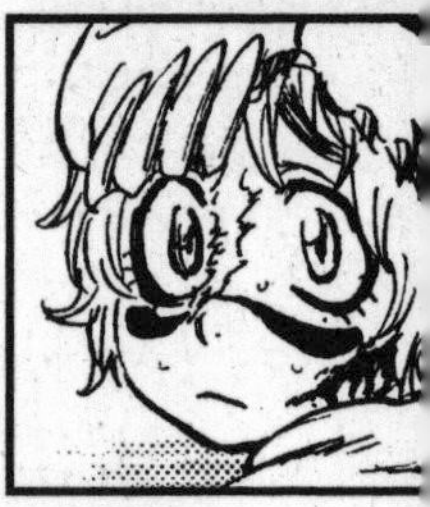

Dordoni

ドルドーニ

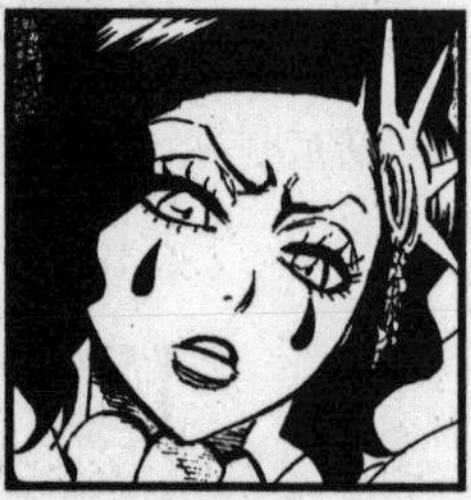

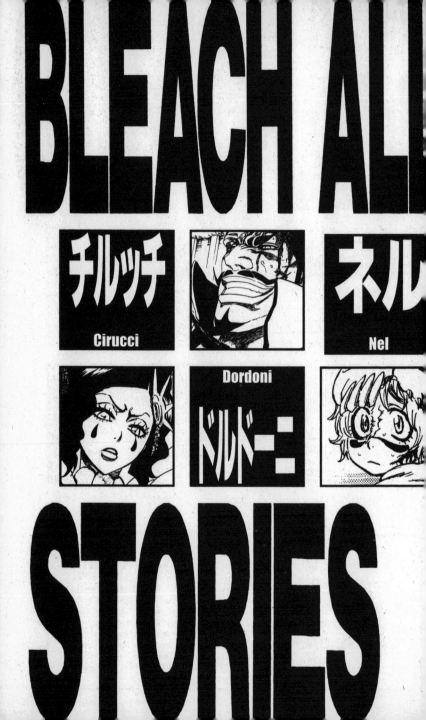

BLEACH 29

THE SLASHING OPERA

Contents

252. REBUT TO THE BARON'S LECTURE	7
253. Don't Call Me Niño	31
254. Leave the Chocolate Here	51
255. DON'T BREATHE IN THE BUSH	71
256. Infinite Slick	91
257. The Slashing Opera	111
258. Seeleschneider	131
259. Flicker Flames	151
260. RIGHTARM OF THE GIANT2	171

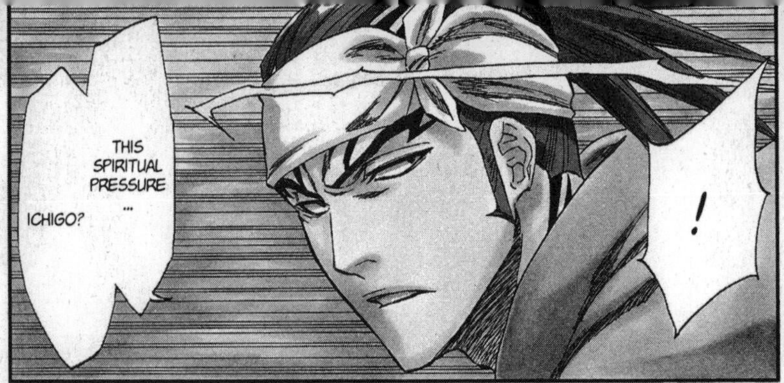
!
THIS SPIRITUAL PRESSURE ...
ICHIGO?

252. REBUT TO THE BARON'S LECTURE

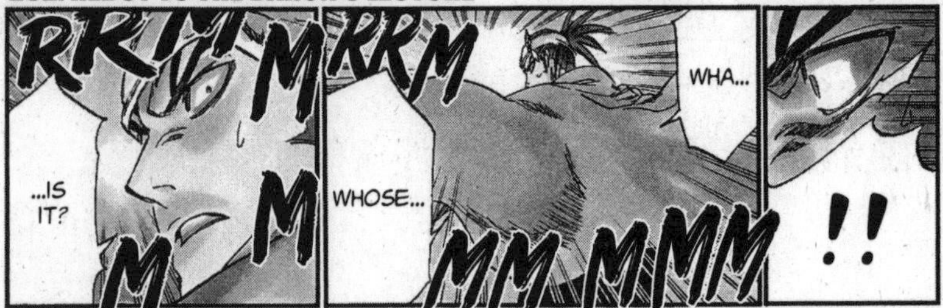
!!
WHA...
WHOSE...
MRRM
MM MMMM
RRMM
M M
...IS IT?
M M

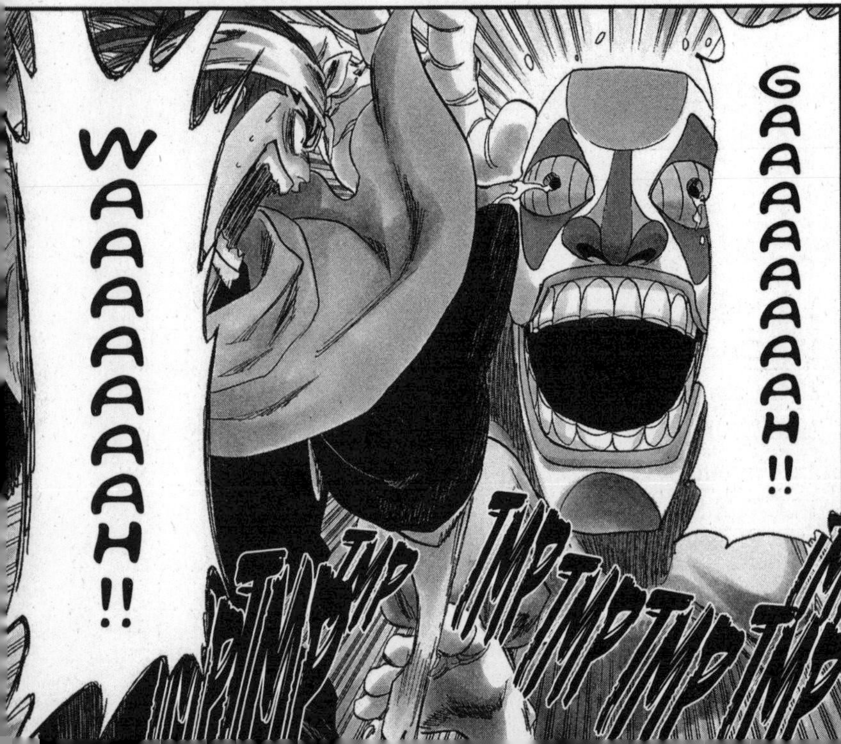
GAAAAAAAAAH!!
WAAAAAAAAAAH!!
THMP THMP THMP THMP THMP THMP

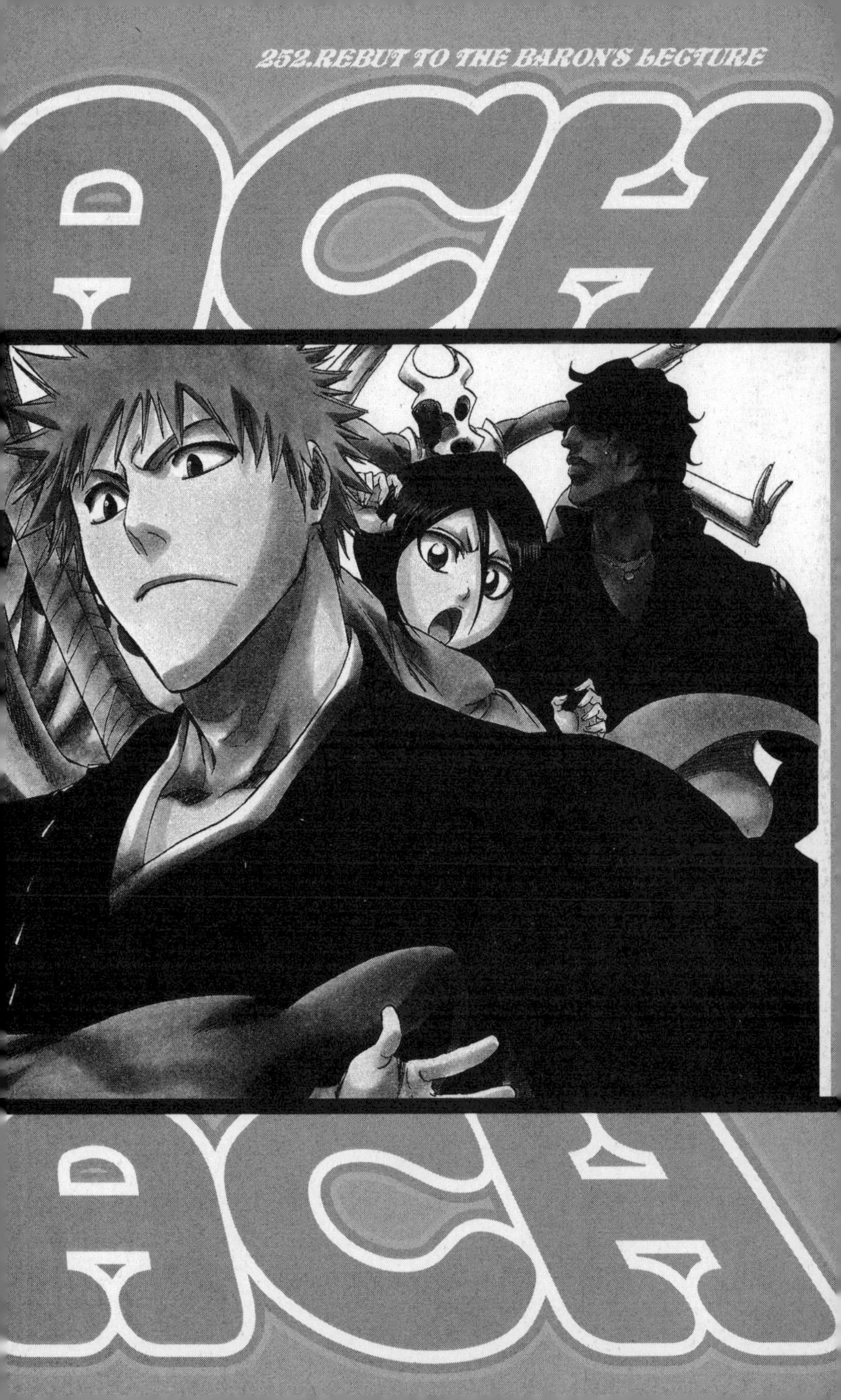
252.REBUT TO THE BARON'S LECTURE

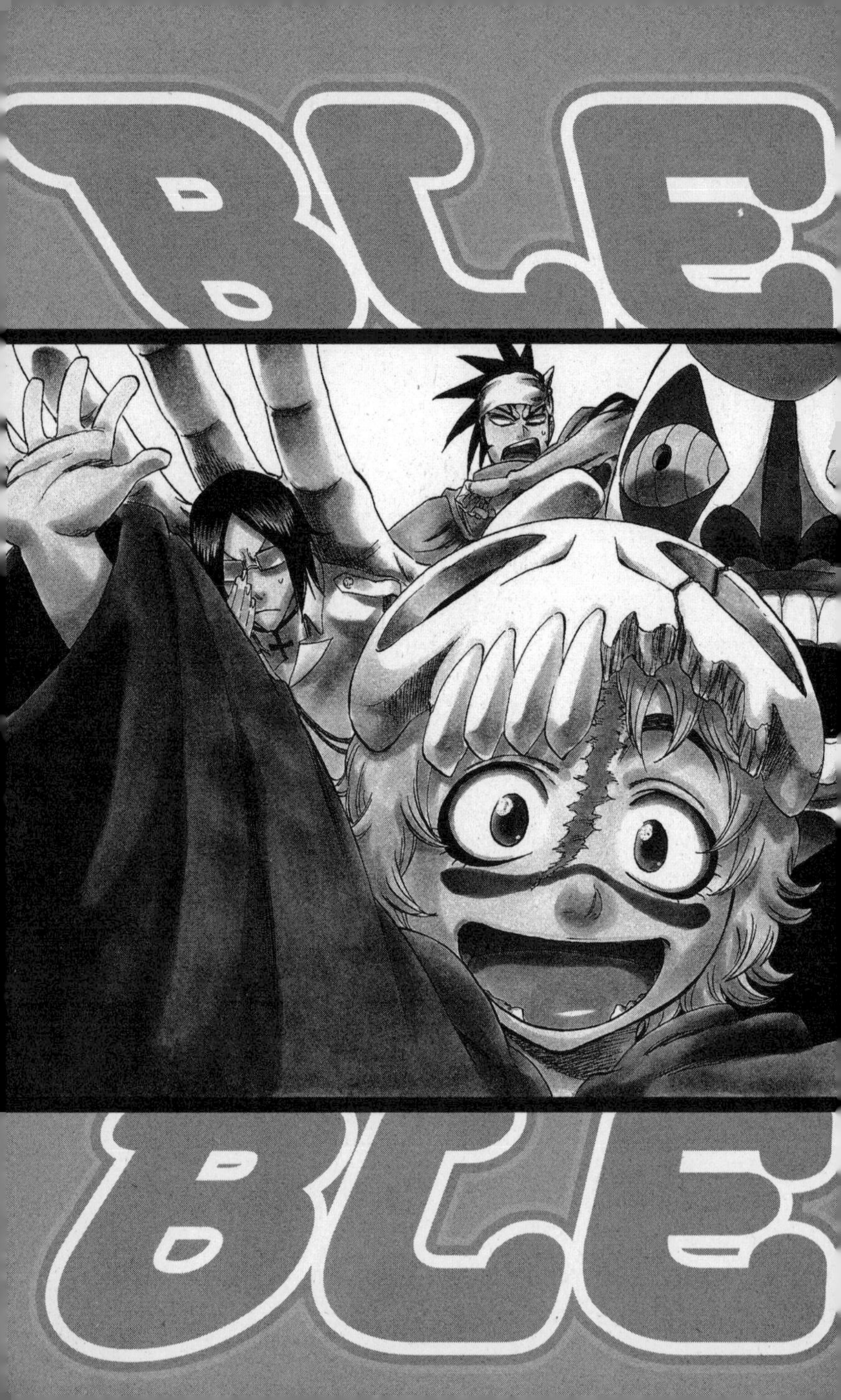
BLE
BLE

BLEACH
ブリーチ

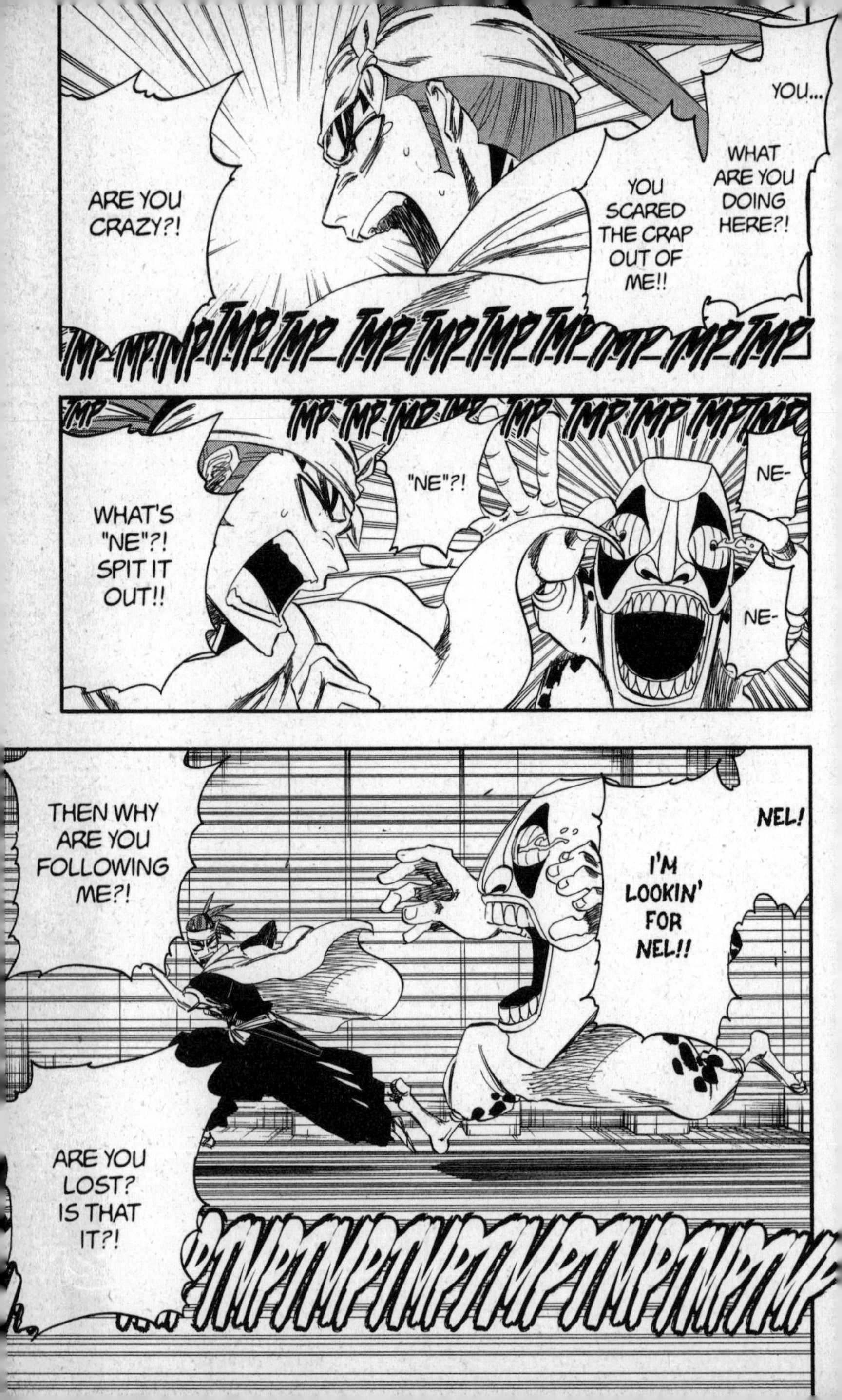
YOU...
WHAT ARE YOU DOING HERE?!
YOU SCARED THE CRAP OUT OF ME!!
ARE YOU CRAZY?!
TMP TMP TMP TMP TMP TMP TMP TMP TMP TMP TMP TMP
TMP TMP TMP TMP TMP TMP TMP TMP
NE-
NE-
"NE"?!
WHAT'S "NE"?! SPIT IT OUT!!
NEL!
I'M LOOKIN' FOR NEL!!
THEN WHY ARE YOU FOLLOWING ME?!
ARE YOU LOST? IS THAT IT?!
TMP TMP TMP TMP TMP TMP TMP TMP TMP TMP

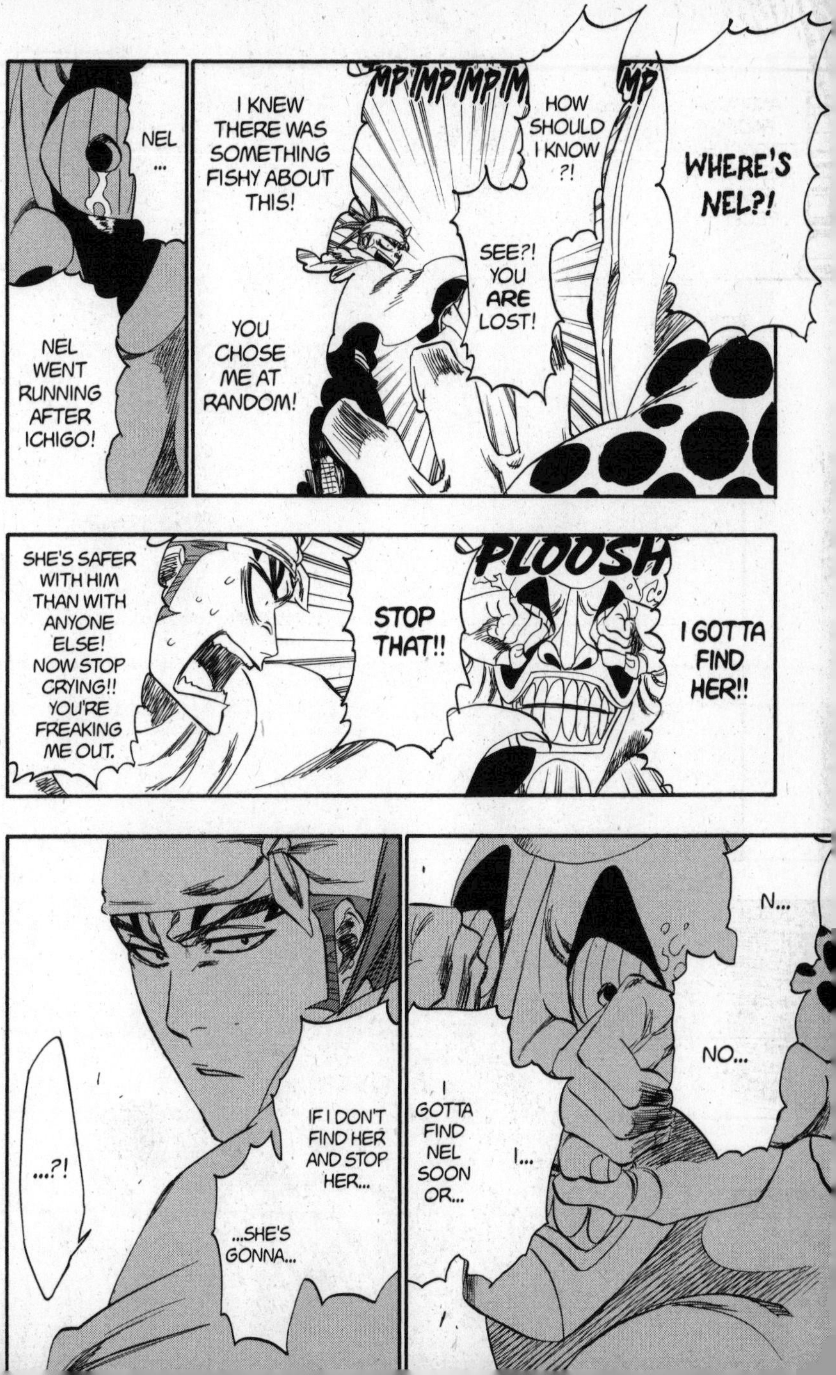
WHERE'S NEL?!
MP IMP IMP IM MP
HOW SHOULD I KNOW ?!
I KNEW THERE WAS SOMETHING FISHY ABOUT THIS!
SEE?! YOU **ARE** LOST!
YOU CHOSE ME AT RANDOM!
NEL ...
NEL WENT RUNNING AFTER ICHIGO!
I GOTTA FIND HER!!
PLOOSH
STOP THAT!!
SHE'S SAFER WITH HIM THAN WITH ANYONE ELSE! NOW STOP CRYING!! YOU'RE FREAKING ME OUT.
N...
NO...
I...
I GOTTA FIND NEL SOON OR...
IF I DON'T FIND HER AND STOP HER...
...SHE'S GONNA...
...?!

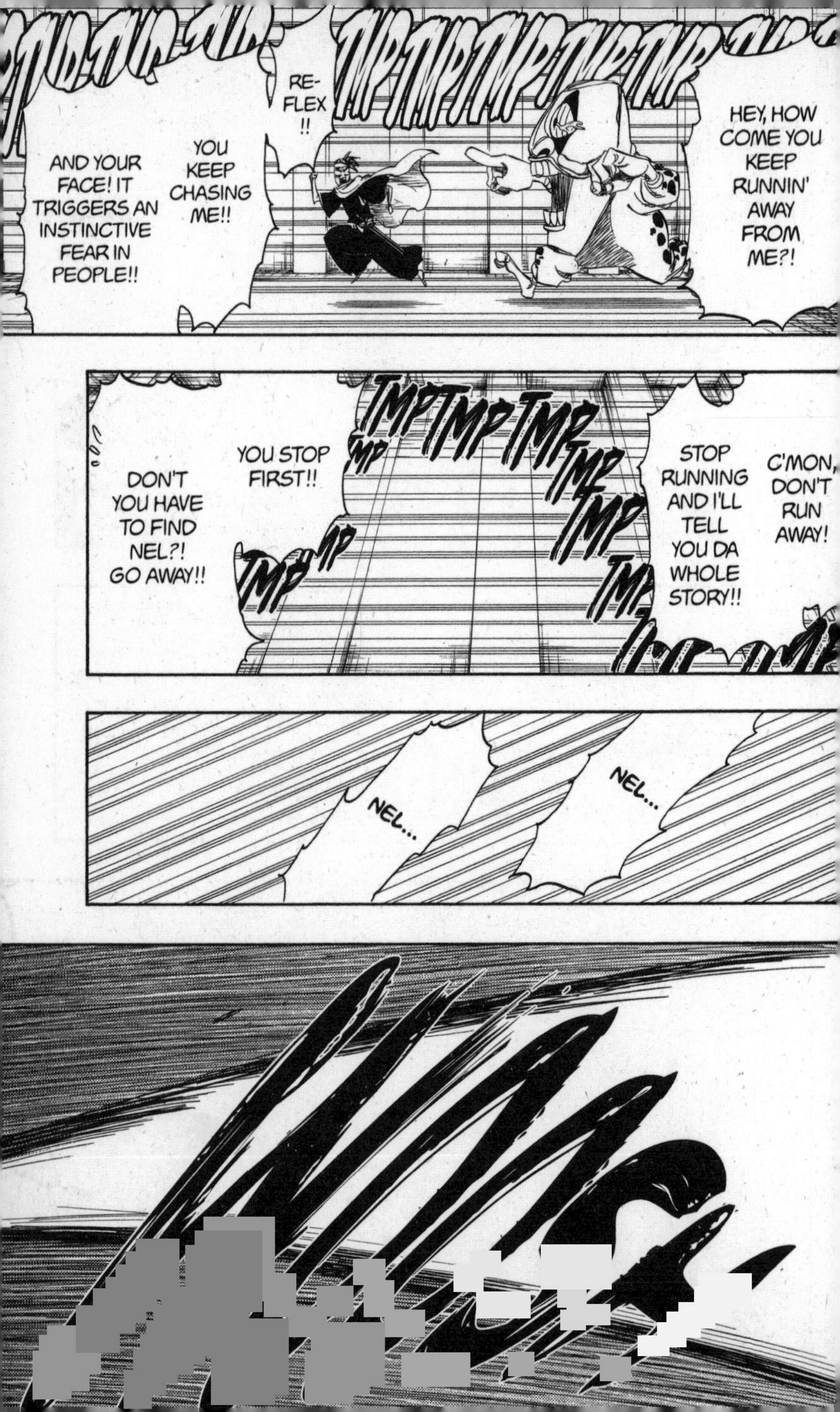

HEY, HOW COME YOU KEEP RUNNIN' AWAY FROM ME?!
RE-FLEX!!
YOU KEEP CHASING ME!!
AND YOUR FACE! IT TRIGGERS AN INSTINCTIVE FEAR IN PEOPLE!!
C'MON, DON'T RUN AWAY!
STOP RUNNING AND I'LL TELL YOU DA WHOLE STORY!!
YOU STOP FIRST!!
DON'T YOU HAVE TO FIND NEL?! GO AWAY!!
NEL...
NEL...

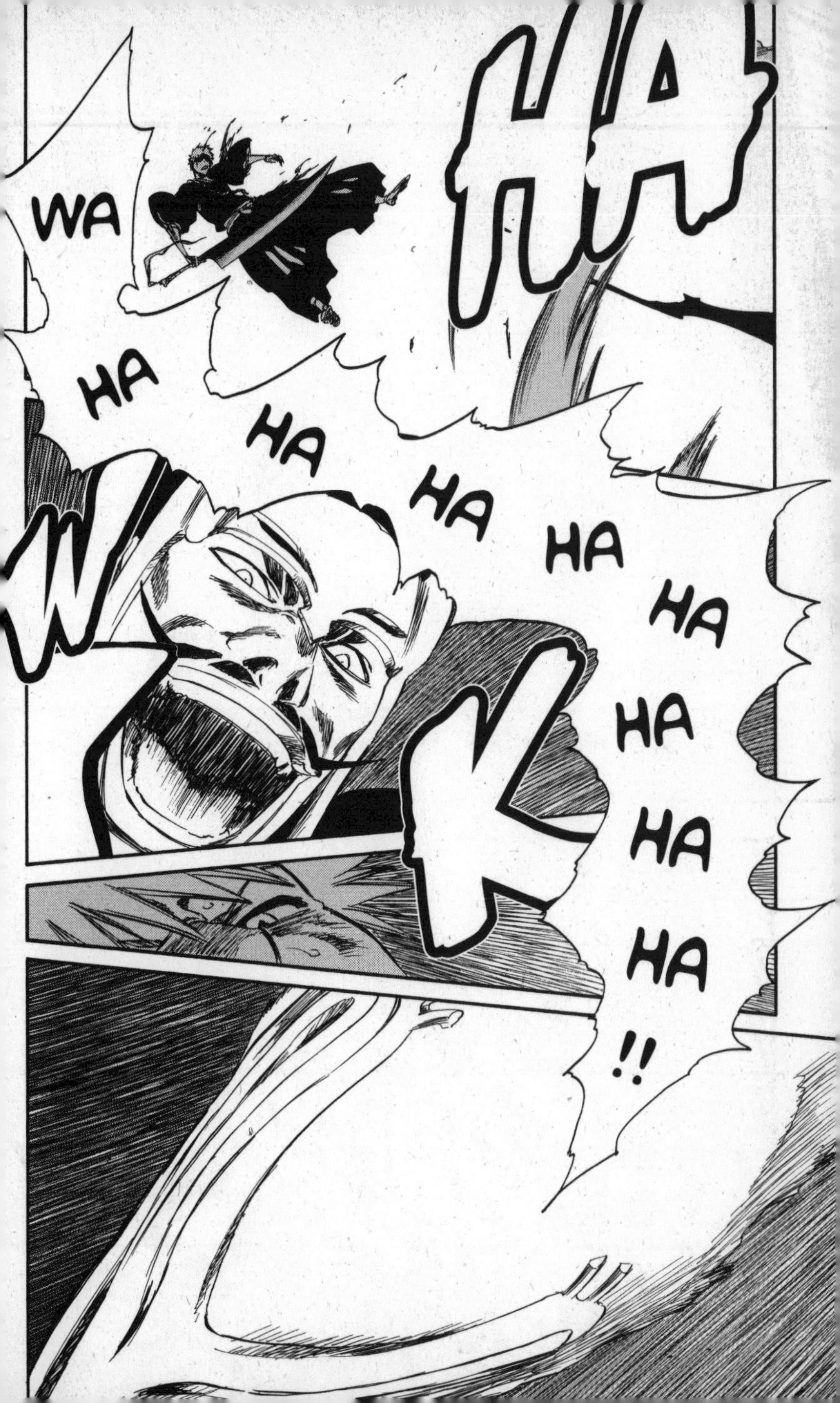
WA
HA
HA
HA
HA
HA
HA
HA
HA
!!

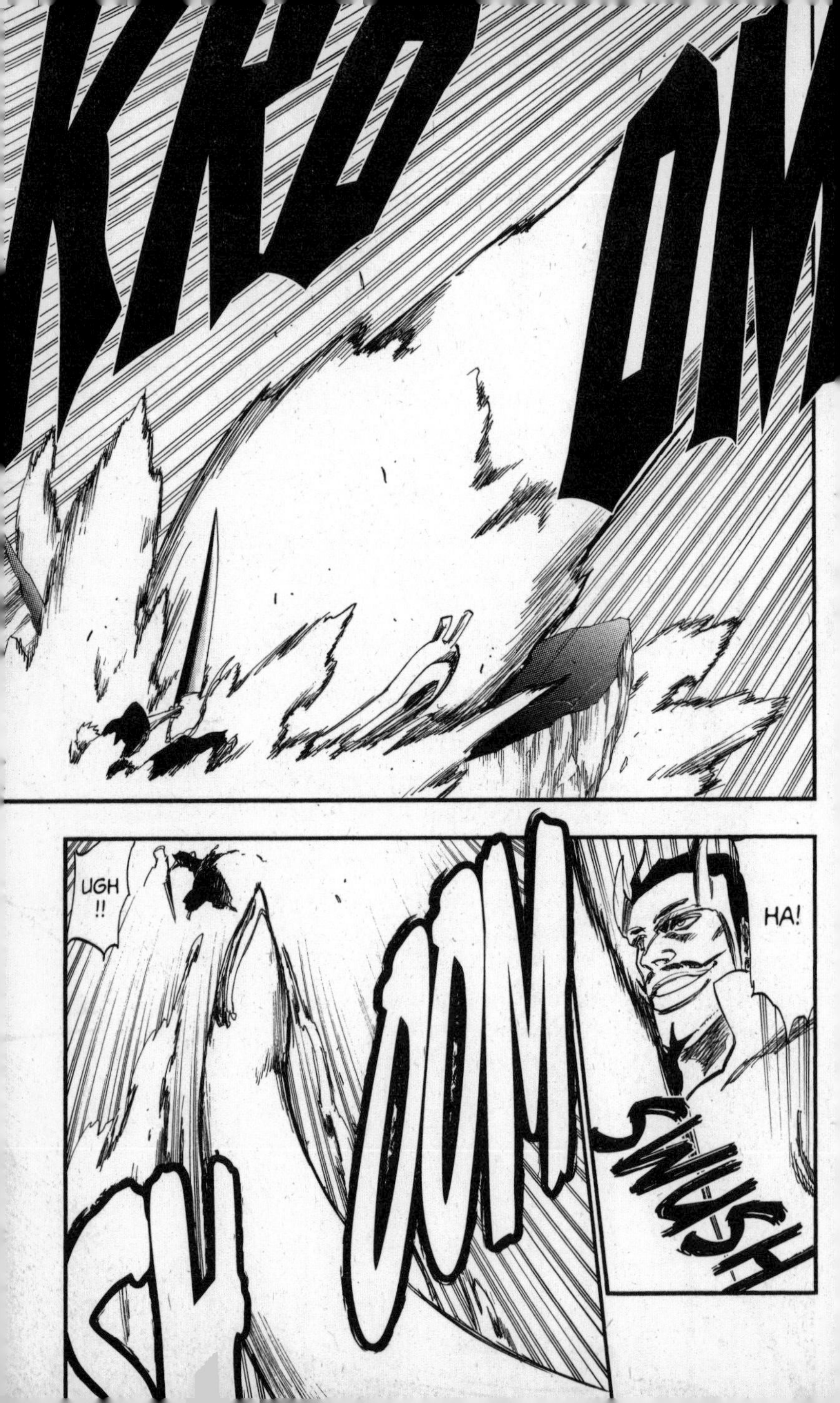
HA!
SWISH
UGH !!
DOOM

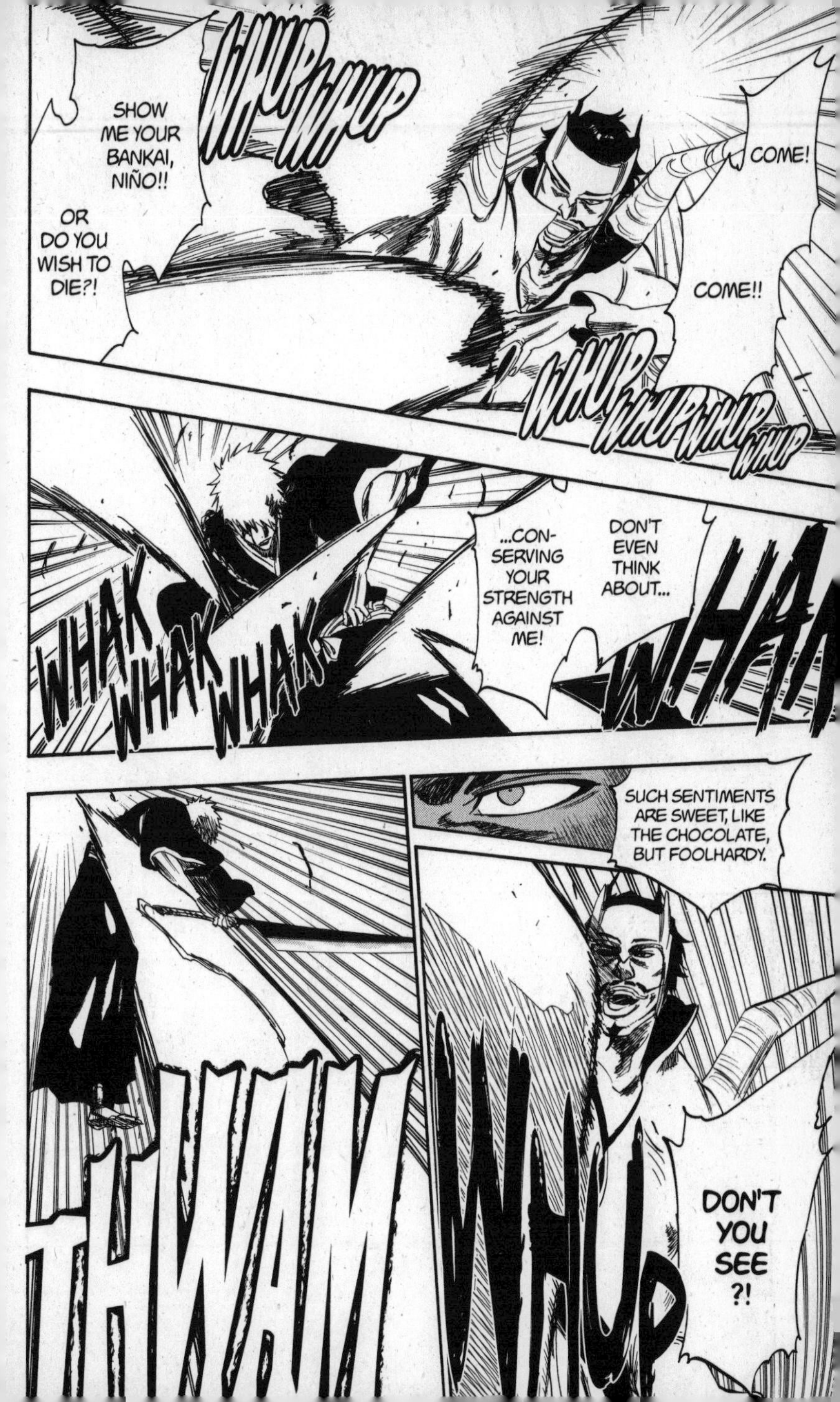
COME!
COME!!
WHUP WHUP
SHOW ME YOUR BANKAI, NIÑO!!
OR DO YOU WISH TO DIE?!
WHUP WHUP WHUP WHUP
WHAK
DON'T EVEN THINK ABOUT...
...CON-SERVING YOUR STRENGTH AGAINST ME!
WHAK WHAK WHAK
SUCH SENTIMENTS ARE SWEET, LIKE THE CHOCOLATE, BUT FOOLHARDY.
DON'T YOU SEE?!
WHUP
THWAM

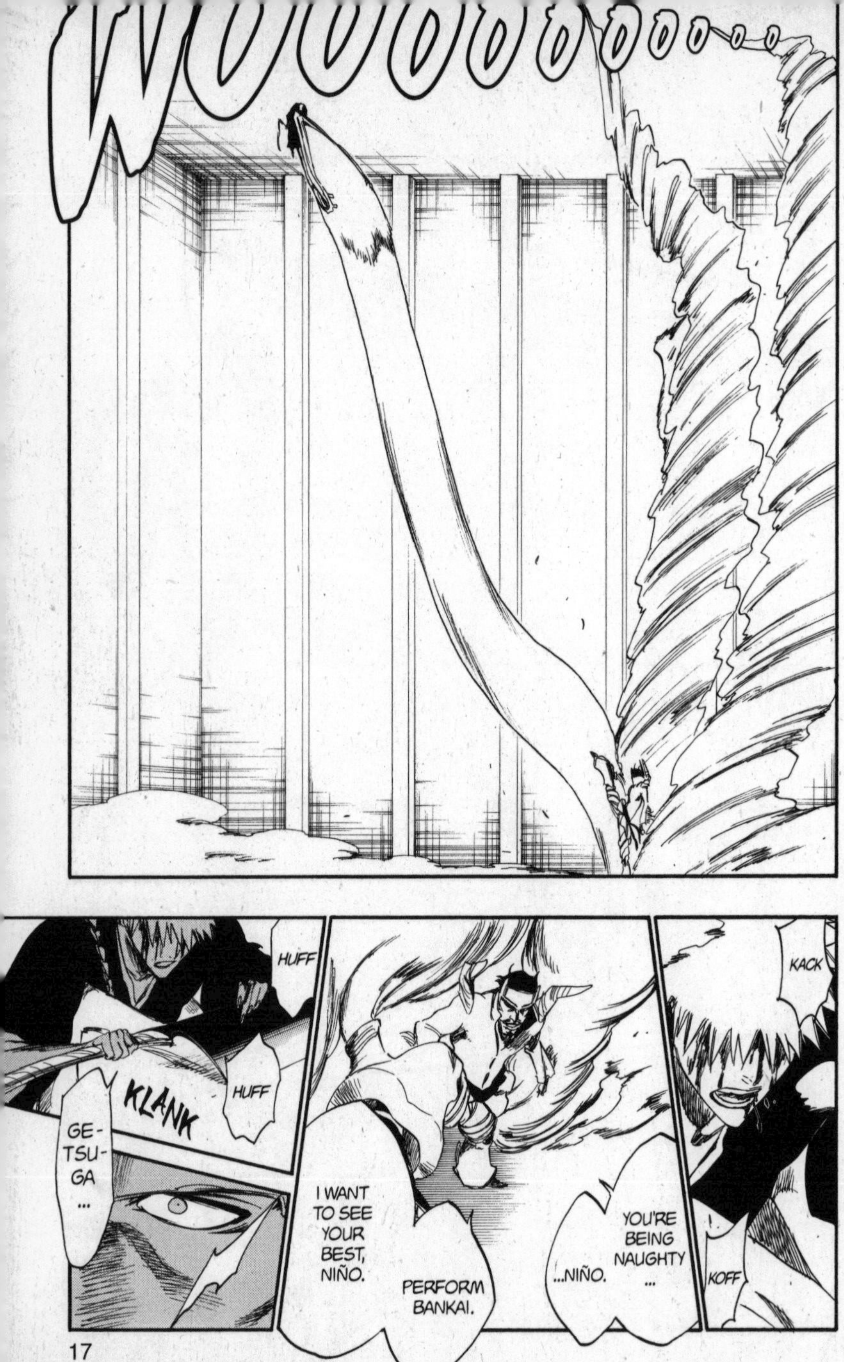
WOOOOOOOOOOO
KACK
KOFF
YOU'RE BEING NAUGHTY ...
...NIÑO.
I WANT TO SEE YOUR BEST, NIÑO.
PERFORM BANKAI.
HUFF
HUFF
KLANK
GE-TSU-GA ...

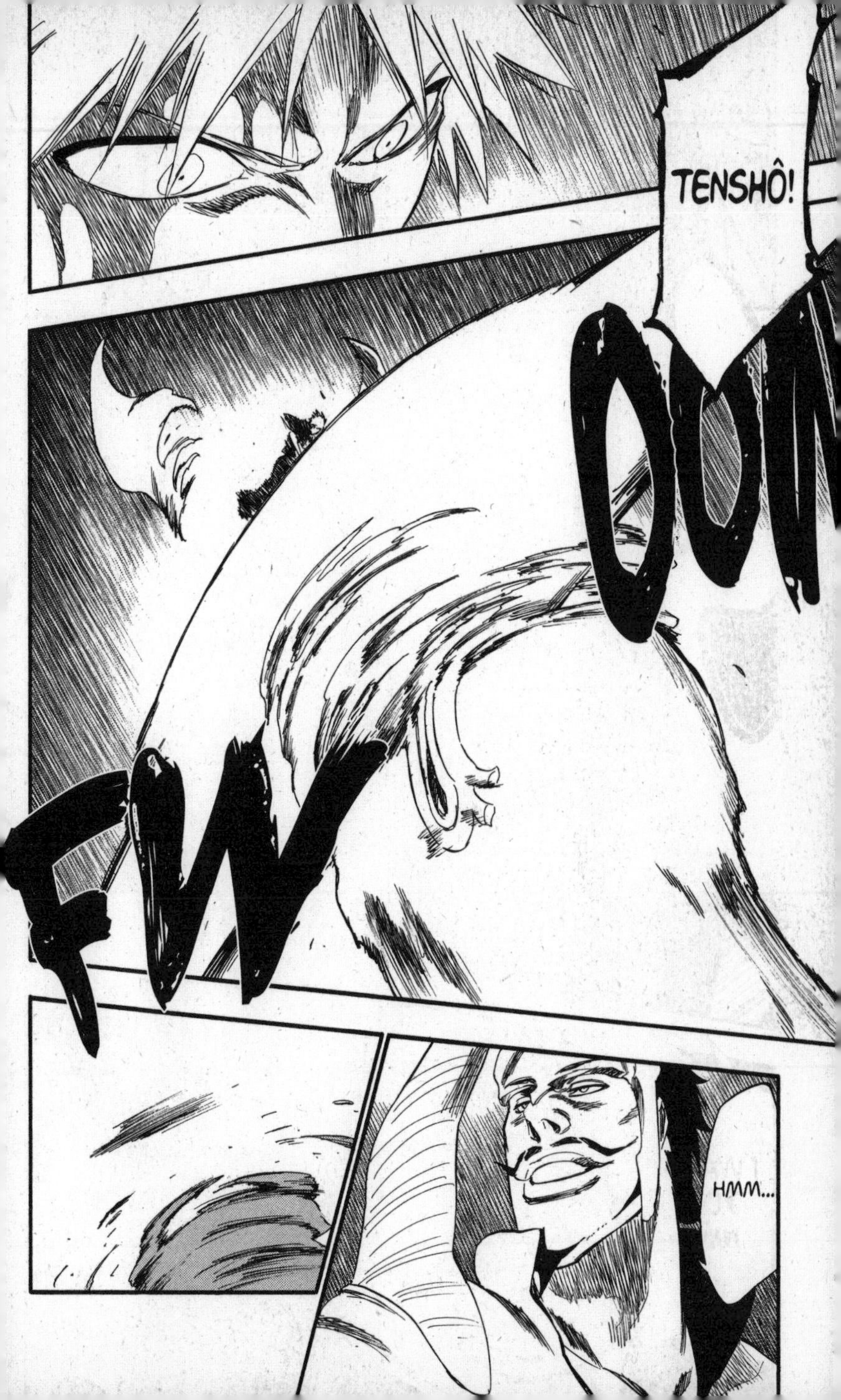
TENSHÔ!
OOM
FW
HMM...

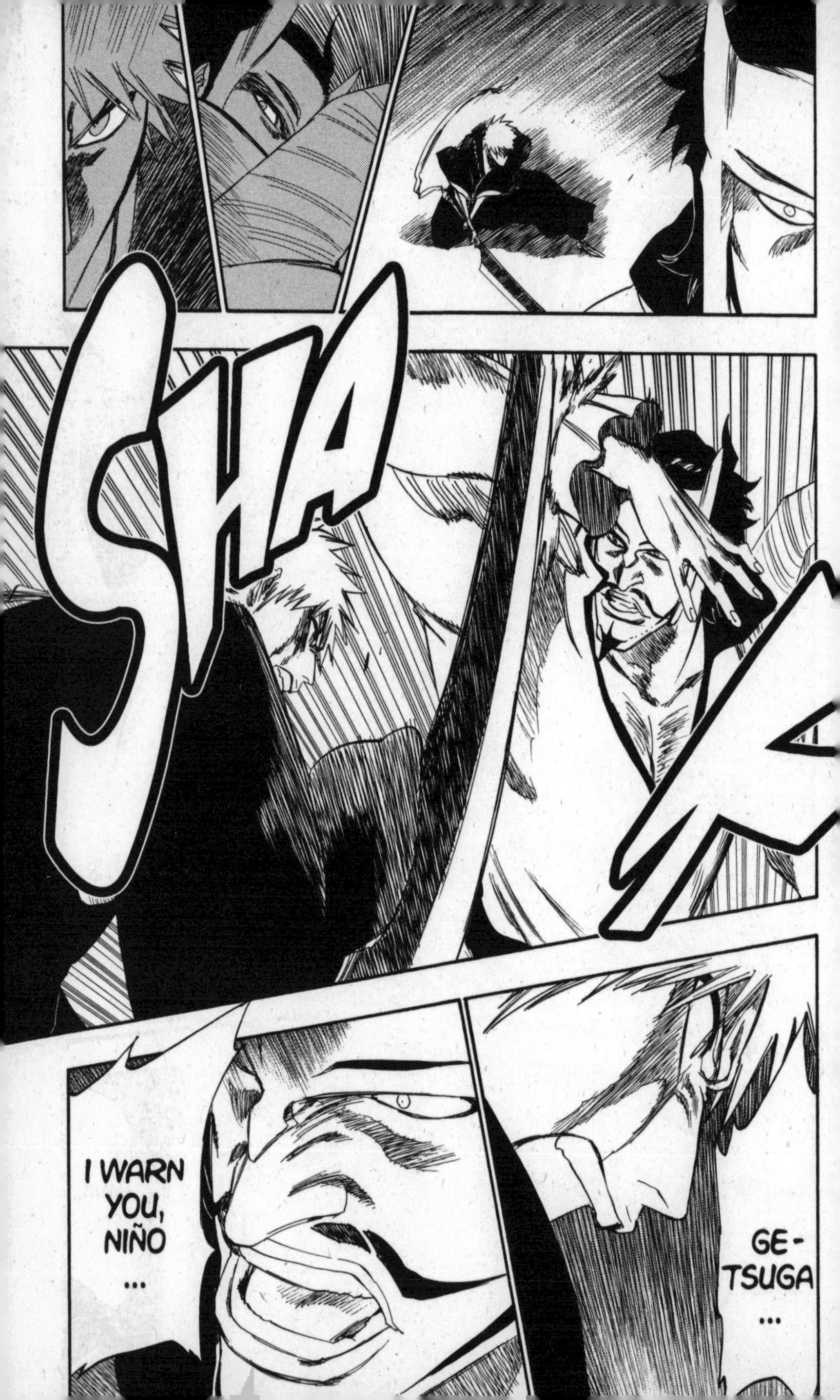
SHA
GE-TSUGA...
I WARN YOU, NIÑO...

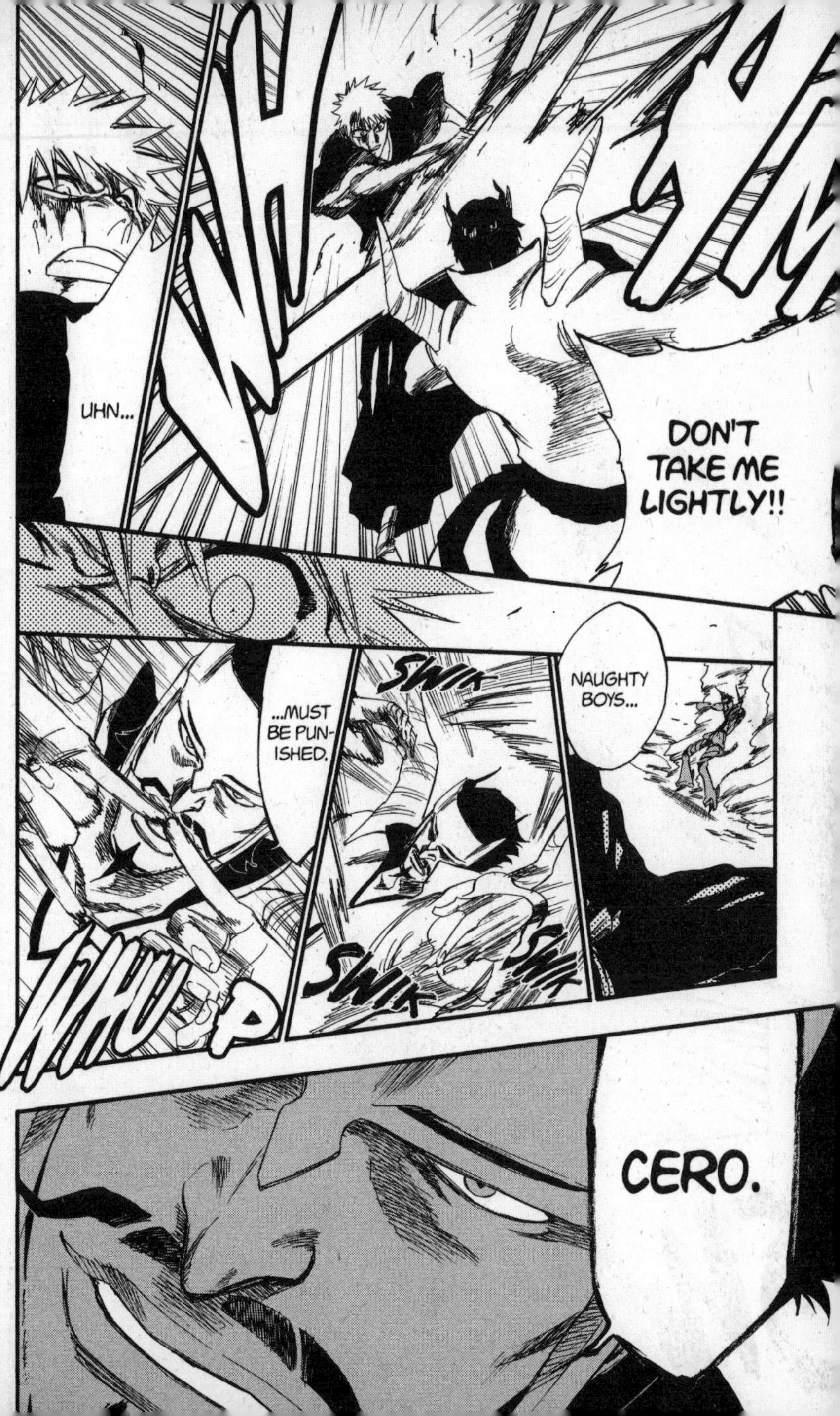
DON'T TAKE ME LIGHTLY!!
UHN...
NAUGHTY BOYS...
SWIK
SWIK
SWIK
...MUST BE PUN-ISHED.
CERO.

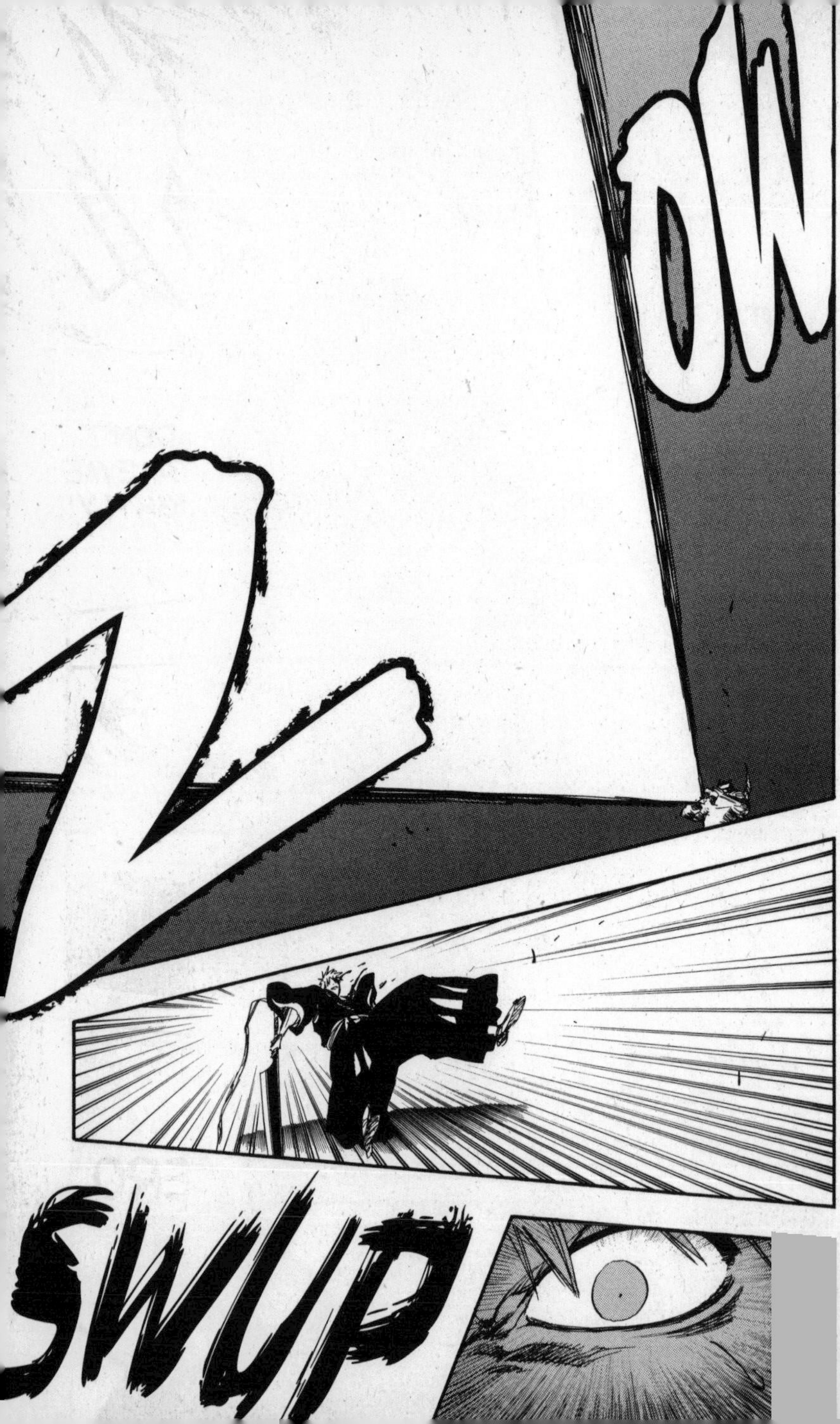
SWUP

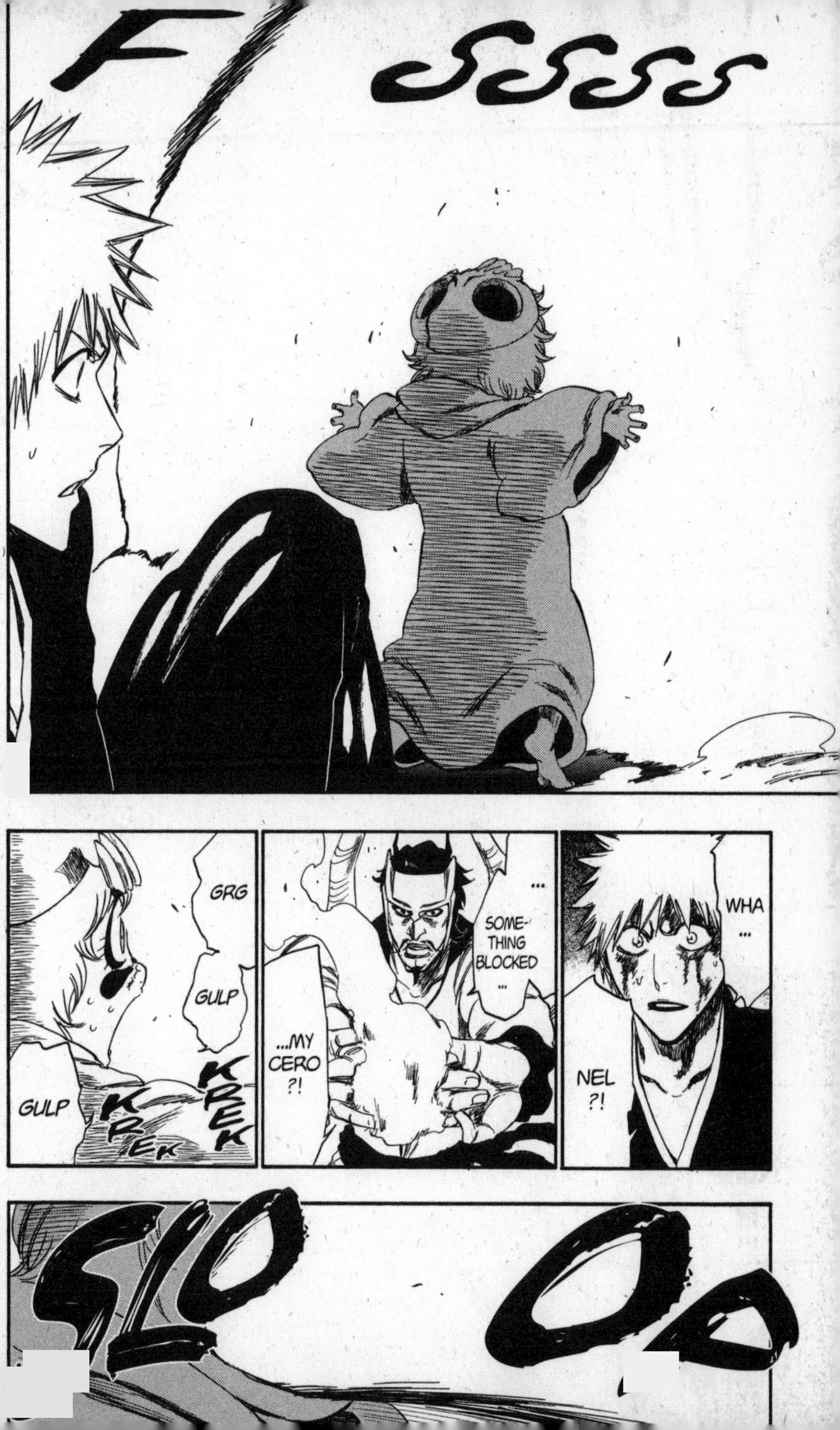
FSSSS
WHA ...
NEL ?!
... SOME-THING BLOCKED ...
...MY CERO ?!
GRG
GULP
KREK KREK
GULP
SLOOOO

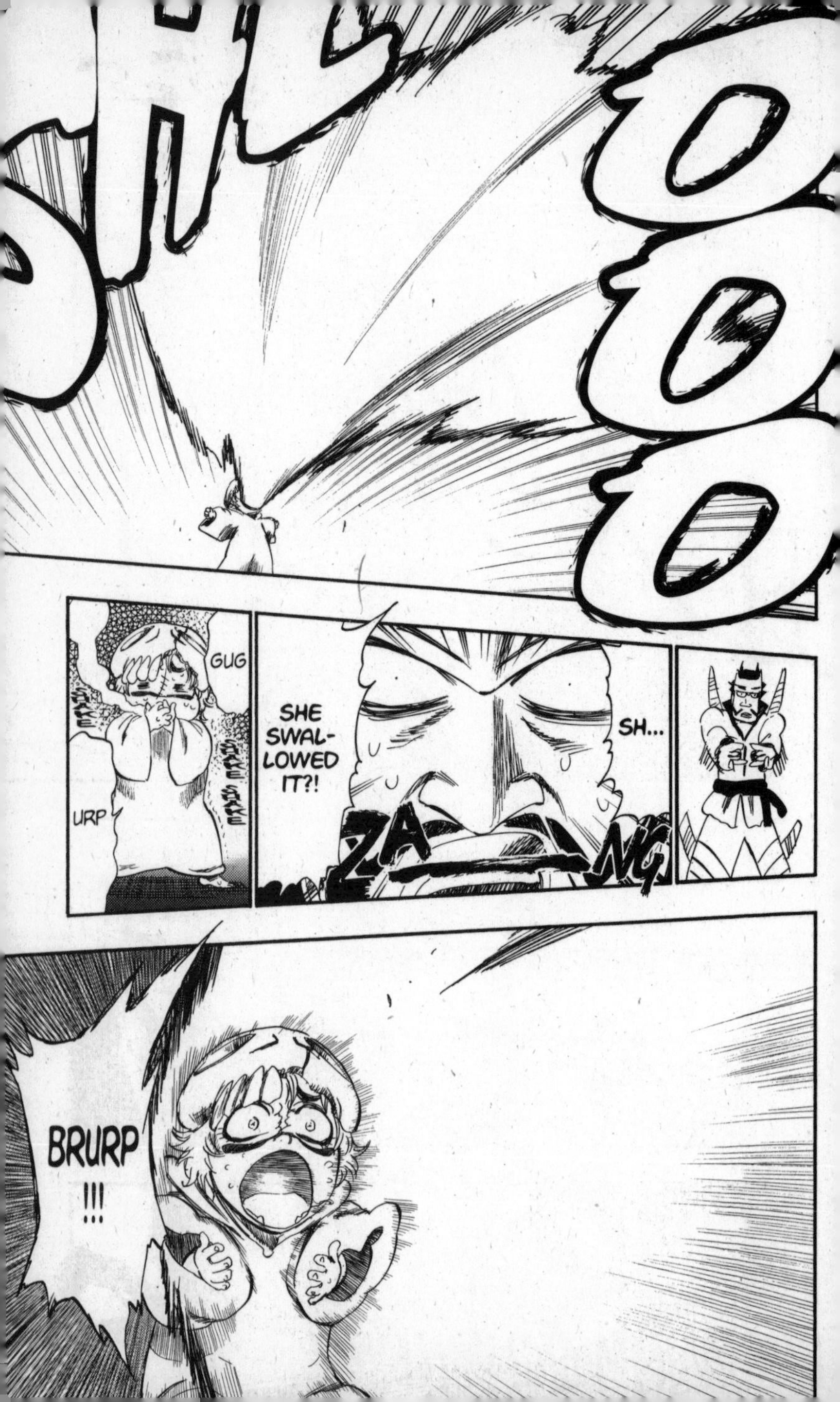
SH...
SHE SWAL-LOWED IT?!
ZANG
GUG
SHAKE
SHAKE SHAKE
URP
BRURP !!!

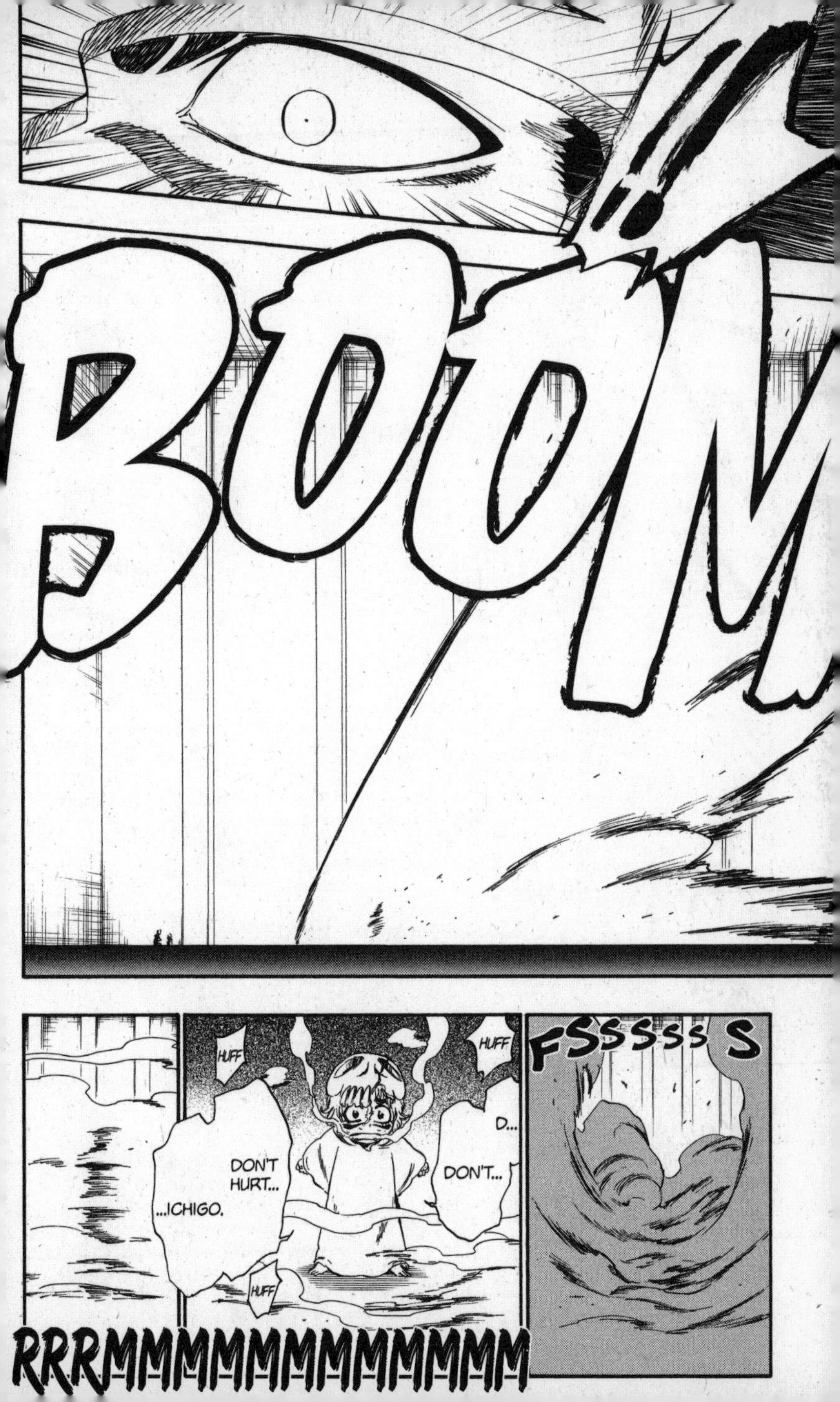
BOOM
FSSSSS S
HUFF
HUFF
D...
DON'T...
DON'T HURT...
...ICHIGO.
HUFF
RRRMMMMMMMMMMMM

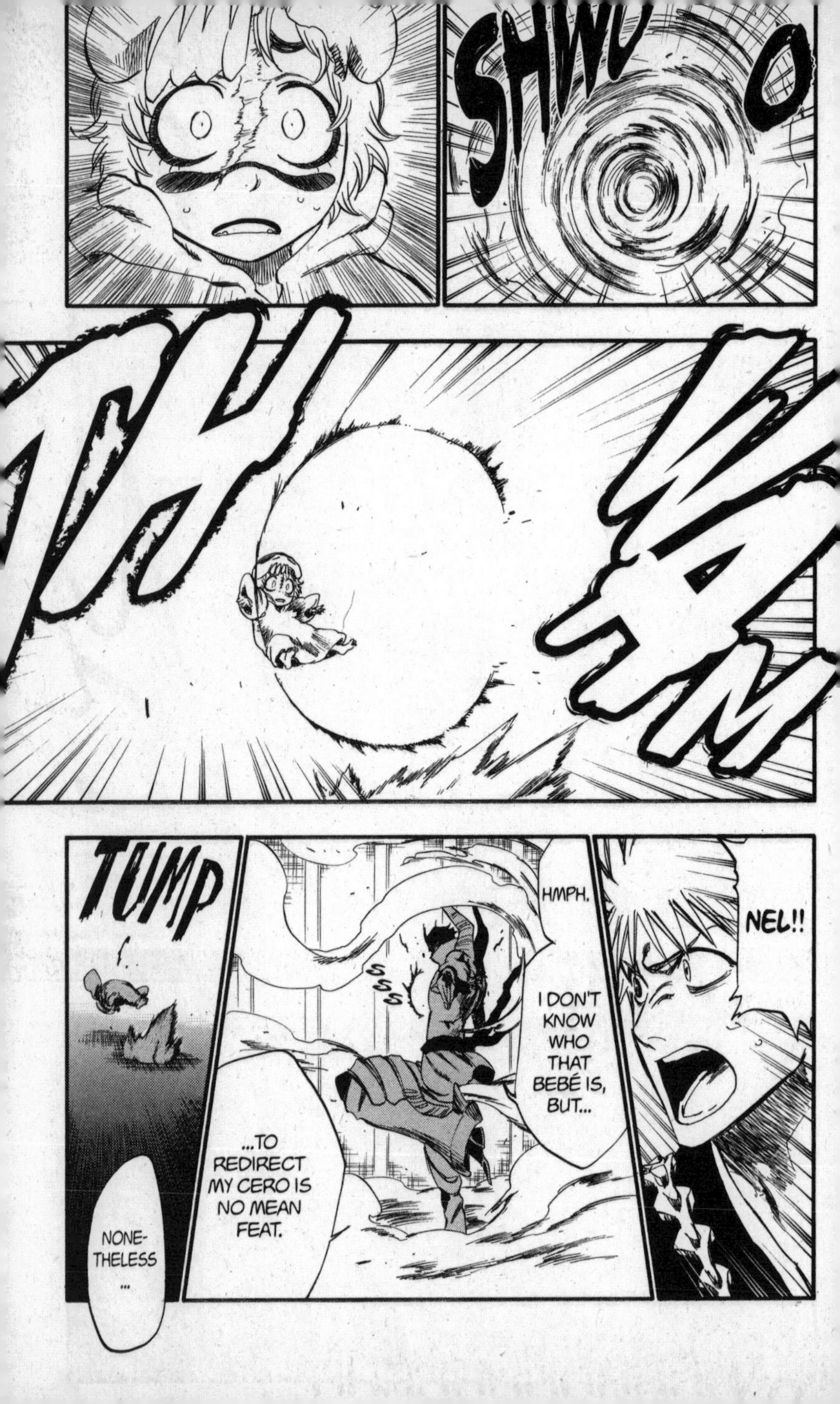
NEL!!
HMPH.
I DON'T KNOW WHO THAT BEBÉ IS, BUT...
SSS
...TO REDIRECT MY CERO IS NO MEAN FEAT.
TUMP
NONE-THELESS ...

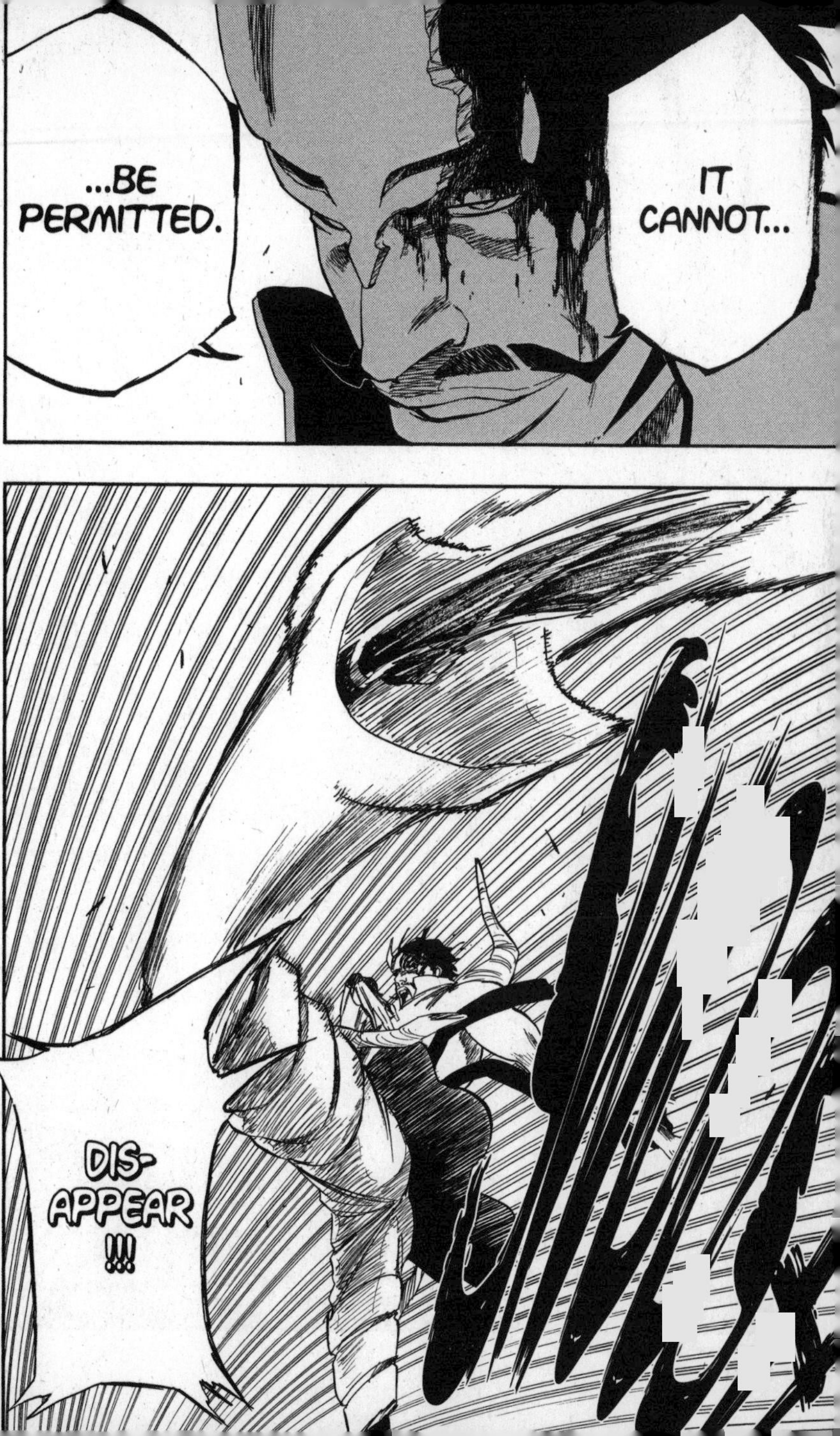
IT CANNOT...
...BE PERMITTED.
DIS-APPEAR!!!

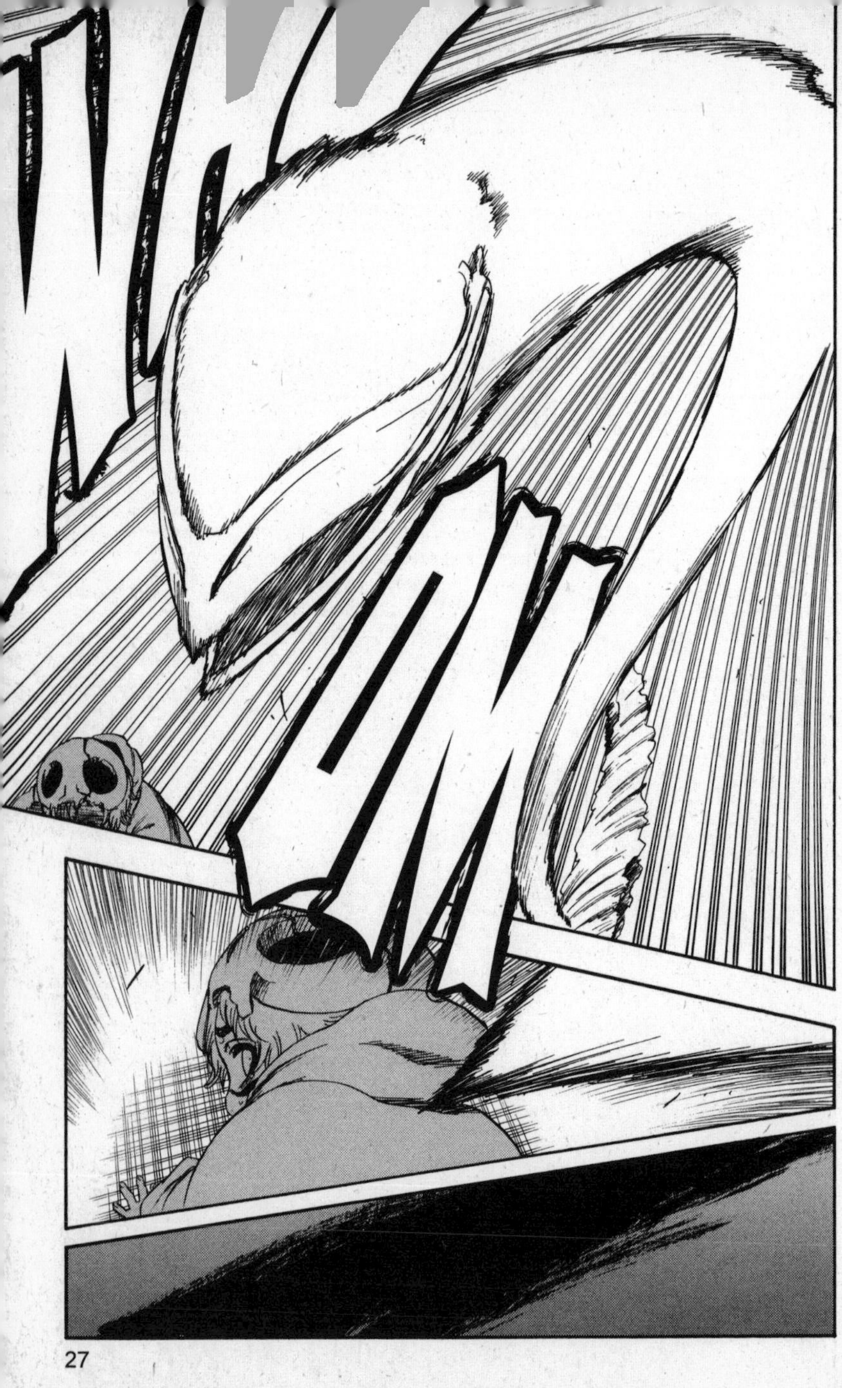

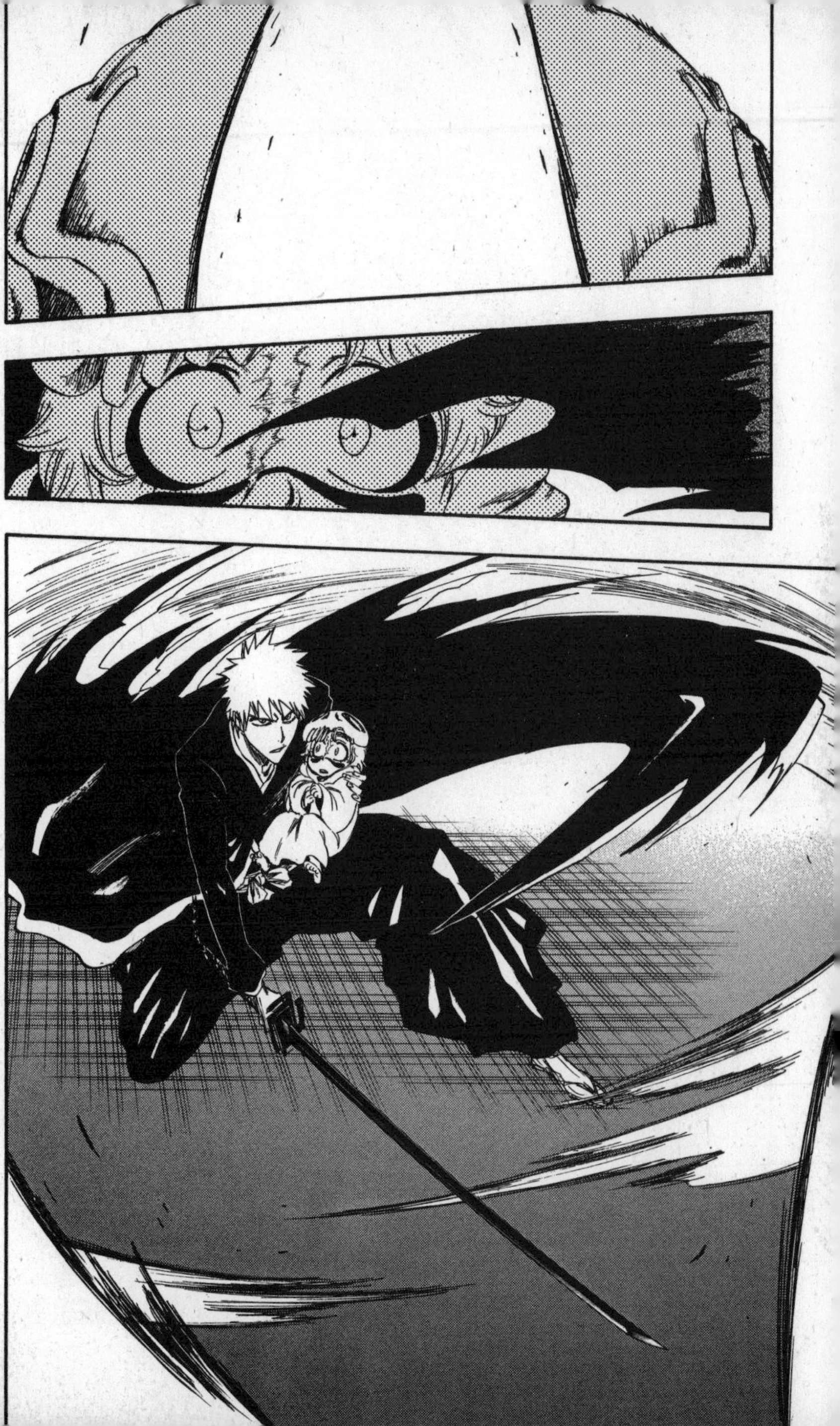

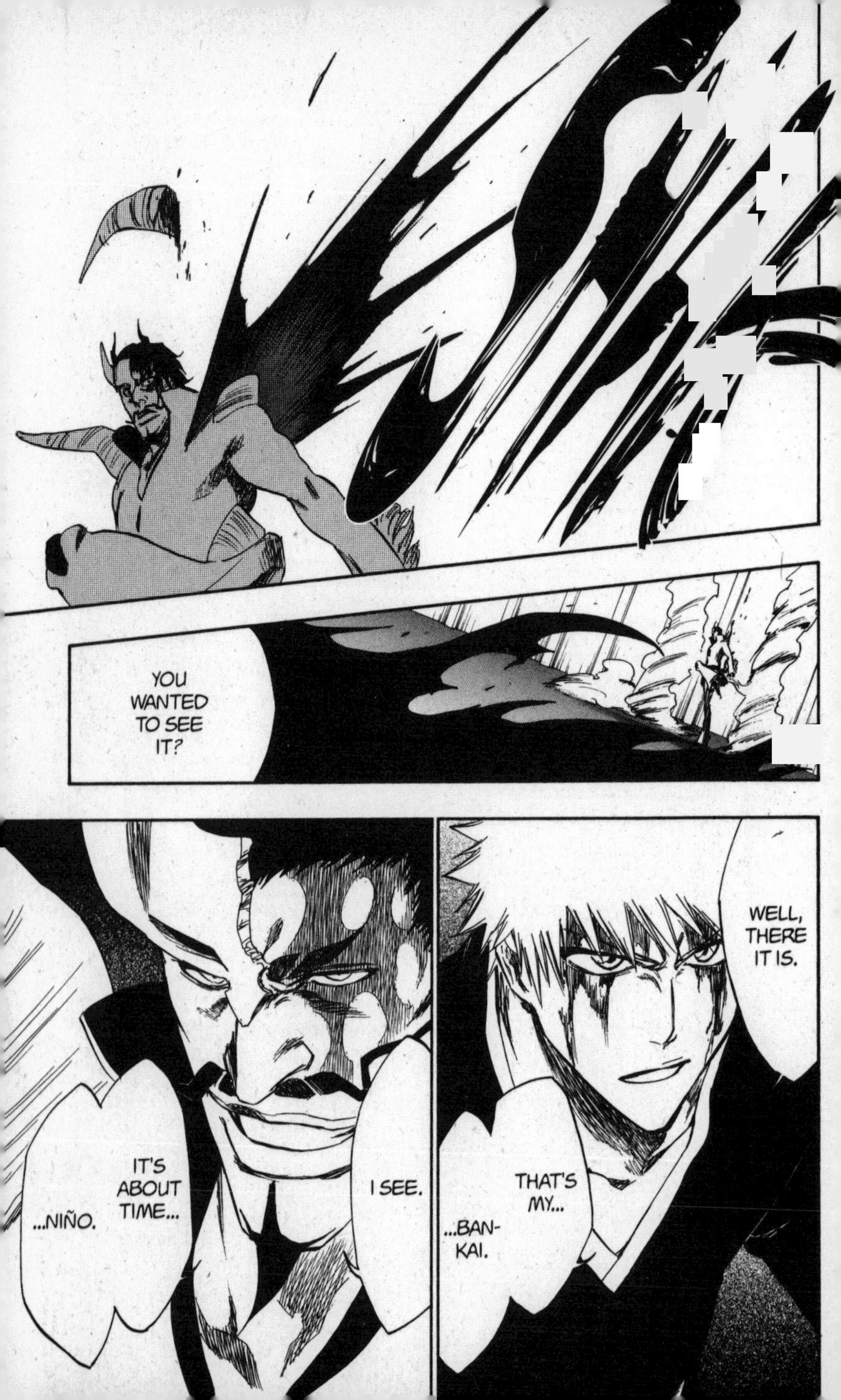
YOU WANTED TO SEE IT?
WELL, THERE IT IS.
THAT'S MY...
...BAN-KAI.
I SEE.
IT'S ABOUT TIME...
...NIÑO.

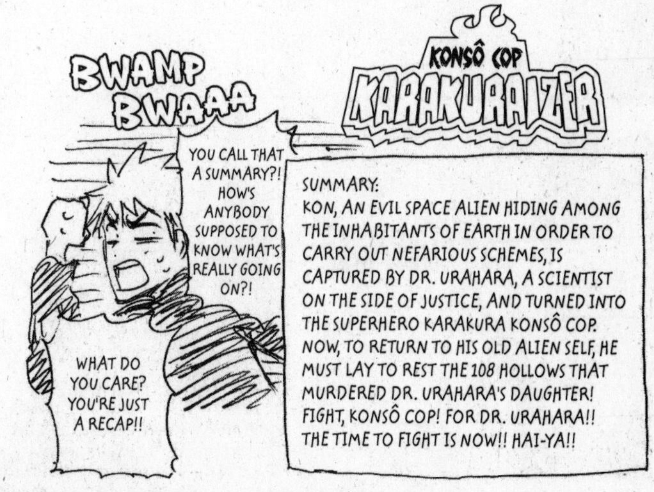
KONSÔ COP KARAKURAIZER
SUMMARY:
KON, AN EVIL SPACE ALIEN HIDING AMONG THE INHABITANTS OF EARTH IN ORDER TO CARRY OUT NEFARIOUS SCHEMES, IS CAPTURED BY DR. URAHARA, A SCIENTIST ON THE SIDE OF JUSTICE, AND TURNED INTO THE SUPERHERO KARAKURA KONSÔ COP. NOW, TO RETURN TO HIS OLD ALIEN SELF, HE MUST LAY TO REST THE 108 HOLLOWS THAT MURDERED DR. URAHARA'S DAUGHTER! FIGHT, KONSÔ COP! FOR DR. URAHARA!! THE TIME TO FIGHT IS NOW!! HAI-YA!!
YOU CALL THAT A SUMMARY?! HOW'S ANYBODY SUPPOSED TO KNOW WHAT'S REALLY GOING ON?!
BWAMP BWAAA
WHAT DO YOU CARE? YOU'RE JUST A RECAP!!

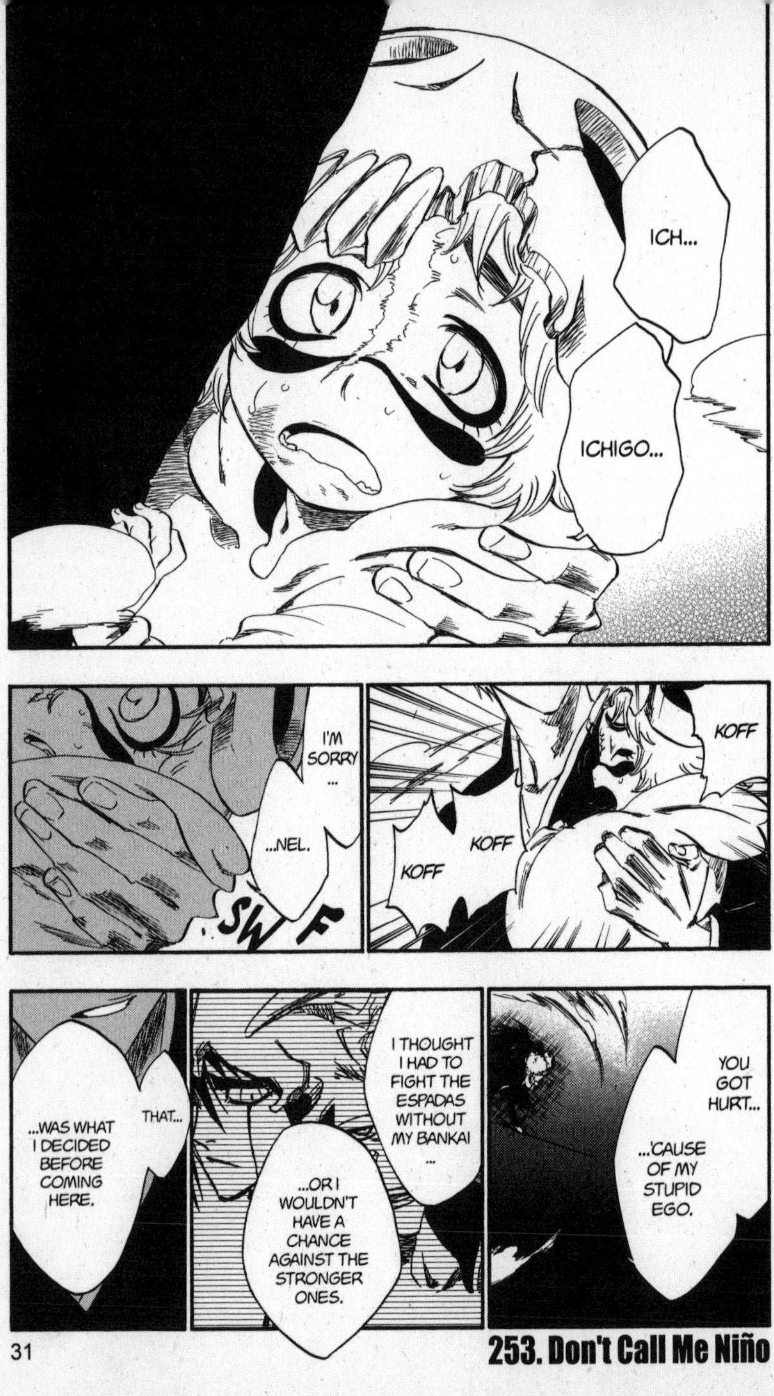
ICH...
ICHIGO...
KOFF
KOFF
KOFF
I'M SORRY ...
...NEL.
SWF
YOU GOT HURT...
...'CAUSE OF MY STUPID EGO.
I THOUGHT I HAD TO FIGHT THE ESPADAS WITHOUT MY BANKAI ...
...OR I WOULDN'T HAVE A CHANCE AGAINST THE STRONGER ONES.
THAT...
...WAS WHAT I DECIDED BEFORE COMING HERE.

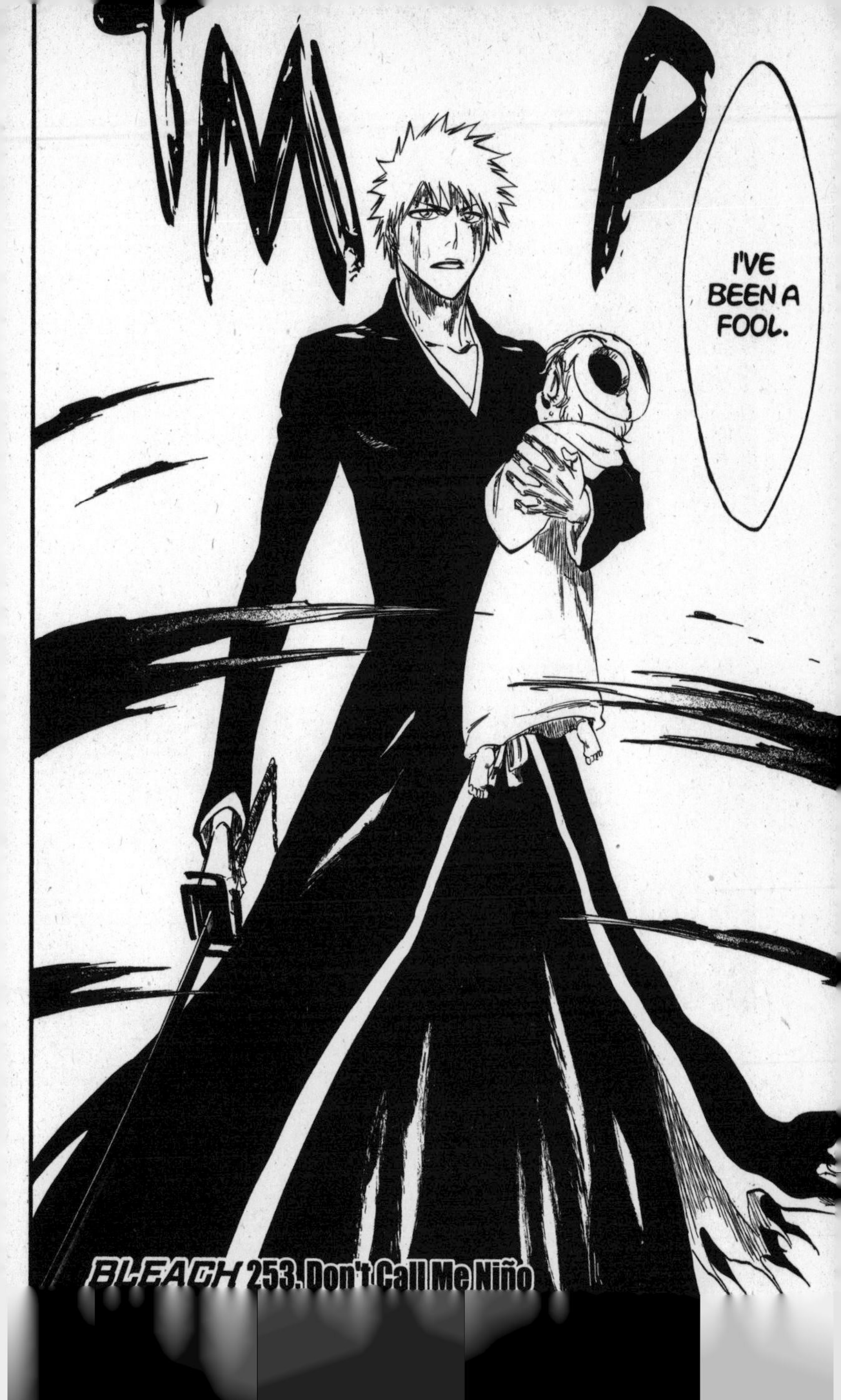
TMP
I'VE BEEN A FOOL.
BLEACH 253. Don't Call Me Niño

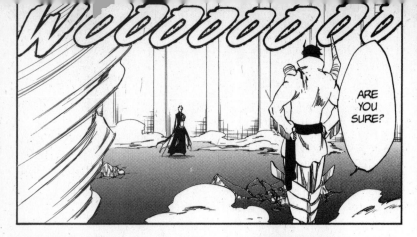

WOOOOOOOO
ARE YOU SURE?
RE-STRAINT IN BATTLE...
...IS REQUIRED OF THOSE WHO SEEK GREAT POWER.
THAT WAS VERY IMPRES-SIVE.
IT'S NOT WORTH LETTING A FRIEND GET HURT.
HUFF
HUFF
THEN YOU DO NOT SEEK POWER FOR YOUR OWN SAKE?
YOU MERELY WISH...
...TO PROTECT YOUR FRIENDS?
YOU ARE KIND, NIÑO.
YOU ARE LIKE A SAINT.
SWUP
BUT...

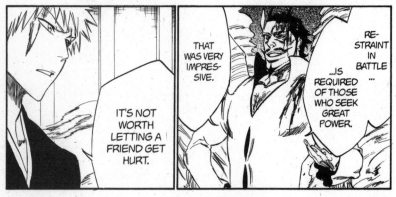

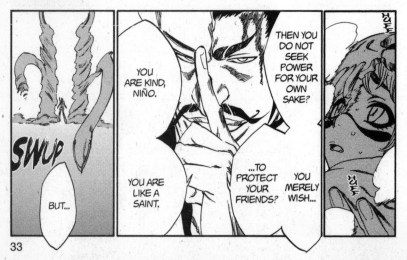

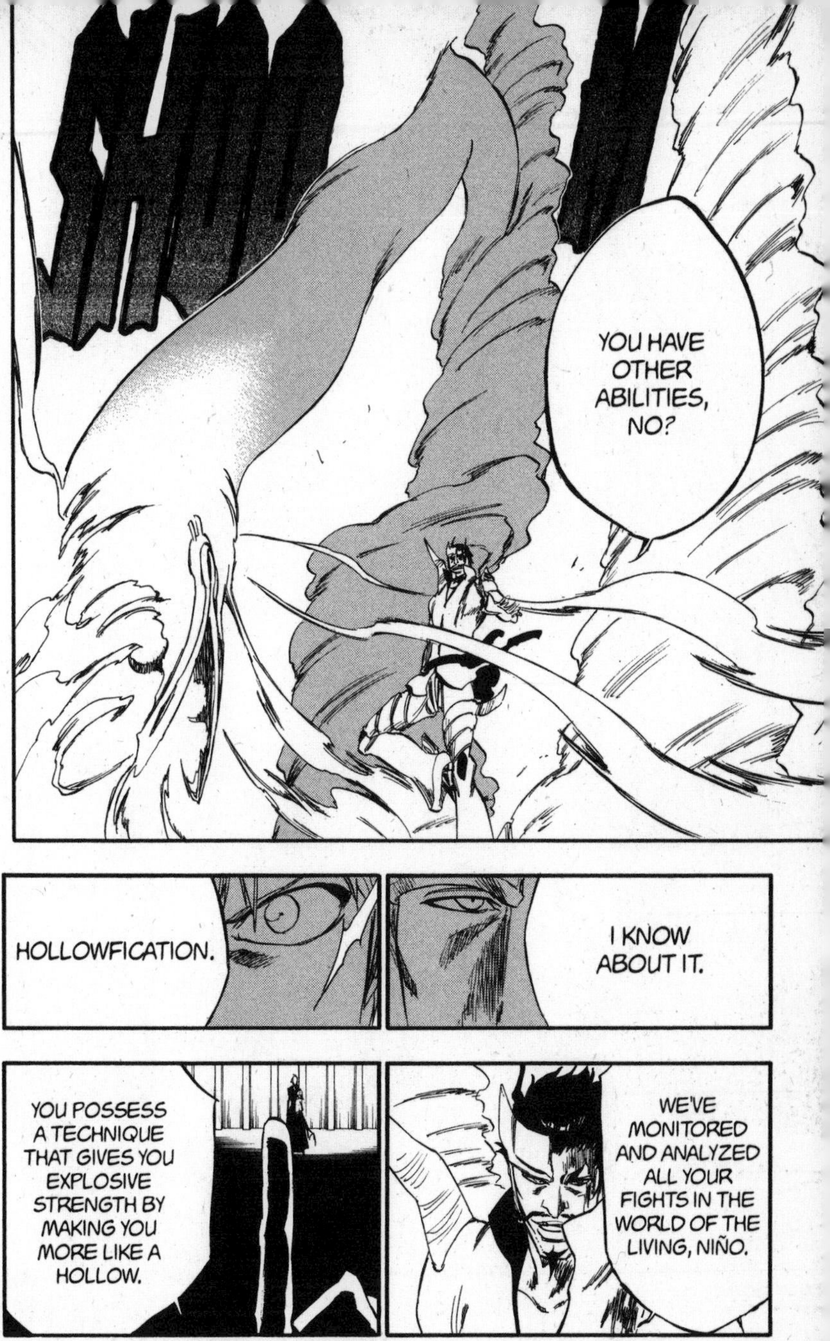
YOU HAVE OTHER ABILITIES, NO?
I KNOW ABOUT IT.
HOLLOWFICATION.
WE'VE MONITORED AND ANALYZED ALL YOUR FIGHTS IN THE WORLD OF THE LIVING, NIÑO.
YOU POSSESS A TECHNIQUE THAT GIVES YOU EXPLOSIVE STRENGTH BY MAKING YOU MORE LIKE A HOLLOW.

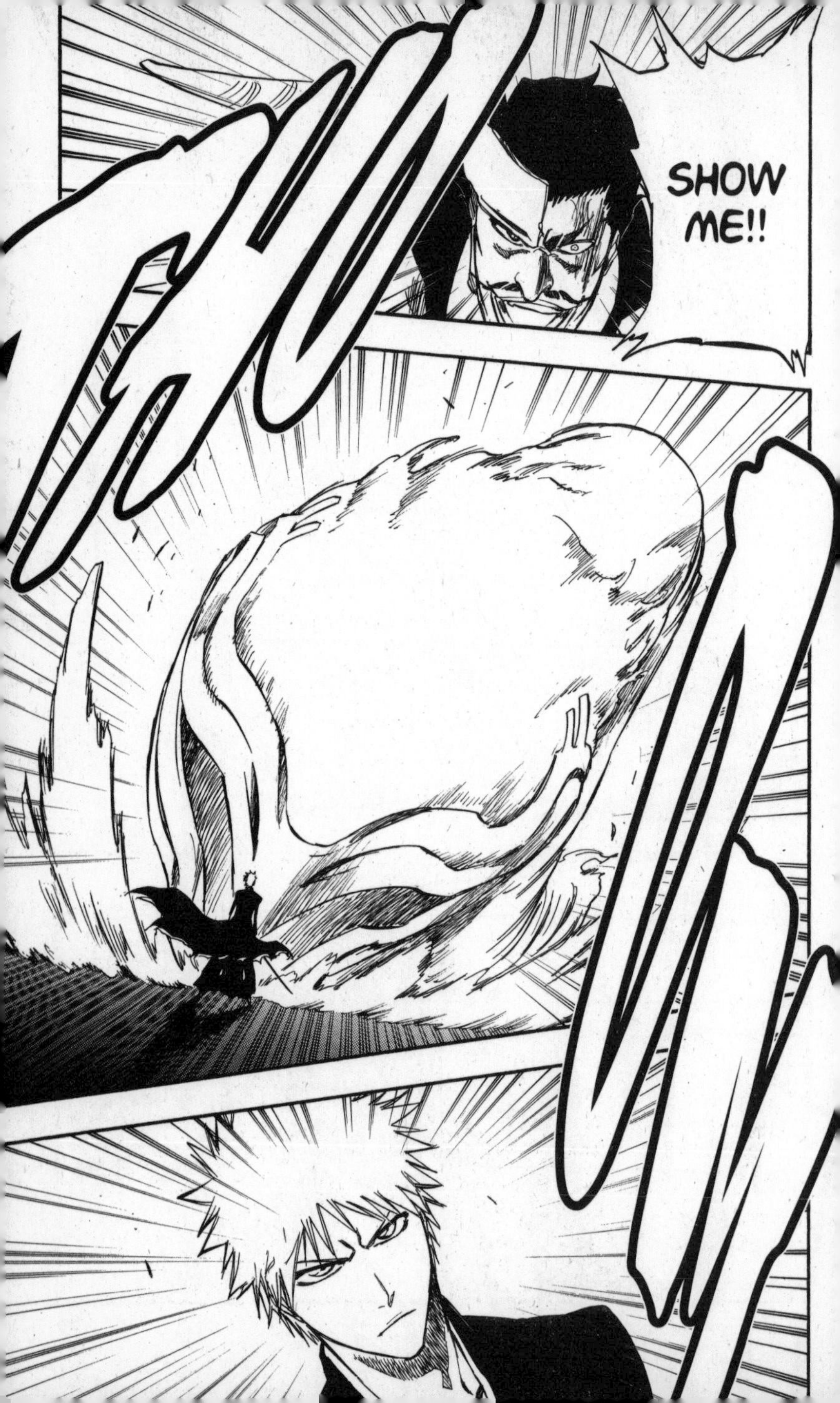
SHOW ME!!

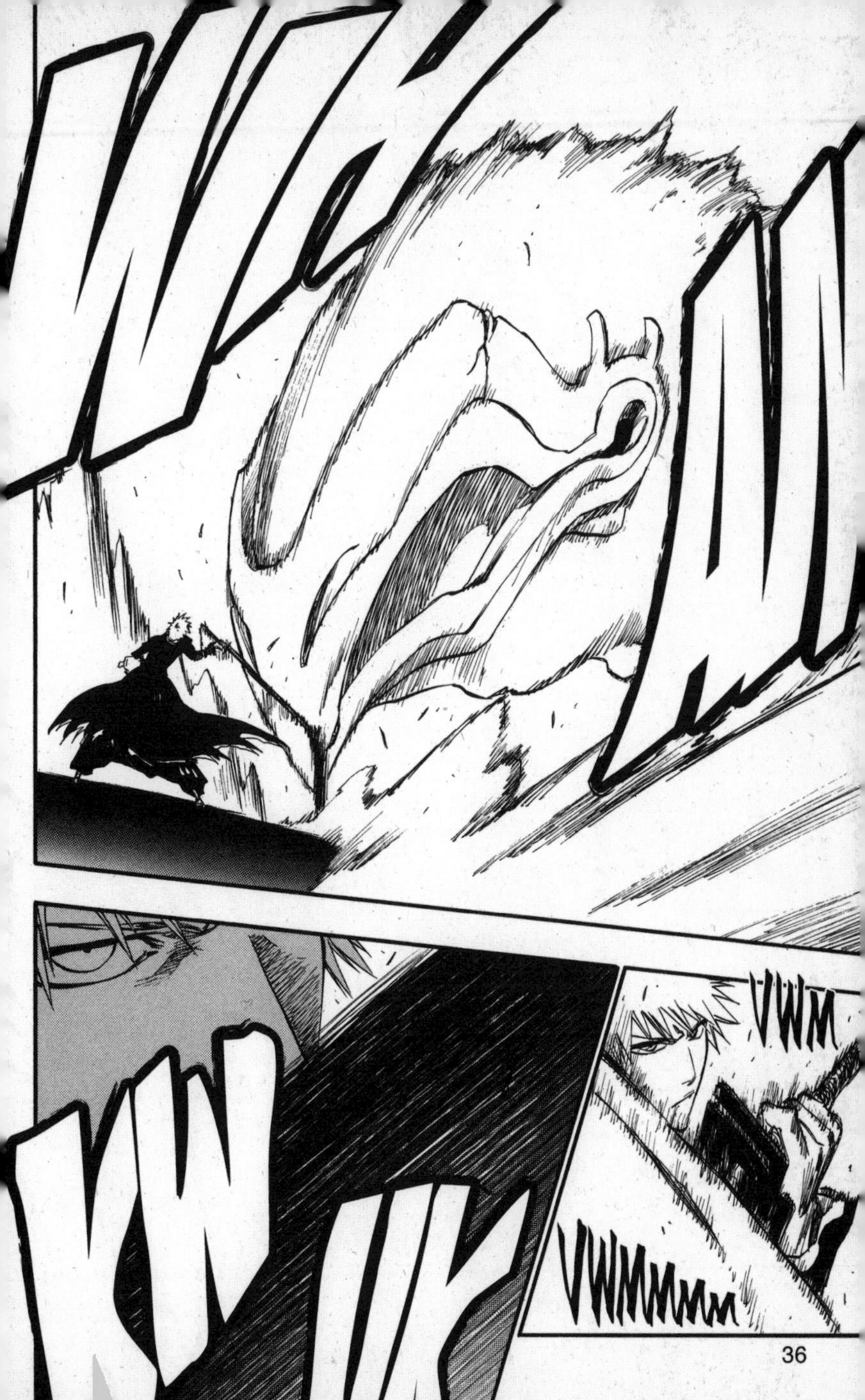
VWM
VWMMMM

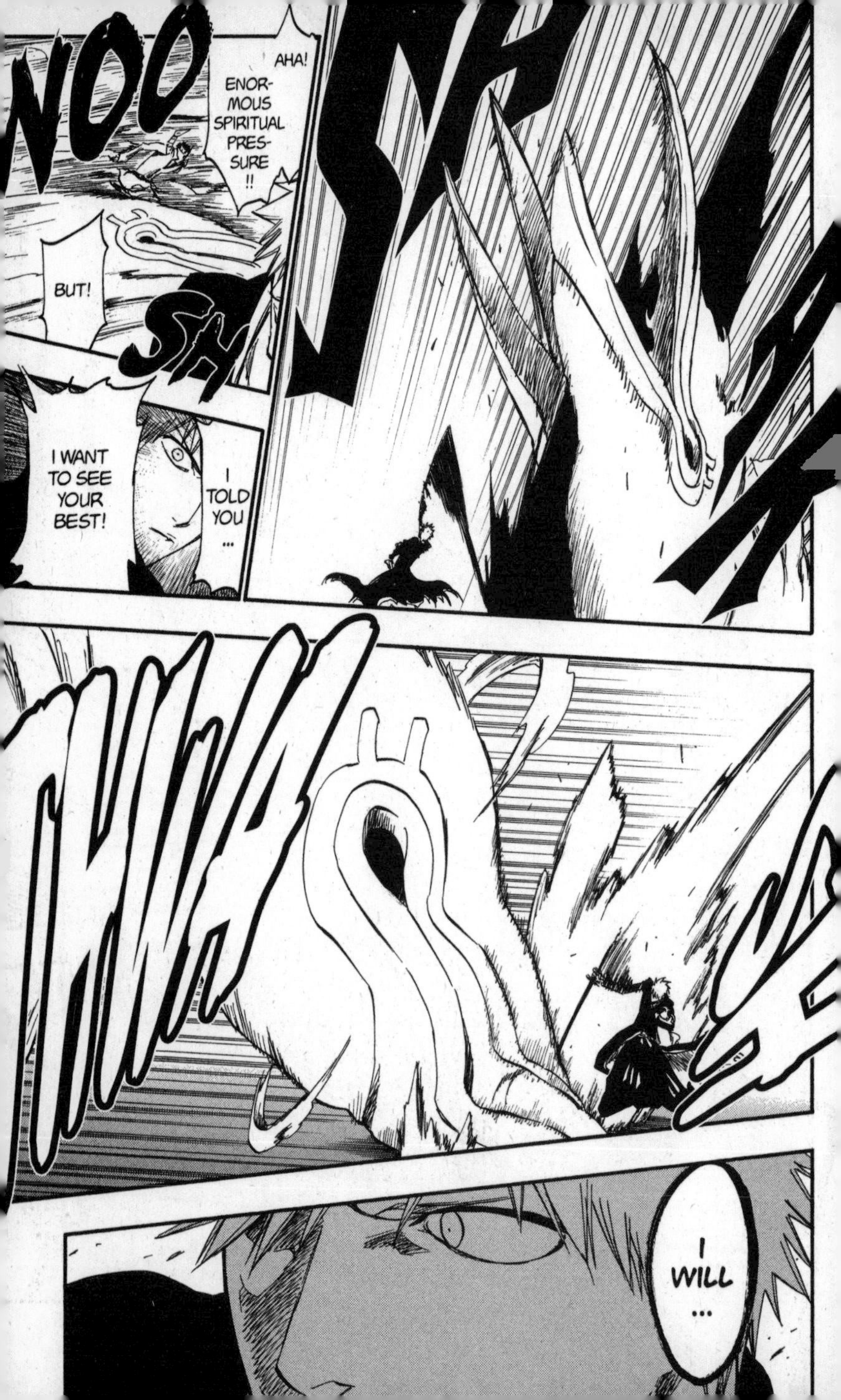
AHA! ENORMOUS SPIRITUAL PRESSURE!!
BUT!
I TOLD YOU...
I WANT TO SEE YOUR BEST!
I WILL...

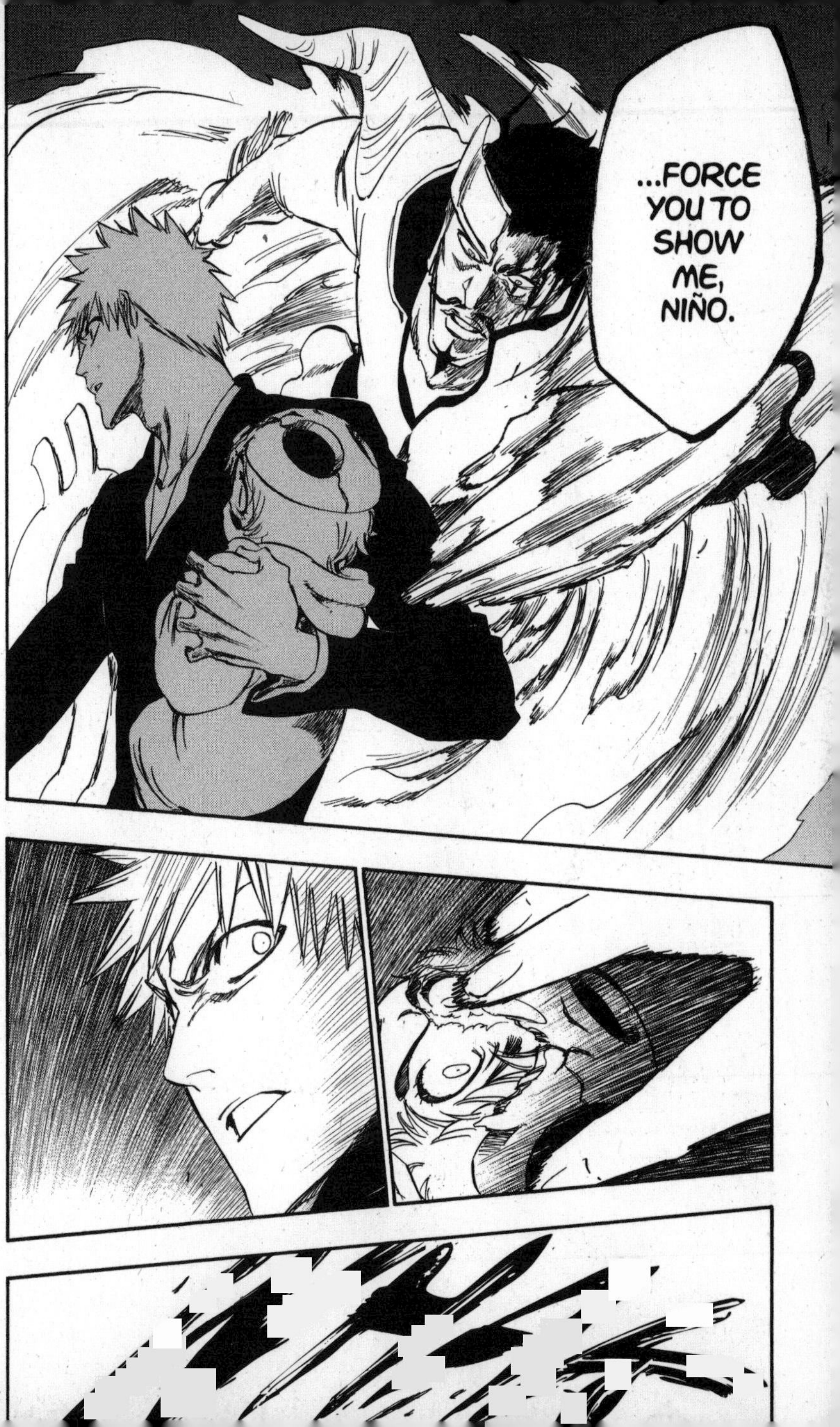
...FORCE YOU TO SHOW ME, NIÑO.

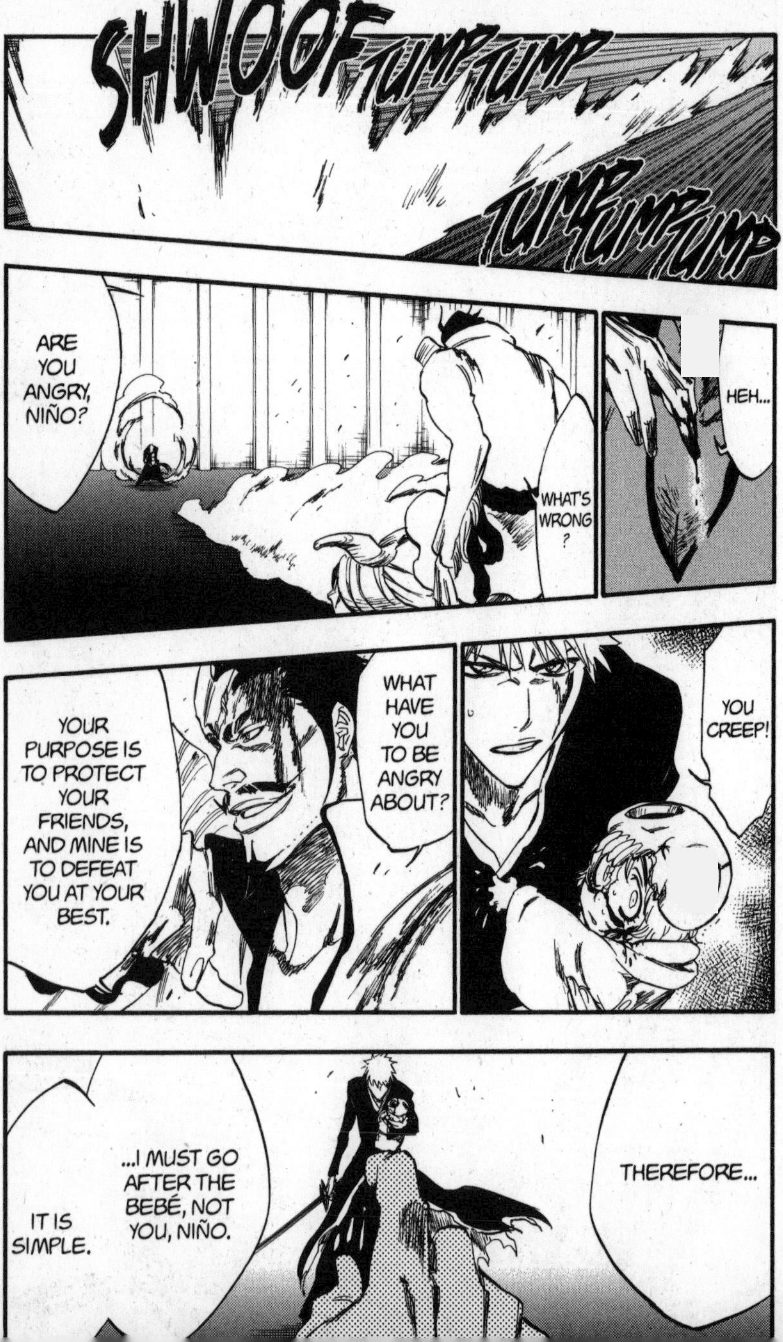
SHWOOF
TUMP TUMP
TUMP TUMP TUMP TUMP
HEH...
WHAT'S WRONG?
ARE YOU ANGRY, NIÑO?
YOU CREEP!
WHAT HAVE YOU TO BE ANGRY ABOUT?
YOUR PURPOSE IS TO PROTECT YOUR FRIENDS, AND MINE IS TO DEFEAT YOU AT YOUR BEST.
THEREFORE...
...I MUST GO AFTER THE BEBÉ, NOT YOU, NIÑO.
IT IS SIMPLE.

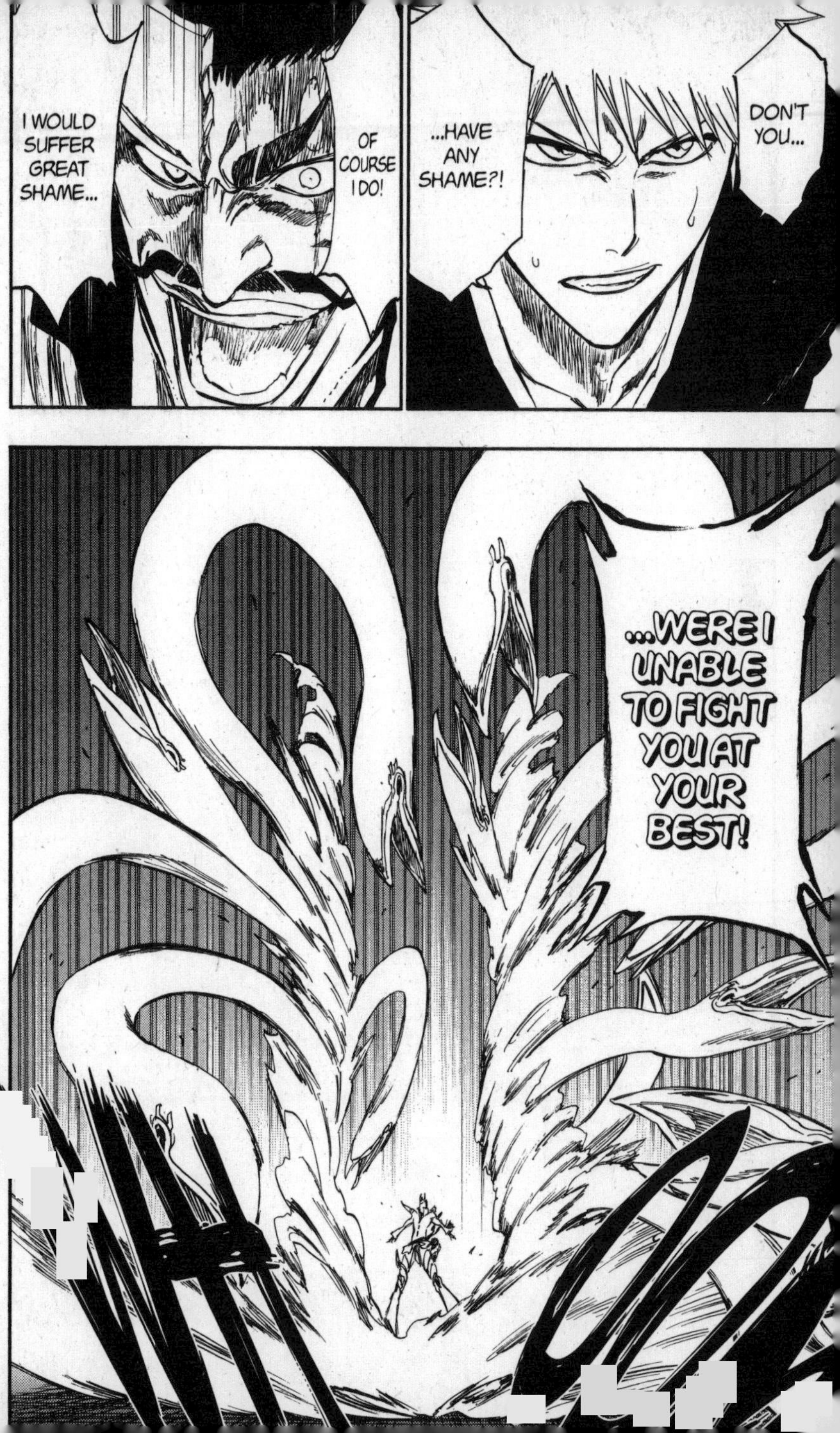
DON'T YOU...
...HAVE ANY SHAME?!
OF COURSE I DO!
I WOULD SUFFER GREAT SHAME...
...WERE I UNABLE TO FIGHT YOU AT YOUR BEST!

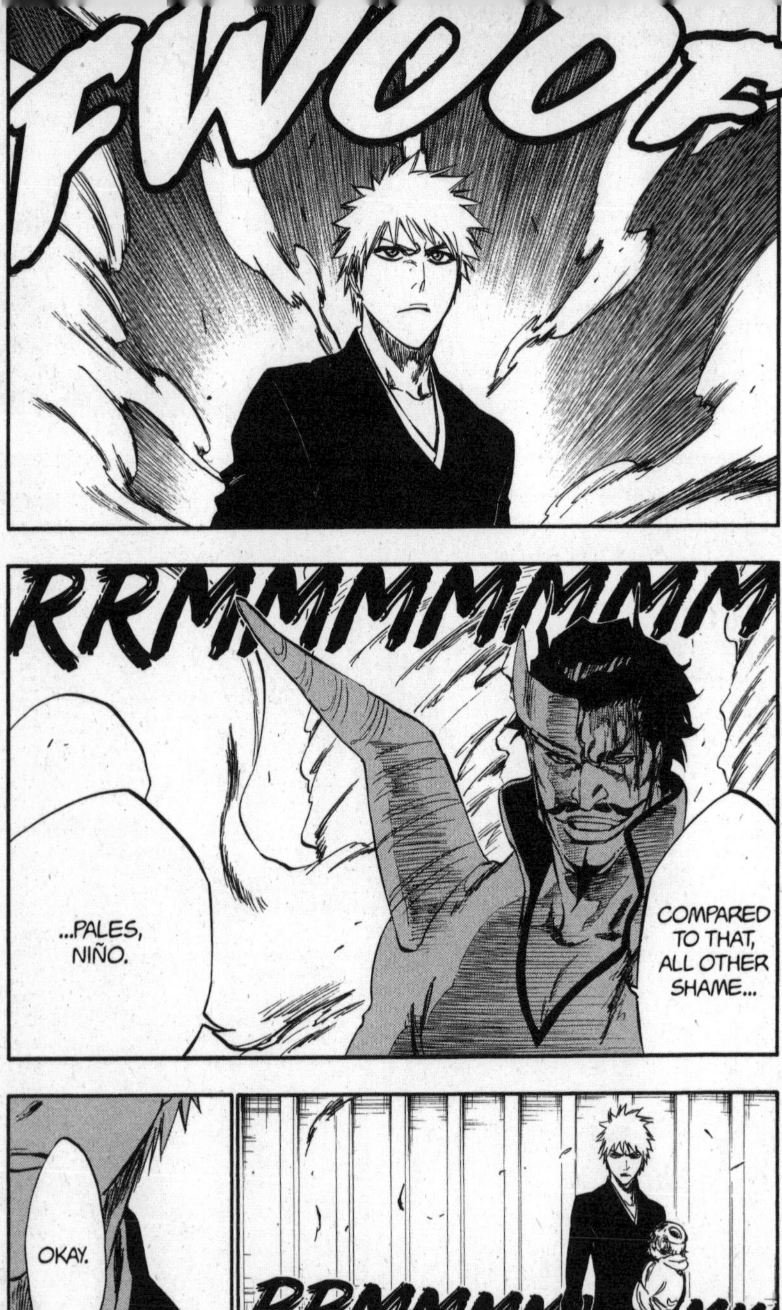

FWOOF
RRMMMMMMMMM
COMPARED TO THAT, ALL OTHER SHAME...
...PALES, NIÑO.
RRMMMMM
MM
OKAY.

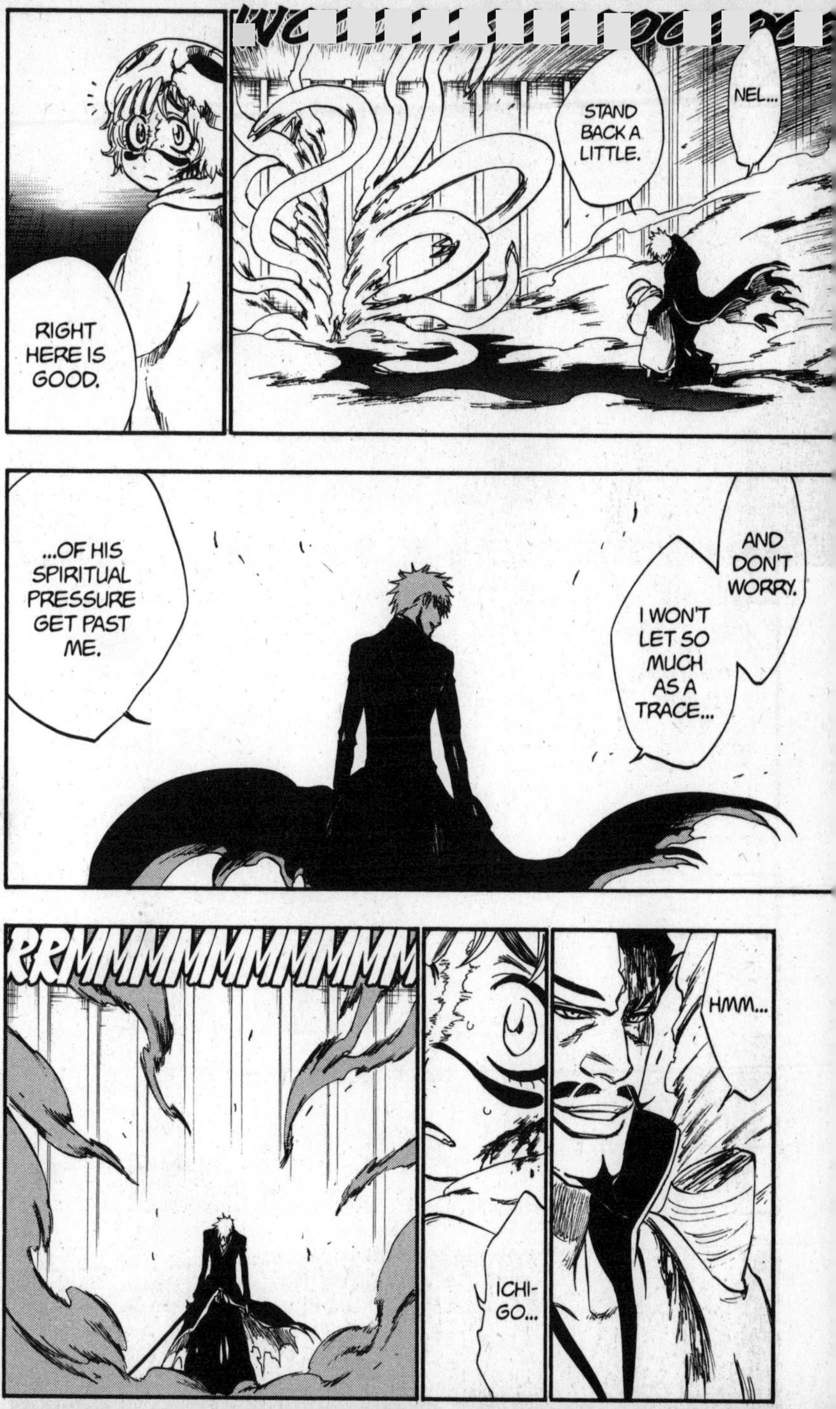
NEL...
STAND BACK A LITTLE.
RIGHT HERE IS GOOD.
AND DON'T WORRY.
I WON'T LET SO MUCH AS A TRACE...
...OF HIS SPIRITUAL PRESSURE GET PAST ME.
HMM...
ICHI-GO...
RRMMMMMMMMMMMM

READ THIS WAY

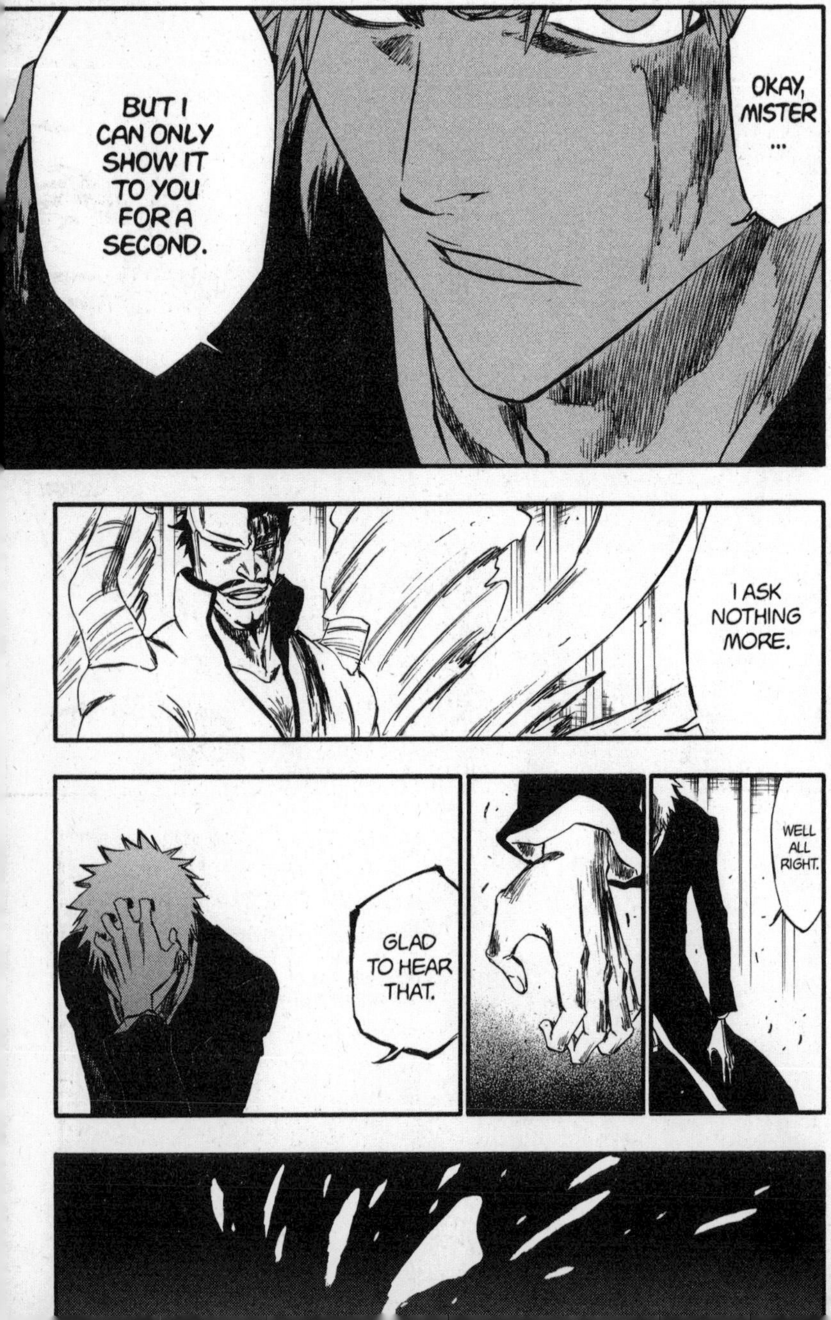
OKAY, MISTER ...
BUT I CAN ONLY SHOW IT TO YOU FOR A SECOND.
I ASK NOTHING MORE.
WELL ALL RIGHT.
GLAD TO HEAR THAT.

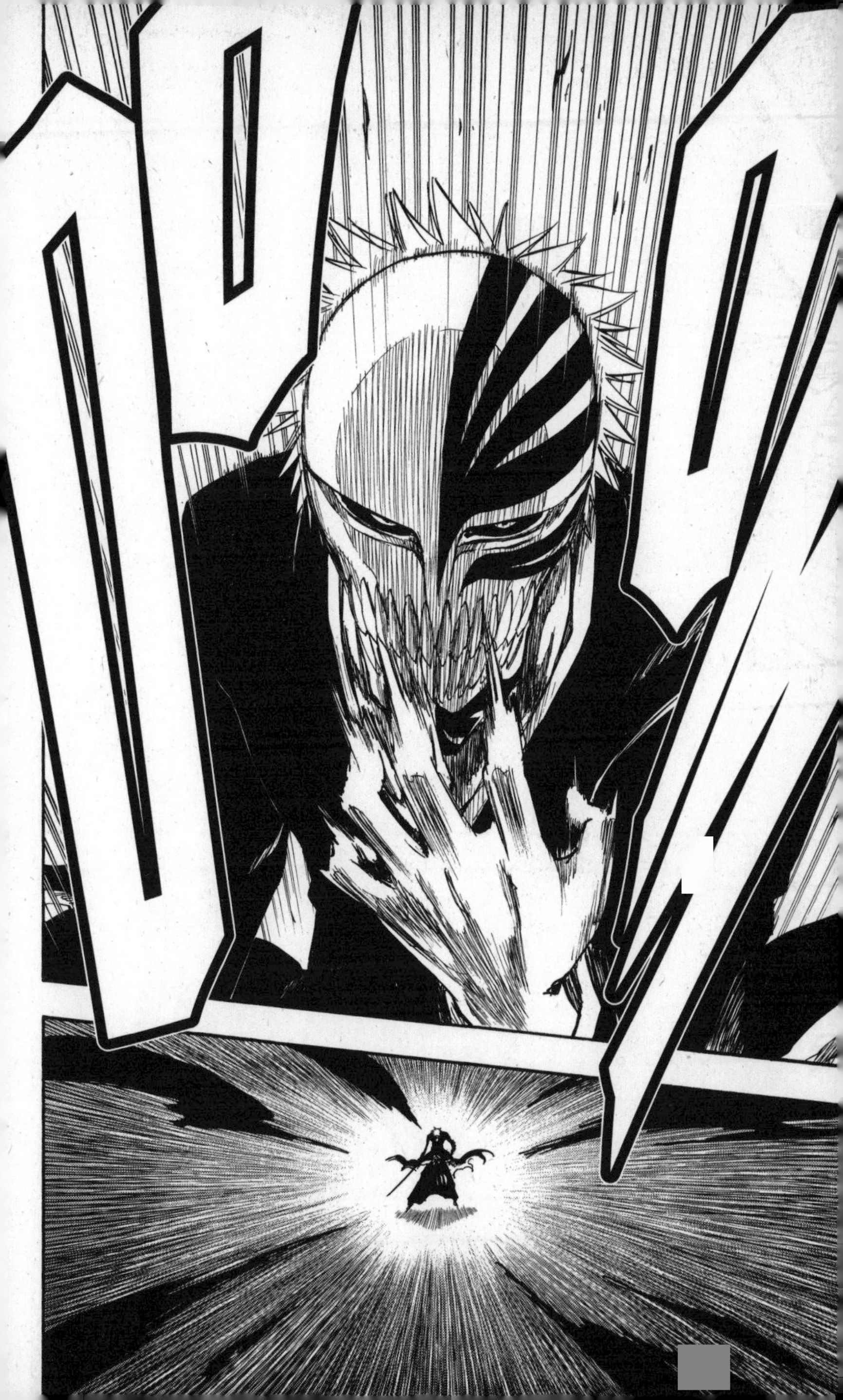

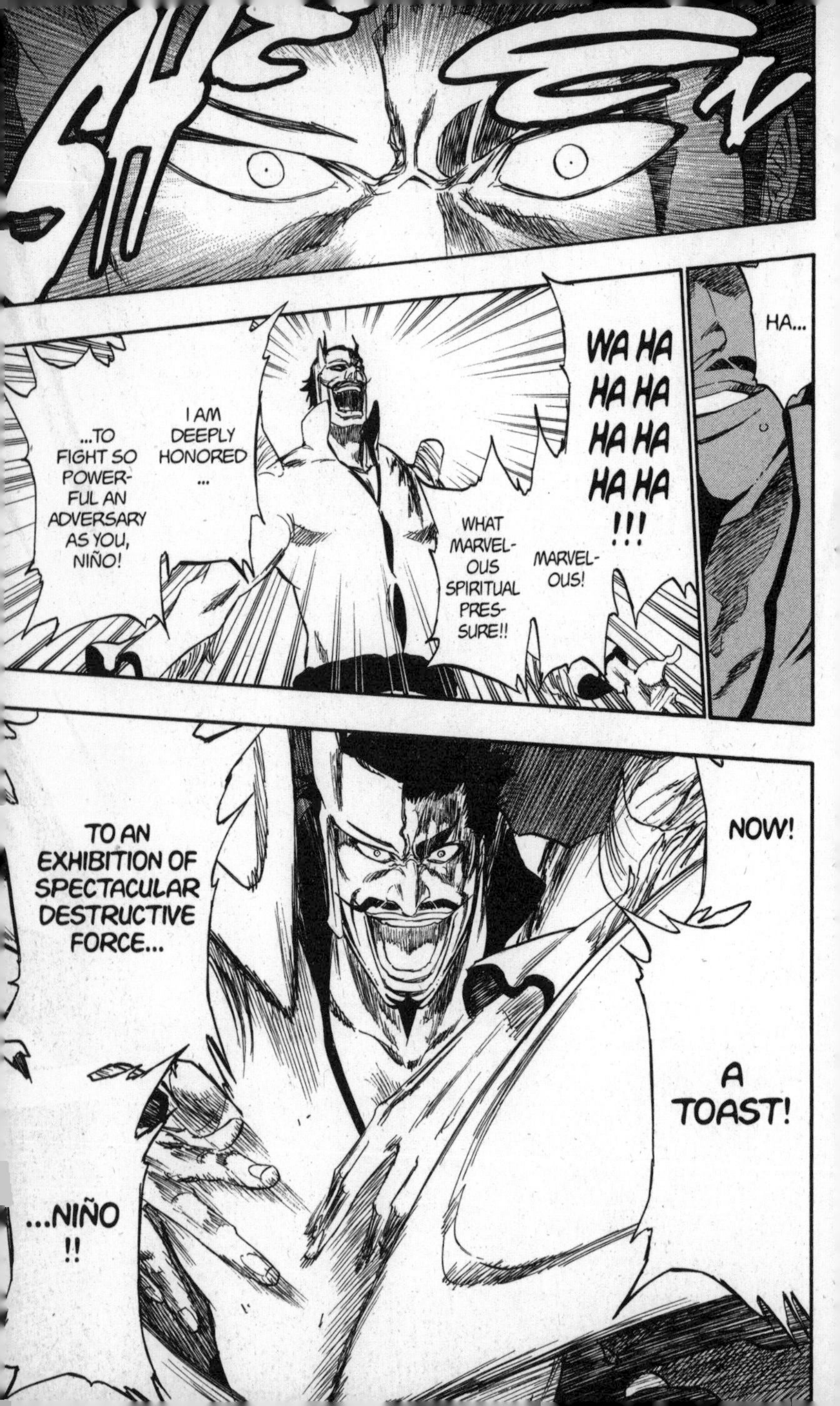

HA...
WA HA HA HA HA HA HA HA!!!
MARVEL-OUS!
WHAT MARVEL-OUS SPIRITUAL PRES-SURE!!
I AM DEEPLY HONORED...
...TO FIGHT SO POWER-FUL AN ADVERSARY AS YOU, NIÑO!
NOW!
A TOAST!
TO AN EXHIBITION OF SPECTACULAR DESTRUCTIVE FORCE...
...NIÑO!!

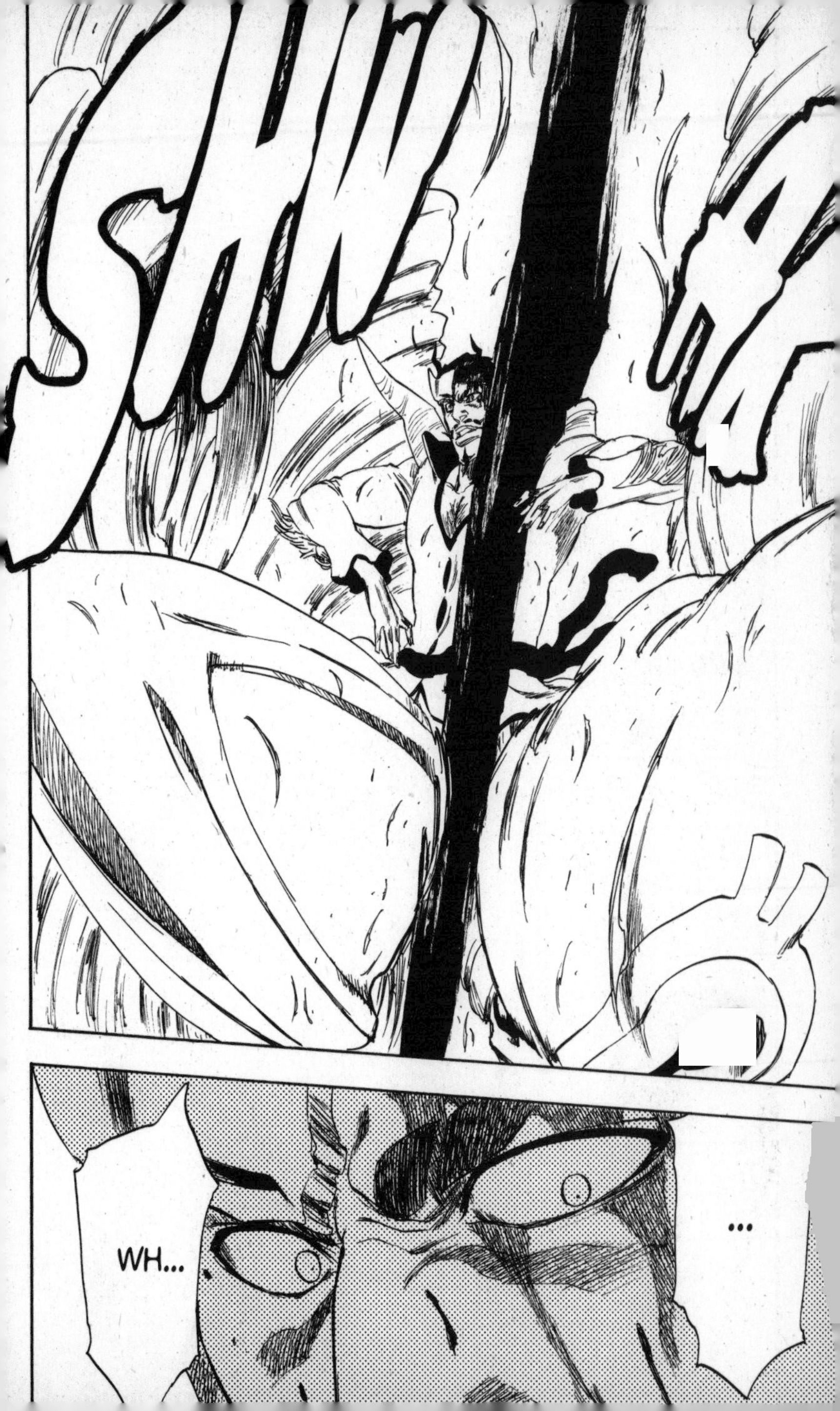
...
WH...

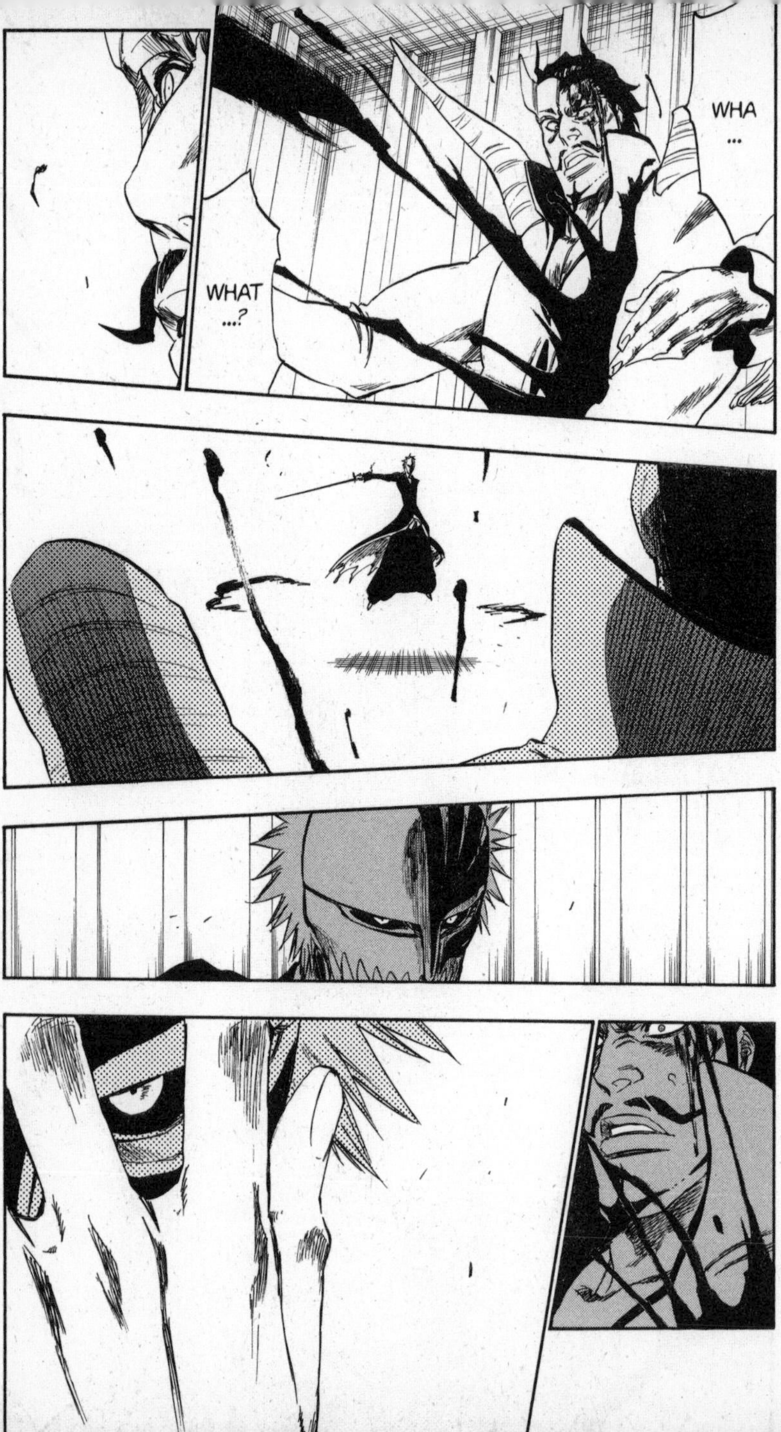
WHA ...
WHAT ...?

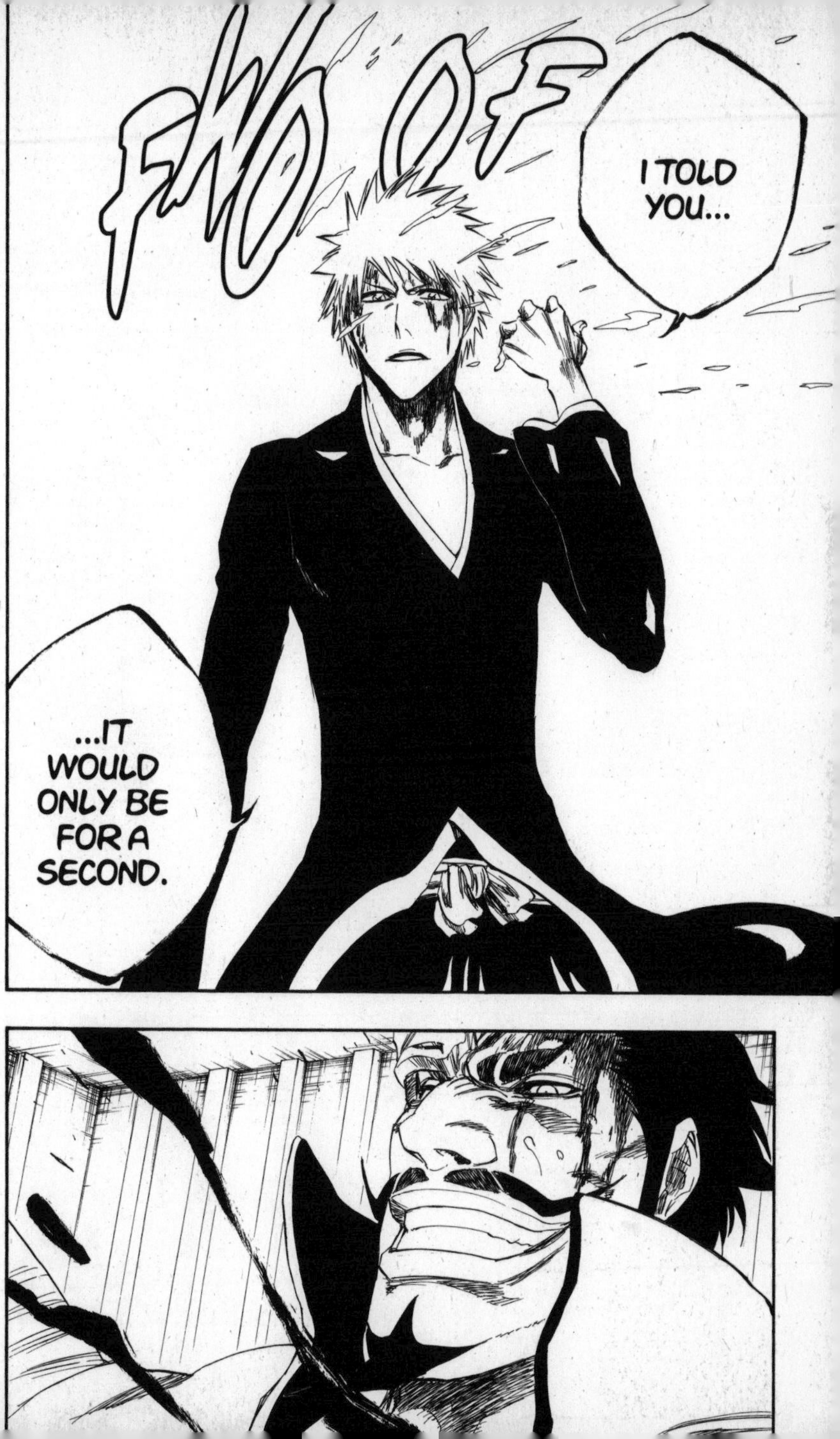
I TOLD YOU...
FWOOF
...IT WOULD ONLY BE FOR A SECOND.

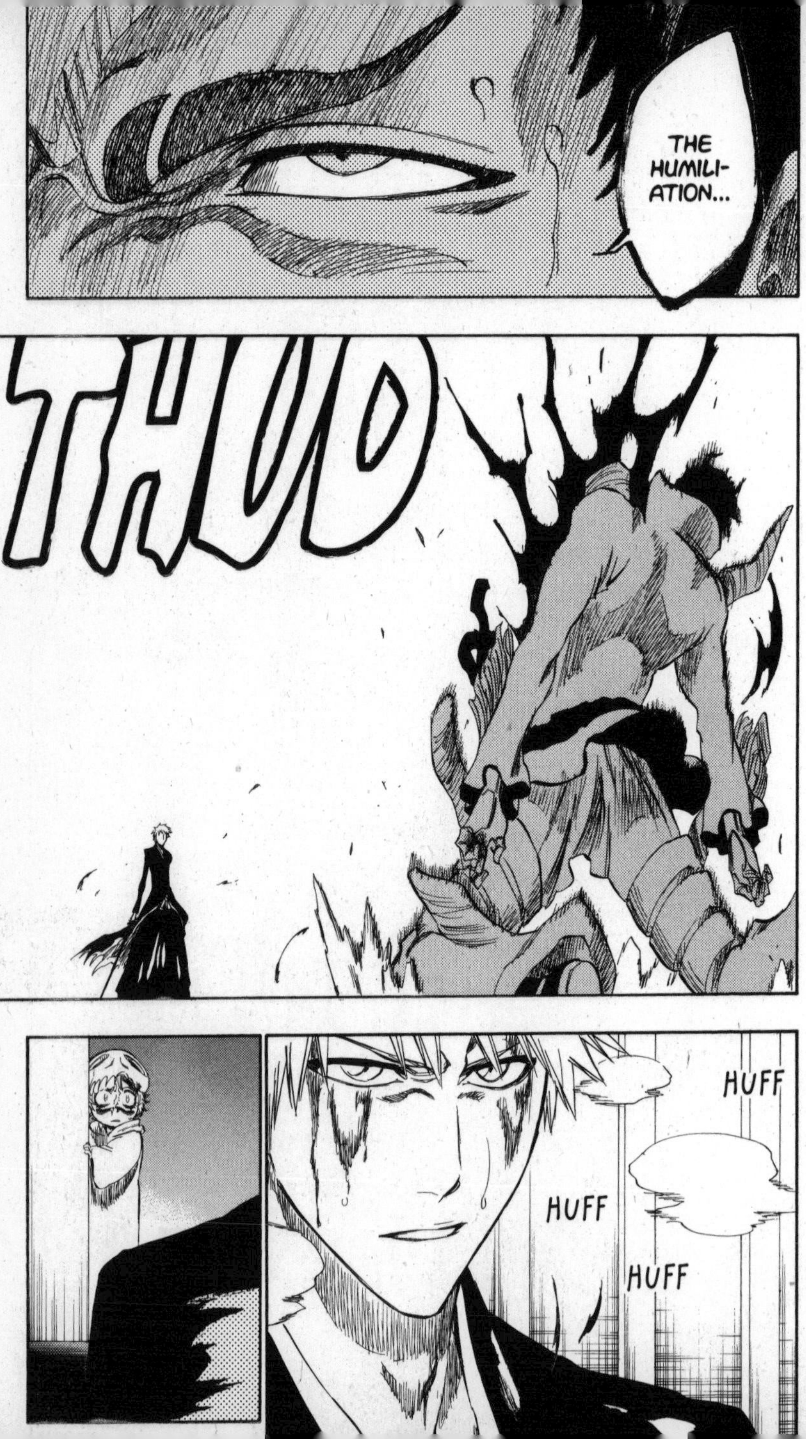
THE HUMILI-ATION...
THUD
HUFF
HUFF
HUFF

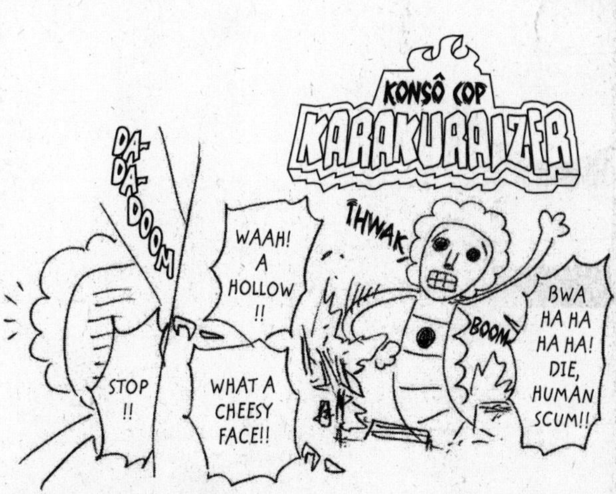
KONSÔ COP
KARAKURAIZER
THWAK
BWA HA HA HA HA! DIE, HUMAN SCUM!!
BOOM
WAAH! A HOLLOW !!
WHAT A CHEESY FACE!!
DA-DA-DOOM
STOP !!

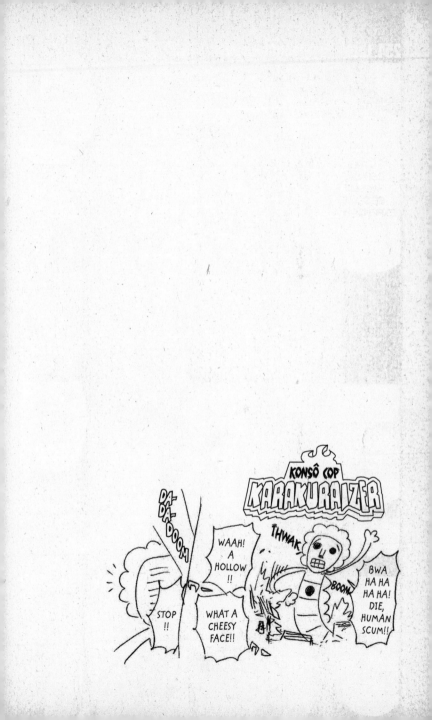

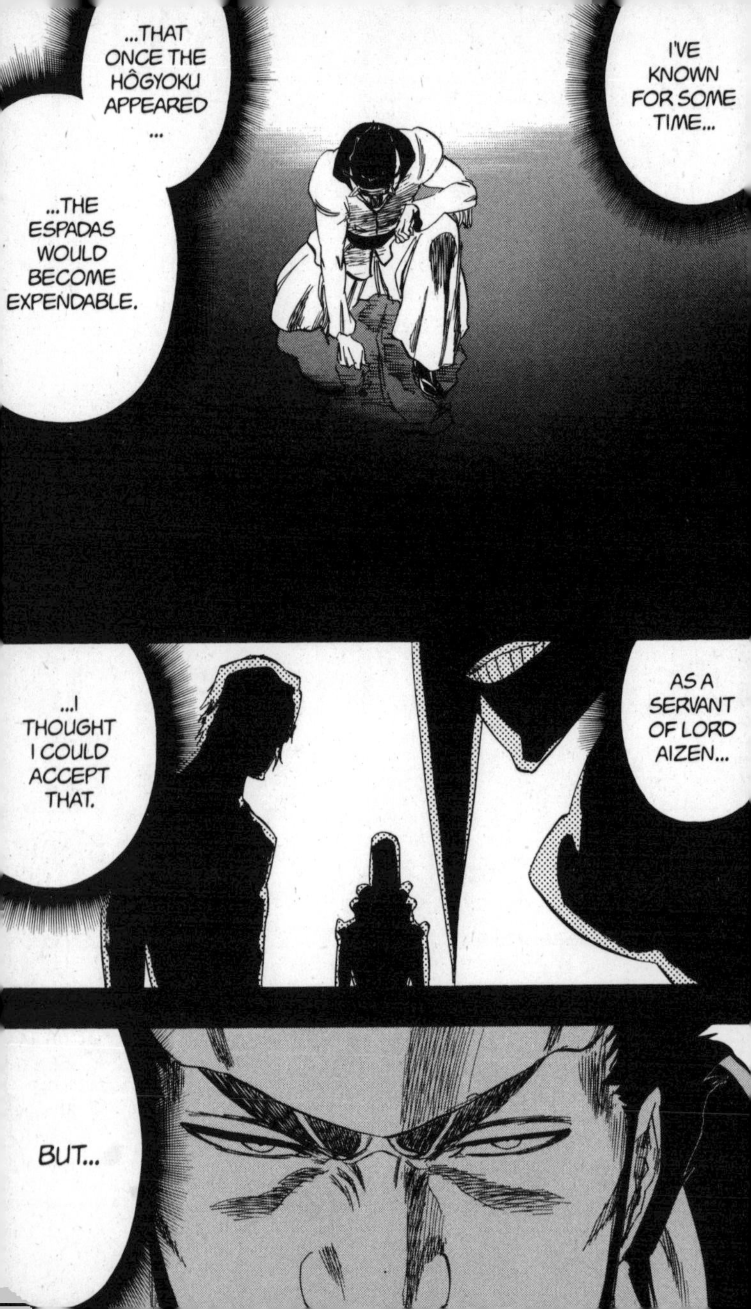
I'VE KNOWN FOR SOME TIME...
...THAT ONCE THE HÔGYOKU APPEARED ...
...THE ESPADAS WOULD BECOME EXPENDABLE.
AS A SERVANT OF LORD AIZEN...
...I THOUGHT I COULD ACCEPT THAT.
BUT...

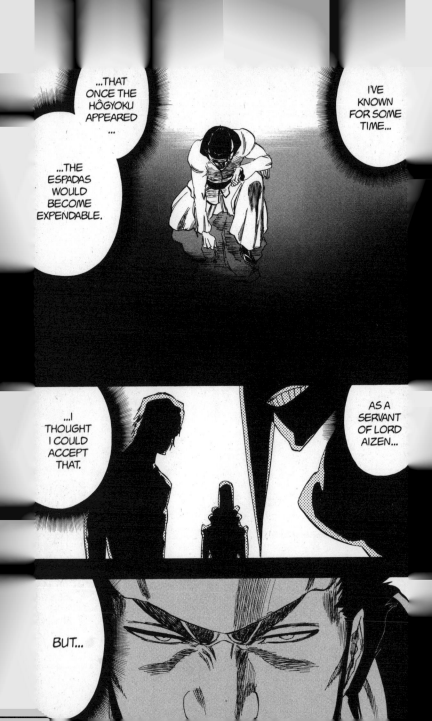

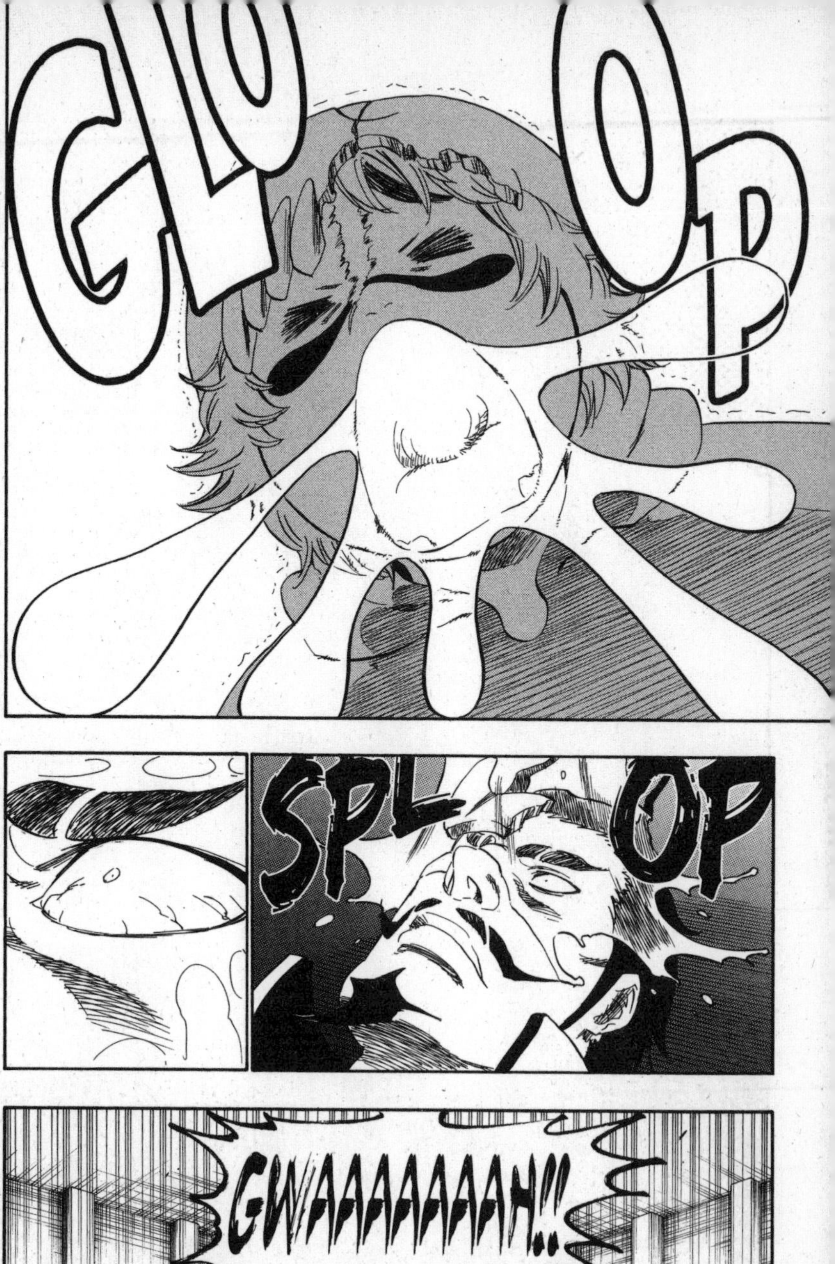
GLUOP
SPLOP
GWAAAAAAAH!!

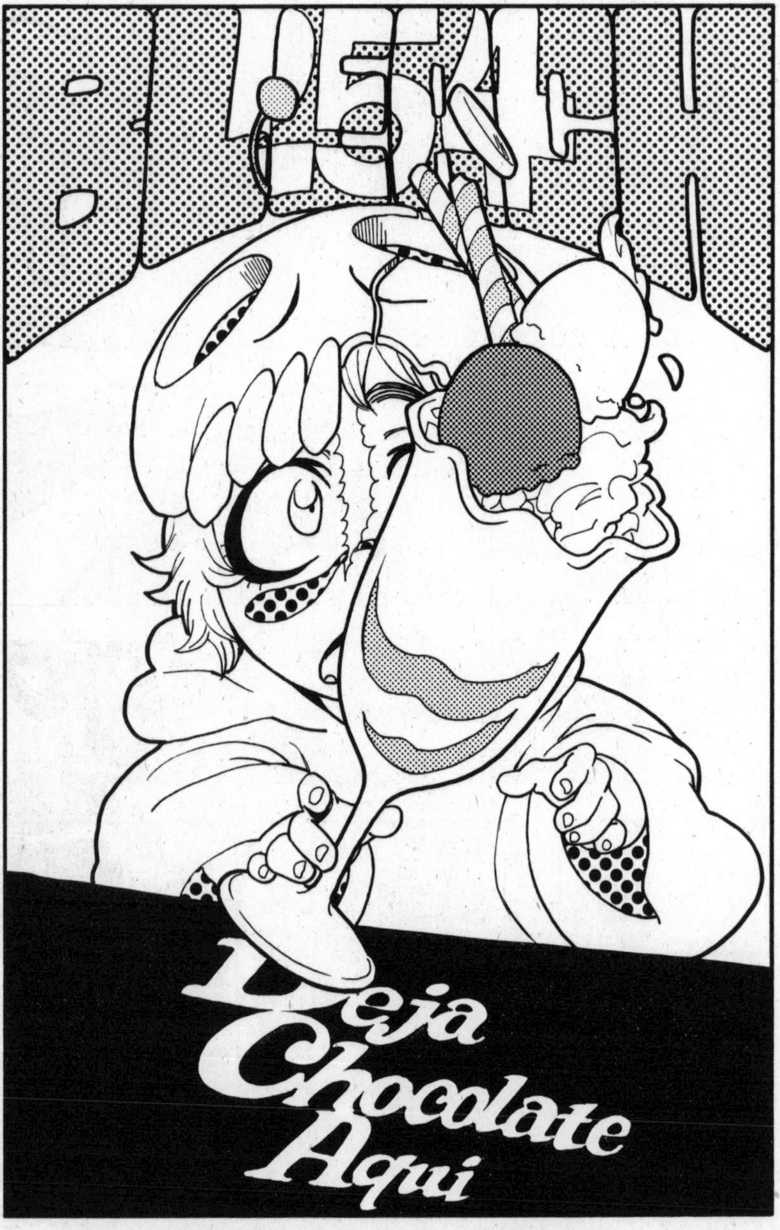
BLEACH
Deja Chocolate Aqui

BLEACH 254. Leave the Chocolate Here

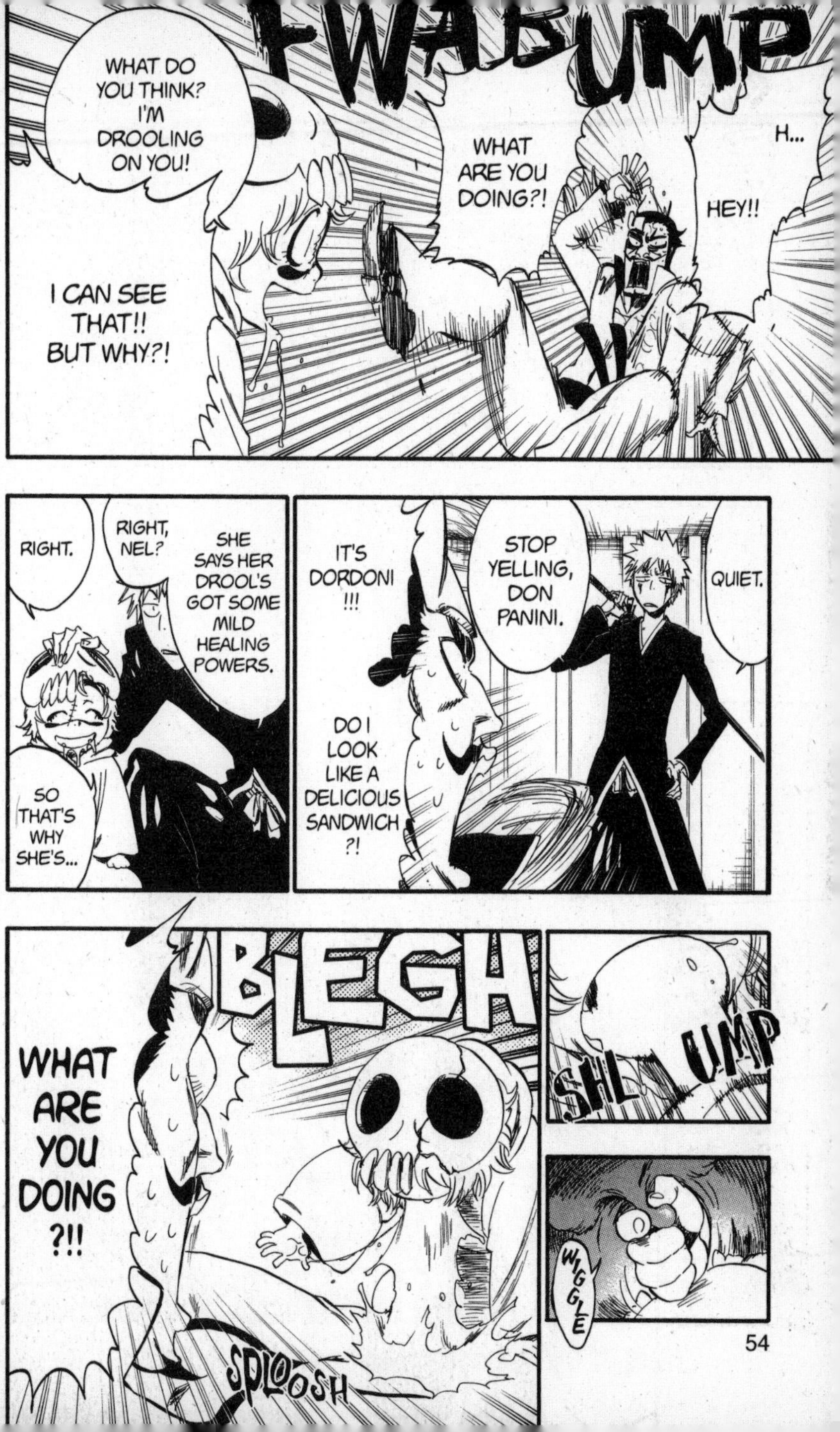

FWABUMP
H...
HEY!!
WHAT ARE YOU DOING?!
WHAT DO YOU THINK? I'M DROOLING ON YOU!
I CAN SEE THAT!! BUT WHY?!
QUIET.
STOP YELLING, DON PANINI.
IT'S DORDONI!!!
DO I LOOK LIKE A DELICIOUS SANDWICH?!
SHE SAYS HER DROOL'S GOT SOME MILD HEALING POWERS.
RIGHT, NEL?
RIGHT.
SO THAT'S WHY SHE'S...
SHLUMP
WIGGLE
BLEGH
WHAT ARE YOU DOING?!!
SPLOOSH

READ THIS WAY

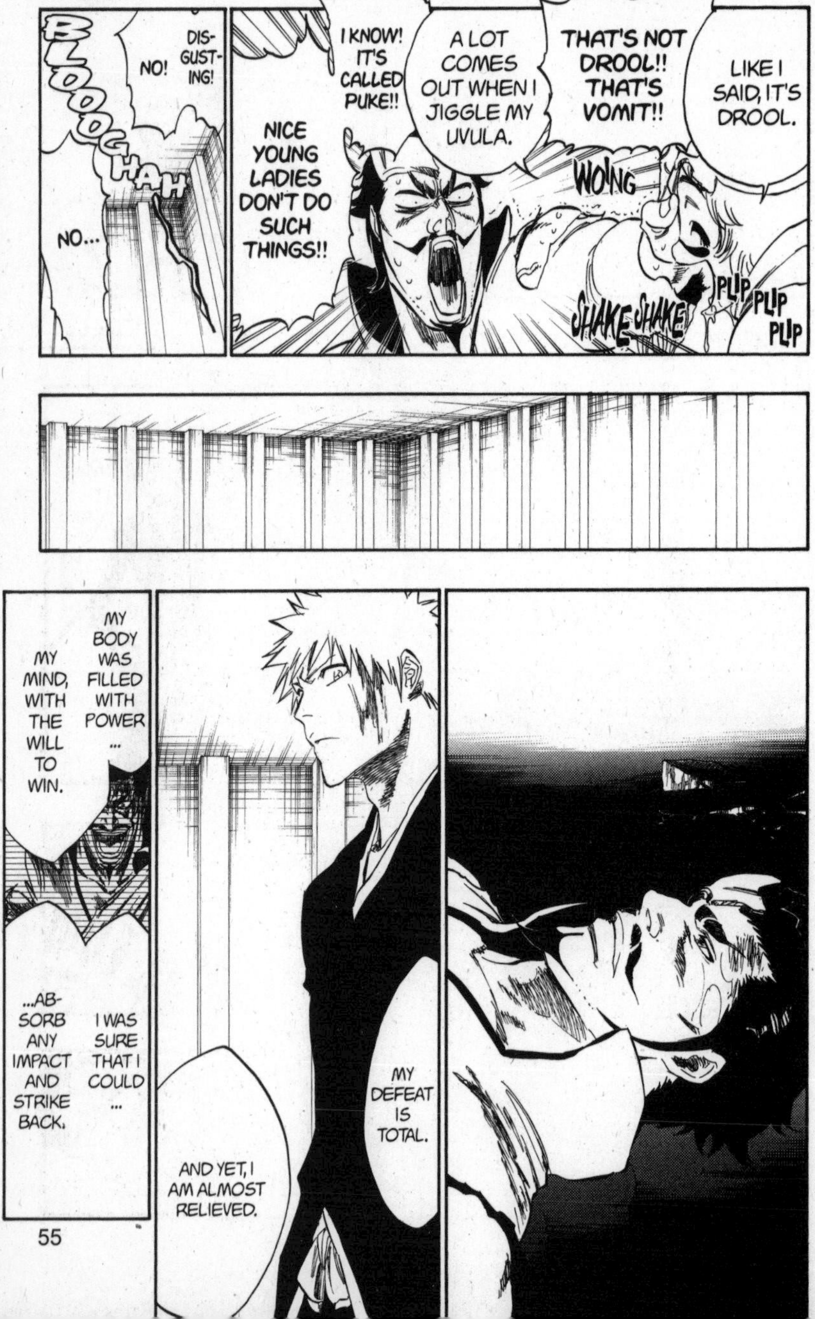
LIKE I SAID, IT'S DROOL.
THAT'S NOT DROOL!! THAT'S VOMIT!!
WOING
A LOT COMES OUT WHEN I JIGGLE MY UVULA.
I KNOW! IT'S CALLED PUKE!!
NICE YOUNG LADIES DON'T DO SUCH THINGS!!
SHAKE SHAKE
PLIP PLIP PLIP
DIS-GUSTING!
NO!
BLOODGHAH
NO...
MY DEFEAT IS TOTAL.
AND YET, I AM ALMOST RELIEVED.
MY BODY WAS FILLED WITH POWER...
MY MIND, WITH THE WILL TO WIN.
I WAS SURE THAT I COULD...
...ABSORB ANY IMPACT AND STRIKE BACK.

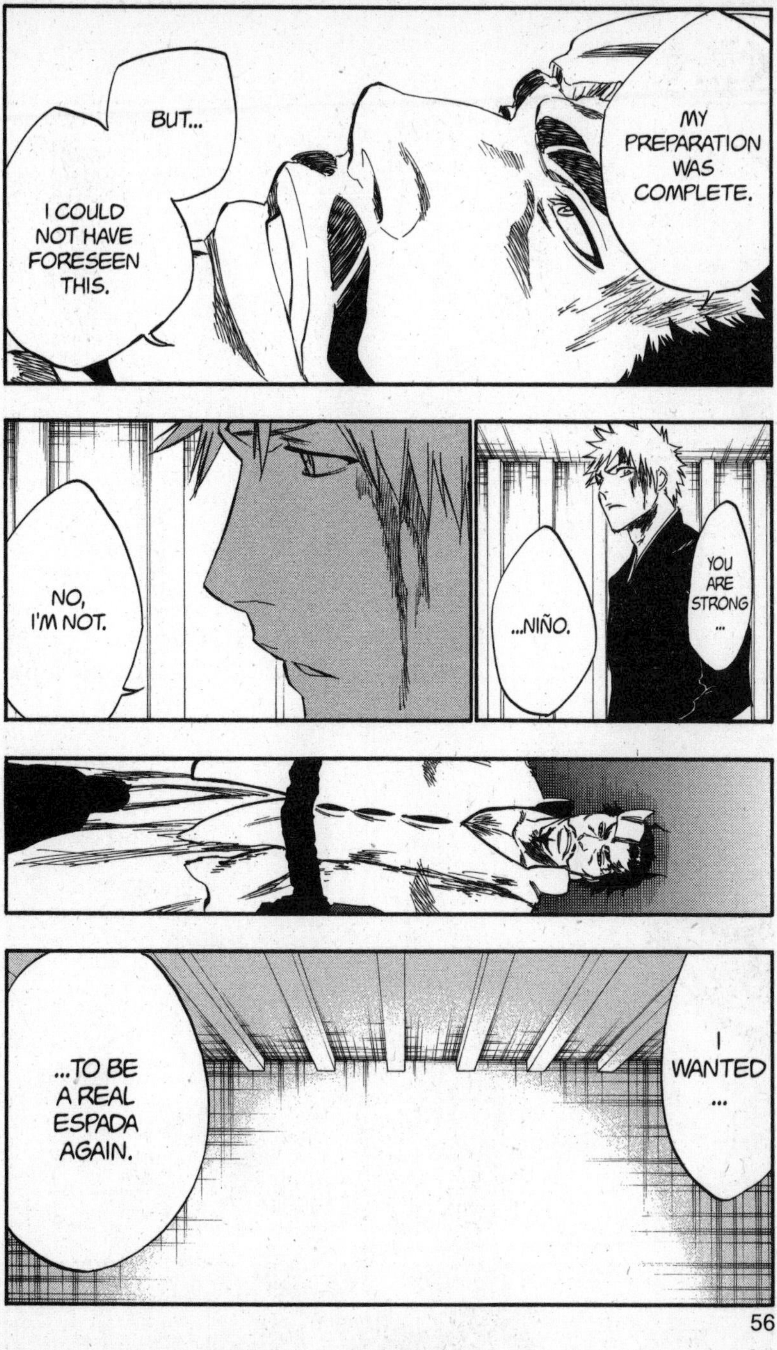
MY PREPARATION WAS COMPLETE.
BUT...
I COULD NOT HAVE FORESEEN THIS.
YOU ARE STRONG ...
...NIÑO.
NO, I'M NOT.
I WANTED ...
...TO BE A REAL ESPADA AGAIN.

READ THIS WAY

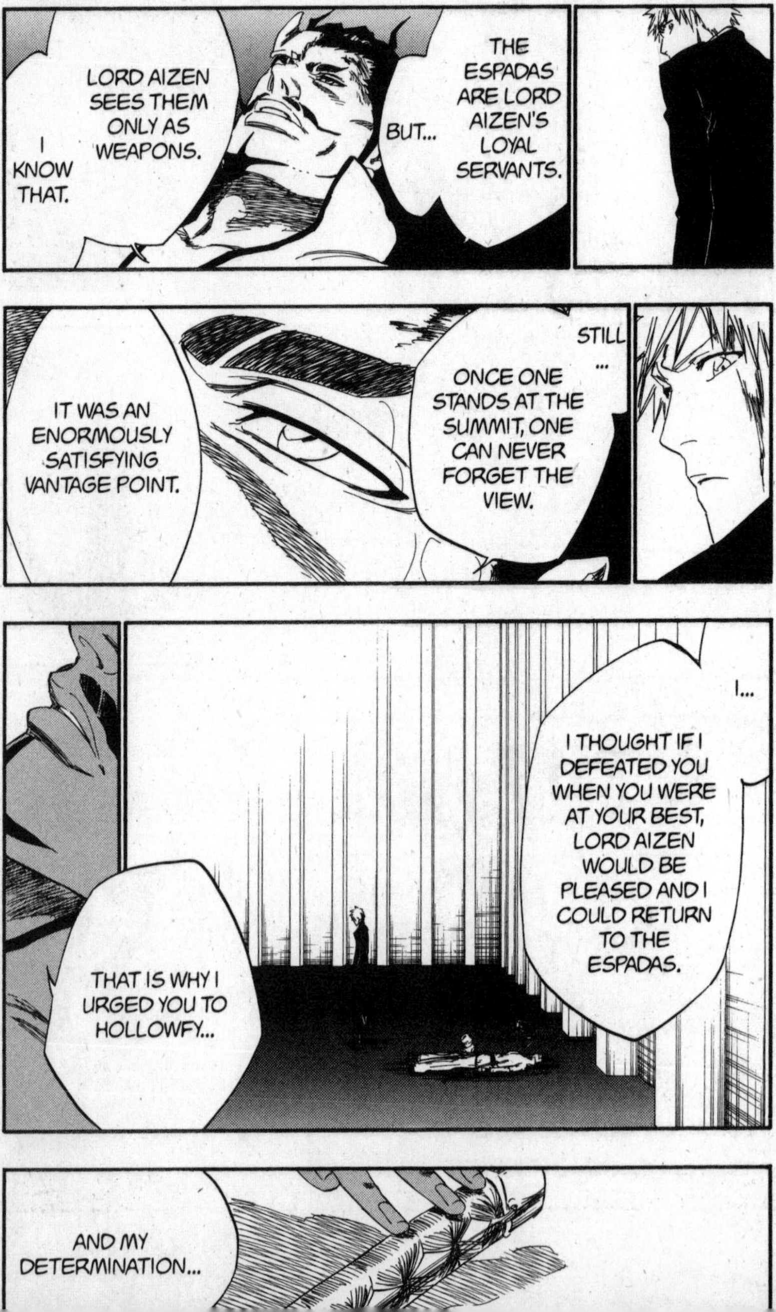
THE ESPADAS ARE LORD AIZEN'S LOYAL SERVANTS.
BUT...
LORD AIZEN SEES THEM ONLY AS WEAPONS.
I KNOW THAT.
STILL...
ONCE ONE STANDS AT THE SUMMIT, ONE CAN NEVER FORGET THE VIEW.
IT WAS AN ENORMOUSLY SATISFYING VANTAGE POINT.
I...
I THOUGHT IF I DEFEATED YOU WHEN YOU WERE AT YOUR BEST, LORD AIZEN WOULD BE PLEASED AND I COULD RETURN TO THE ESPADAS.
THAT IS WHY I URGED YOU TO HOLLOWFY...
AND MY DETERMINATION...

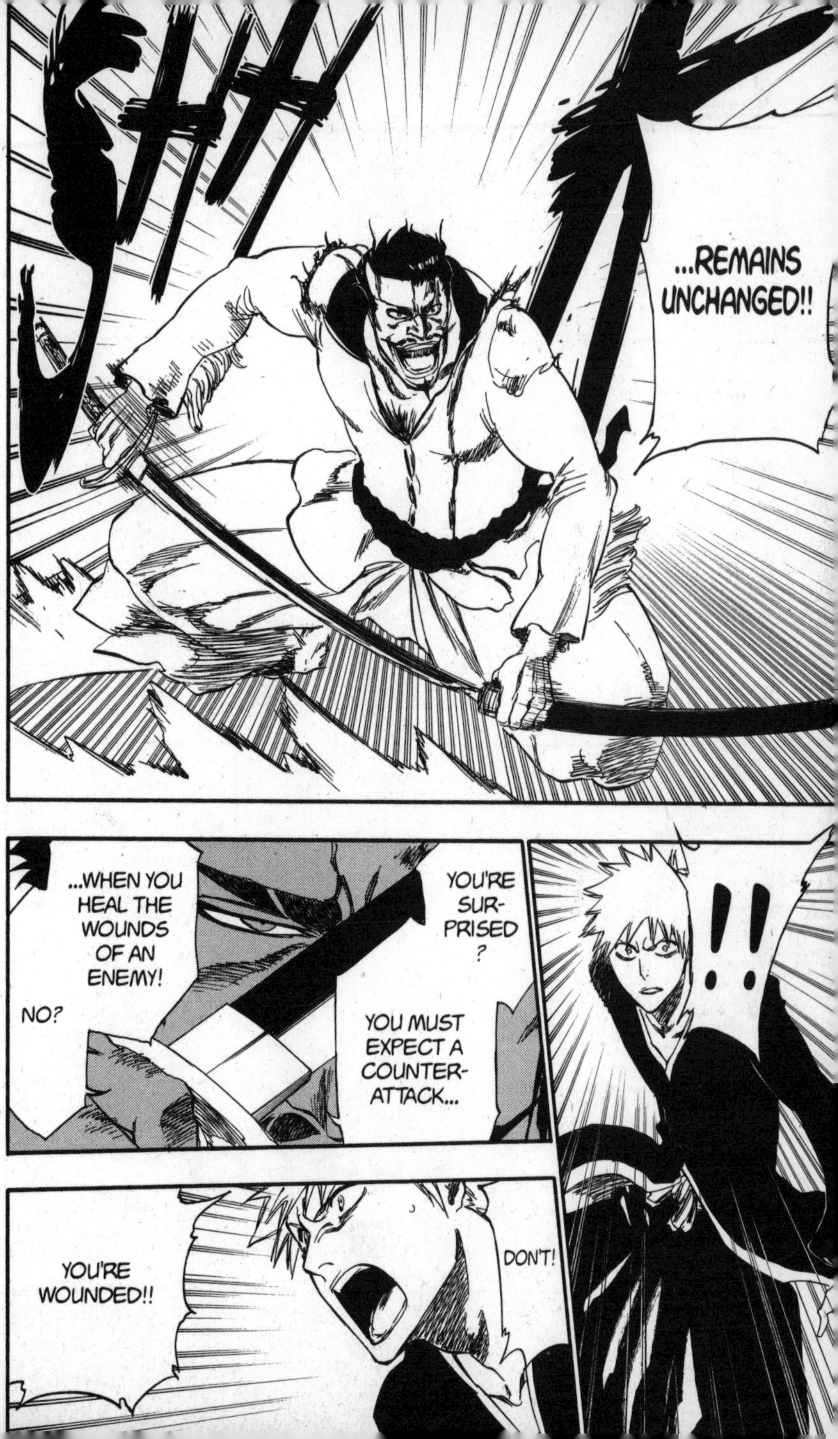
...REMAINS UNCHANGED!!
!!
YOU'RE SUR-PRISED?
...WHEN YOU HEAL THE WOUNDS OF AN ENEMY!
YOU MUST EXPECT A COUNTER-ATTACK...
NO?
DON'T!
YOU'RE WOUNDED!!

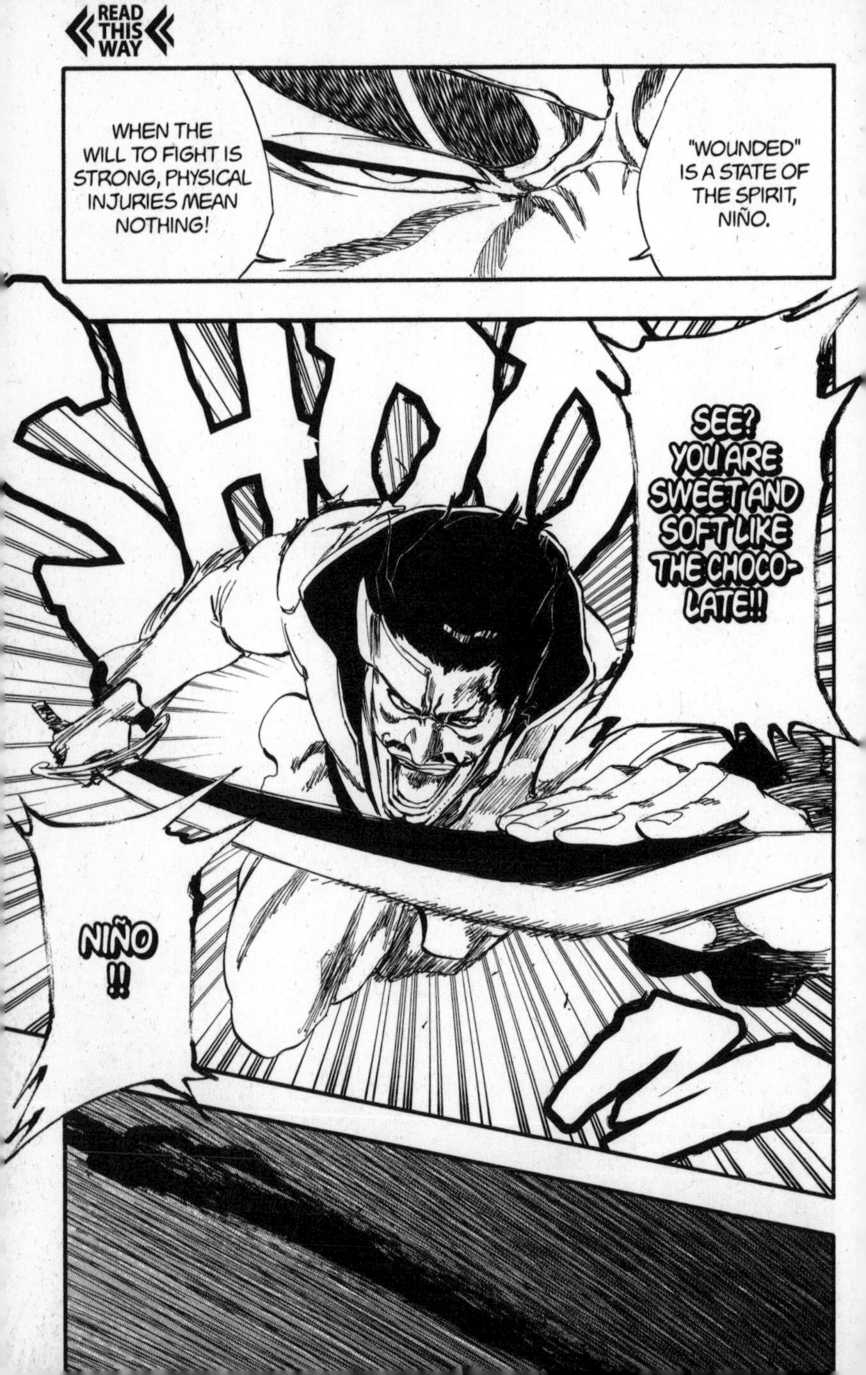
READ THIS WAY
"WOUNDED" IS A STATE OF THE SPIRIT, NIÑO.
WHEN THE WILL TO FIGHT IS STRONG, PHYSICAL INJURIES MEAN NOTHING!
SEE? YOU ARE SWEET AND SOFT LIKE THE CHOCO-LATE!!
NIÑO !!

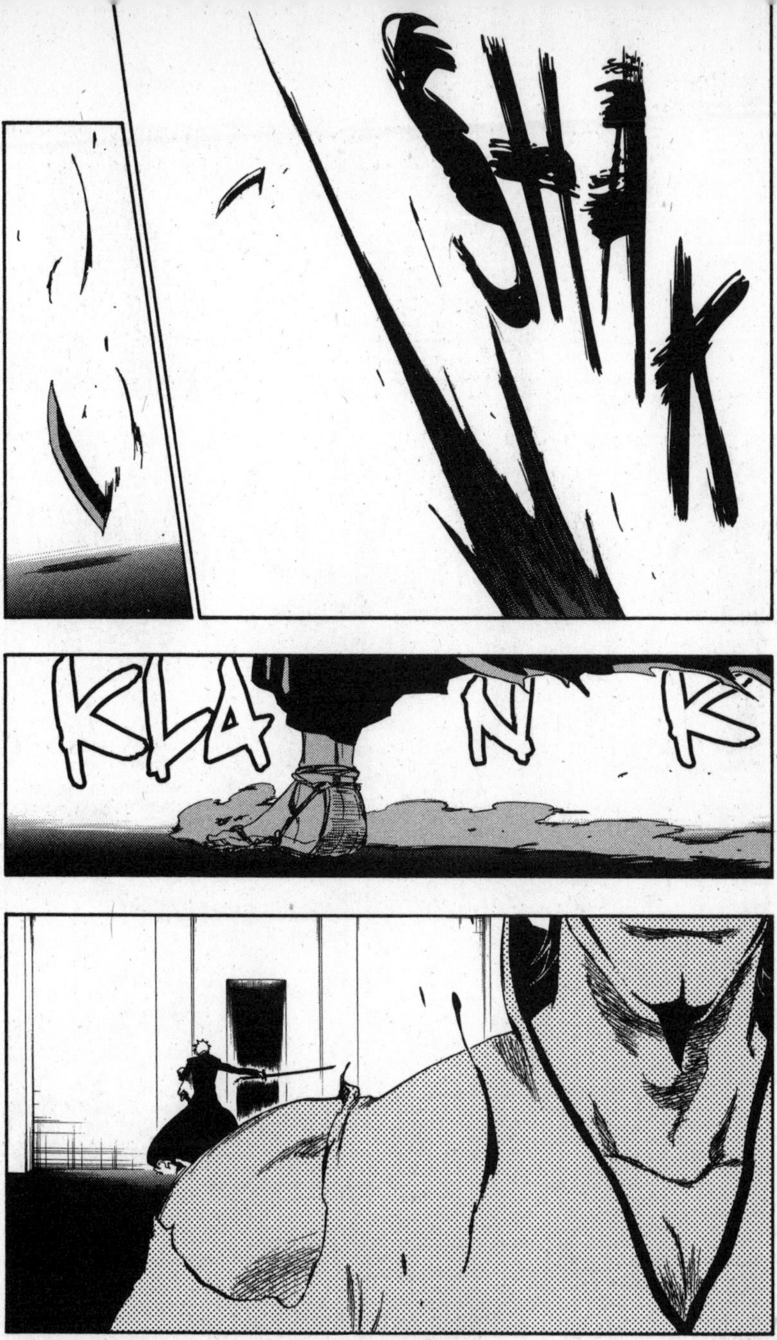
SHNK
KLANK

READ THIS WAY

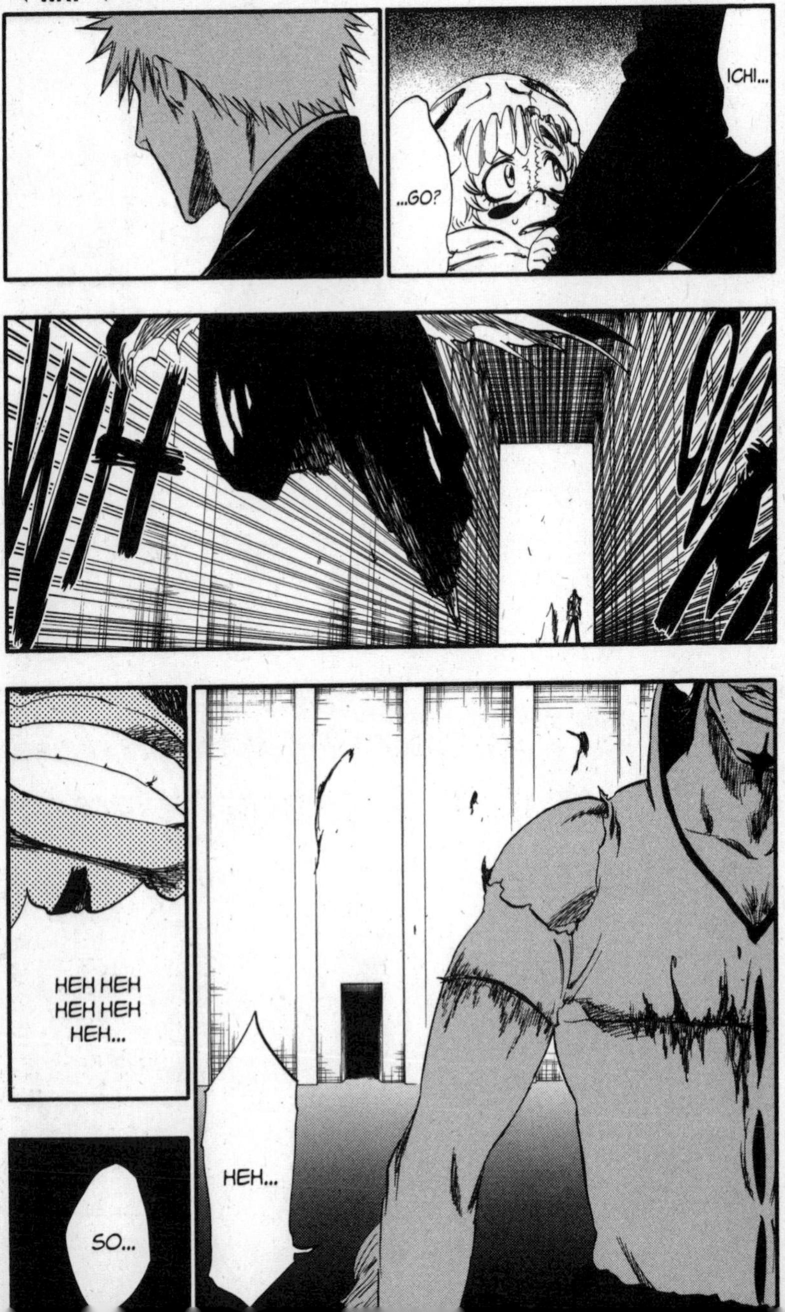
ICHI...
...GO?
HEH...
HEH HEH HEH HEH HEH...
SO...

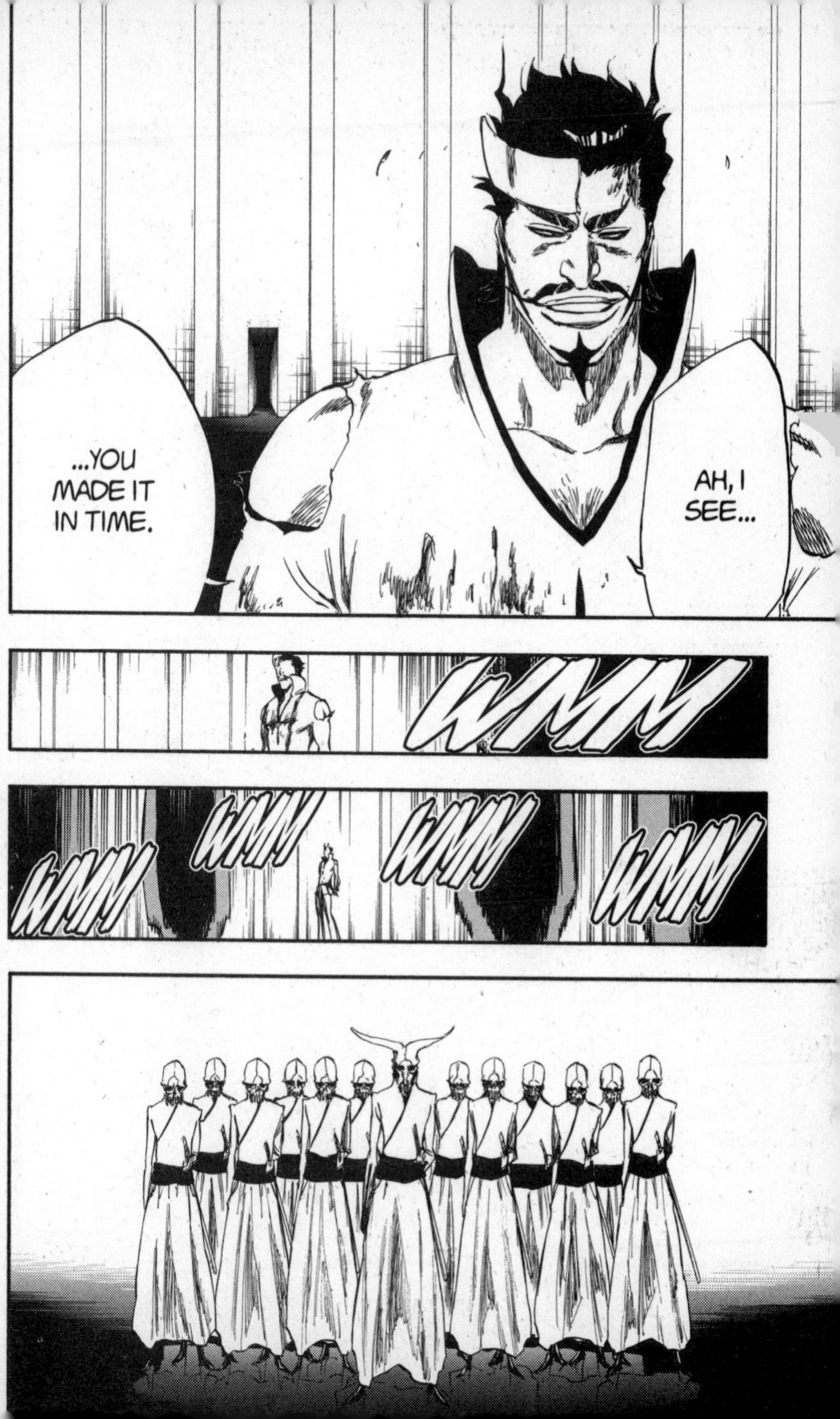
AH, I SEE...
...YOU MADE IT IN TIME.
WMM
WMM
WMM
WMM
WMM

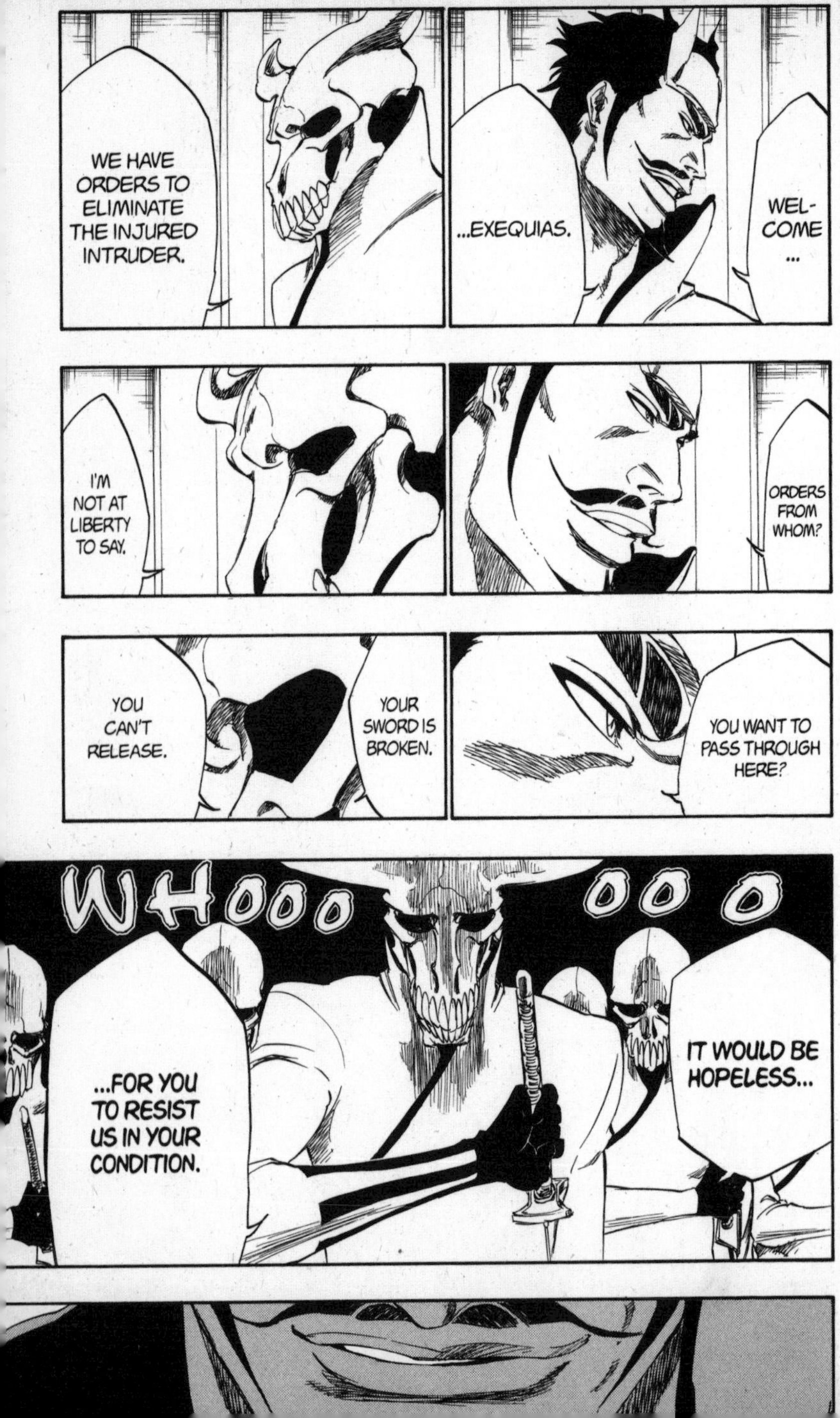
WEL-COME ...
...EXEQUIAS.
WE HAVE ORDERS TO ELIMINATE THE INJURED INTRUDER.
ORDERS FROM WHOM?
I'M NOT AT LIBERTY TO SAY.
YOU WANT TO PASS THROUGH HERE?
YOUR SWORD IS BROKEN.
YOU CAN'T RELEASE.
WHOOO OO O
IT WOULD BE HOPELESS...
...FOR YOU TO RESIST US IN YOUR CONDITION.

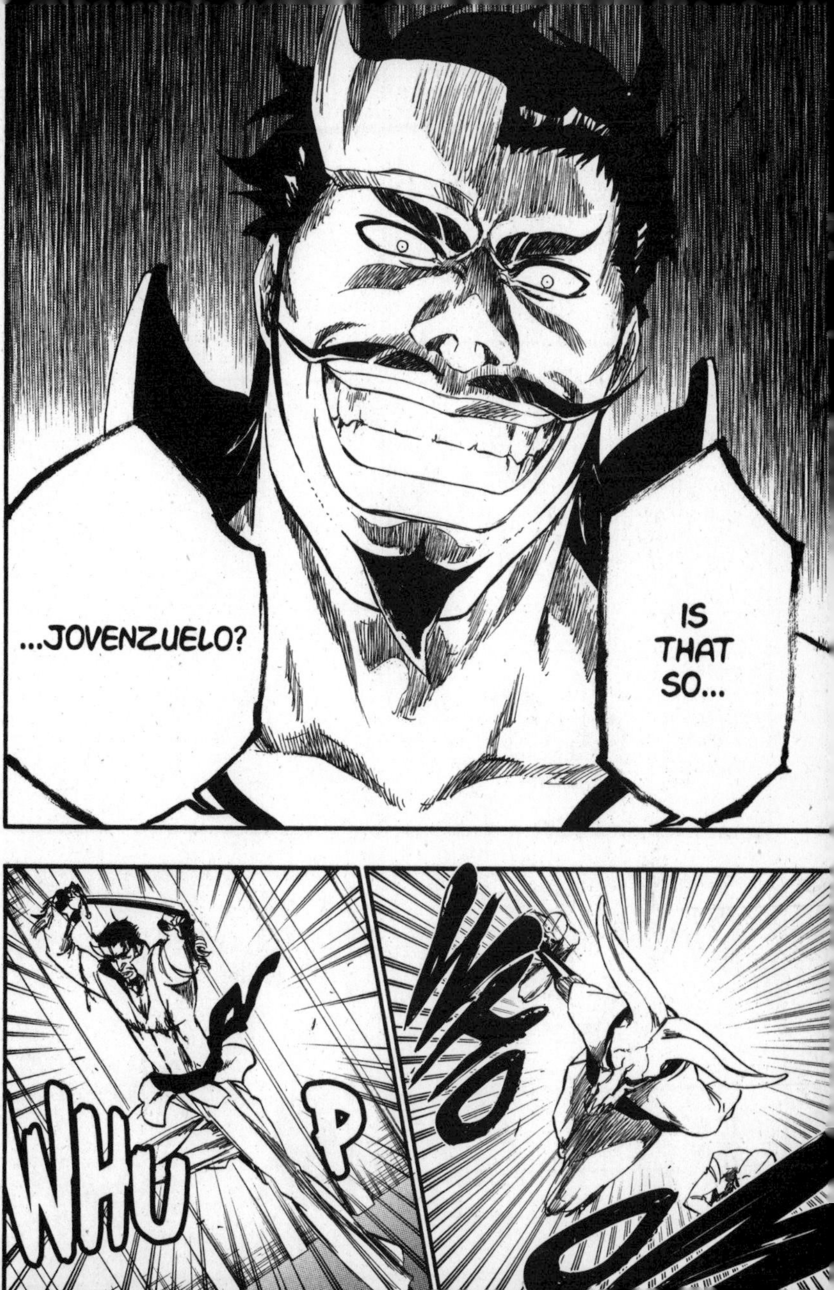
IS THAT SO...
...JOVENZUELO?
WHUP

READ THIS WAY

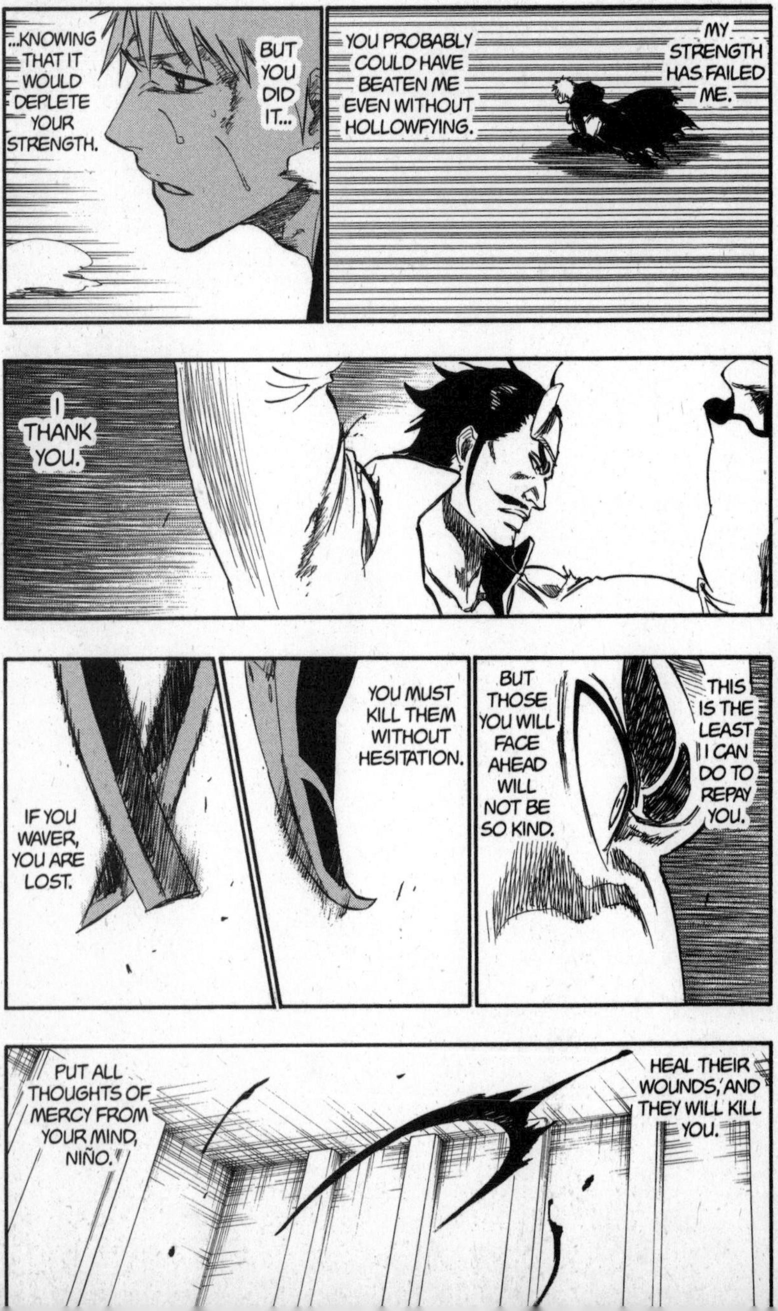
MY STRENGTH HAS FAILED ME.
YOU PROBABLY COULD HAVE BEATEN ME EVEN WITHOUT HOLLOWFYING.
BUT YOU DID IT...
...KNOWING THAT IT WOULD DEPLETE YOUR STRENGTH.
I THANK YOU.
THIS IS THE LEAST I CAN DO TO REPAY YOU.
BUT THOSE YOU WILL FACE AHEAD WILL NOT BE SO KIND.
YOU MUST KILL THEM WITHOUT HESITATION.
IF YOU WAVER, YOU ARE LOST.
HEAL THEIR WOUNDS, AND THEY WILL KILL YOU.
PUT ALL THOUGHTS OF MERCY FROM YOUR MIND, NIÑO.

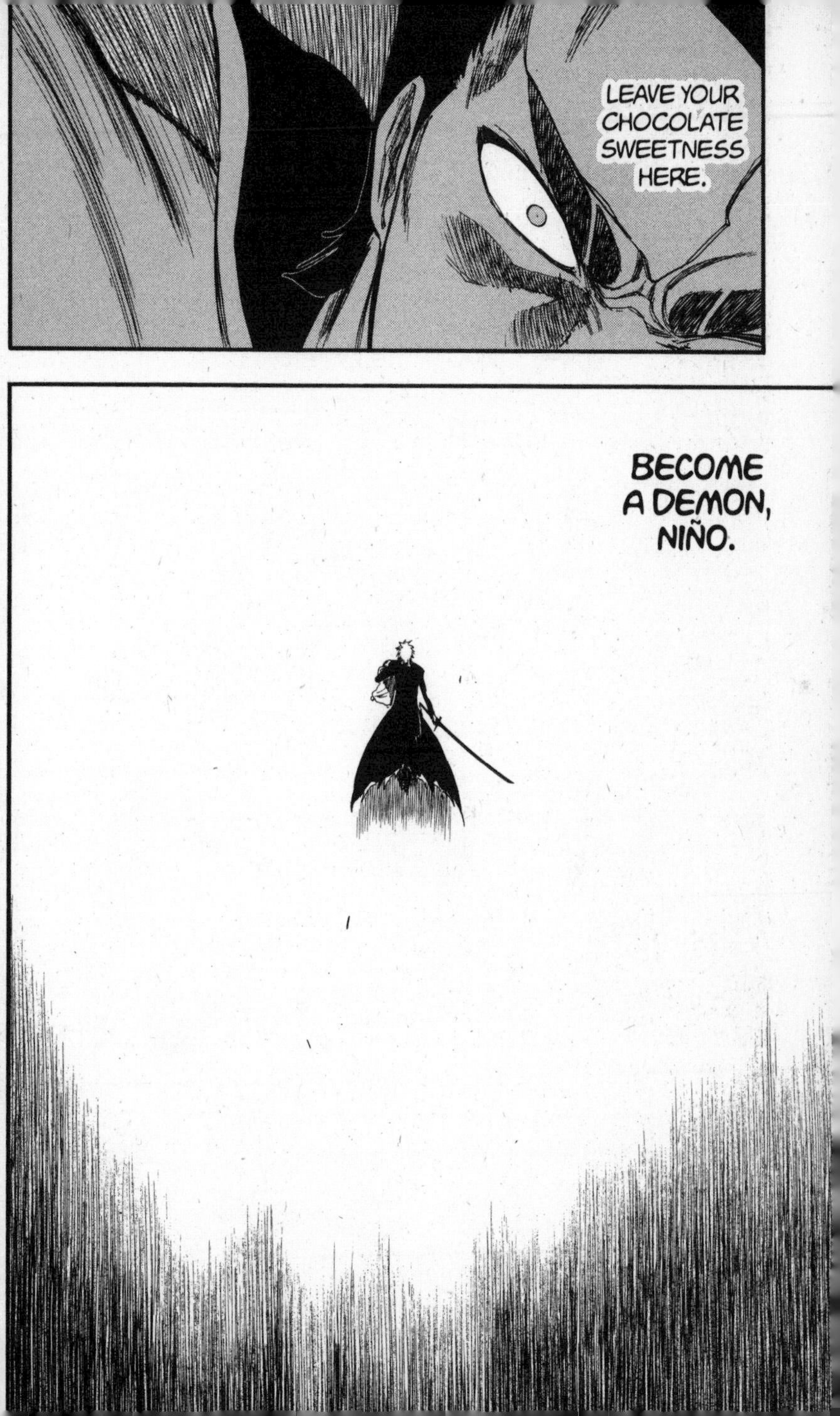
LEAVE YOUR CHOCOLATE SWEETNESS HERE.
BECOME A DEMON, NIÑO.

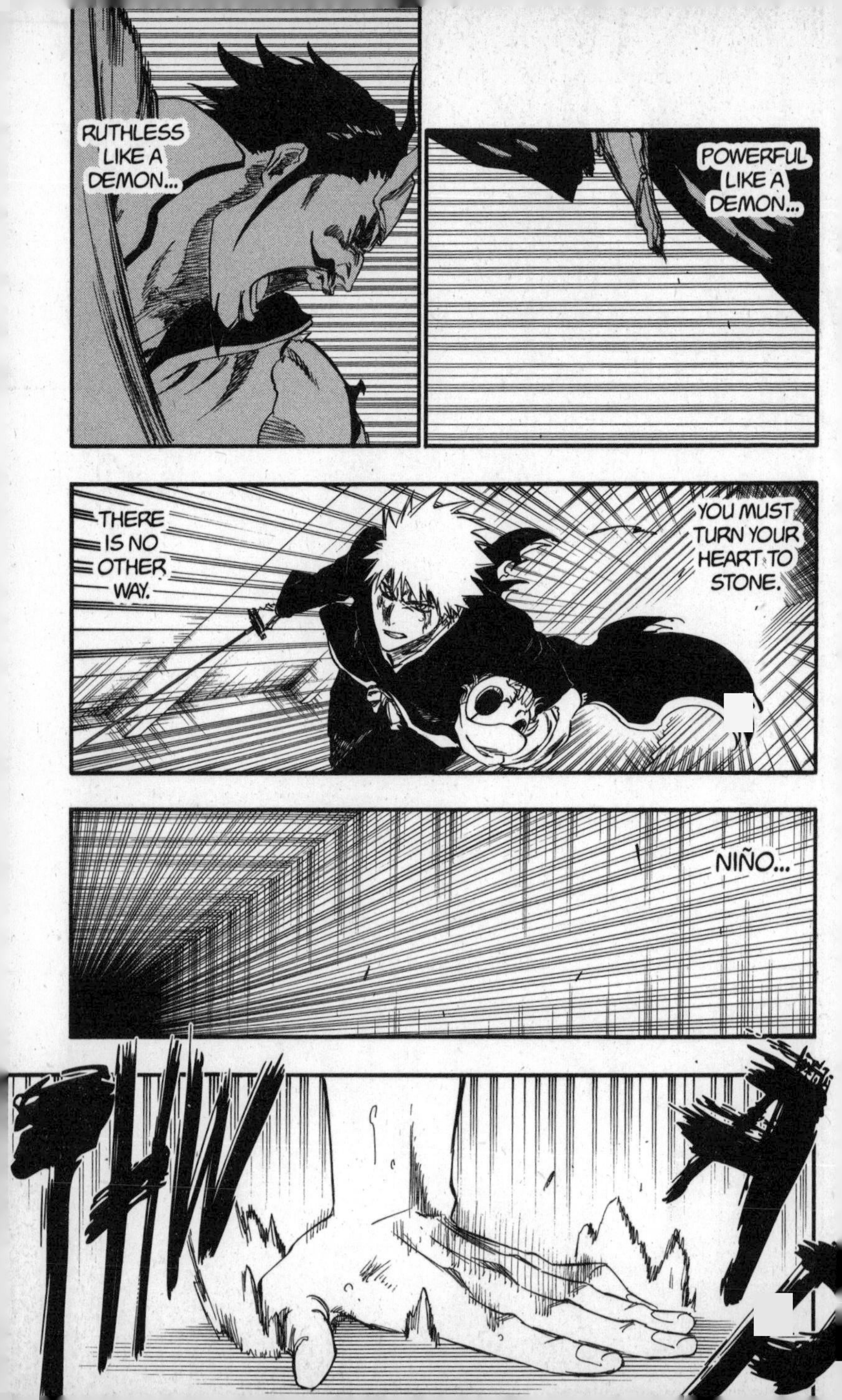
POWERFUL LIKE A DEMON...
RUTHLESS LIKE A DEMON...
YOU MUST TURN YOUR HEART TO STONE.
THERE IS NO OTHER WAY.
NIÑO...

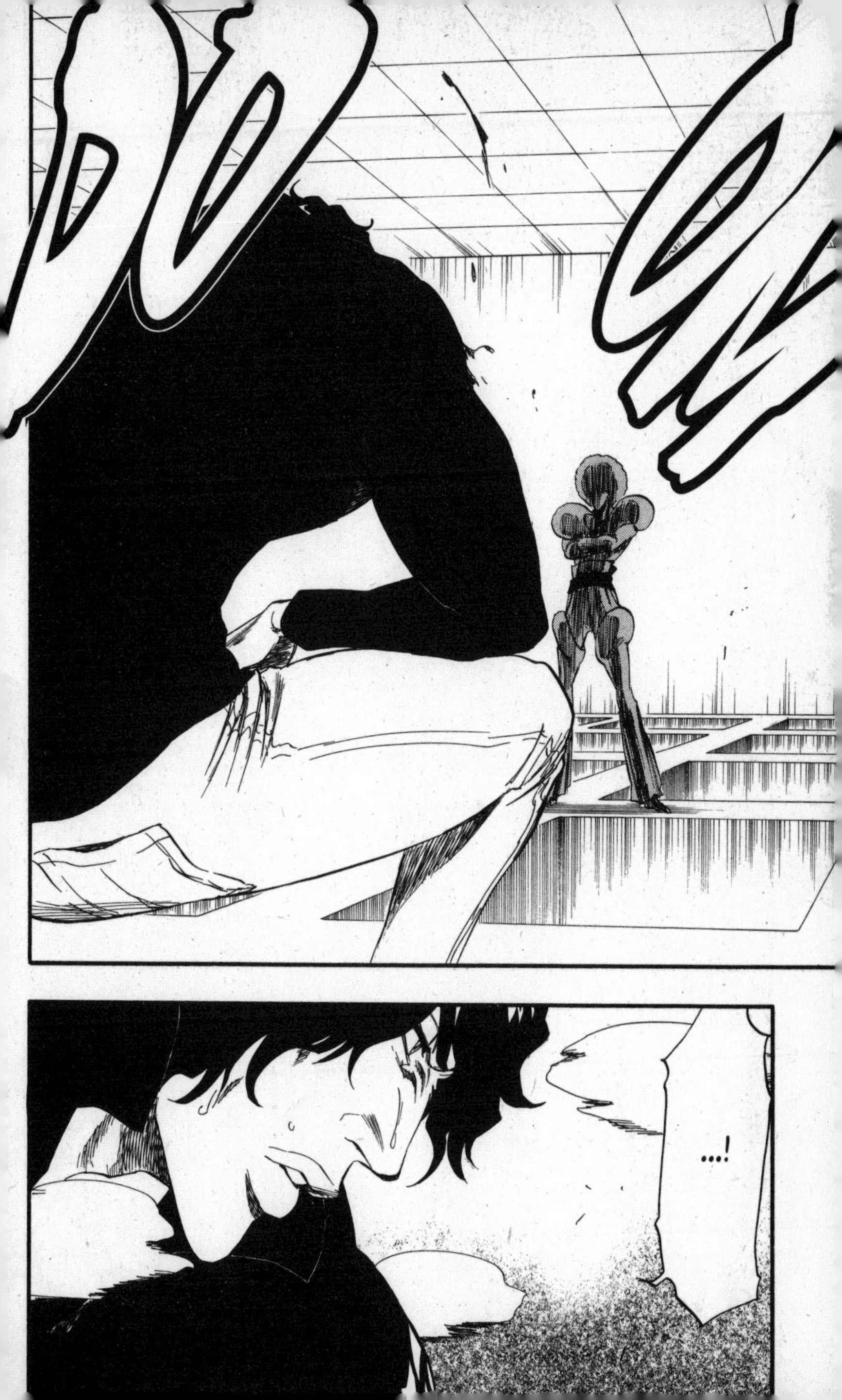
...!

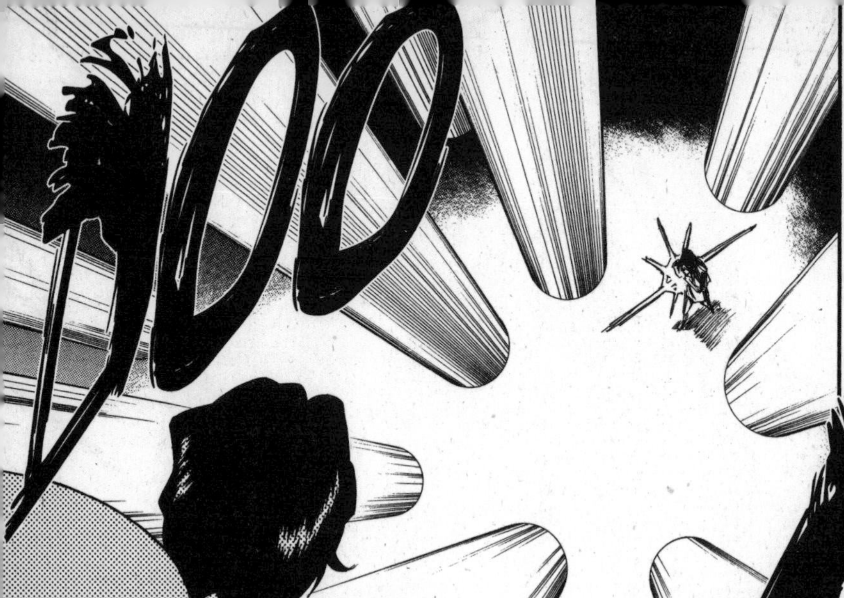
DOOM

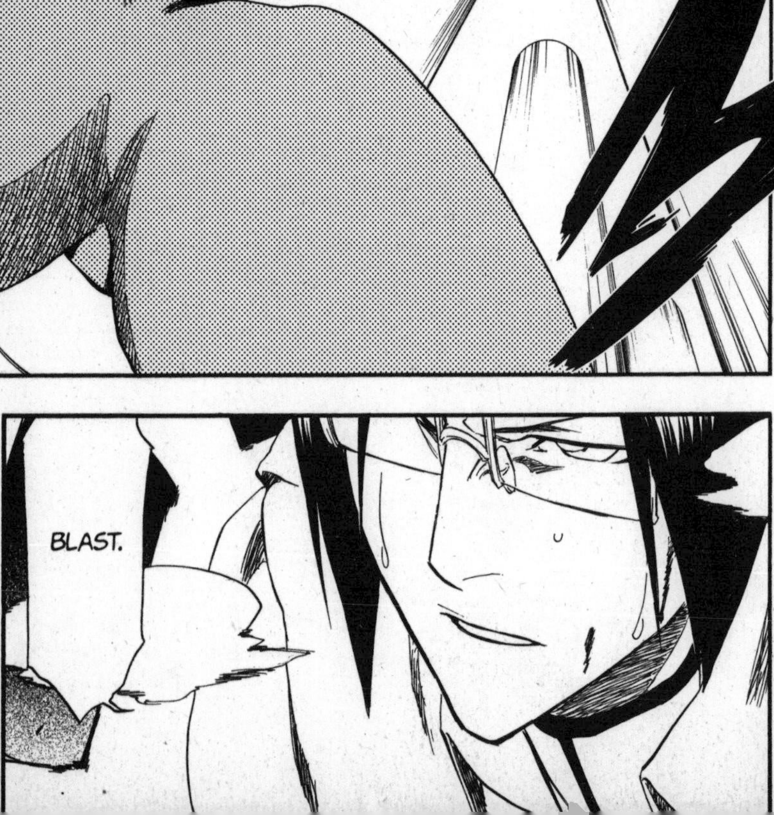
BLAST.

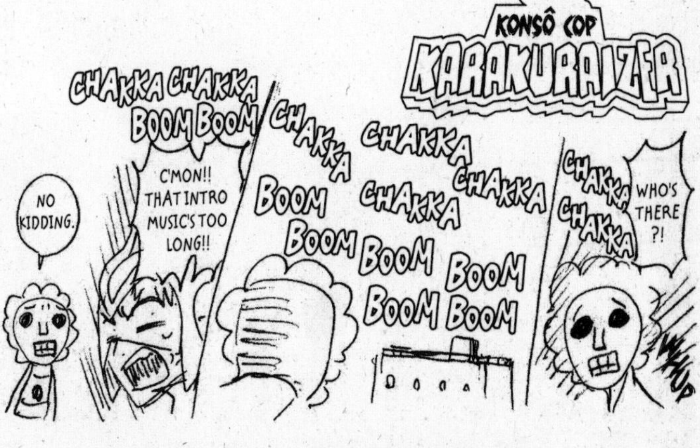
KONSÔ COP
KARAKURAIZER
CHAKKA CHAKKA
WHO'S THERE ?!
CHAKKA CHAKKA CHAKKA CHAKKA
BOOM BOOM BOOM BOOM BOOM BOOM
CHAKKA CHAKKA BOOM BOOM
C'MON!! THAT INTRO MUSIC'S TOO LONG!!
NO KIDDING.

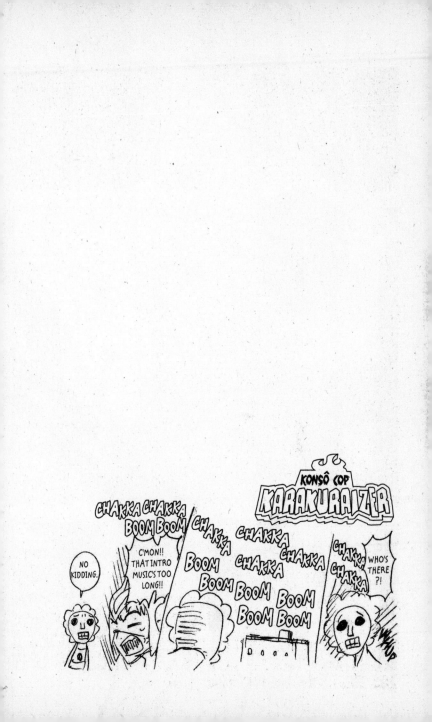

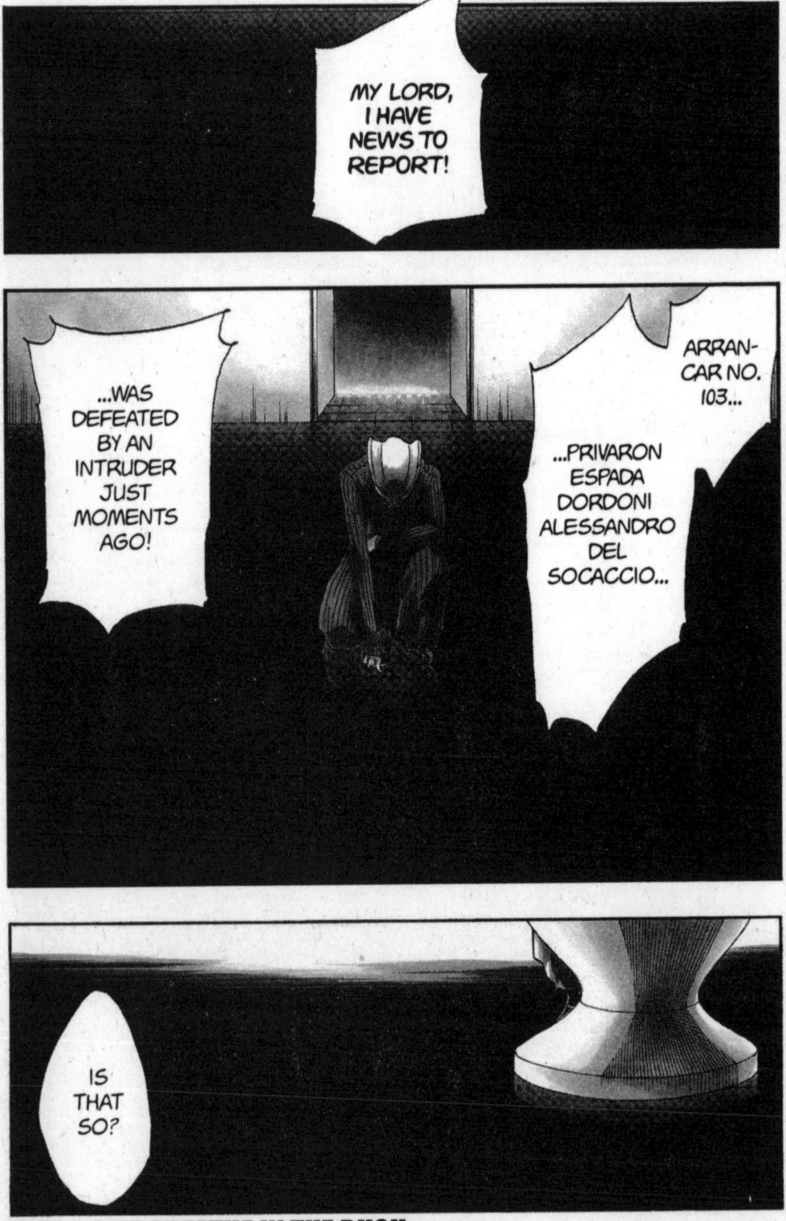
MY LORD, I HAVE NEWS TO REPORT!
ARRAN-CAR NO. 103...
...PRIVARON ESPADA DORDONI ALESSANDRO DEL SOCACCIO...
...WAS DEFEATED BY AN INTRUDER JUST MOMENTS AGO!
IS THAT SO?

255. DON'T BREATHE IN THE BUSH

255

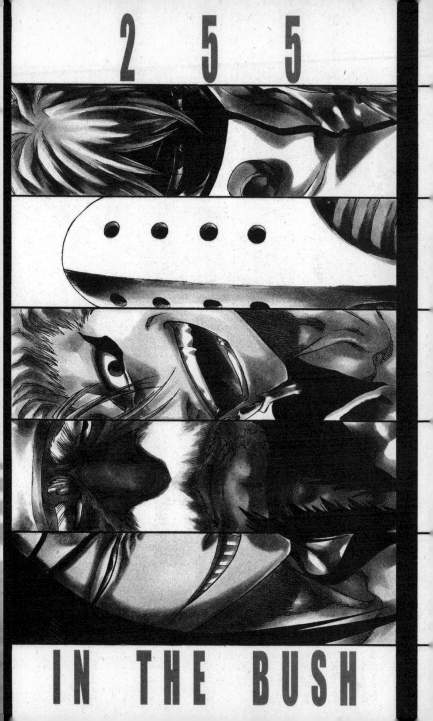

IN THE BUSH

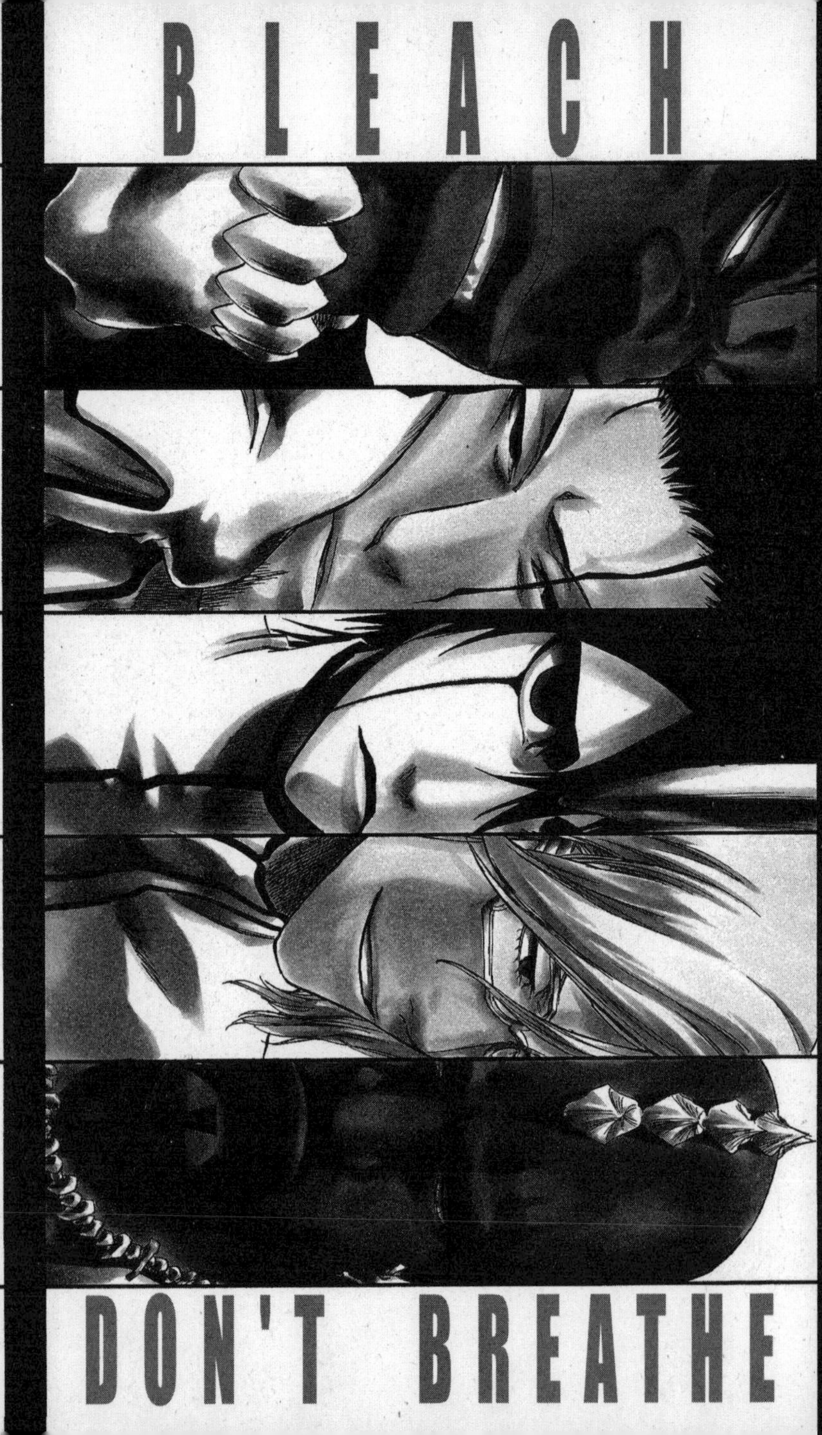
BLEACH
DON'T BREATHE

BLEACH
ブリーチ

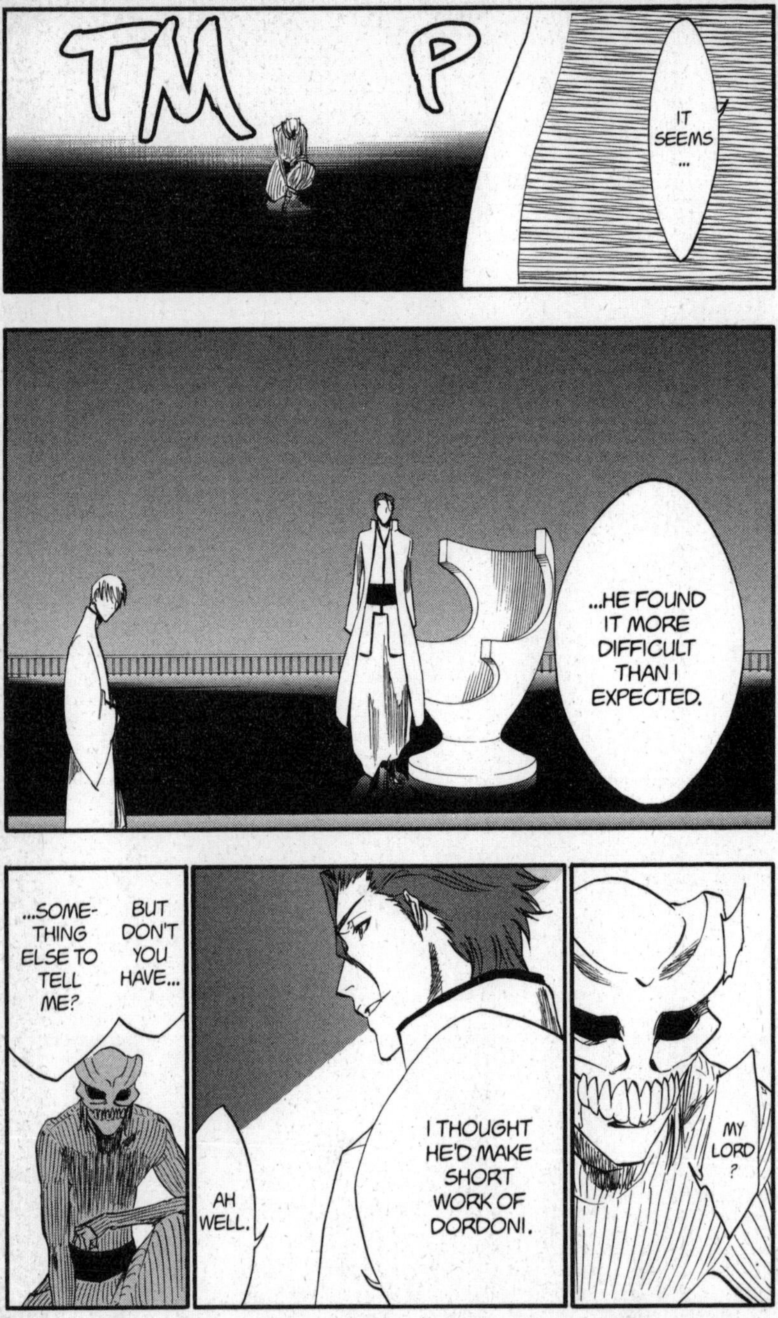
IT SEEMS ...
TM P
...HE FOUND IT MORE DIFFICULT THAN I EXPECTED.
MY LORD ?
I THOUGHT HE'D MAKE SHORT WORK OF DORDONI.
AH WELL.
BUT DON'T YOU HAVE...
...SOME-THING ELSE TO TELL ME?

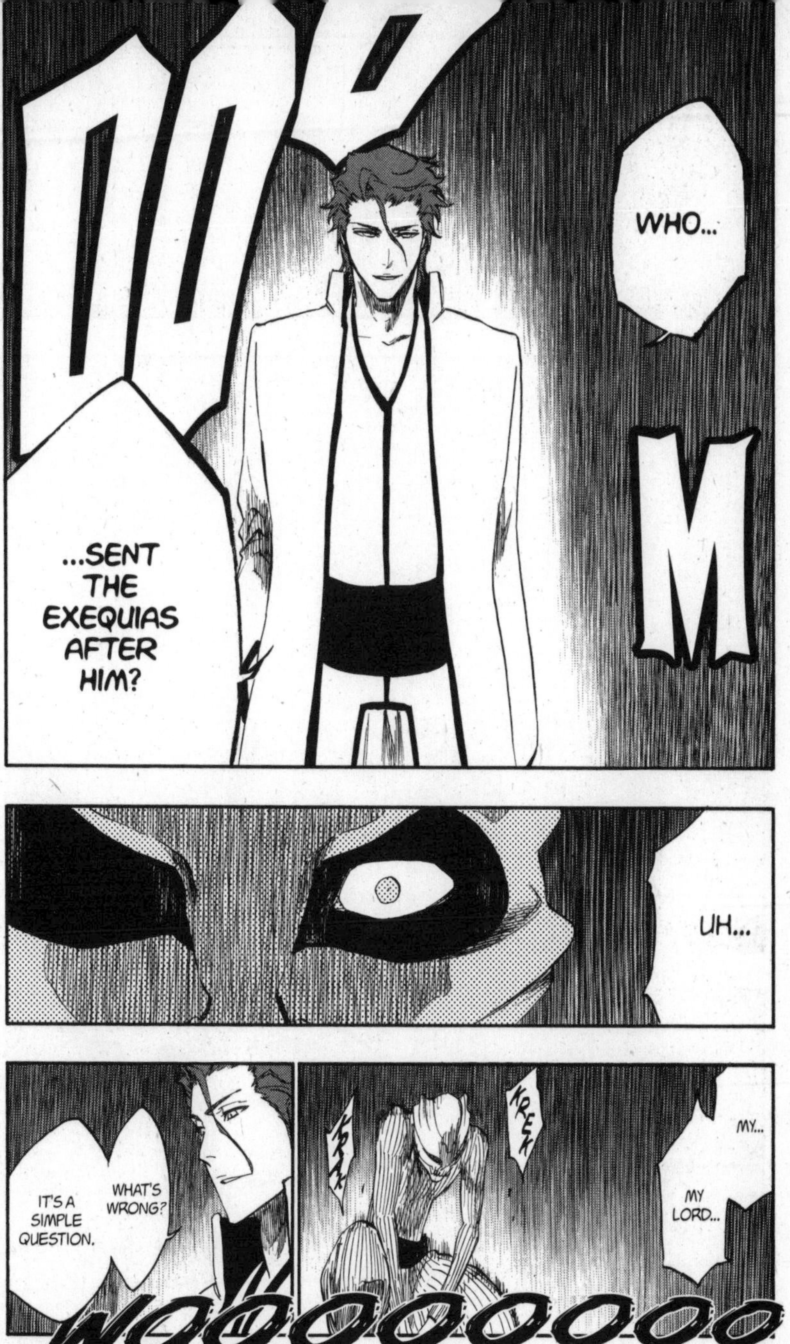
WHO...
...SENT THE EXEQUIAS AFTER HIM?
M
UH...
MY...
MY LORD...
KREK
KREK
WHAT'S WRONG?
IT'S A SIMPLE QUESTION.
WOOOOOOOOOO

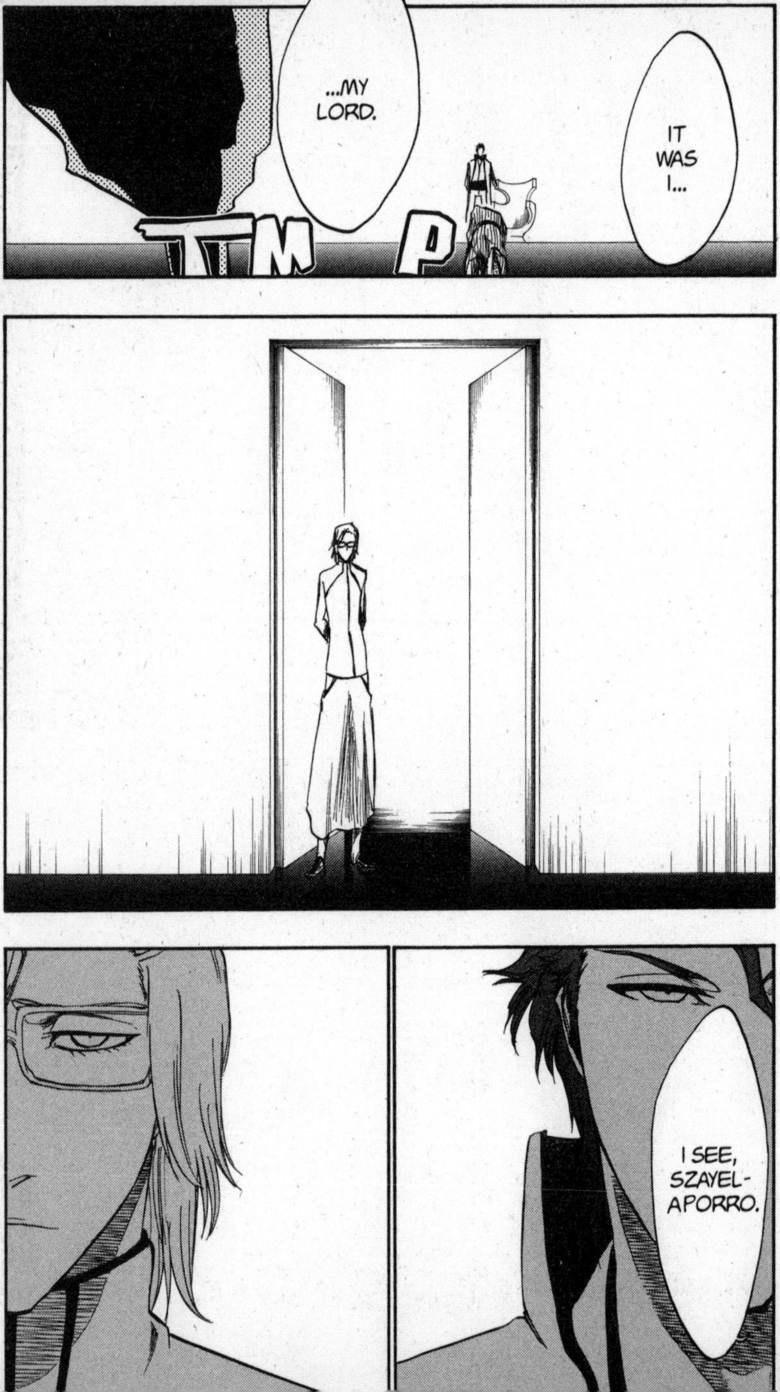
IT WAS I...
...MY LORD.
TMP
I SEE, SZAYEL-APORRO.

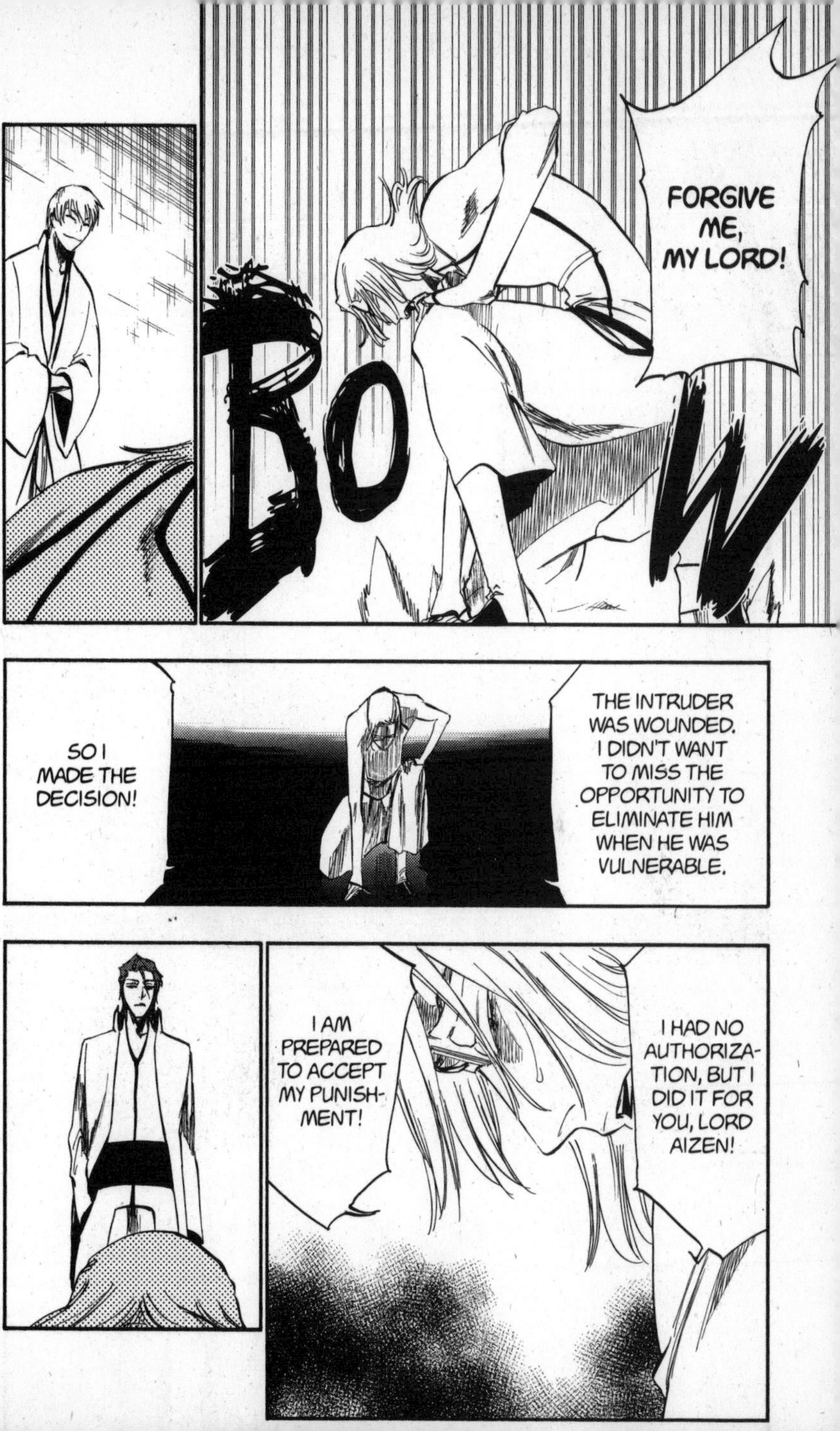
FORGIVE ME, MY LORD!
BOW
THE INTRUDER WAS WOUNDED. I DIDN'T WANT TO MISS THE OPPORTUNITY TO ELIMINATE HIM WHEN HE WAS VULNERABLE.
SO I MADE THE DECISION!
I HAD NO AUTHORIZA-TION, BUT I DID IT FOR YOU, LORD AIZEN!
I AM PREPARED TO ACCEPT MY PUNISH-MENT!

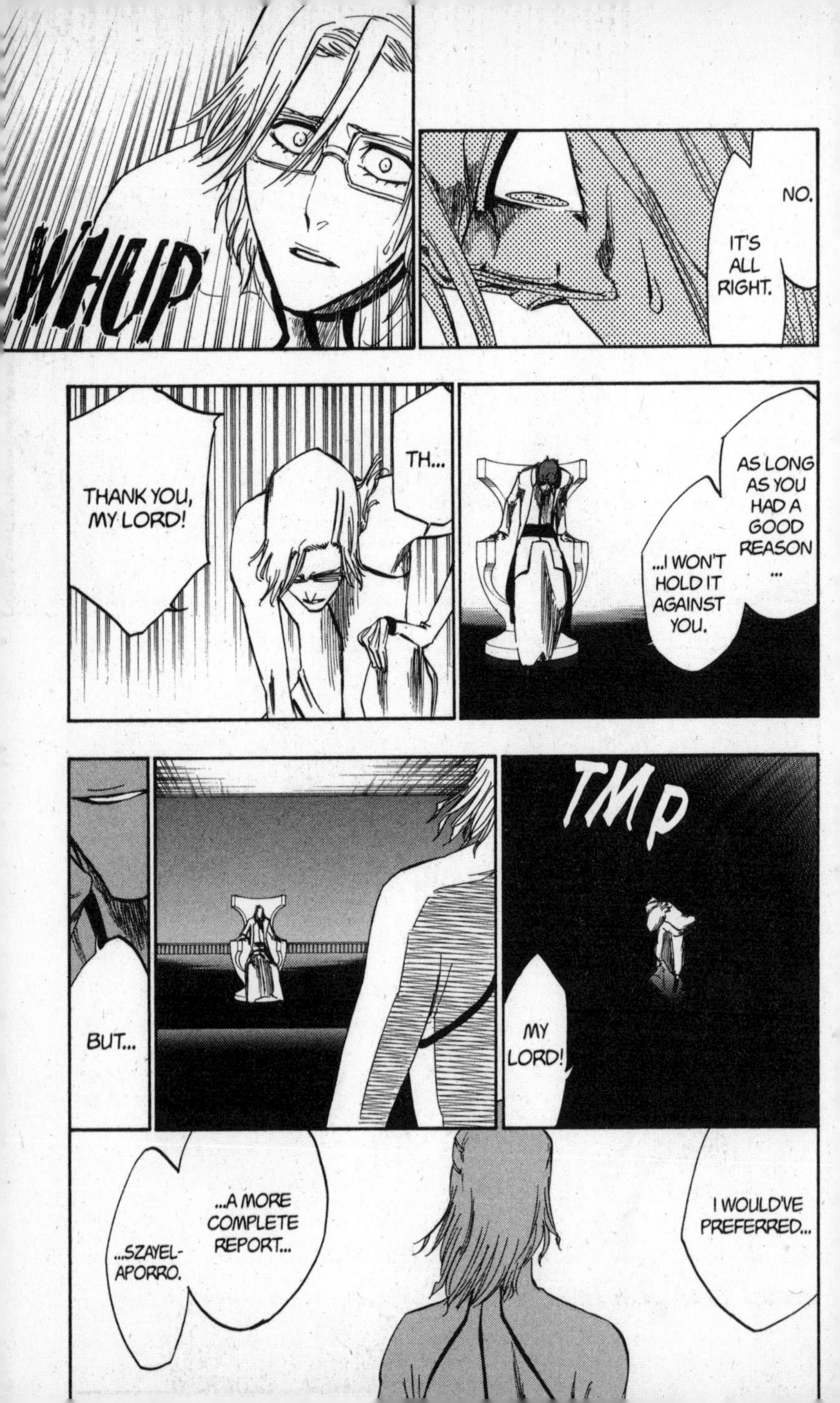
NO.
IT'S ALL RIGHT.
WHUP
AS LONG AS YOU HAD A GOOD REASON...
...I WON'T HOLD IT AGAINST YOU.
TH...
THANK YOU, MY LORD!
TMP
MY LORD!
BUT...
I WOULD'VE PREFERRED...
...A MORE COMPLETE REPORT...
...SZAYEL-APORRO.

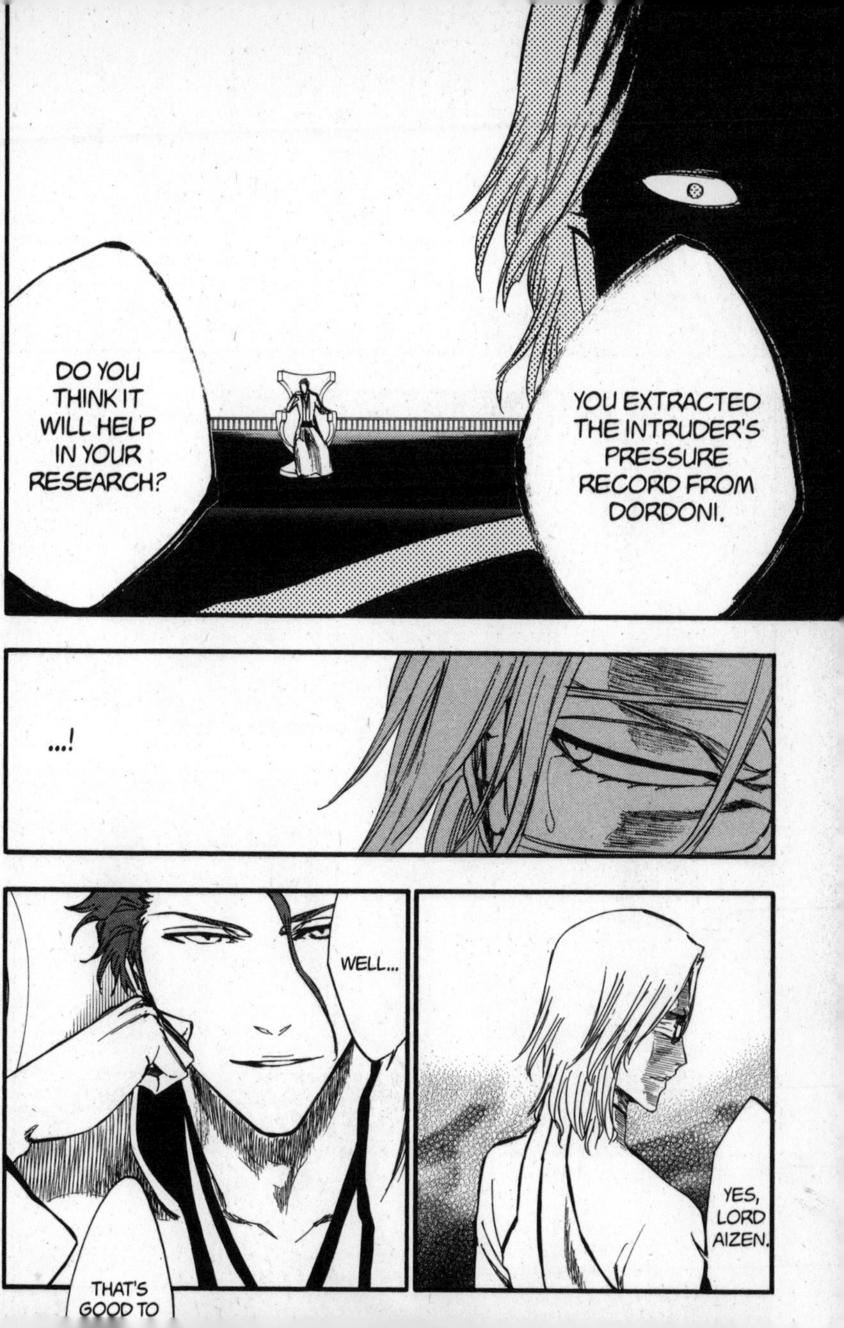
YOU EXTRACTED THE INTRUDER'S PRESSURE RECORD FROM DORDONI.
DO YOU THINK IT WILL HELP IN YOUR RESEARCH?
...!
YES, LORD AIZEN.
WELL...
THAT'S GOOD TO

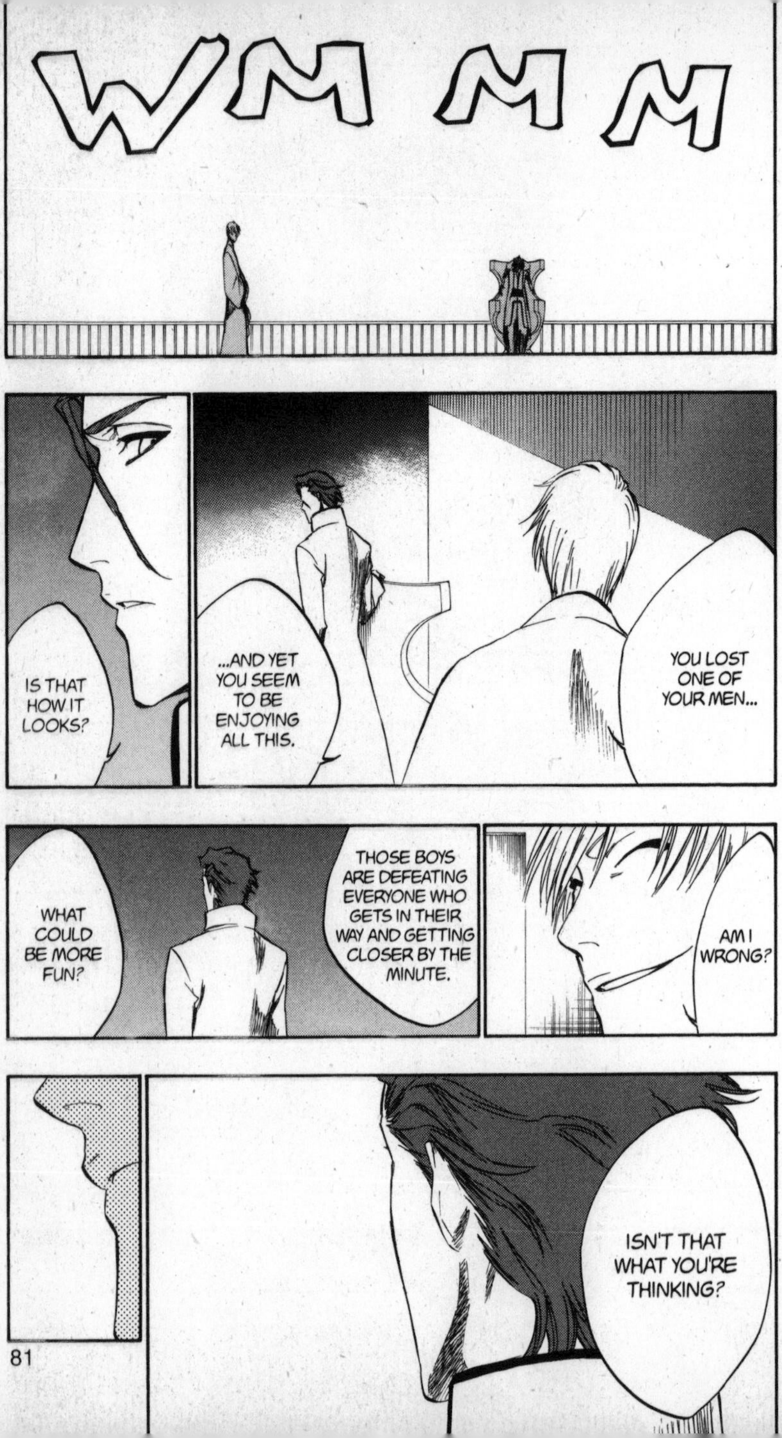
WMMM
YOU LOST ONE OF YOUR MEN...
...AND YET YOU SEEM TO BE ENJOYING ALL THIS.
IS THAT HOW IT LOOKS?
AM I WRONG?
THOSE BOYS ARE DEFEATING EVERYONE WHO GETS IN THEIR WAY AND GETTING CLOSER BY THE MINUTE.
WHAT COULD BE MORE FUN?
ISN'T THAT WHAT YOU'RE THINKING?

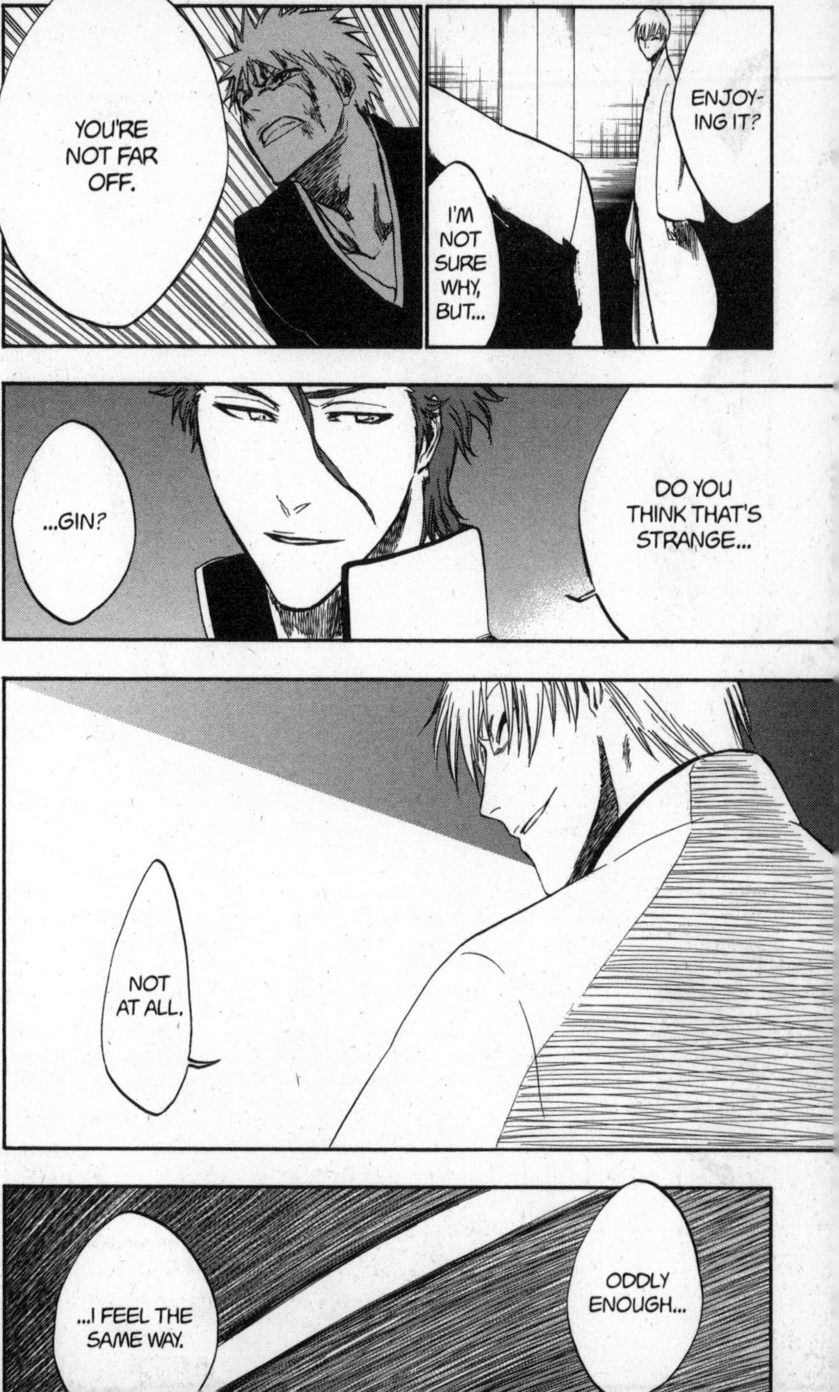
ENJOY-ING IT?
I'M NOT SURE WHY, BUT...
YOU'RE NOT FAR OFF.
DO YOU THINK THAT'S STRANGE...
...GIN?
NOT AT ALL.
ODDLY ENOUGH...
...I FEEL THE SAME WAY.

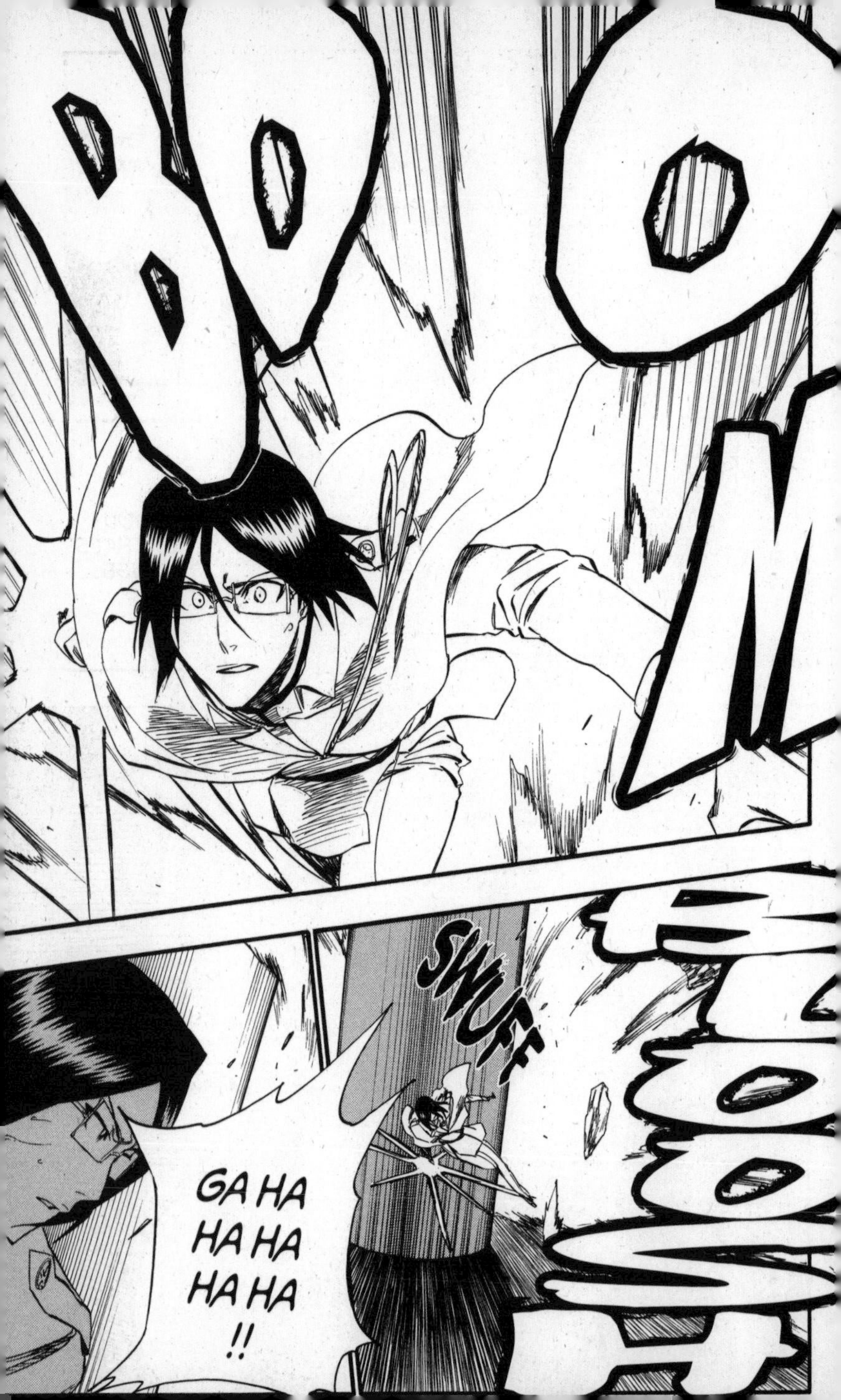
BOOM
WHOOSH
SWUFF
GA HA HA HA HA HA!!

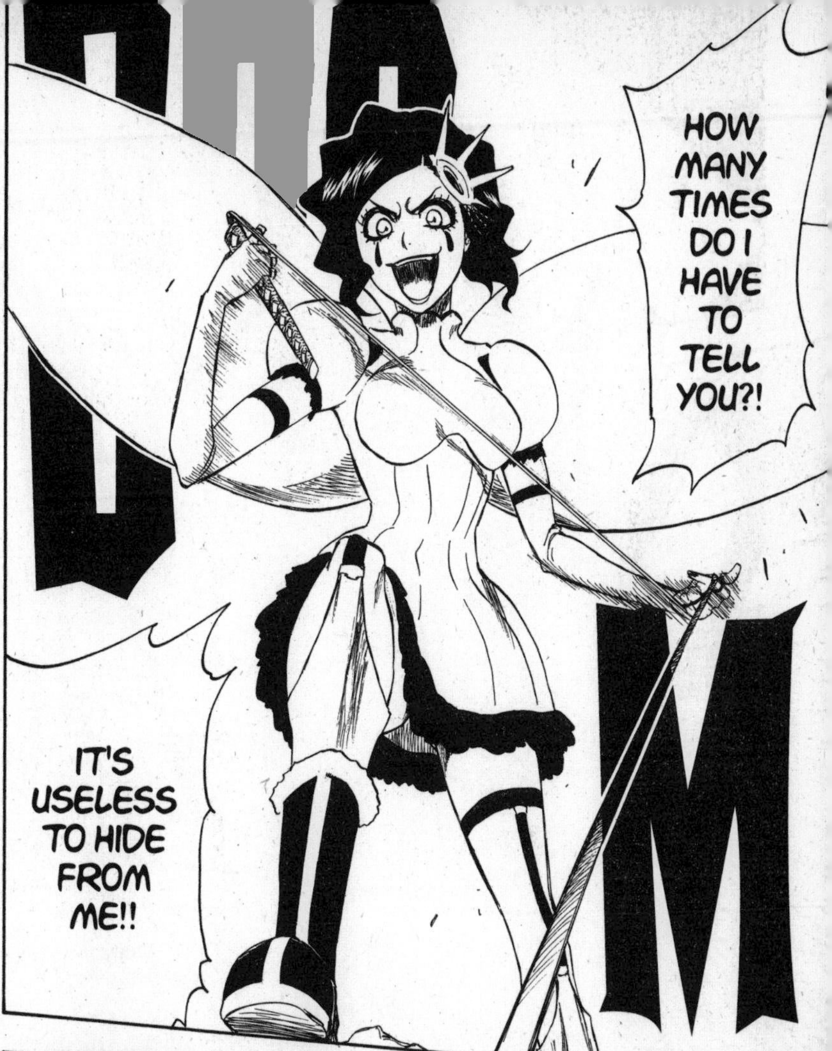
HOW MANY TIMES DO I HAVE TO TELL YOU?!
IT'S USELESS TO HIDE FROM ME!!

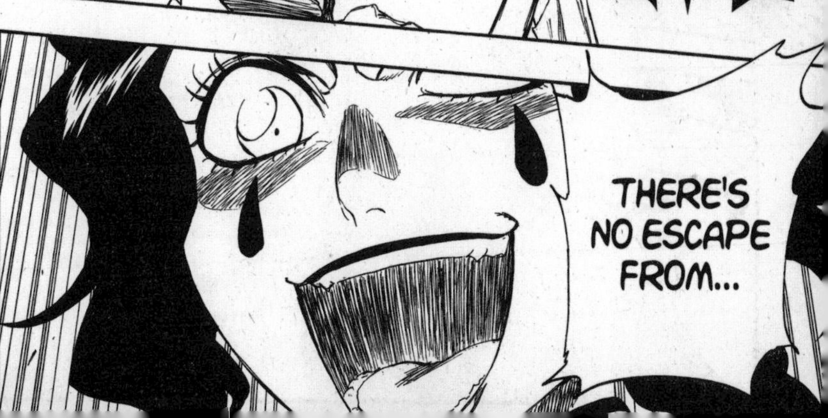
THERE'S NO ESCAPE FROM...

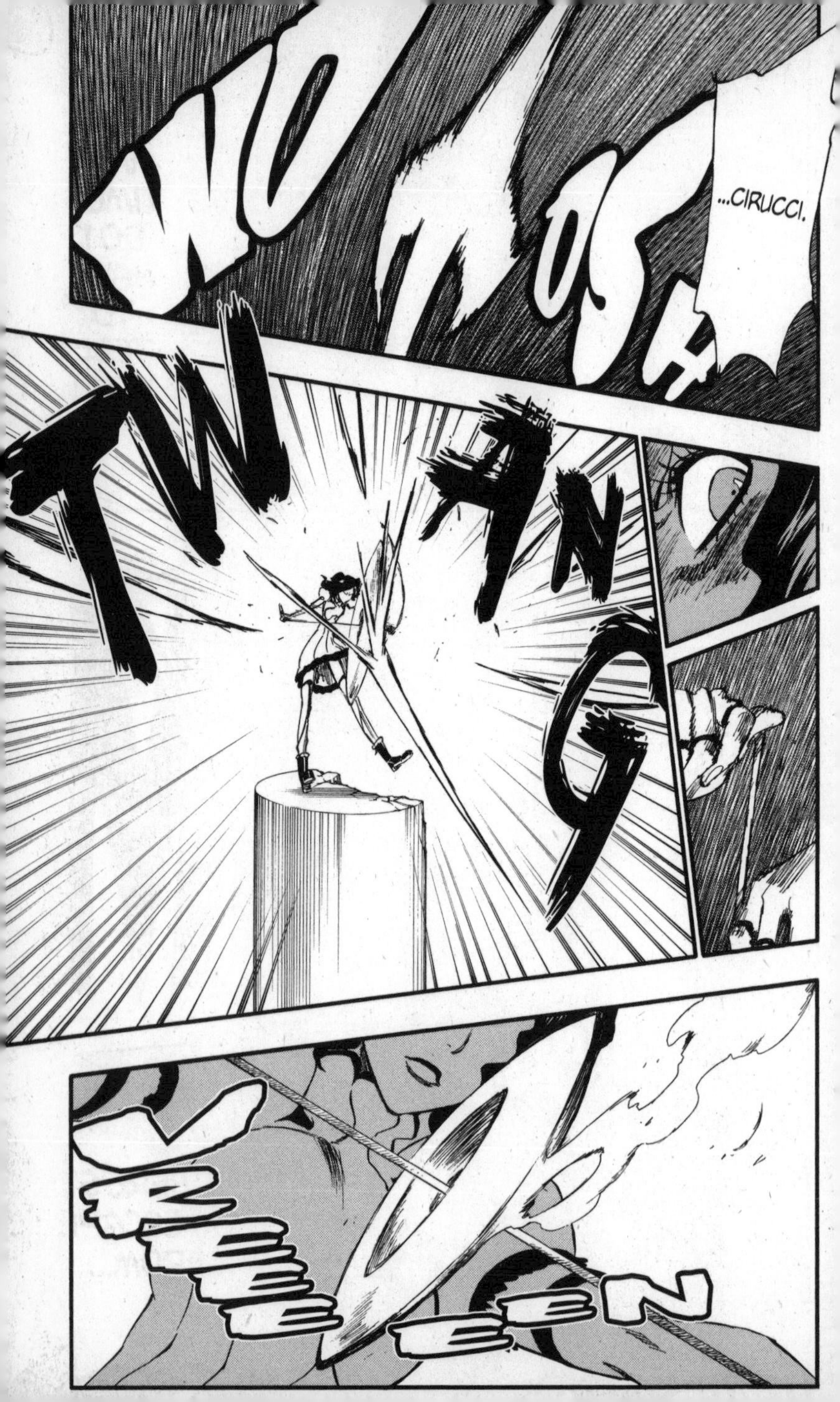
...CIRUCCI.
TWANG

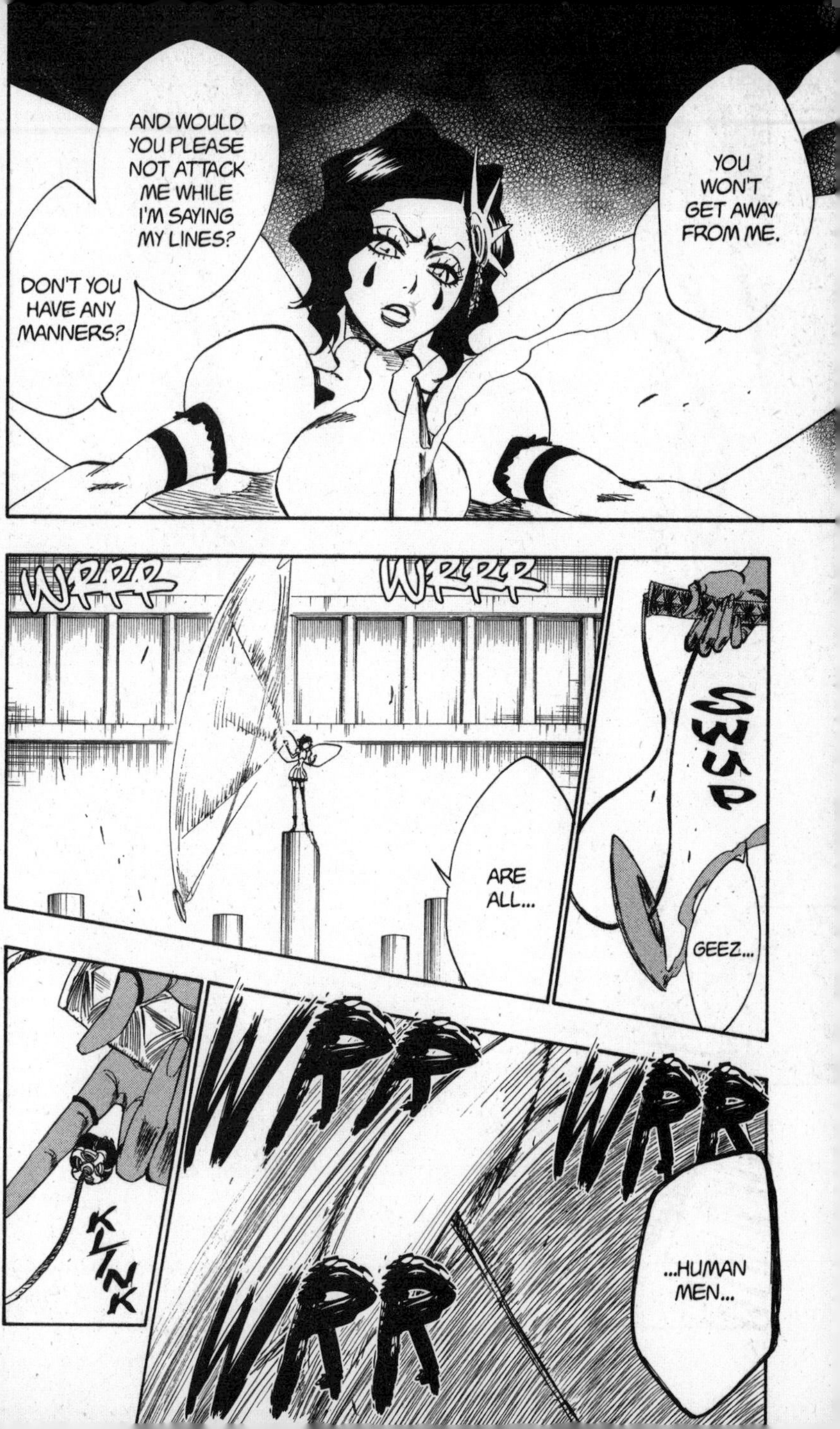
YOU WON'T GET AWAY FROM ME.
AND WOULD YOU PLEASE NOT ATTACK ME WHILE I'M SAYING MY LINES?
DON'T YOU HAVE ANY MANNERS?
SWUP
GEEZ...
WRRR
WRRR
ARE ALL...
WRR
WRR
...HUMAN MEN...
WRR
KLINK

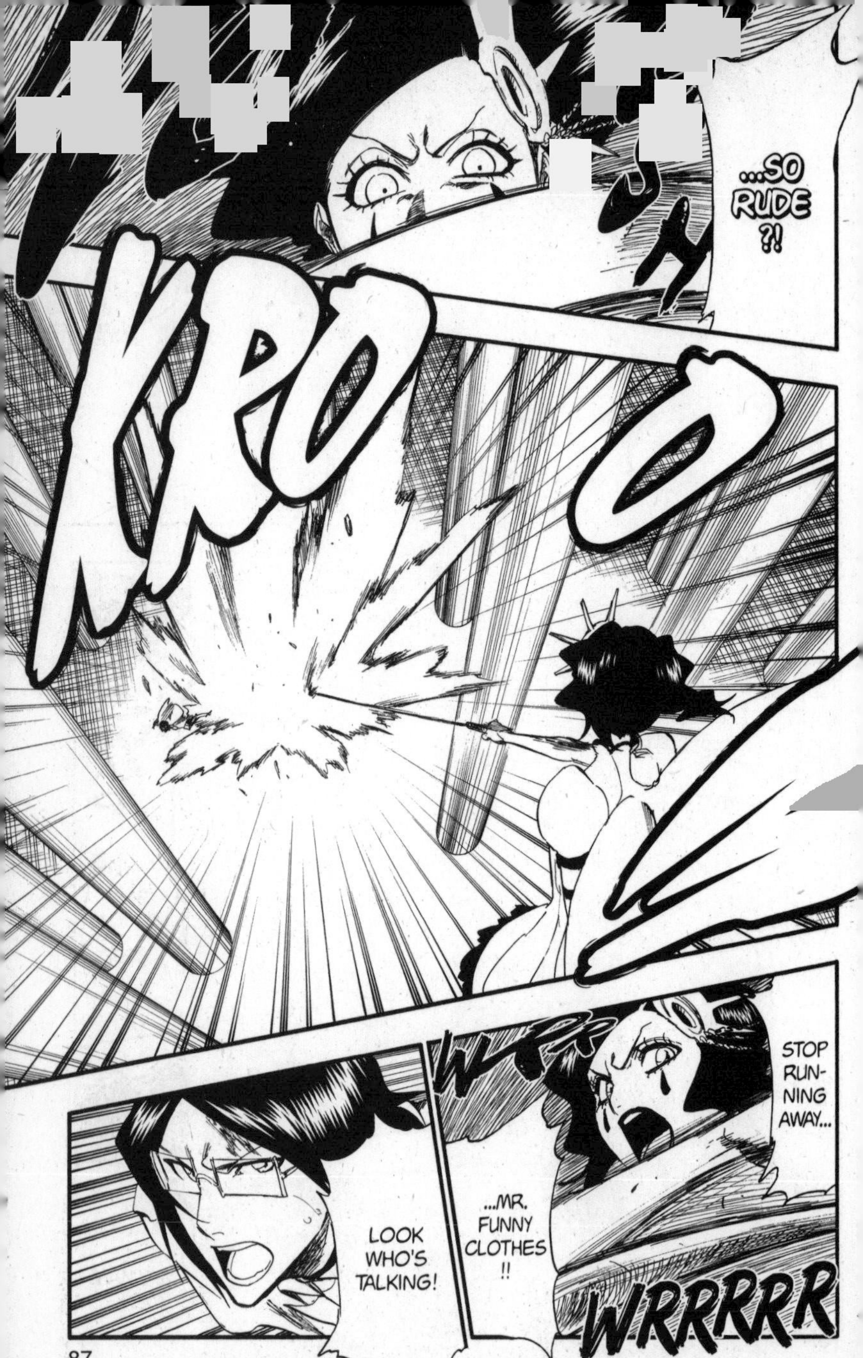
...SO RUDE ?!
STOP RUN-NING AWAY...
...MR. FUNNY CLOTHES !!
WRRRRR
LOOK WHO'S TALKING!

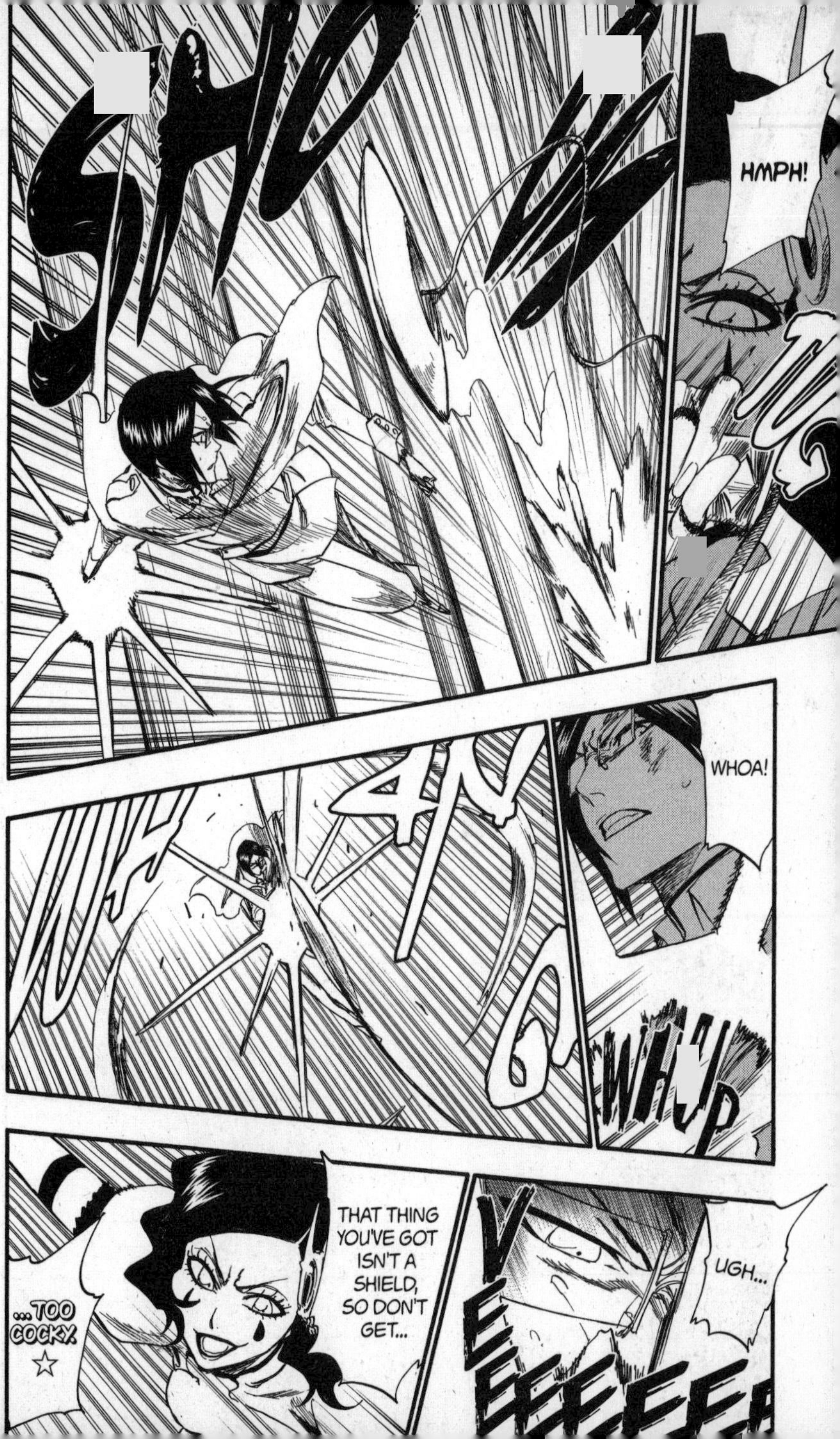

HMPH!
WHOA!
UGH...
THAT THING YOU'VE GOT ISN'T A SHIELD, SO DON'T GET...
...TOO COCKY. ☆

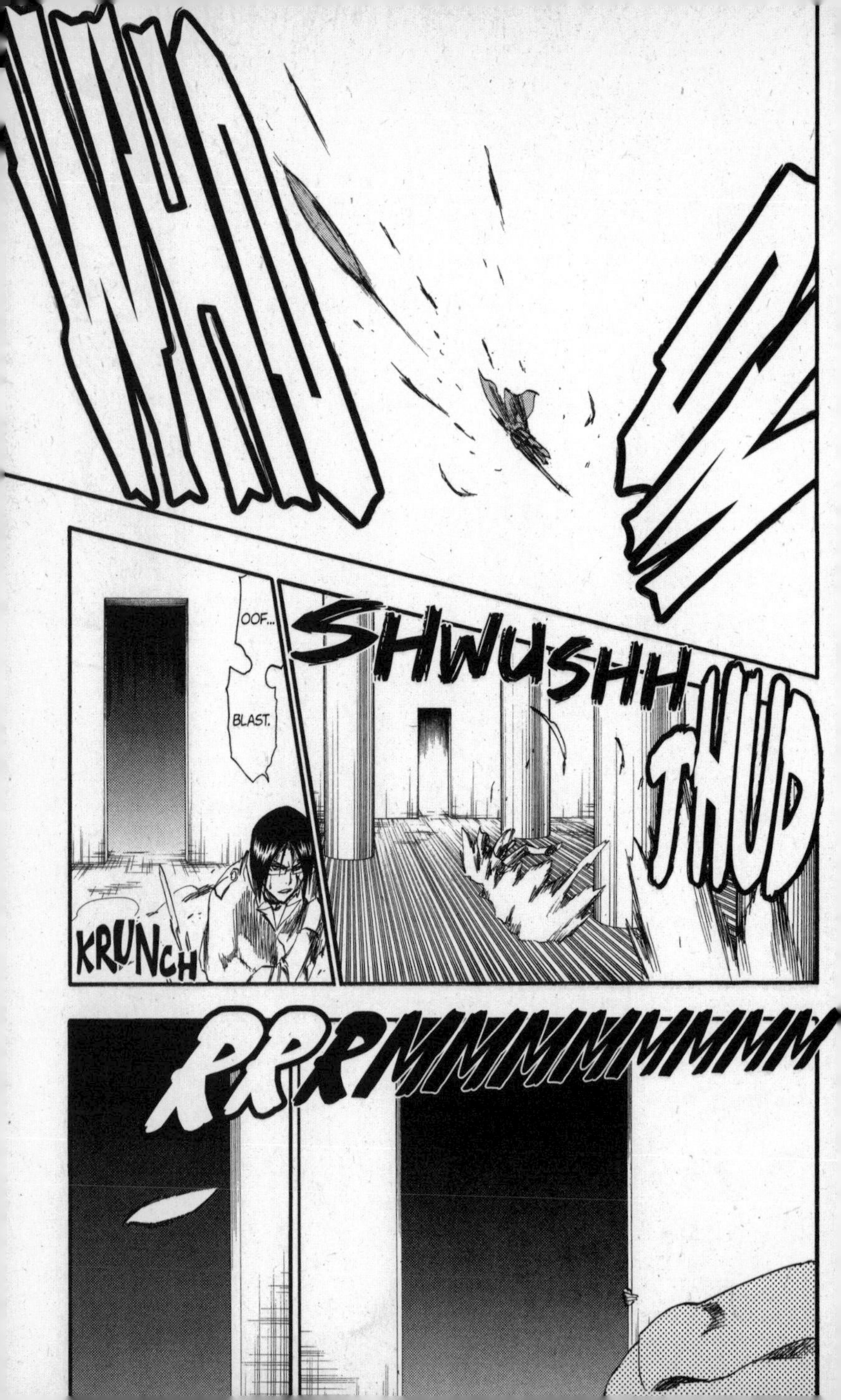
SHWUSHH
THUD
OOF...
BLAST.
KRUNCH
RRRMMMMMMMMMM

WHO ARE YOU?!
HEH HEH... WHO, ME? I'M...
KONSÔ COP KARAKURAIZER
...A SUPER-HERO WHO'S GONNA TAKE YOU DOWN!!
I AM KARAKURA KONSÔ COP!!
TA DAH
K
I THOUGHT SO.
THAT EXPLAINS THE FLOATING LOGO.
HEH HEH ...
MR. KON SEEMS TO BE GETTING INTO THIS.

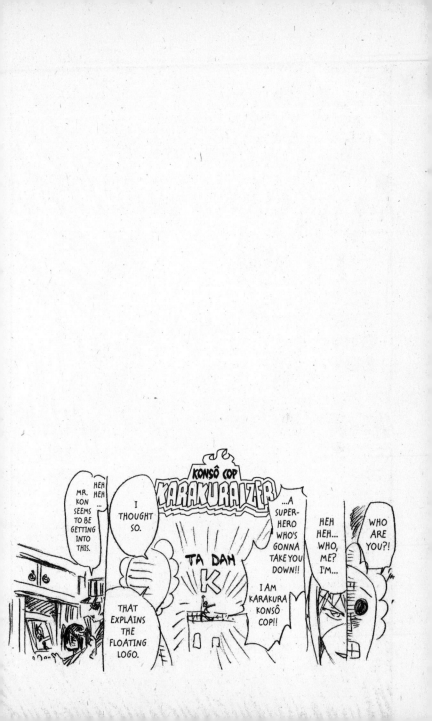

256. Infinite Slick

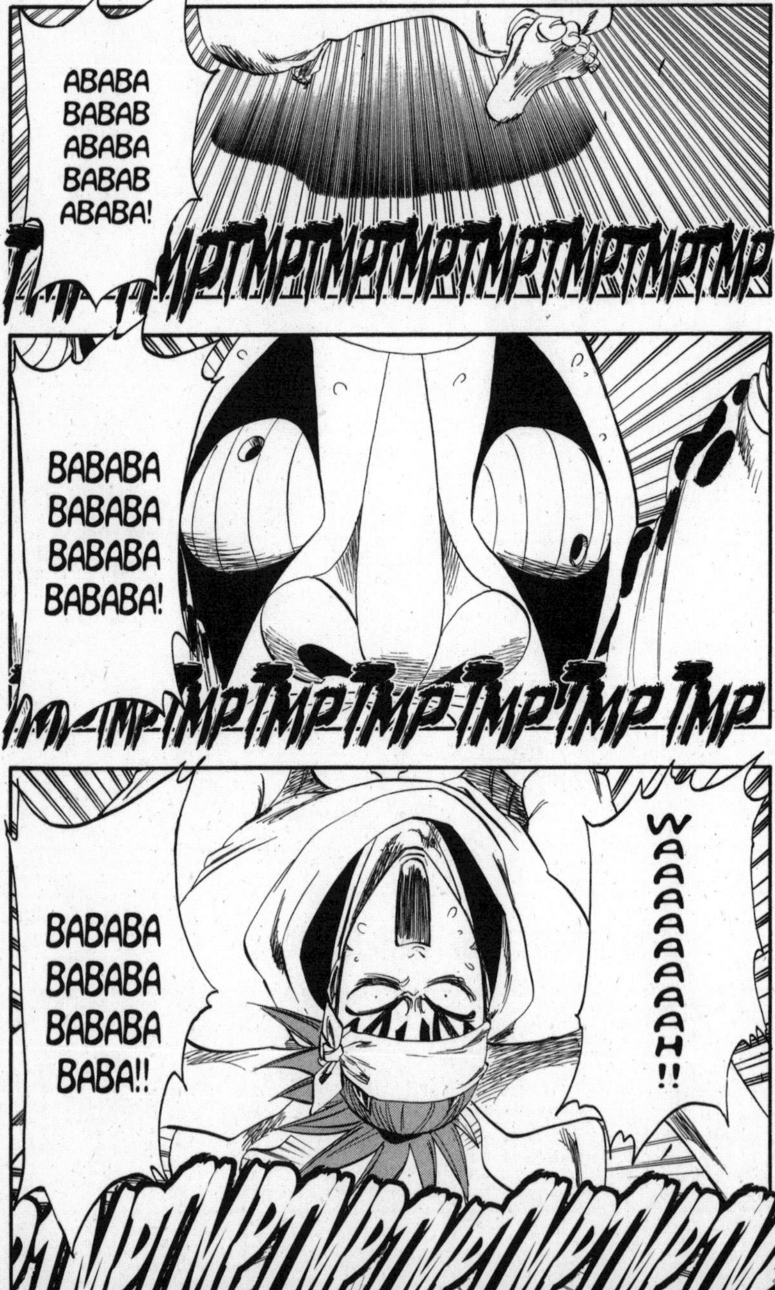
ABABA BABAB ABABA BABAB ABABA!
TMPTMPTMPTMPTMPTMPTMPTMPTMPTMP
BABABA BABABA BABABA BABABA!
TMPTMPTMPTMPTMPTMPTMPTMP
WAAAAAAAAAH!!
BABABA BABABA BABABA BABA!!

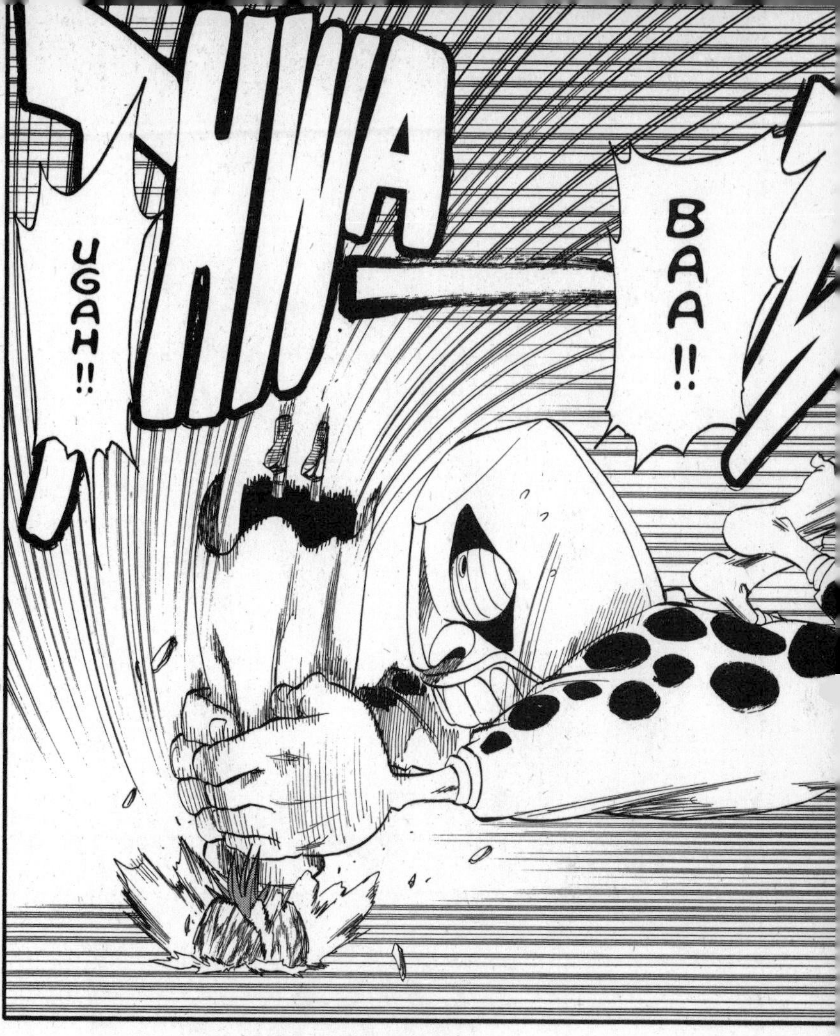
BAA!!
THWA
UGAH!!

BLEACH 256. Infinite Slick

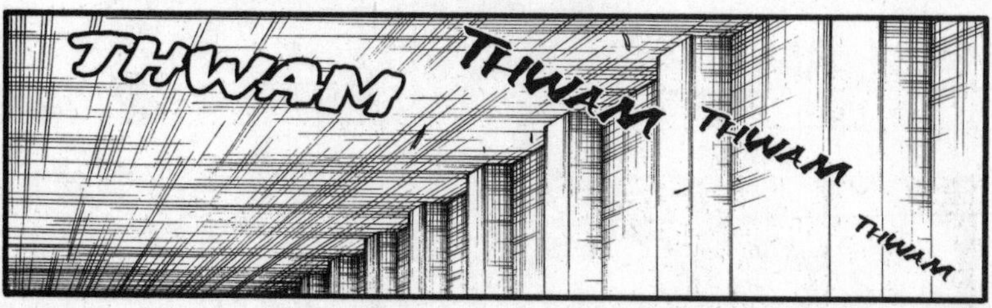
THWAM
THWAM
THWAM
THWAM

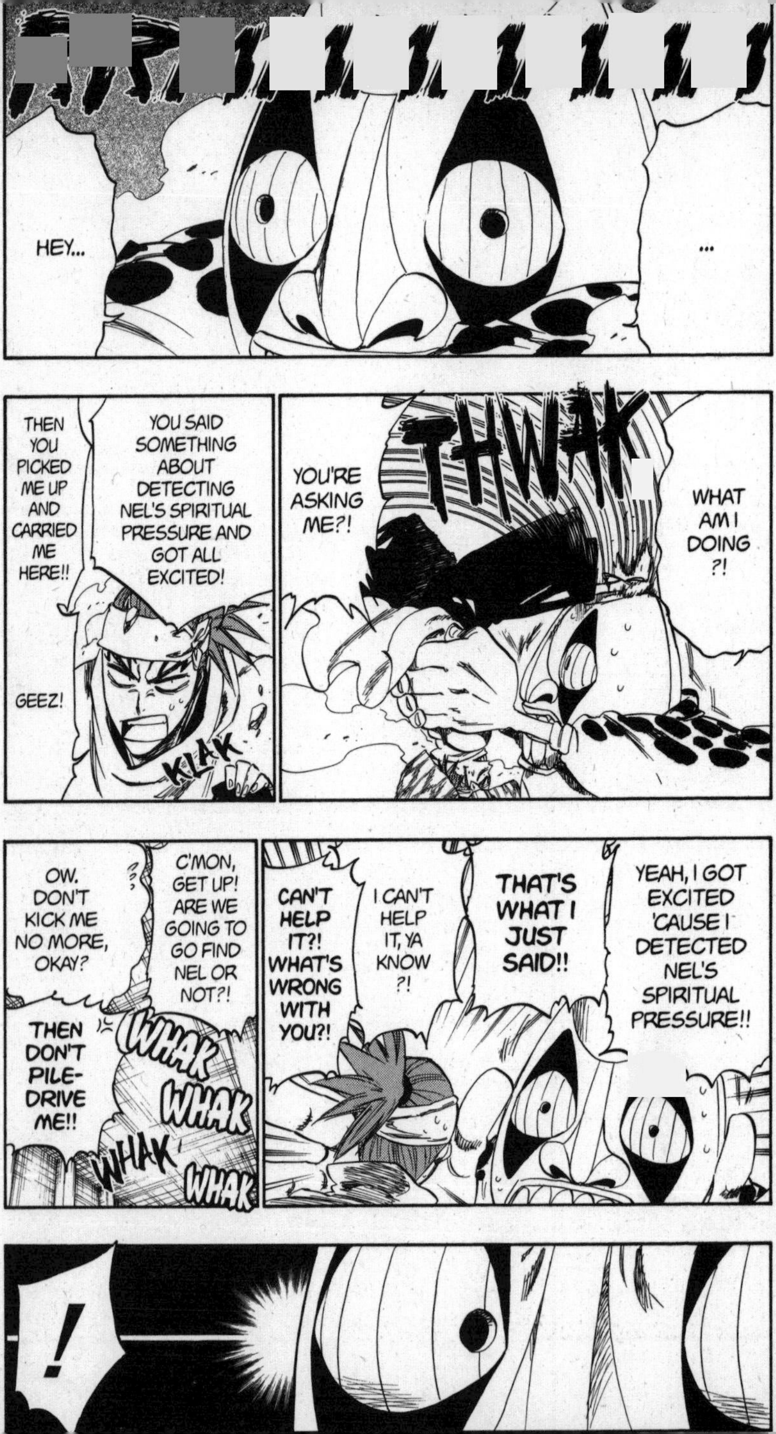
...
HEY...
WHAT AM I DOING ?!
THWAK
YOU'RE ASKING ME?!
YOU SAID SOMETHING ABOUT DETECTING NEL'S SPIRITUAL PRESSURE AND GOT ALL EXCITED!
THEN YOU PICKED ME UP AND CARRIED ME HERE!!
GEEZ!
KLAK
YEAH, I GOT EXCITED 'CAUSE I DETECTED NEL'S SPIRITUAL PRESSURE!!
THAT'S WHAT I JUST SAID!!
I CAN'T HELP IT, YA KNOW ?!
CAN'T HELP IT?! WHAT'S WRONG WITH YOU?!
C'MON, GET UP! ARE WE GOING TO GO FIND NEL OR NOT?!
OW. DON'T KICK ME NO MORE, OKAY?
WHAK
WHAK
WHAK
WHAK
THEN DON'T PILE-DRIVE ME!!
!

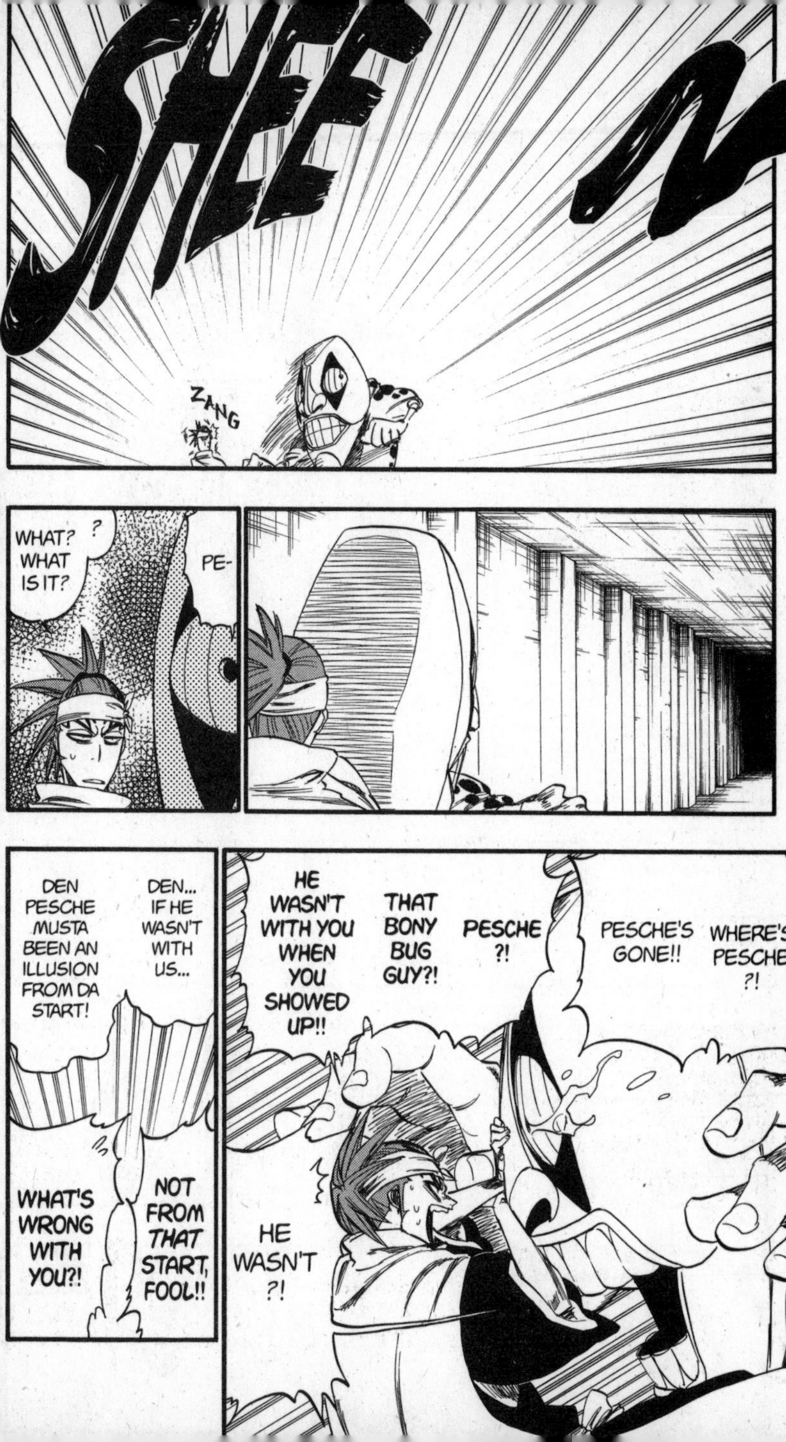
SHEEN
ZANG
PE-
?
WHAT? WHAT IS IT?
WHERE'S PESCHE ?!
PESCHE'S GONE!!
PESCHE ?!
THAT BONY BUG GUY?!
HE WASN'T WITH YOU WHEN YOU SHOWED UP!!
HE WASN'T ?!
DEN... IF HE WASN'T WITH US...
DEN PESCHE MUSTA BEEN AN ILLUSION FROM DA START!
NOT FROM THAT START, FOOL!!
WHAT'S WRONG WITH YOU?!

READ THIS WAY

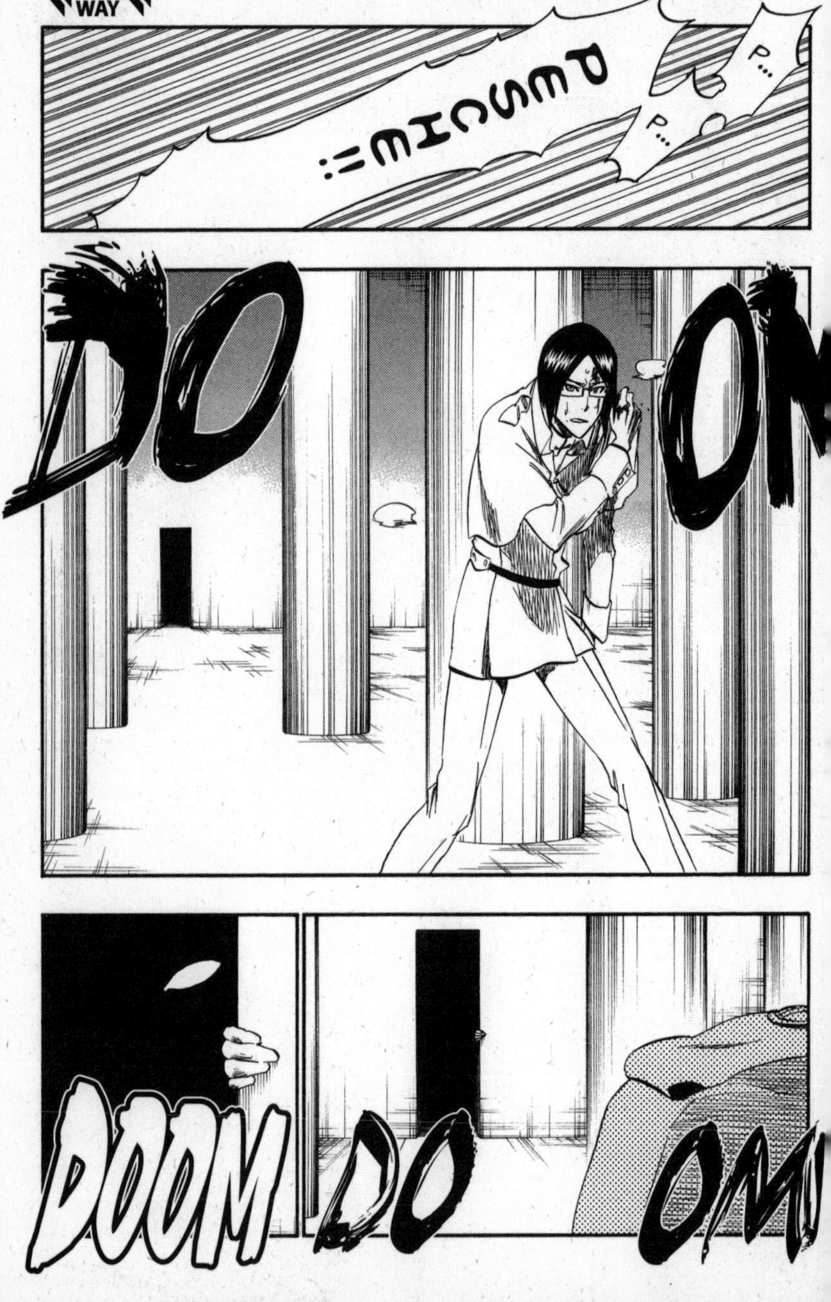
P...
P...
PESCHE!!
DO OM
DO OM
DOOM

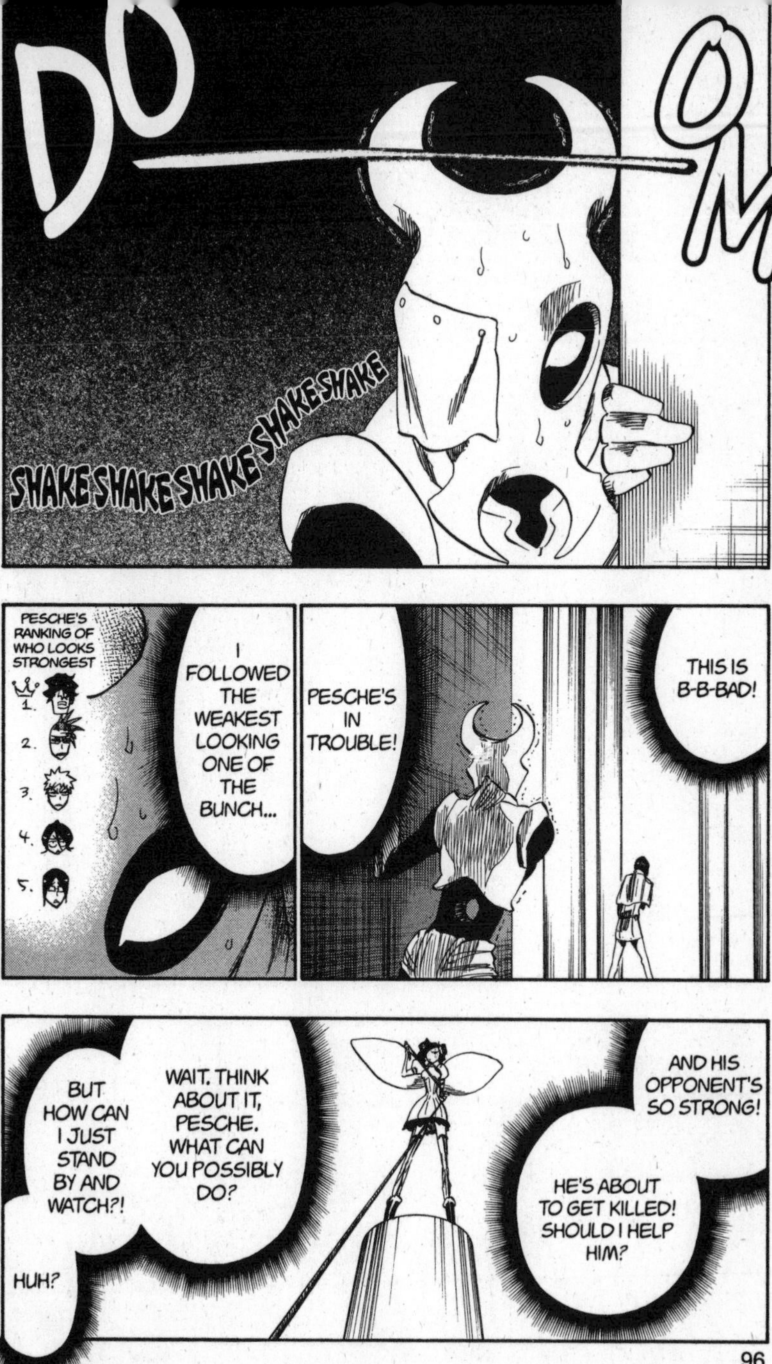
DOOM
SHAKE SHAKE SHAKE SHAKE SHAKE SHAKE
THIS IS B-B-BAD!
PESCHE'S IN TROUBLE!
I FOLLOWED THE WEAKEST LOOKING ONE OF THE BUNCH...
PESCHE'S RANKING OF WHO LOOKS STRONGEST
1.
2.
3.
4.
5.
AND HIS OPPONENT'S SO STRONG!
HE'S ABOUT TO GET KILLED! SHOULD I HELP HIM?
WAIT. THINK ABOUT IT, PESCHE. WHAT CAN YOU POSSIBLY DO?
BUT HOW CAN I JUST STAND BY AND WATCH?!
HUH?

READ THIS WAY

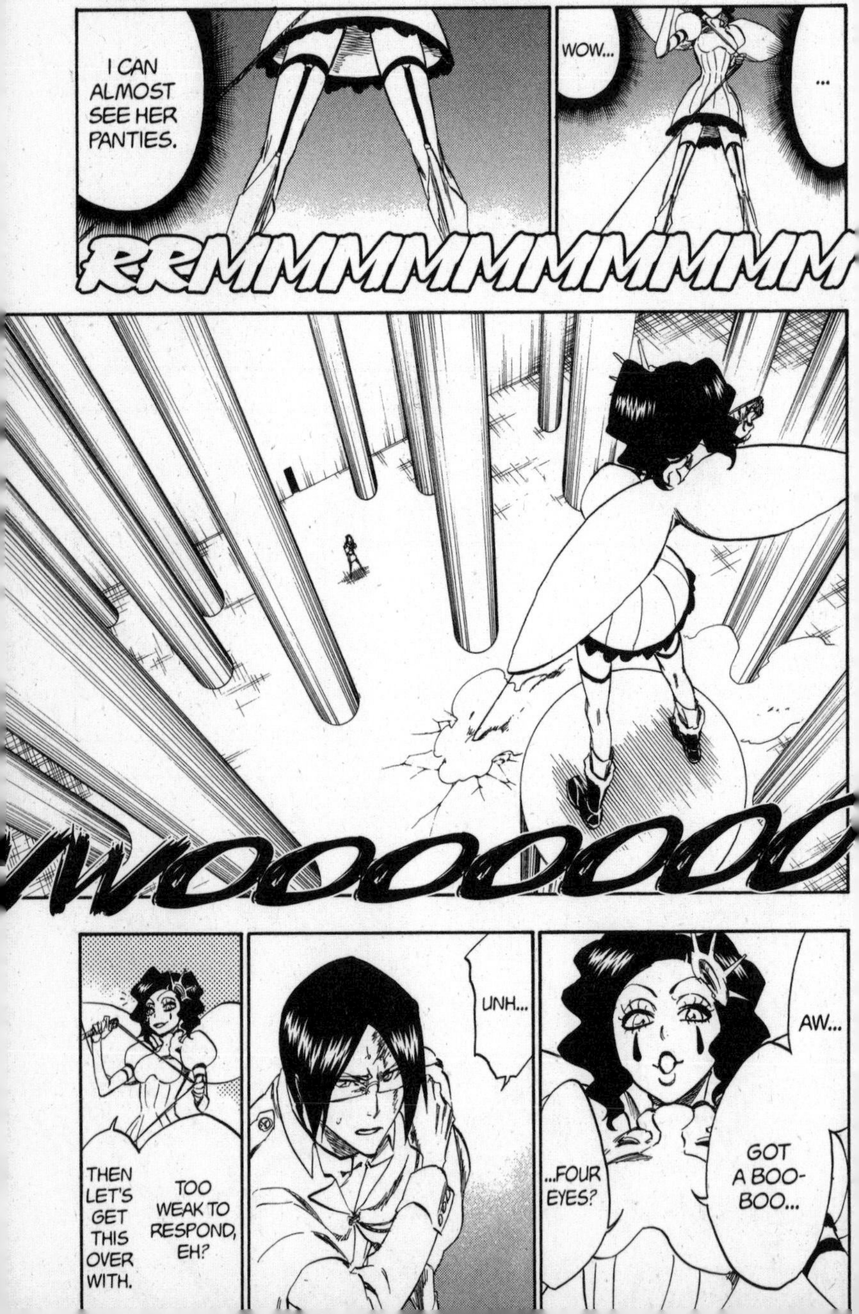
...
WOW...
I CAN ALMOST SEE HER PANTIES.
RRMMMMMMMMMMMMMM
WOOOOOOOOO
AW...
GOT A BOO-BOO...
...FOUR EYES?
UNH...
TOO WEAK TO RESPOND, EH?
THEN LET'S GET THIS OVER WITH.

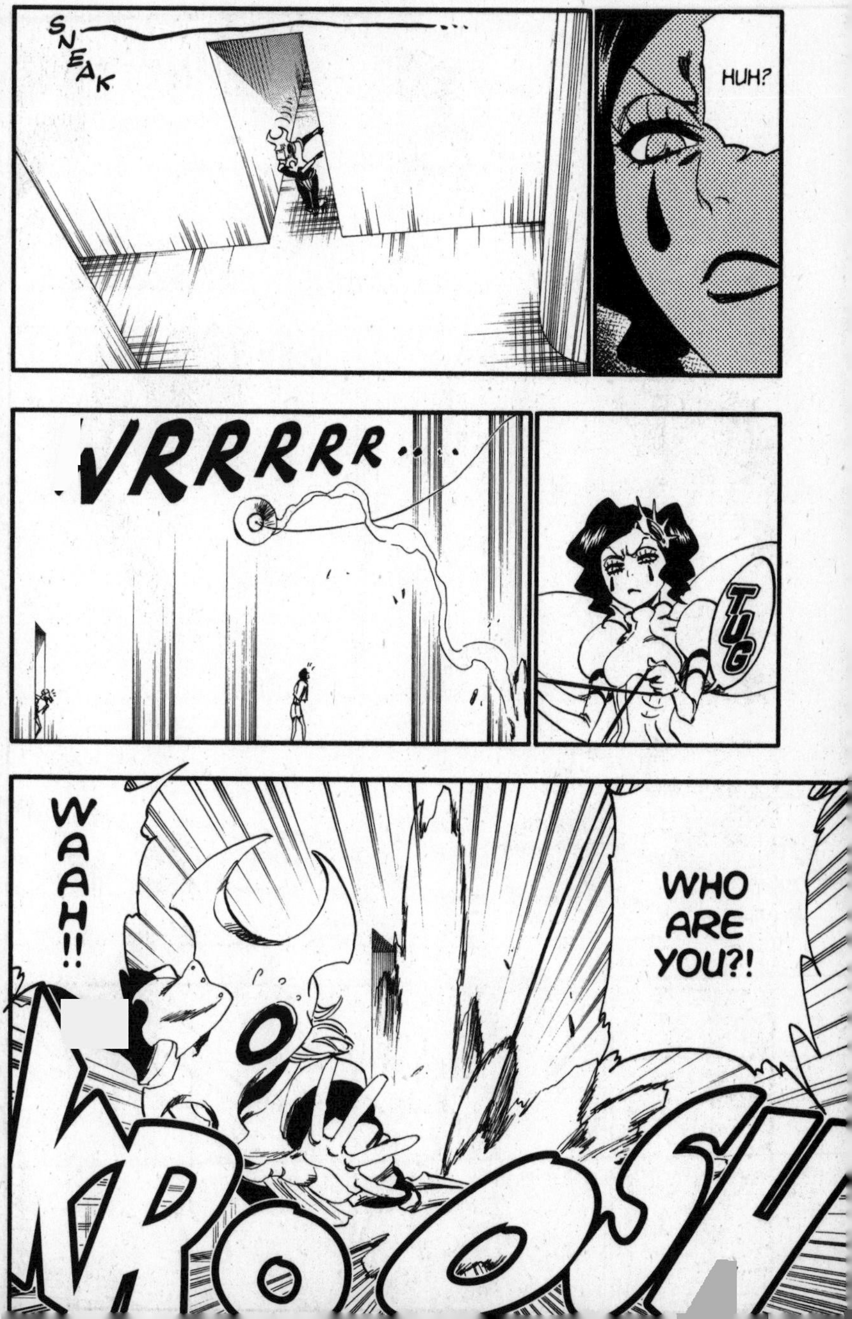
HUH?
SNEAK...
TUG
VRRRRR...
WHO ARE YOU?!
WAAAH!!
VROOSH

READ THIS WAY

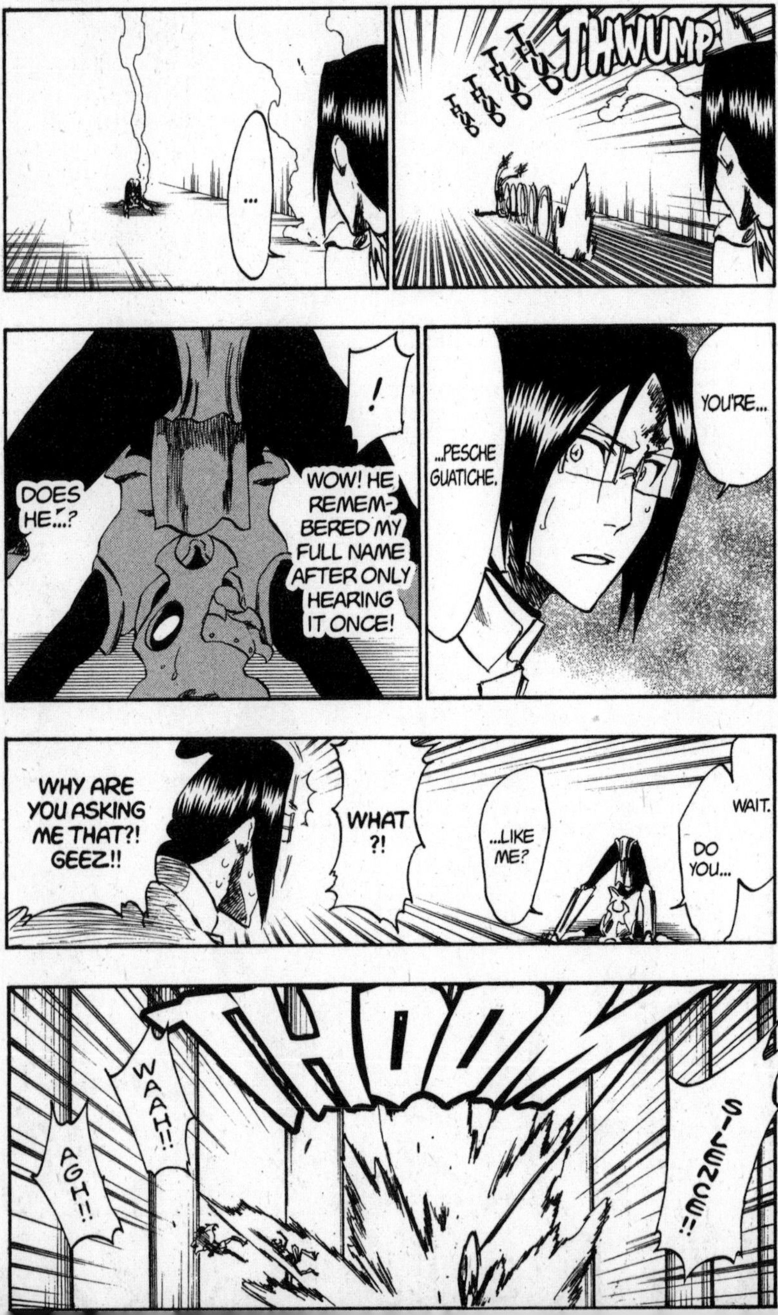

THUD THUD THUD THUD
THWUMP
...
YOU'RE...
...PESCHE GUATICHE.
!
WOW! HE REMEMBERED MY FULL NAME AFTER ONLY HEARING IT ONCE!
DOES HE...?
WAIT.
DO YOU...
...LIKE ME?
WHAT?!
WHY ARE YOU ASKING ME THAT?! GEEZ!!
SILENCE!!
WAAH!!
AGH!!

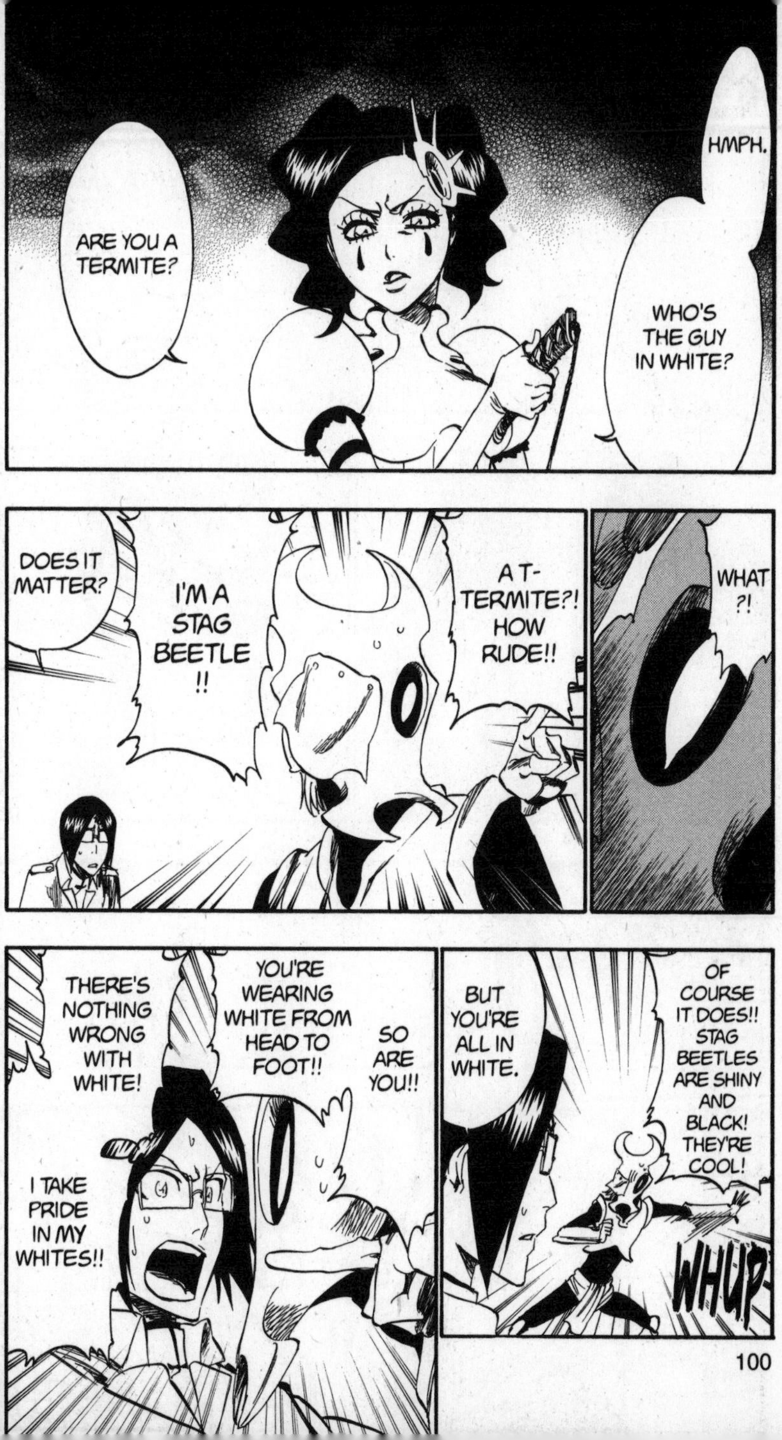
HMPH.
WHO'S THE GUY IN WHITE?
ARE YOU A TERMITE?
WHAT ?!
A T- TERMITE?! HOW RUDE!!
I'M A STAG BEETLE !!
DOES IT MATTER?
OF COURSE IT DOES!! STAG BEETLES ARE SHINY AND BLACK! THEY'RE COOL!
BUT YOU'RE ALL IN WHITE.
WHUP
SO ARE YOU!!
YOU'RE WEARING WHITE FROM HEAD TO FOOT!!
THERE'S NOTHING WRONG WITH WHITE!
I TAKE PRIDE IN MY WHITES!!

READ THIS WAY

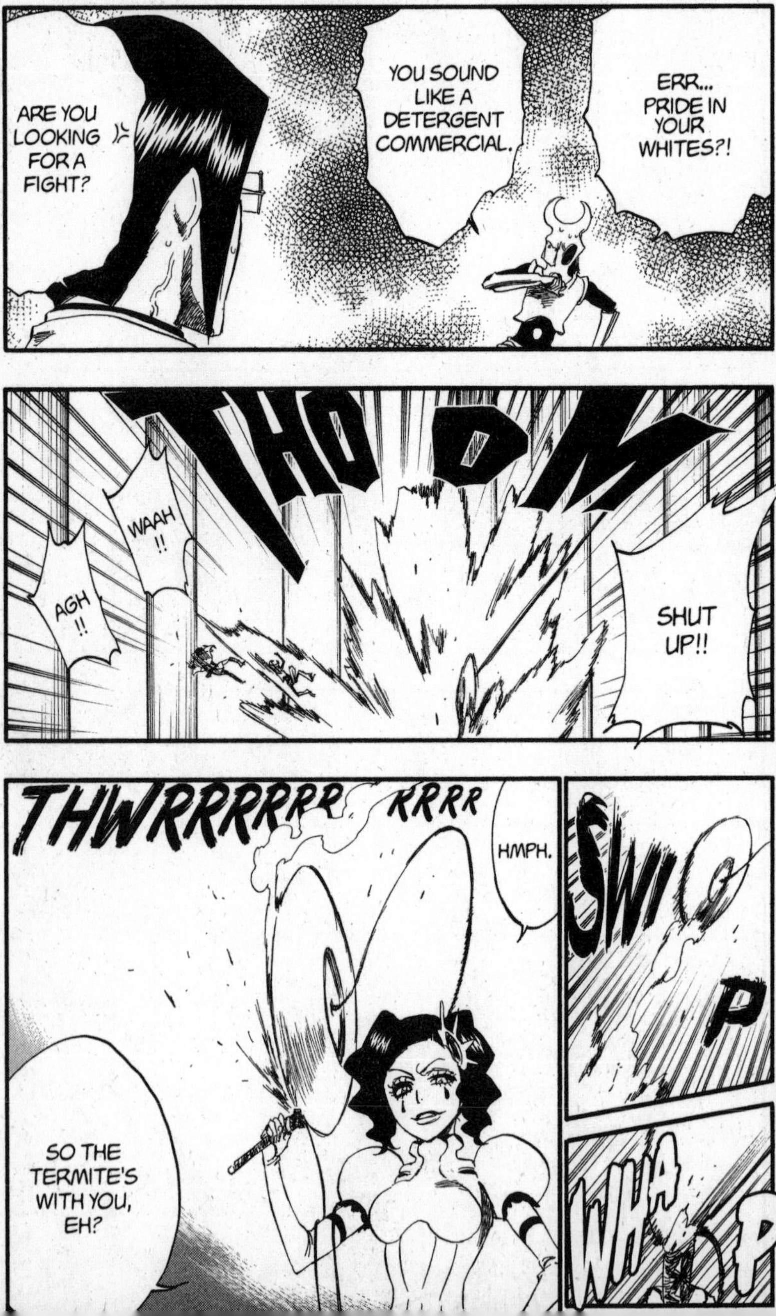

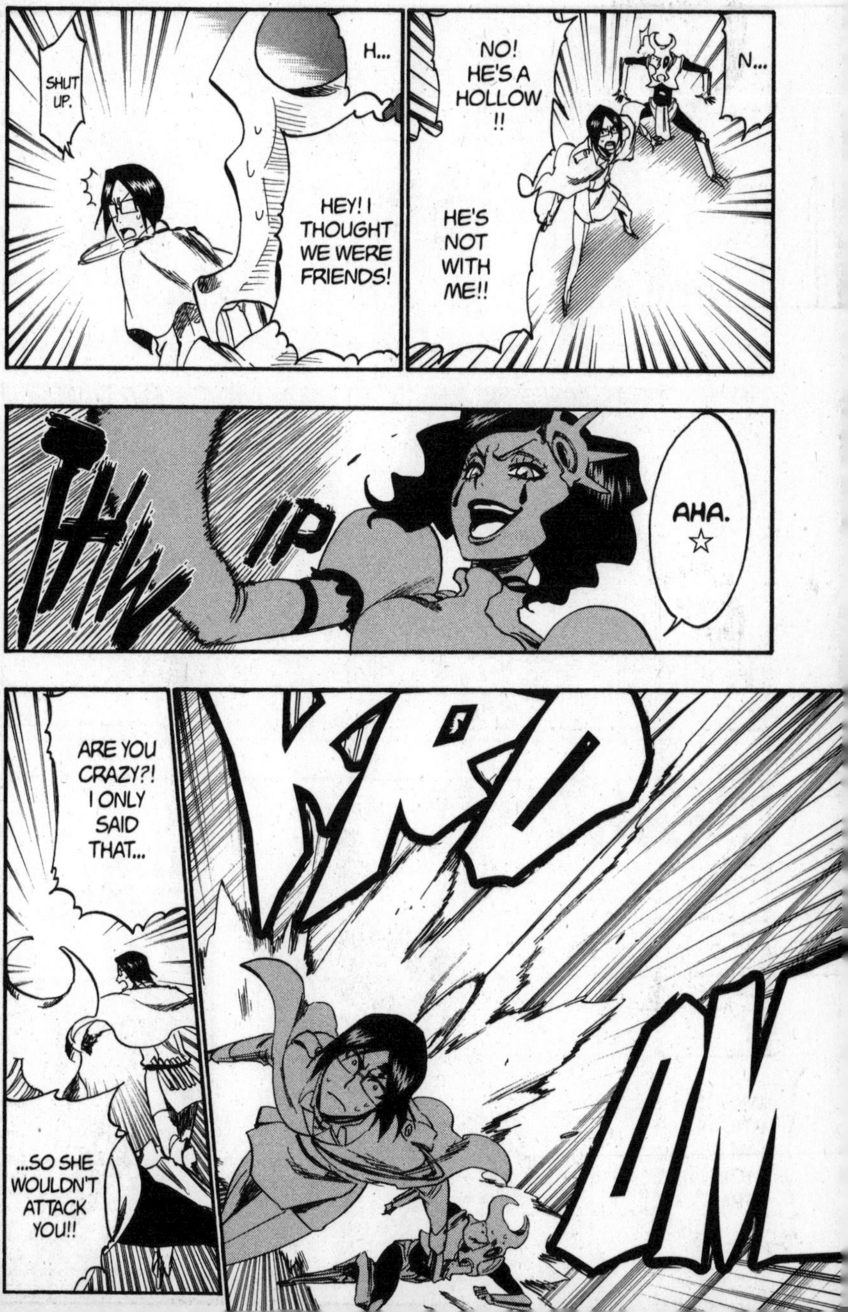
N...
NO! HE'S A HOLLOW !!
HE'S NOT WITH ME!!
H...
HEY! I THOUGHT WE WERE FRIENDS!
SHUT UP.
AHA. ☆
THWIP
KRDOM
ARE YOU CRAZY?! I ONLY SAID THAT...
...SO SHE WOULDN'T ATTACK YOU!!

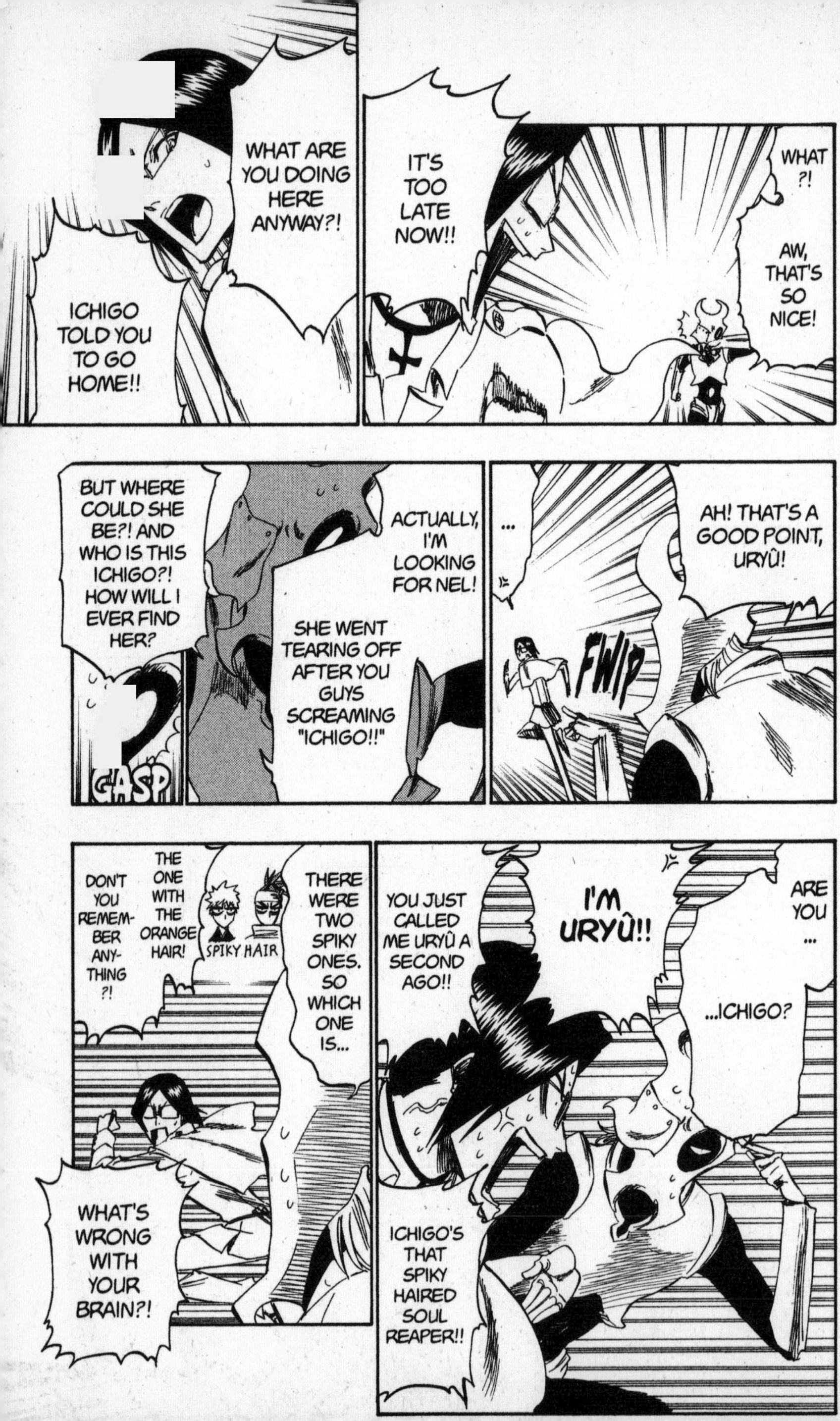
WHAT ?!
AW, THAT'S SO NICE!
IT'S TOO LATE NOW!!
WHAT ARE YOU DOING HERE ANYWAY?!
ICHIGO TOLD YOU TO GO HOME!!
AH! THAT'S A GOOD POINT, URYÛ!
...
FWIP
ACTUALLY, I'M LOOKING FOR NEL!
SHE WENT TEARING OFF AFTER YOU GUYS SCREAMING "ICHIGO!!"
BUT WHERE COULD SHE BE?! AND WHO IS THIS ICHIGO?! HOW WILL I EVER FIND HER?
GASP
ARE YOU ...
I'M URYÛ!!
YOU JUST CALLED ME URYÛ A SECOND AGO!!
...ICHIGO?
ICHIGO'S THAT SPIKY HAIRED SOUL REAPER!!
THERE WERE TWO SPIKY ONES. SO WHICH ONE IS...
SPIKY HAIR
THE ONE WITH THE ORANGE HAIR!
DON'T YOU REMEMBER ANYTHING ?!
WHAT'S WRONG WITH YOUR BRAIN?!

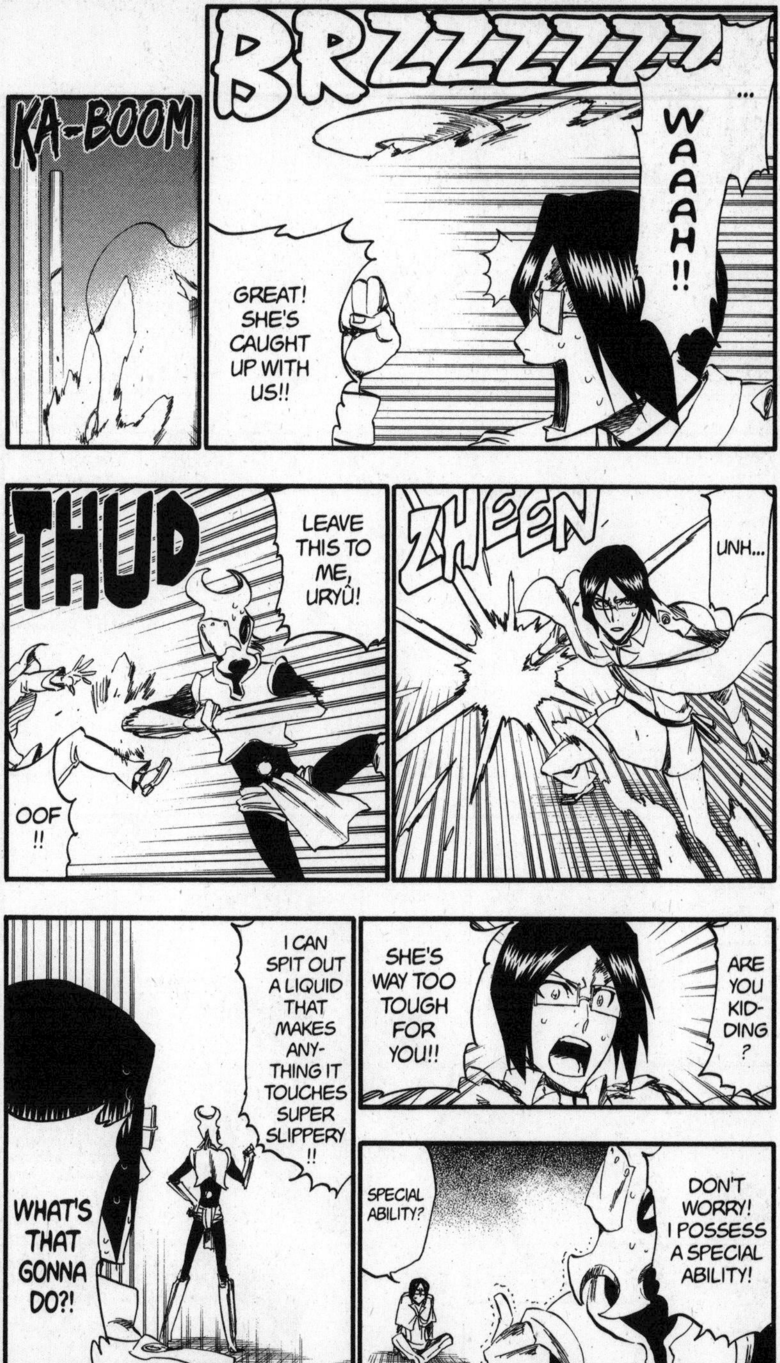

BRZZZZZZ
...WAAAH!!
GREAT! SHE'S CAUGHT UP WITH US!!
KA-BOOM
ZHEEN
UNH...
THUD
LEAVE THIS TO ME, URYŪ!
OOF!!
ARE YOU KID-DING?
SHE'S WAY TOO TOUGH FOR YOU!!
DON'T WORRY! I POSSESS A SPECIAL ABILITY!
SPECIAL ABILITY?
I CAN SPIT OUT A LIQUID THAT MAKES ANY-THING IT TOUCHES SUPER SLIPPERY!!
WHAT'S THAT GONNA DO?!

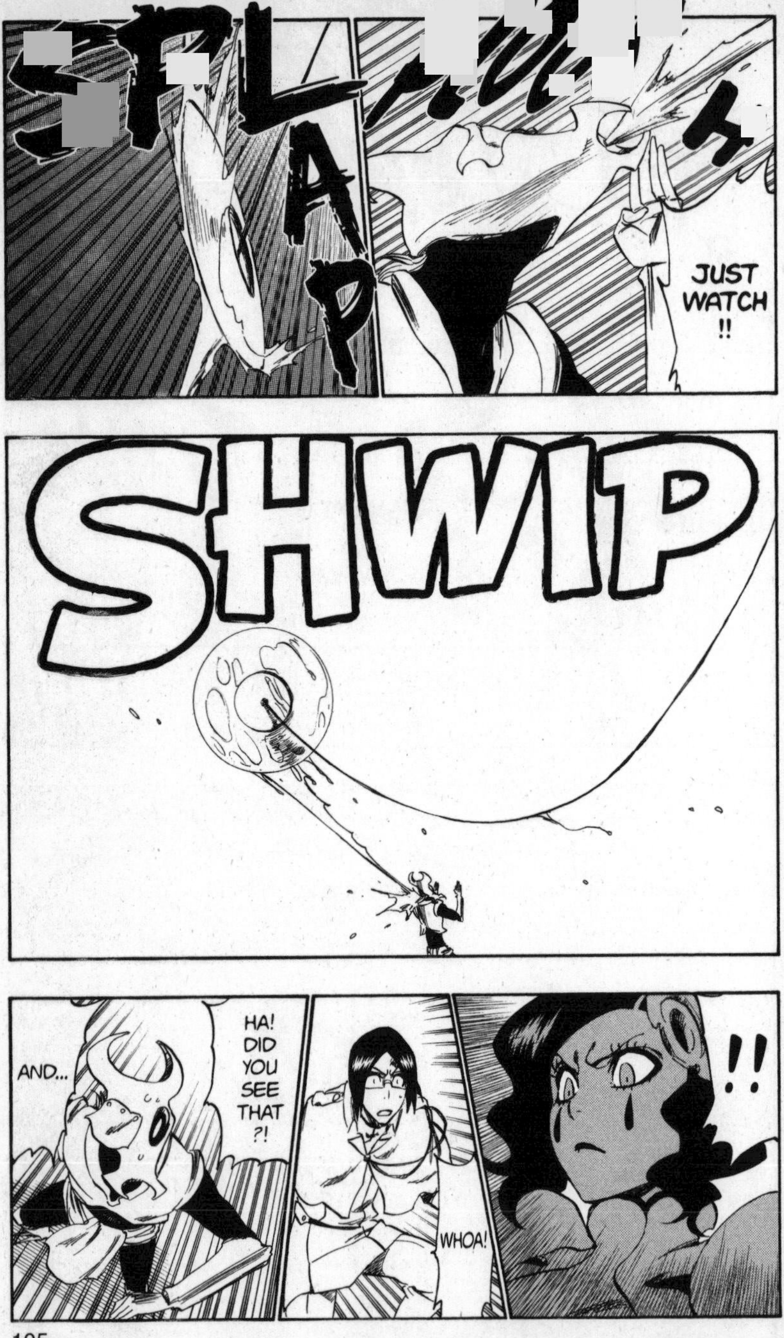

JUST WATCH !!
SHWIP
!!
WHOA!
HA! DID YOU SEE THAT ?!
AND...

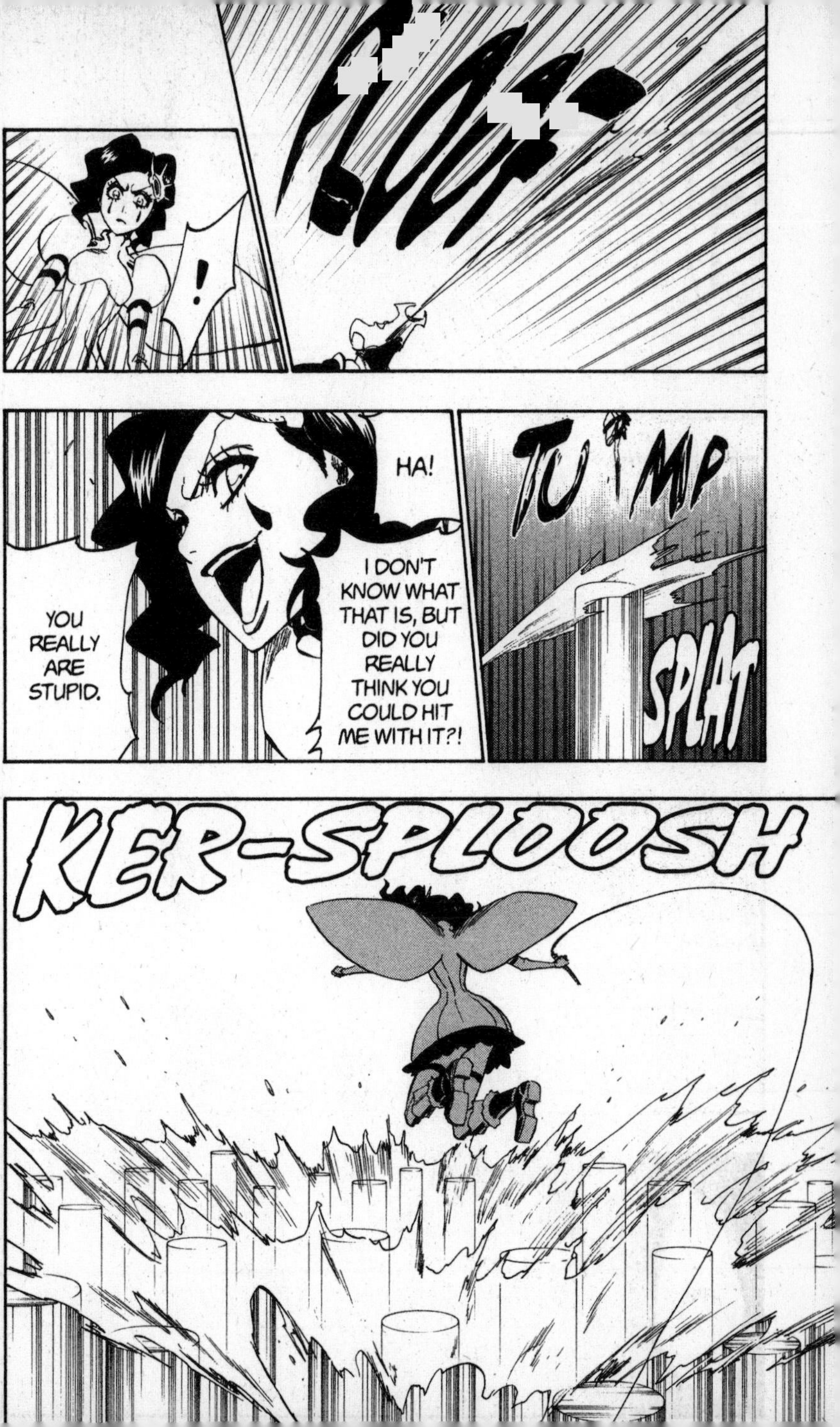
!
TUMP
SPLAT
HA!
I DON'T KNOW WHAT THAT IS, BUT DID YOU REALLY THINK YOU COULD HIT ME WITH IT?!
YOU REALLY ARE STUPID.
KER-SPLOOSH

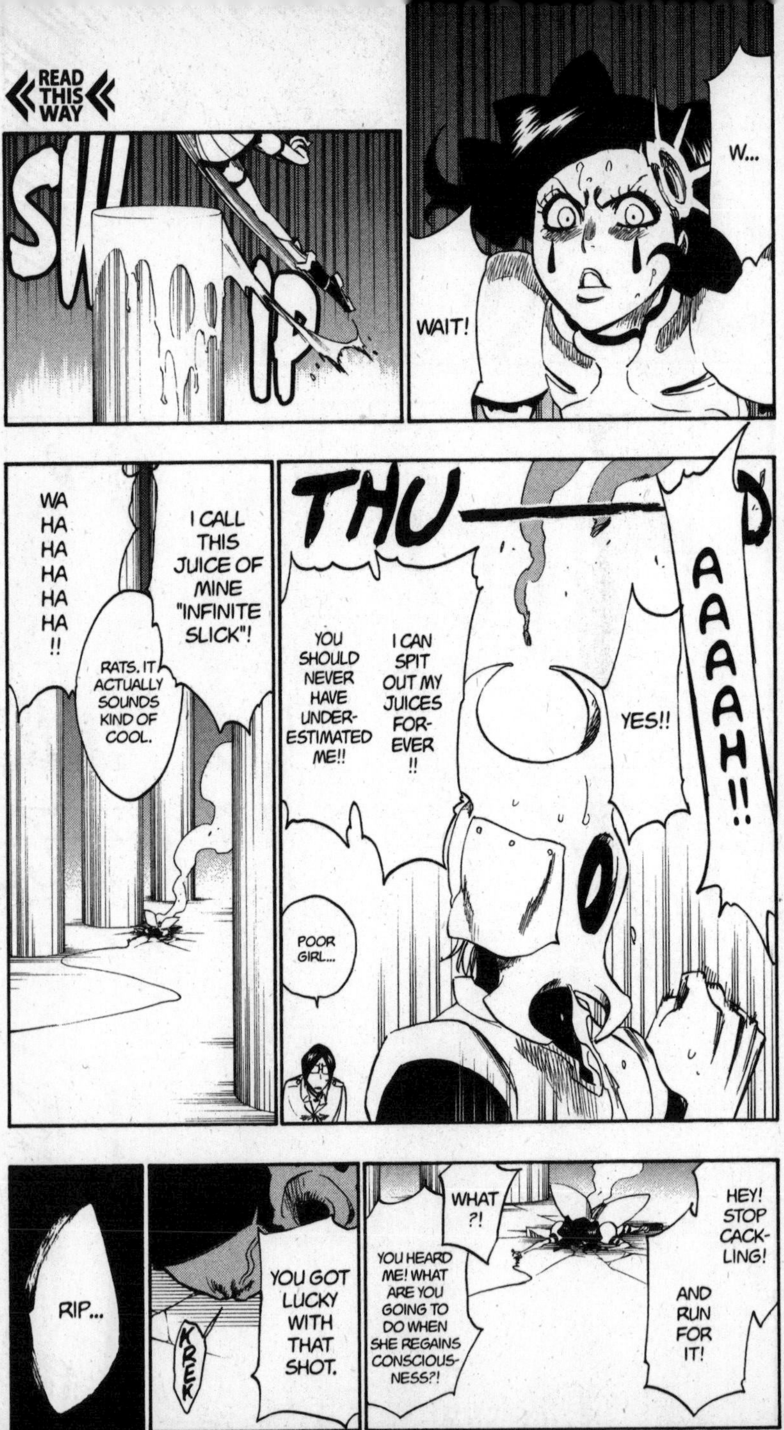
READ THIS WAY
W...
WAIT!
SWIP
THU——D
AAAAAH!!
YES!!
I CAN SPIT OUT MY JUICES FOR-EVER!!
YOU SHOULD NEVER HAVE UNDER-ESTIMATED ME!!
POOR GIRL...
I CALL THIS JUICE OF MINE "INFINITE SLICK"!
WA HA HA HA HA HA!!
RATS. IT ACTUALLY SOUNDS KIND OF COOL.
HEY! STOP CACK-LING!
AND RUN FOR IT!
WHAT?!
YOU HEARD ME! WHAT ARE YOU GOING TO DO WHEN SHE REGAINS CONSCIOUS-NESS?!
YOU GOT LUCKY WITH THAT SHOT.
KREK
RIP...

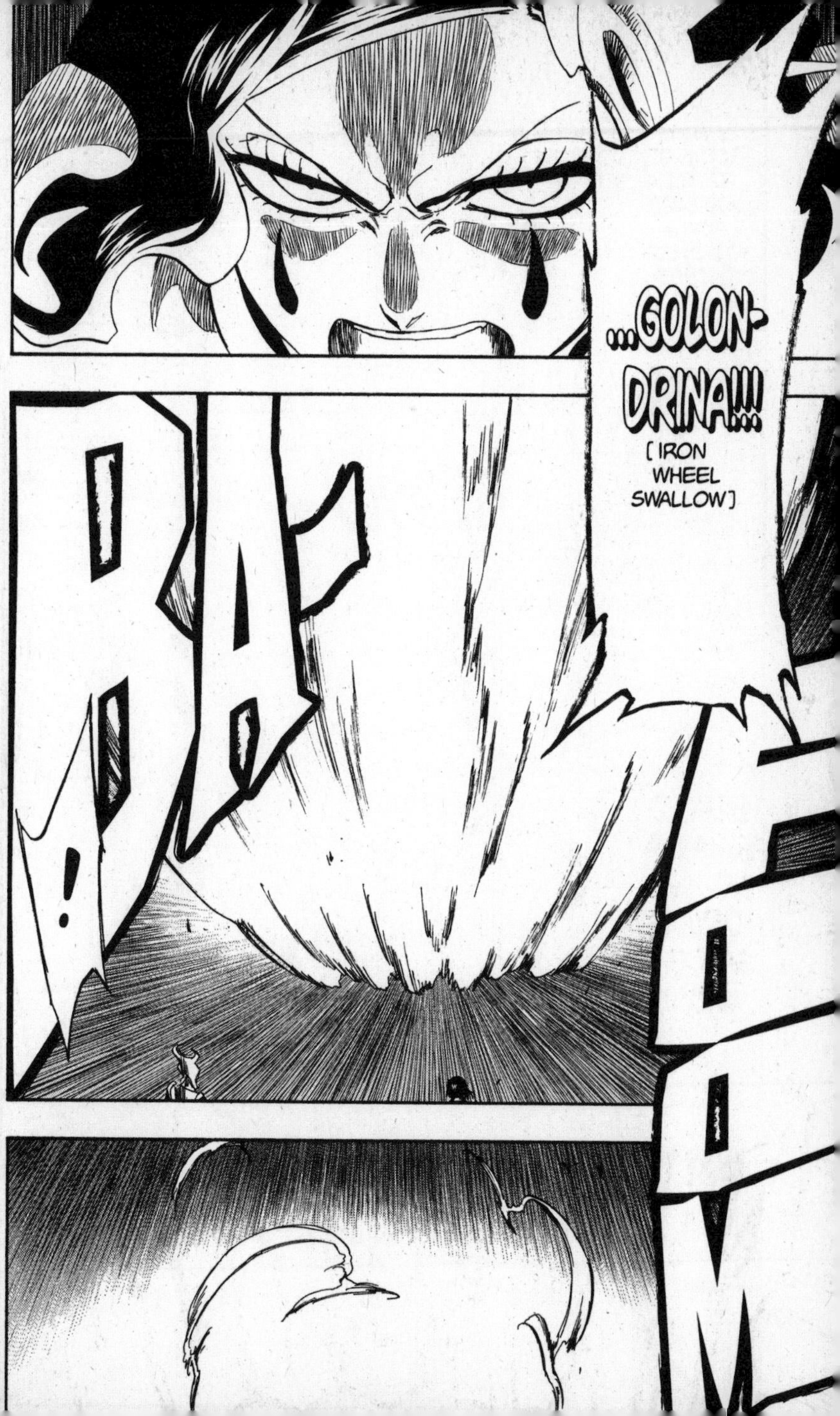

...GOLON-DRINA!!!
[IRON WHEEL SWALLOW]
BA!
BOOM

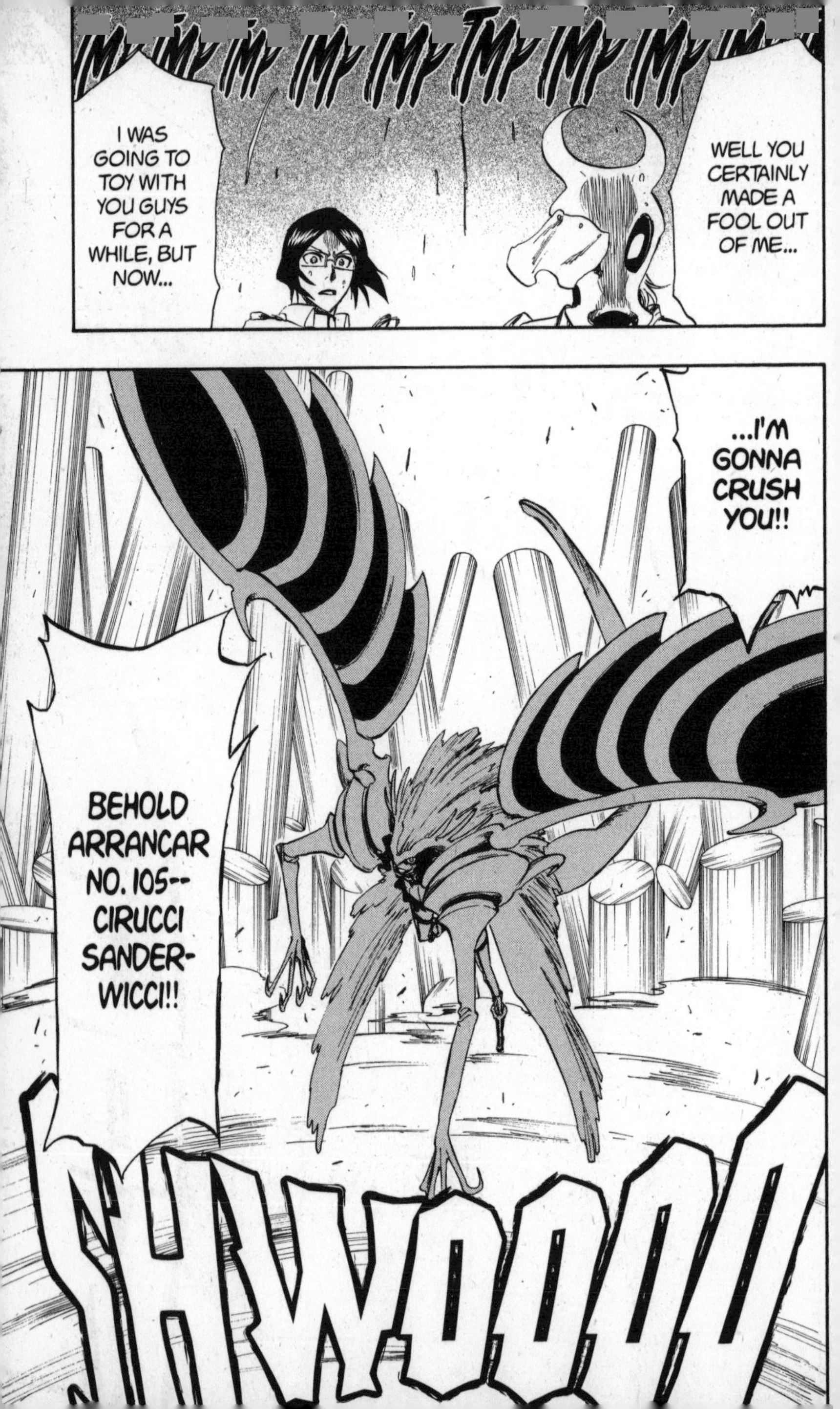
WELL YOU CERTAINLY MADE A FOOL OUT OF ME...
I WAS GOING TO TOY WITH YOU GUYS FOR A WHILE, BUT NOW...
...I'M GONNA CRUSH YOU!!
BEHOLD ARRANCAR NO. 105-- CIRUCCI SANDER-WICCI!!

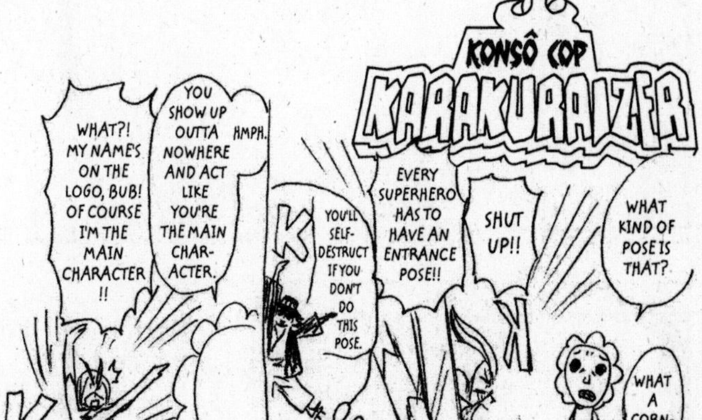
KONSÔ COP KARAKURAIZER
WHAT KIND OF POSE IS THAT?
SHUT UP!!
EVERY SUPERHERO HAS TO HAVE AN ENTRANCE POSE!!
WHAT A CORN-BALL.
YOU'LL SELF-DESTRUCT IF YOU DON'T DO THIS POSE.
HMPH.
YOU SHOW UP OUTTA NOWHERE AND ACT LIKE YOU'RE THE MAIN CHAR-ACTER.
WHAT?! MY NAME'S ON THE LOGO, BUB! OF COURSE I'M THE MAIN CHARACTER !!

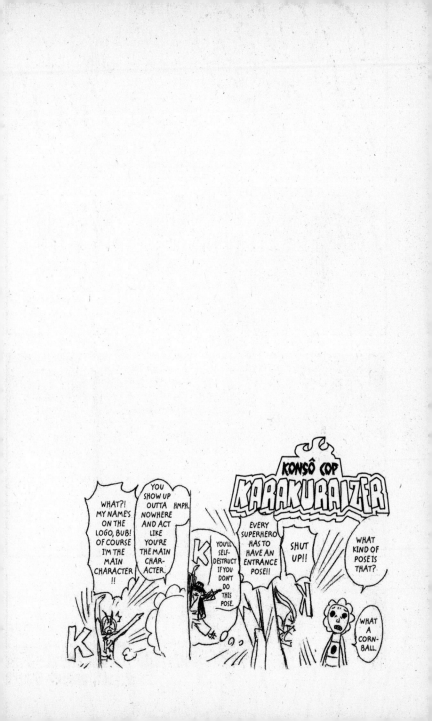

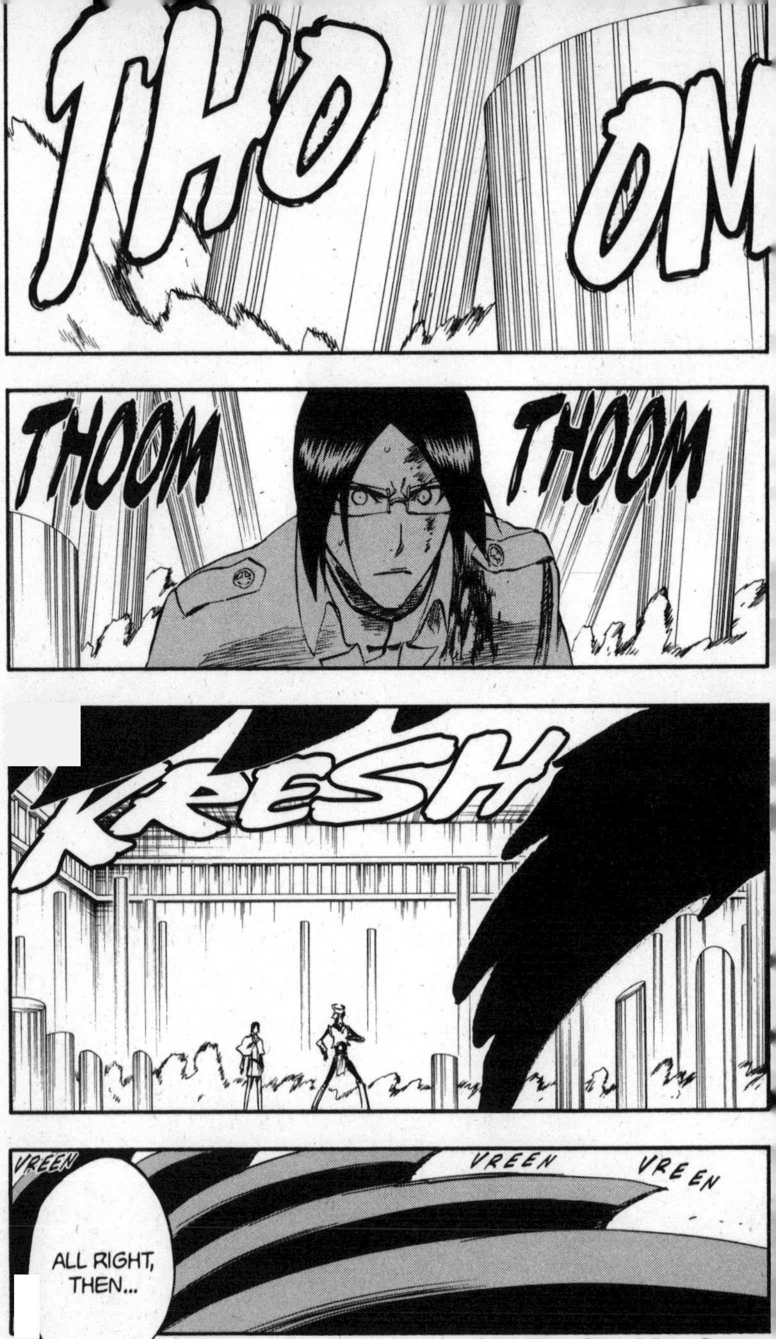
THO OM
THOOM
THOOM
KRESH
VREEN
VREEN
VREEN
ALL RIGHT, THEN...

257. The Slashing Opera

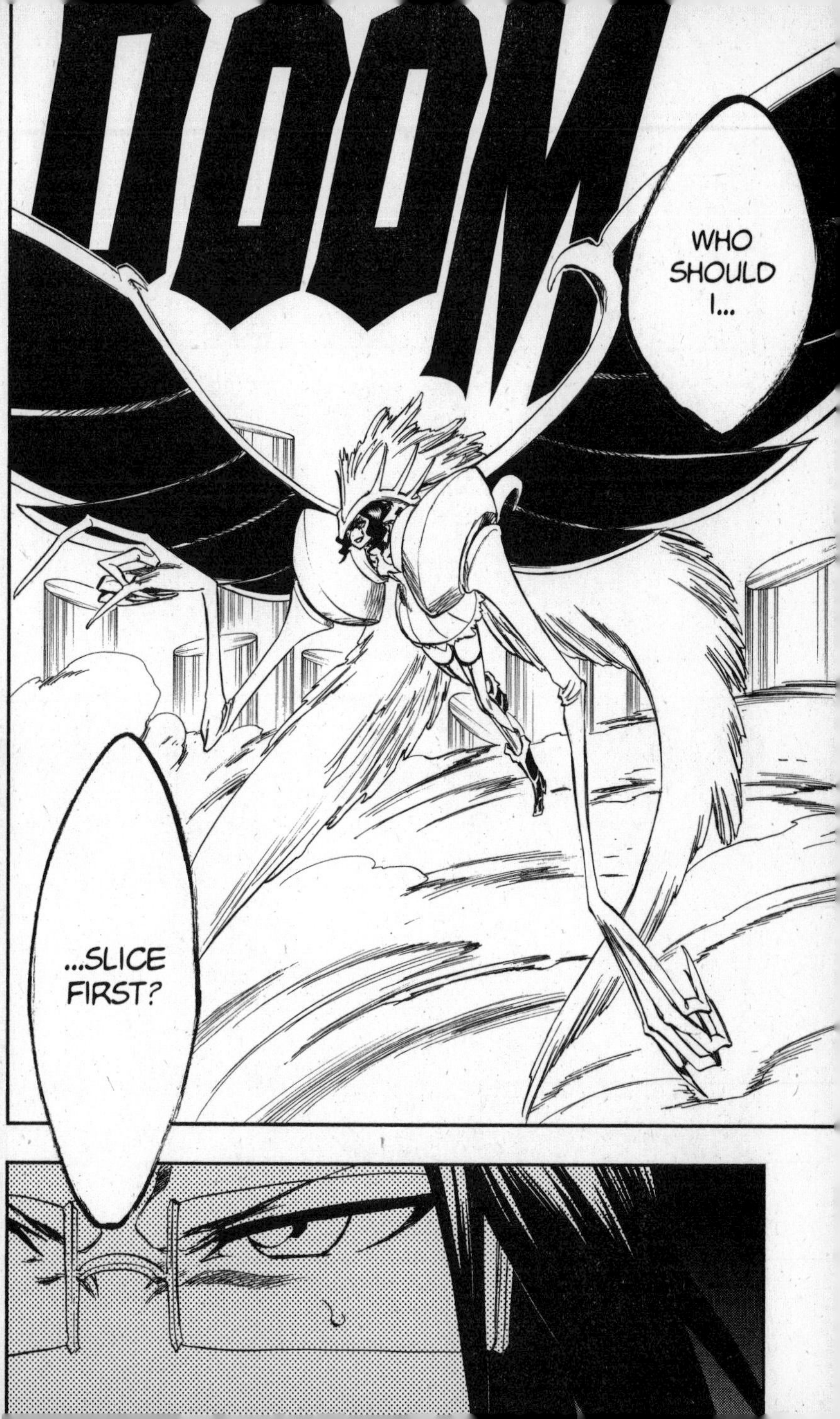
DOOM
WHO SHOULD I...
...SLICE FIRST?

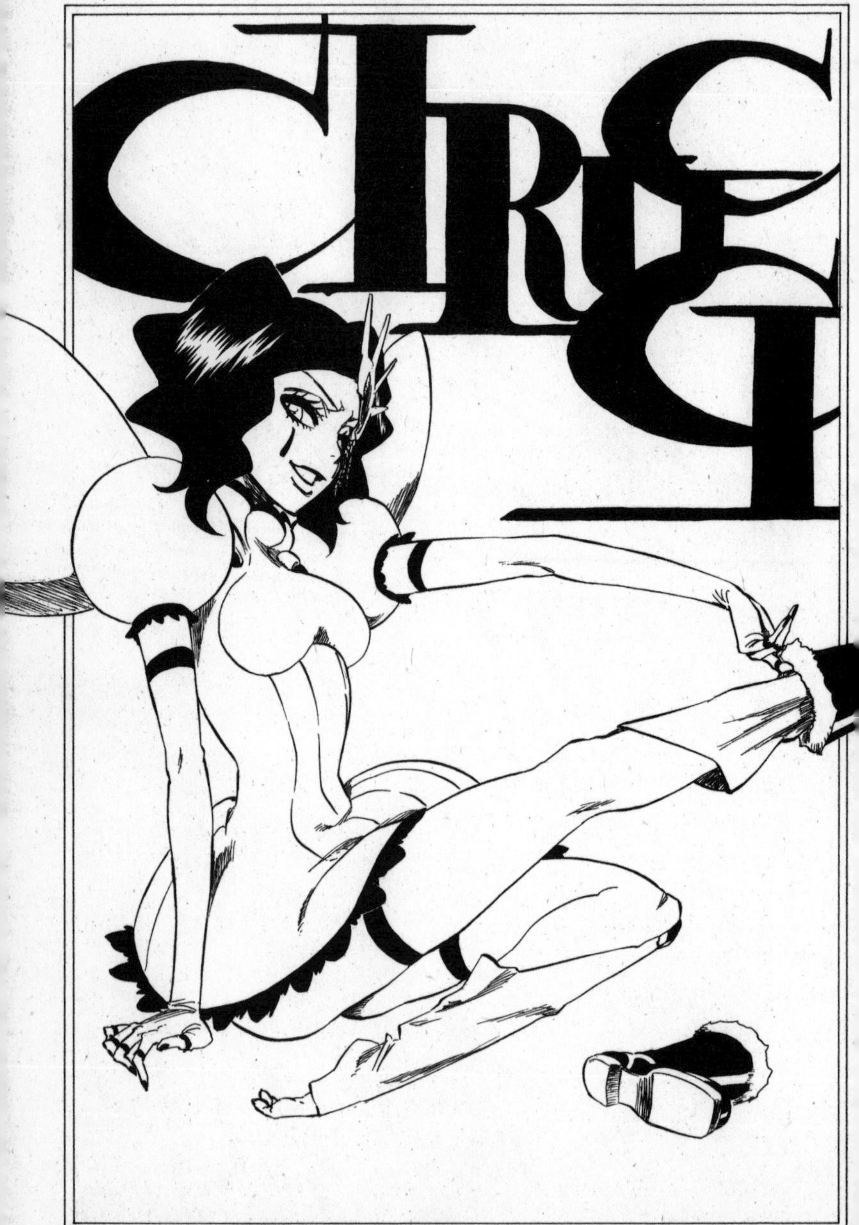

Bleach 257. The Slashing Opera

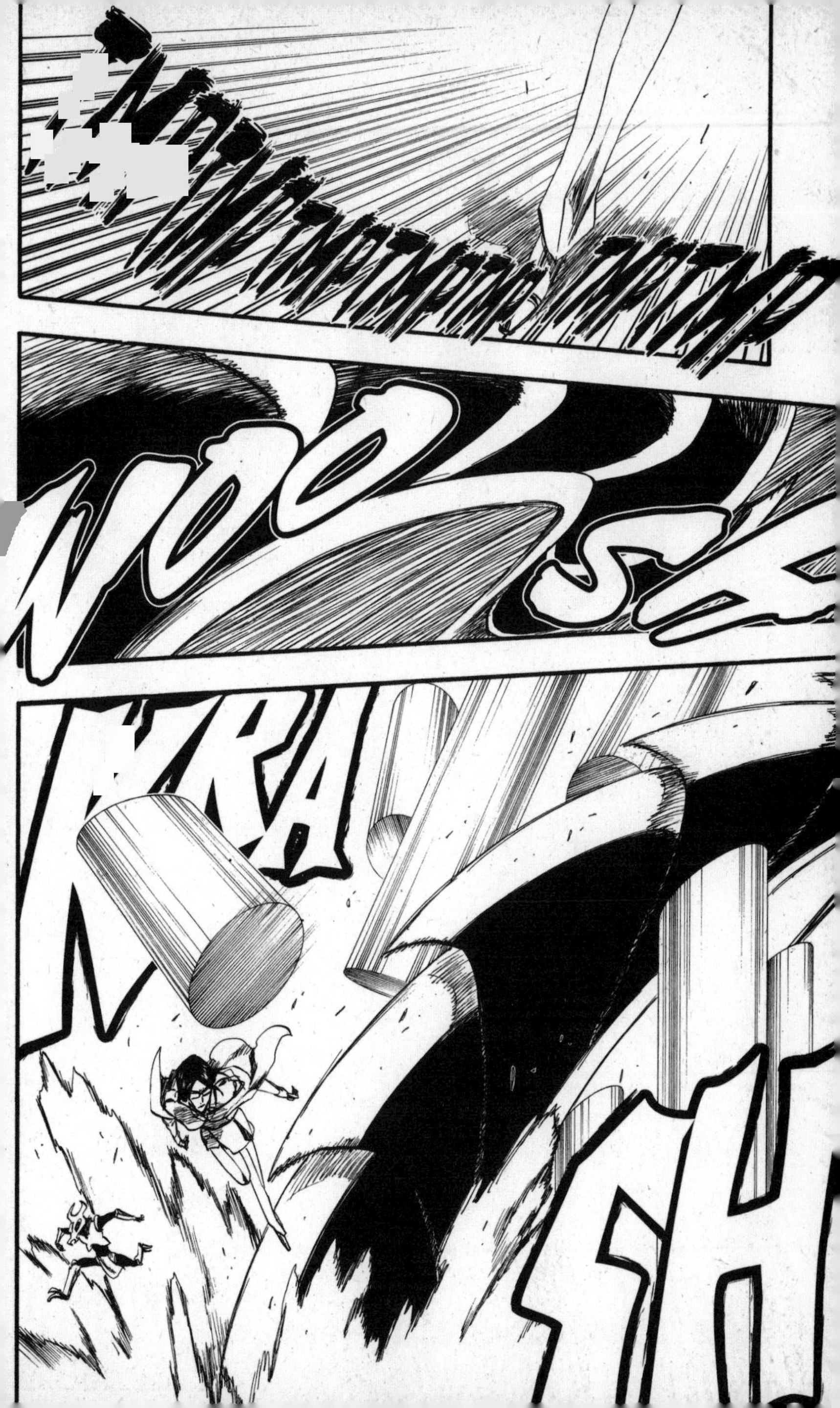
KRA

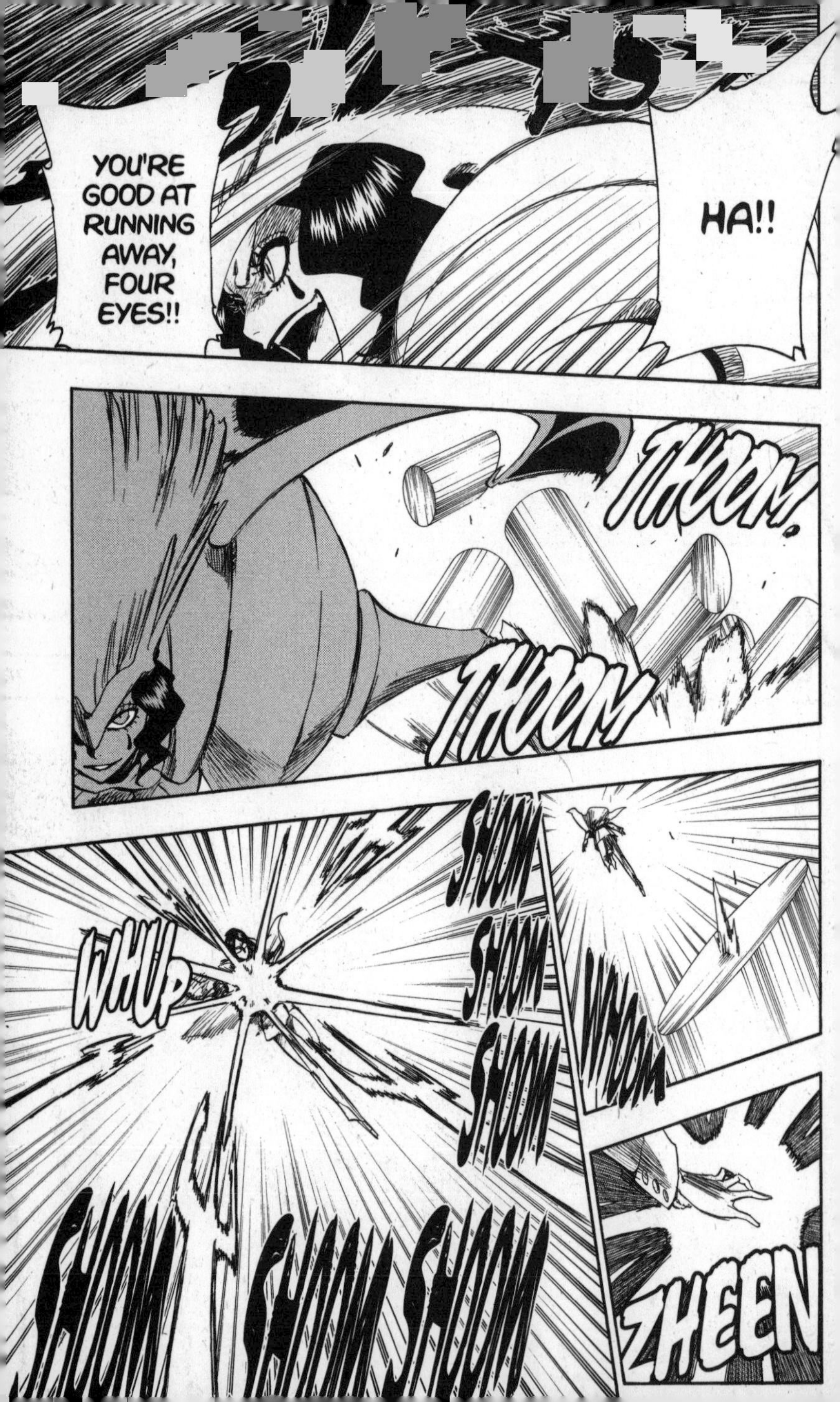
HA!!
YOU'RE GOOD AT RUNNING AWAY, FOUR EYES!!
THOOM
THOOM
WHOOM
ZHEEN
SHOOM SHOOM SHOOM
WHUP
SHOOM SHOOM SHOOM

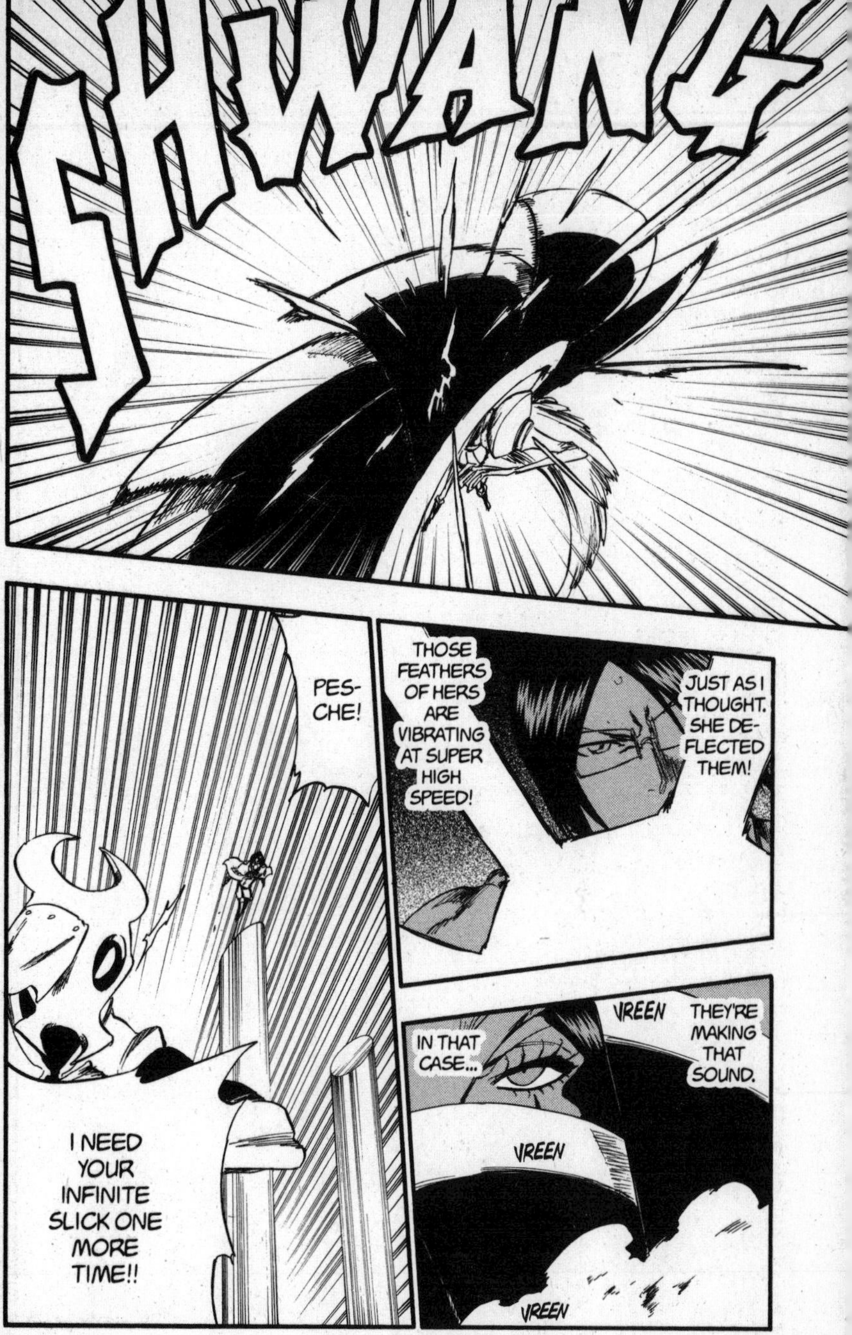
SHWANG
JUST AS I THOUGHT. SHE DEFLECTED THEM!
THOSE FEATHERS OF HERS ARE VIBRATING AT SUPER HIGH SPEED!
VREEN
THEY'RE MAKING THAT SOUND.
IN THAT CASE...
VREEN
VREEN
PES-CHE!
I NEED YOUR INFINITE SLICK ONE MORE TIME!!

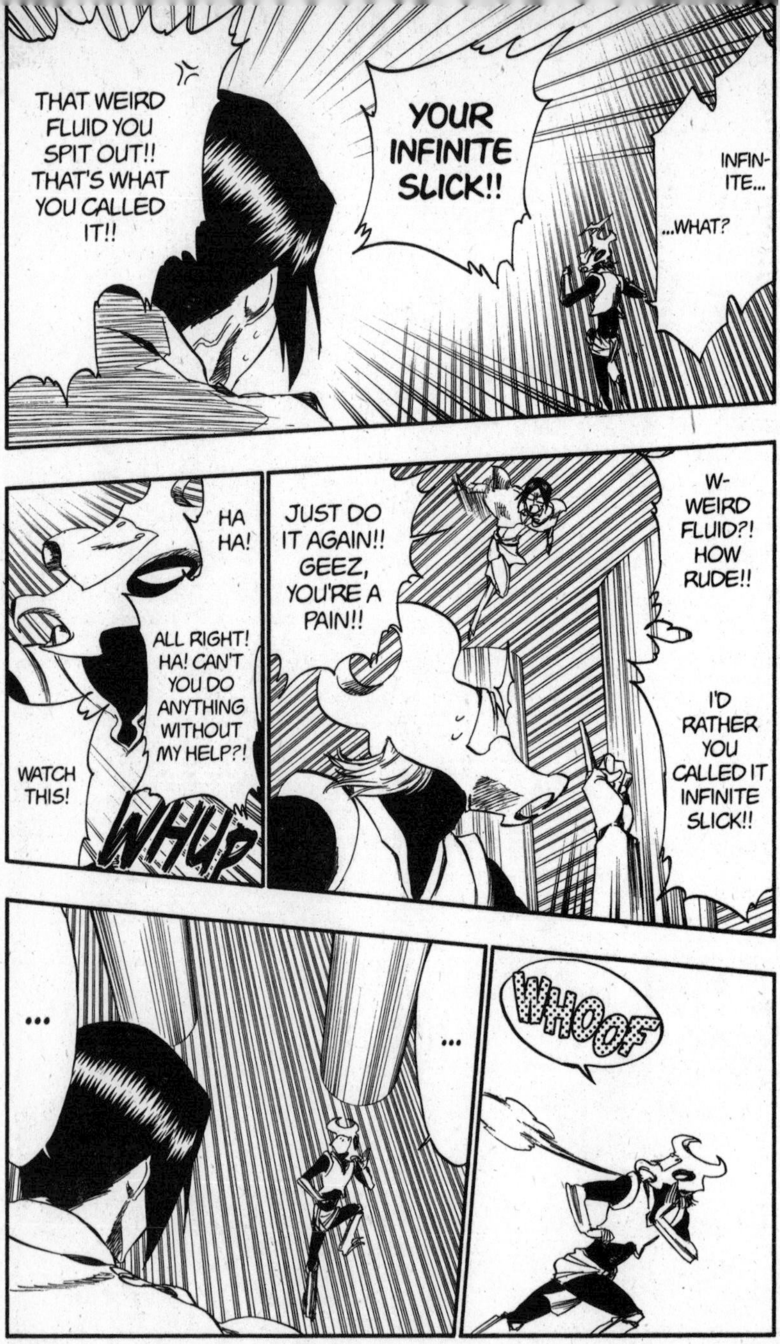
INFINITE...
...WHAT?
YOUR INFINITE SLICK!!
THAT WEIRD FLUID YOU SPIT OUT!! THAT'S WHAT YOU CALLED IT!!
W-WEIRD FLUID?! HOW RUDE!!
I'D RATHER YOU CALLED IT INFINITE SLICK!!
JUST DO IT AGAIN!! GEEZ, YOU'RE A PAIN!!
HA HA!
ALL RIGHT! HA! CAN'T YOU DO ANYTHING WITHOUT MY HELP?!
WATCH THIS!
WHUP
WHOOF
...
...

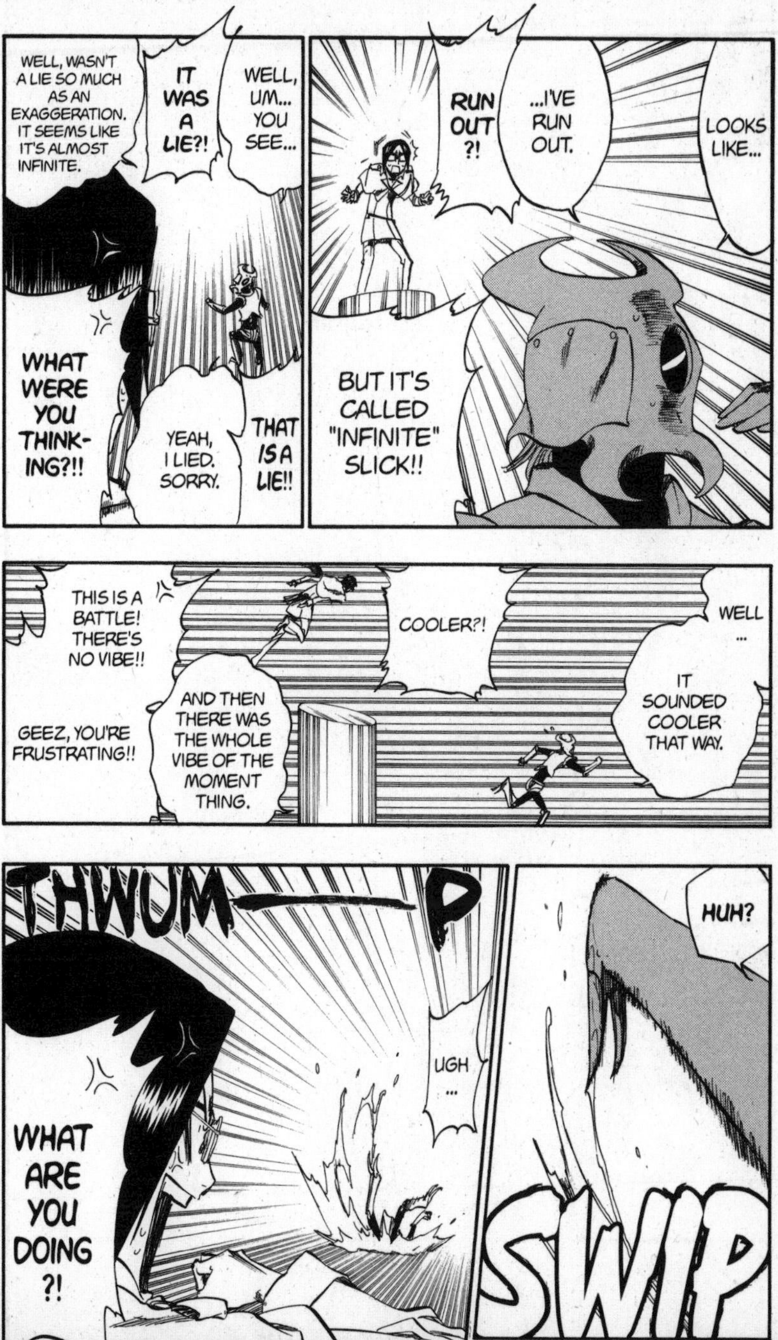
LOOKS LIKE...
...I'VE RUN OUT.
RUN OUT?!
BUT IT'S CALLED "INFINITE" SLICK!!
WELL, UM... YOU SEE...
IT WAS A LIE?!
WELL, WASN'T A LIE SO MUCH AS AN EXAGGERATION. IT SEEMS LIKE IT'S ALMOST INFINITE.
THAT IS A LIE!!
YEAH, I LIED. SORRY.
WHAT WERE YOU THINKING?!!
WELL ...
IT SOUNDED COOLER THAT WAY.
COOLER?!
AND THEN THERE WAS THE WHOLE VIBE OF THE MOMENT THING.
THIS IS A BATTLE! THERE'S NO VIBE!!
GEEZ, YOU'RE FRUSTRATING!!
HUH?
SWIP
THWUM—P
UGH ...
WHAT ARE YOU DOING ?!

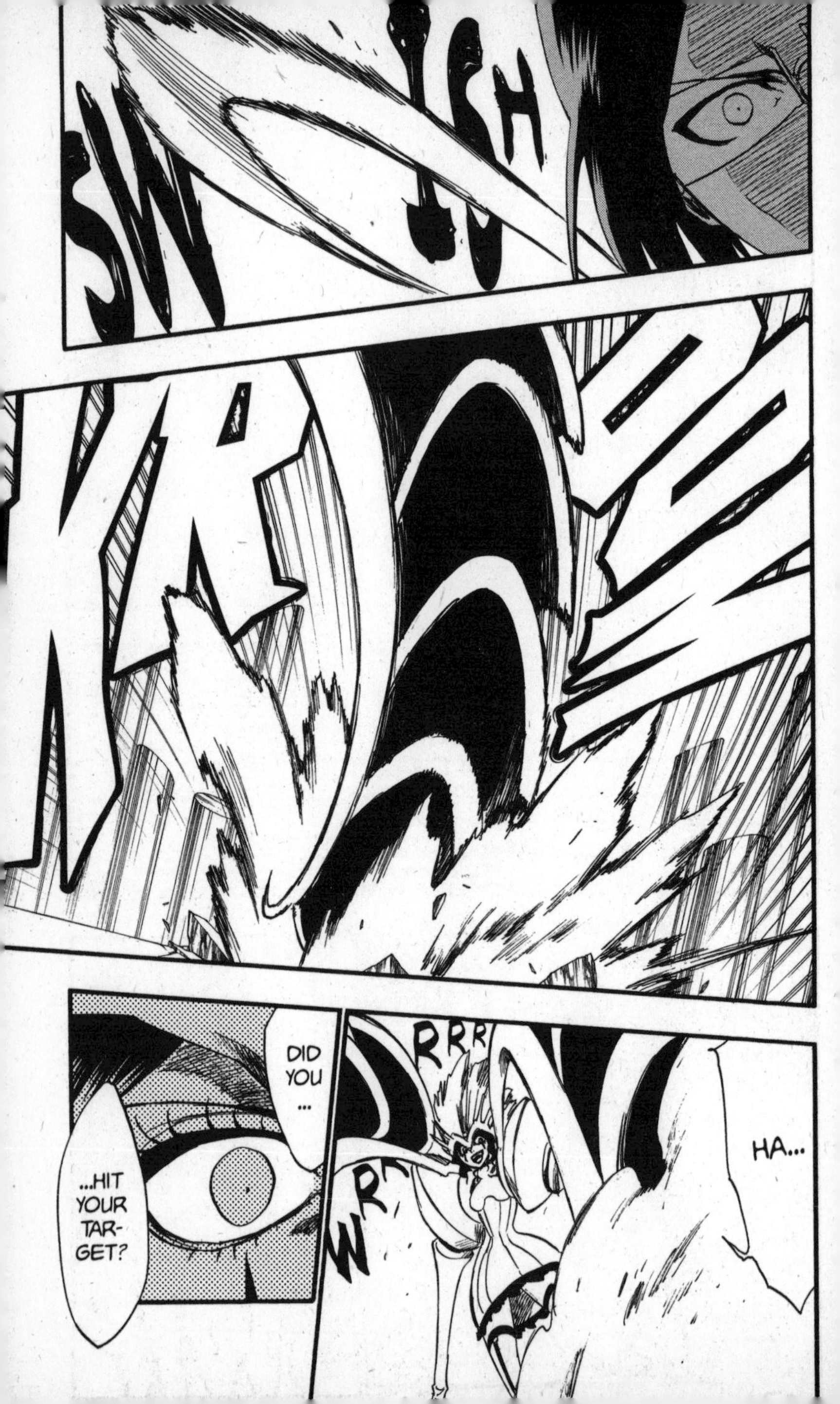
SWISH
RRR
WR
HA...
DID YOU ...
...HIT YOUR TAR- GET?

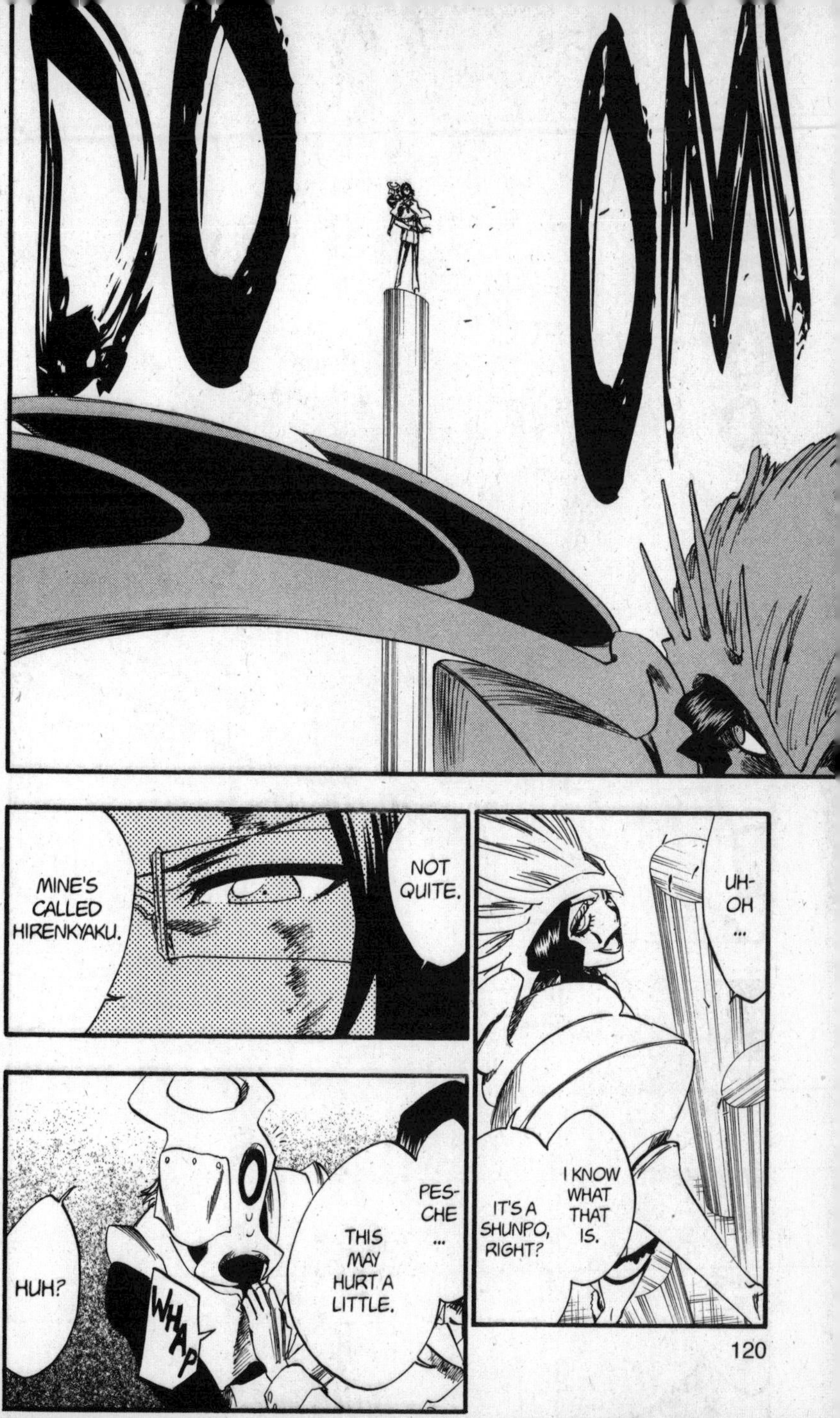
DOOM
UH-OH ...
I KNOW WHAT THAT IS.
IT'S A SHUNPO, RIGHT?
NOT QUITE.
MINE'S CALLED HIRENKYAKU.
PES-CHE ...
THIS MAY HURT A LITTLE.
WHAP
HUH?

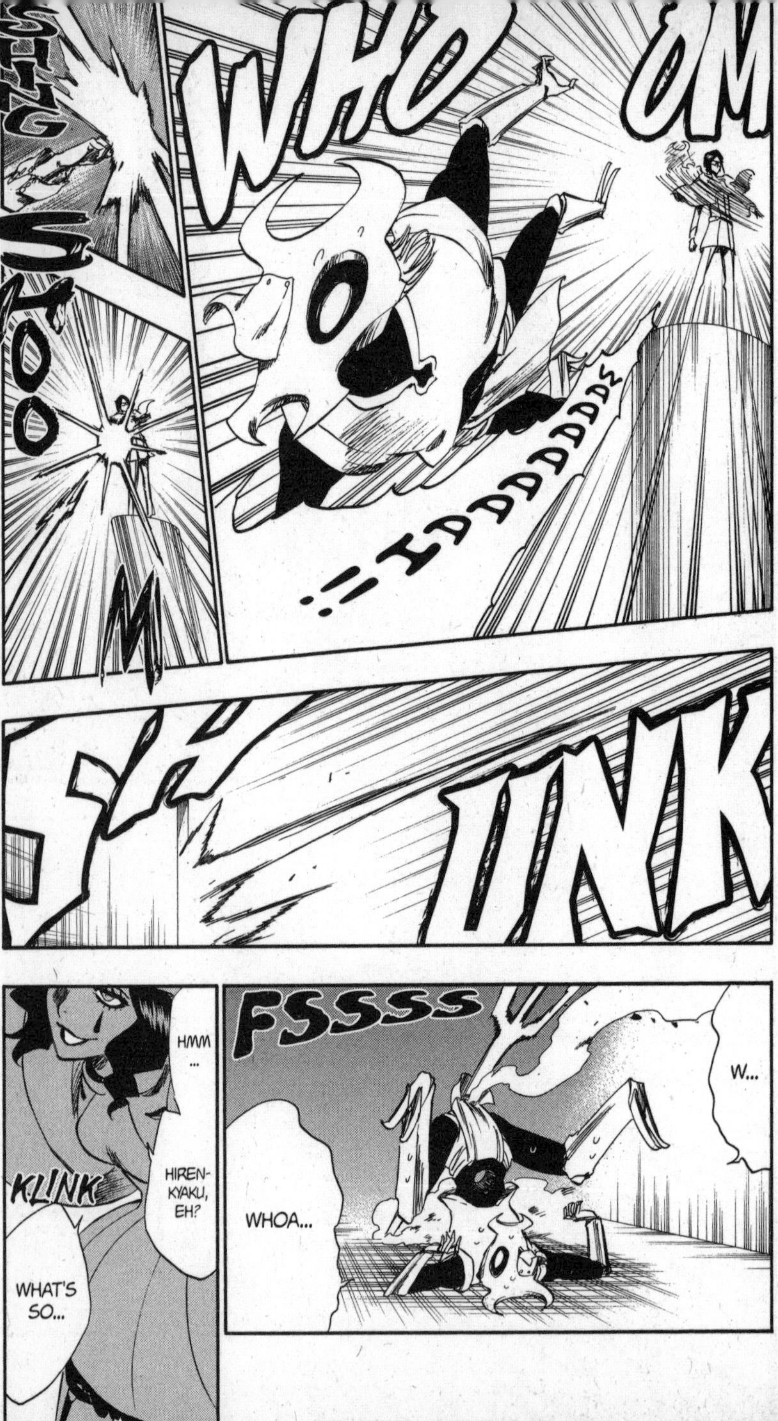
WHOOM
SHING
SHOOOM
FSSSS
W...
WHOA...
HMM...
KLINK
HIREN-KYAKU, EH?
WHAT'S SO...

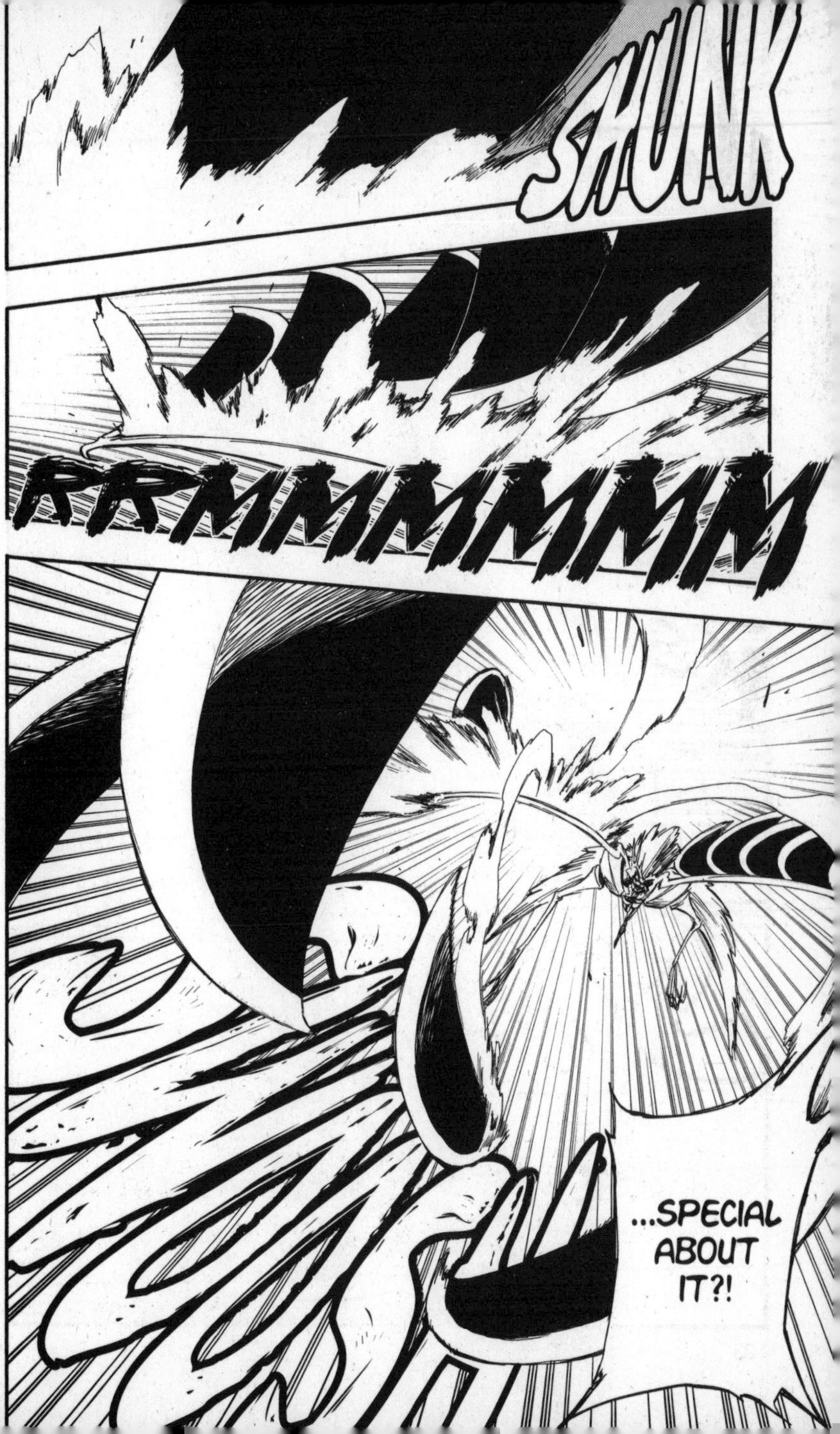
SHUNK
RRMMMMMMM
...SPECIAL ABOUT IT?!

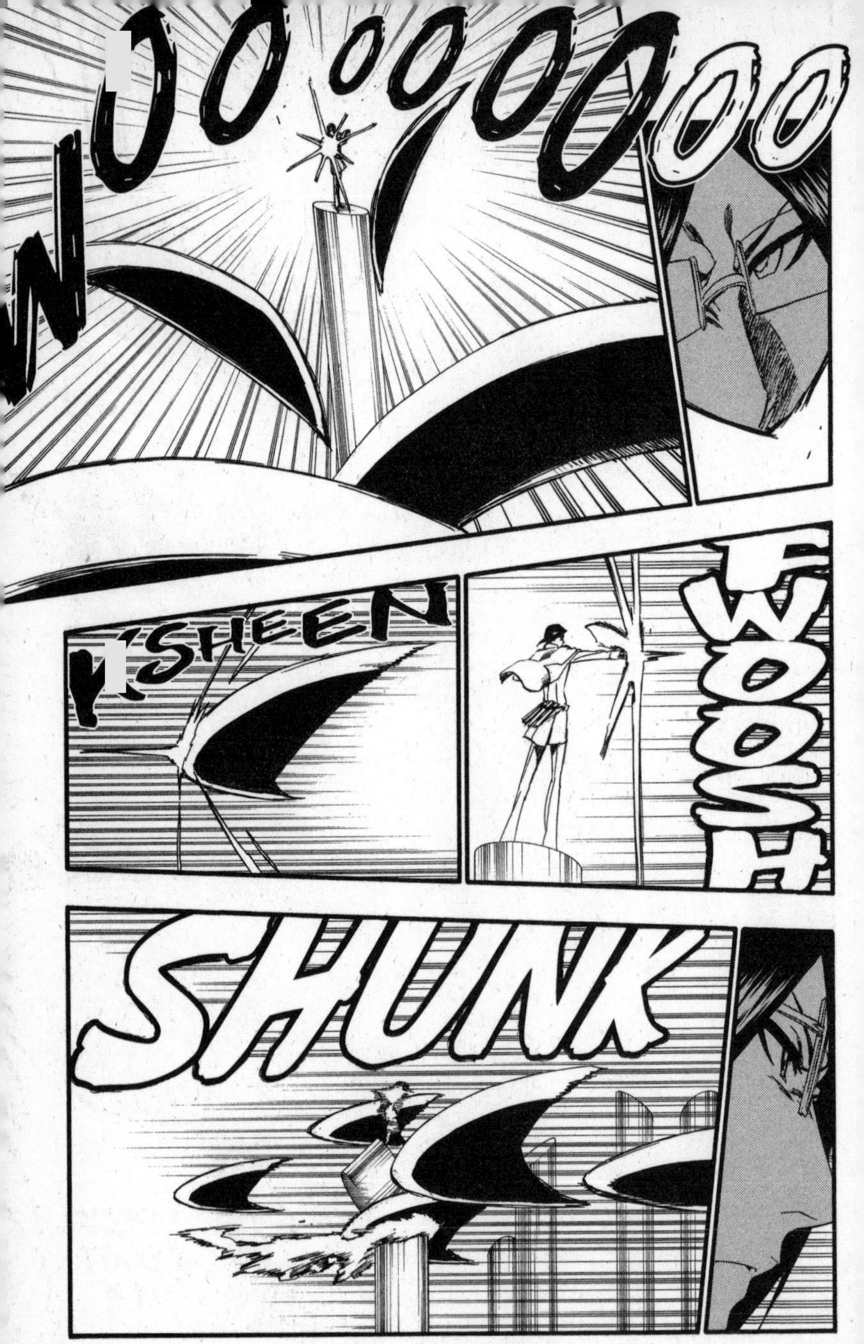
WOOSH
SHEEN
SHUNK

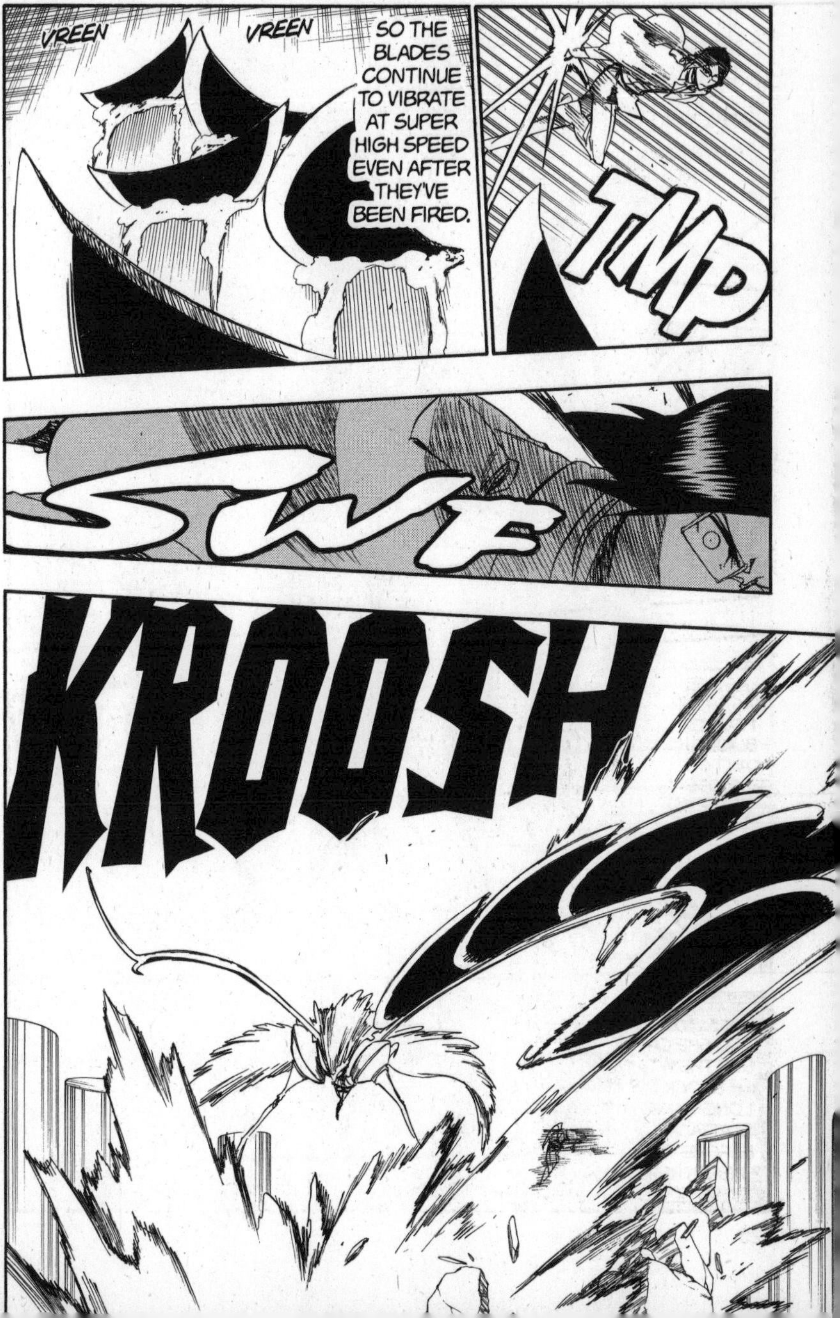
TMP
VREEN
VREEN
SO THE BLADES CONTINUE TO VIBRATE AT SUPER HIGH SPEED EVEN AFTER THEY'VE BEEN FIRED.
SWF
KROOSH

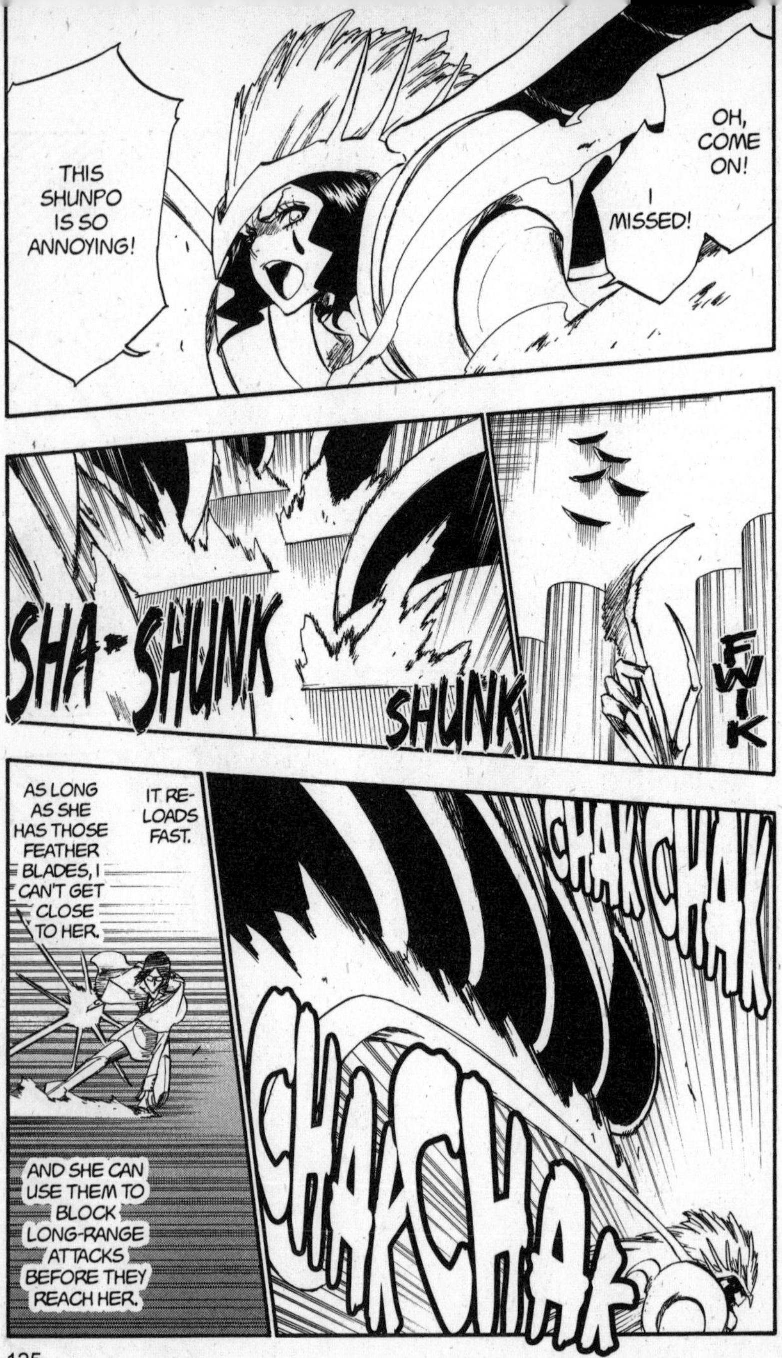
OH, COME ON!
I MISSED!
THIS SHUNPO IS SO ANNOYING!
FWIK
SHA-SHUNK
SHUNK
CHAK CHAK
CHAKCHAK
IT RE-LOADS FAST.
AS LONG AS SHE HAS THOSE FEATHER BLADES, I CAN'T GET CLOSE TO HER.
AND SHE CAN USE THEM TO BLOCK LONG-RANGE ATTACKS BEFORE THEY REACH HER.

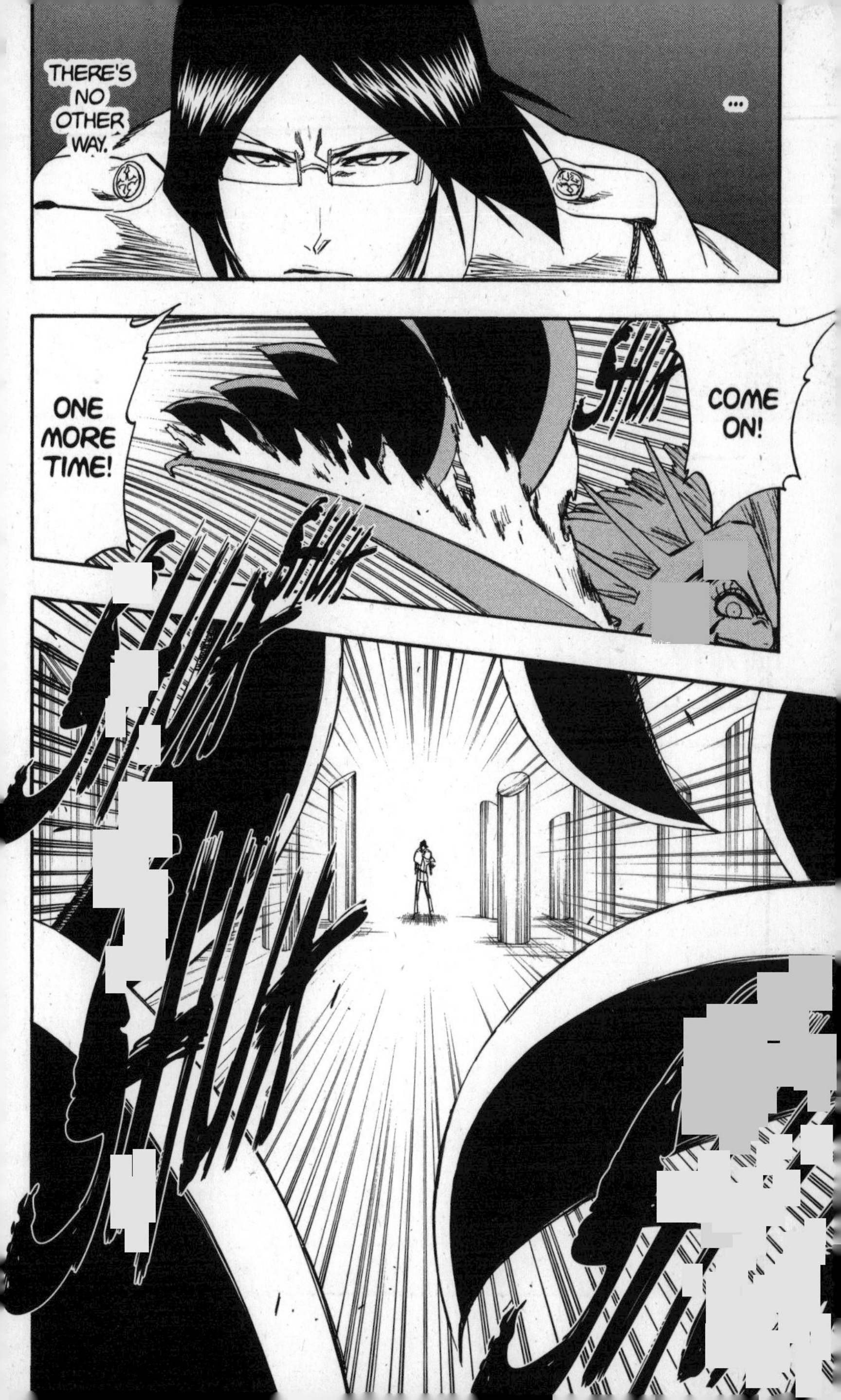
...
THERE'S NO OTHER WAY.
COME ON!
SHUK
ONE MORE TIME!
SHUK

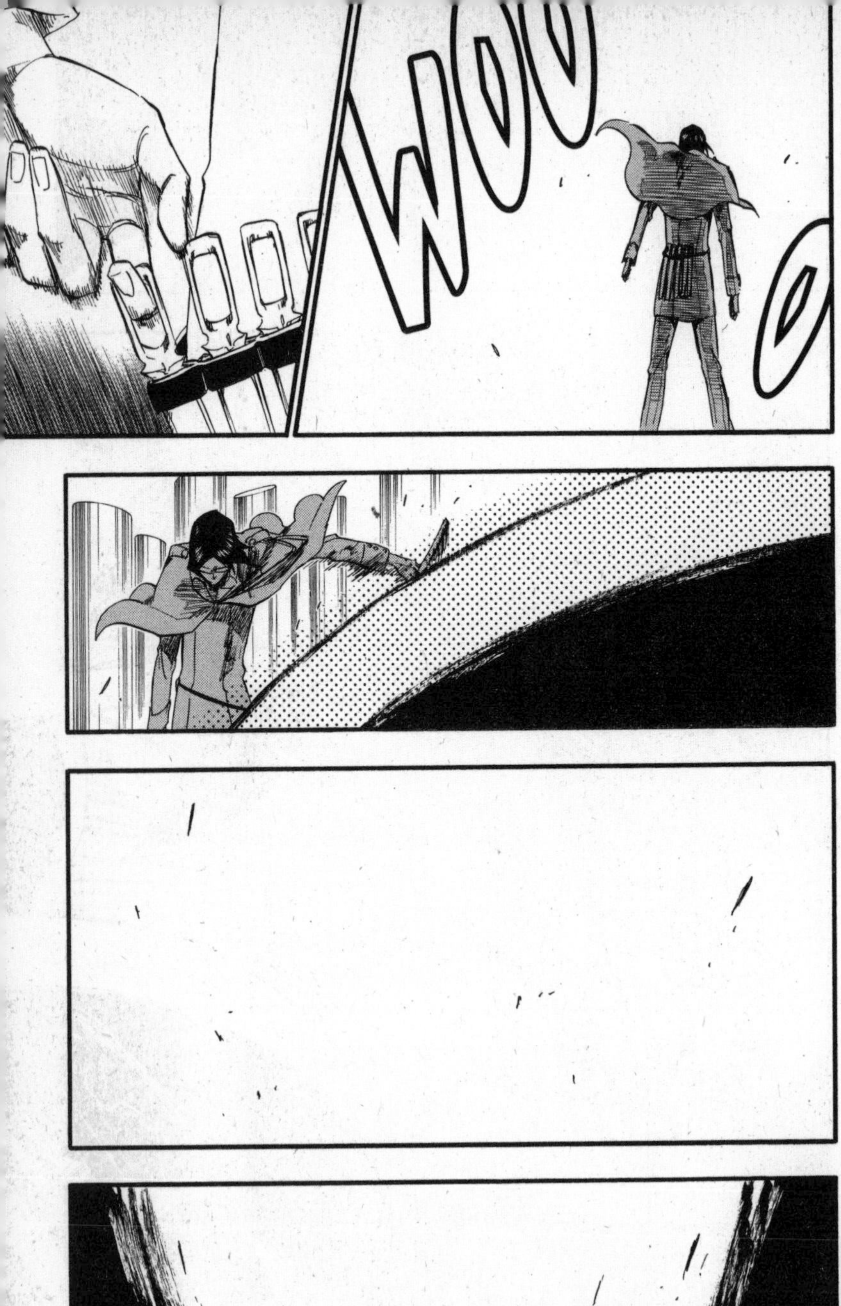
WOOO

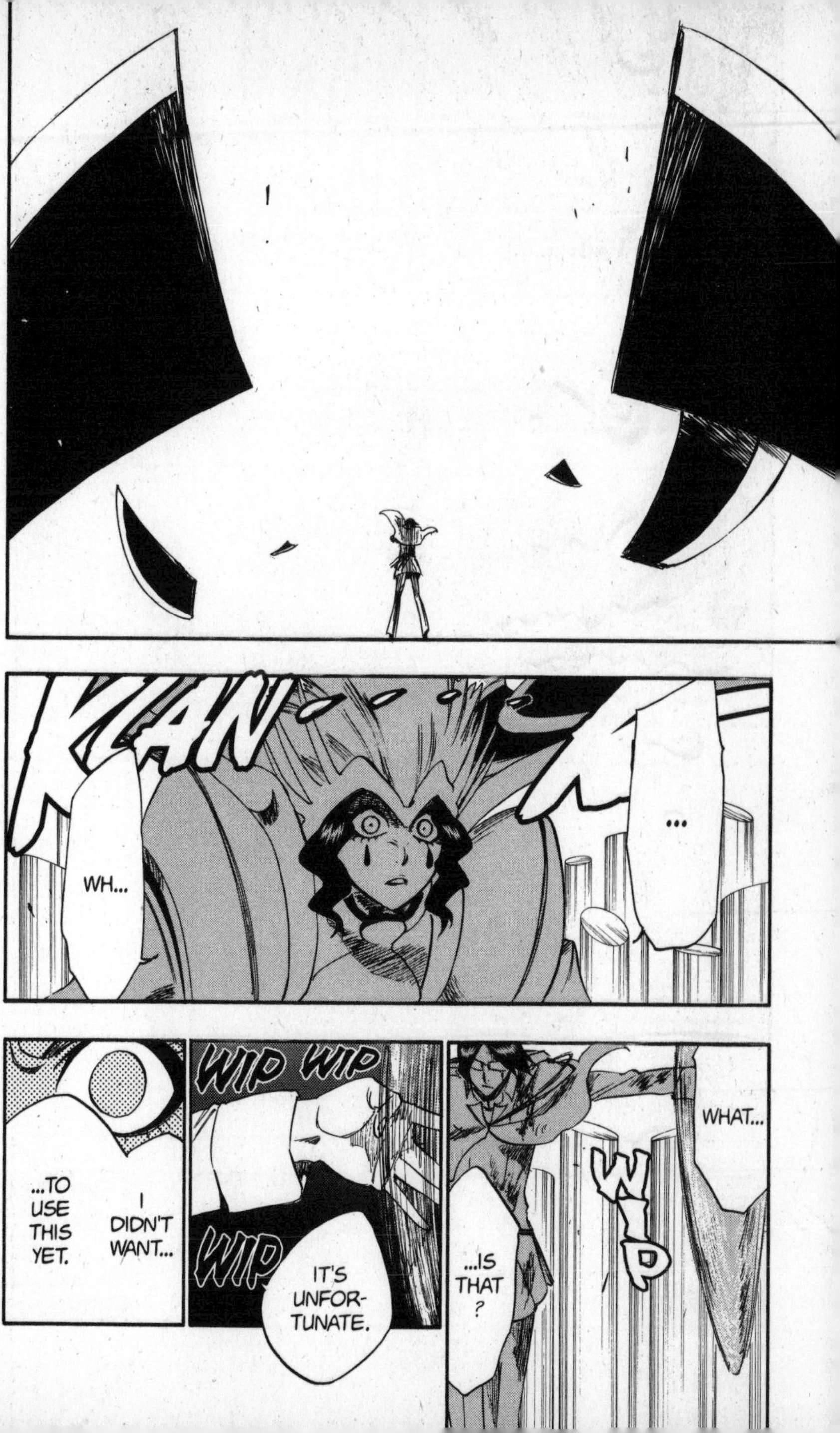
...
WH...
WHAT...
WIP
...IS THAT ?
WIP WIP
WIP
IT'S UNFOR-TUNATE.
I DIDN'T WANT...
...TO USE THIS YET.

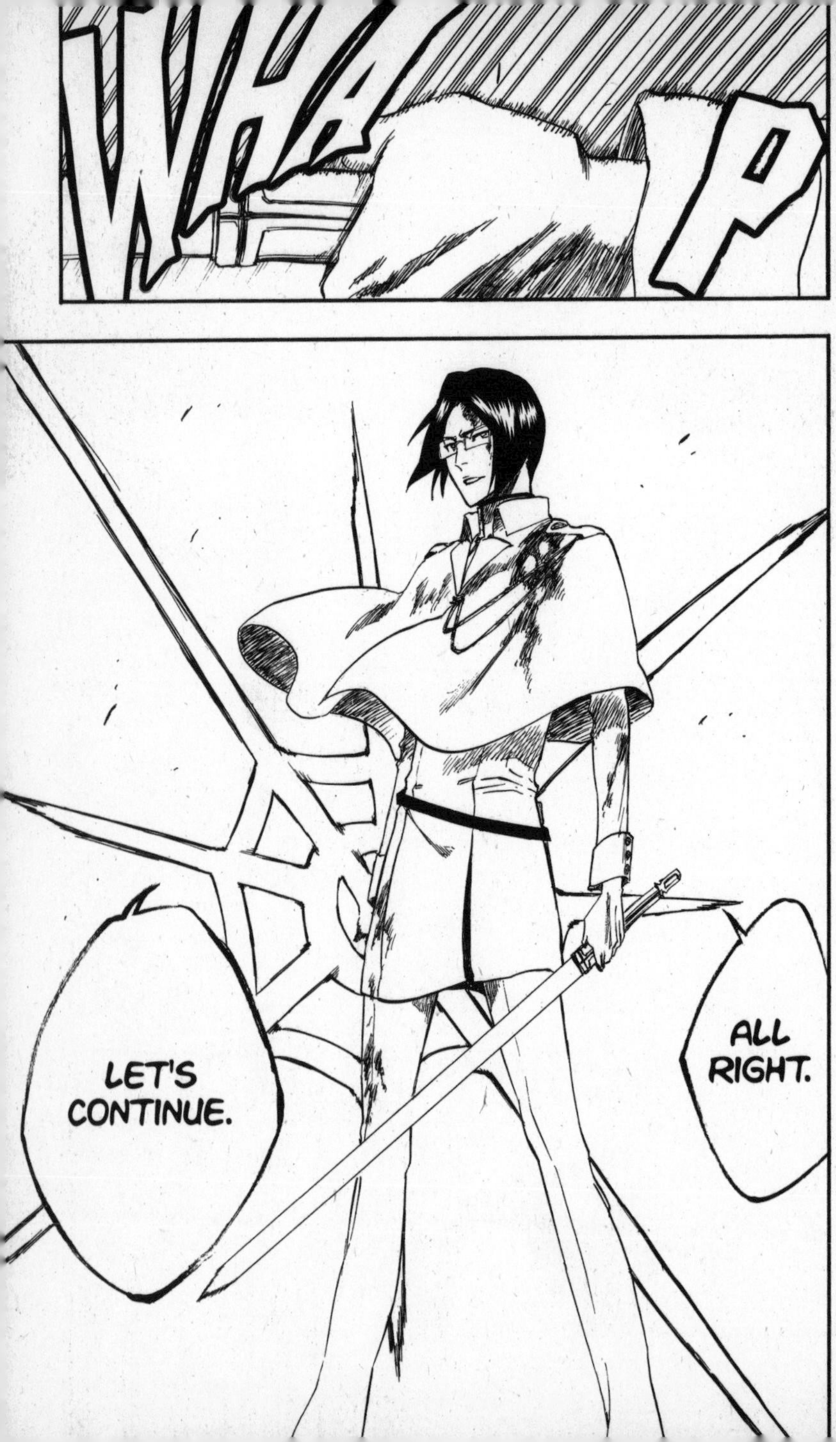
WHAP
ALL RIGHT.
LET'S CONTINUE.

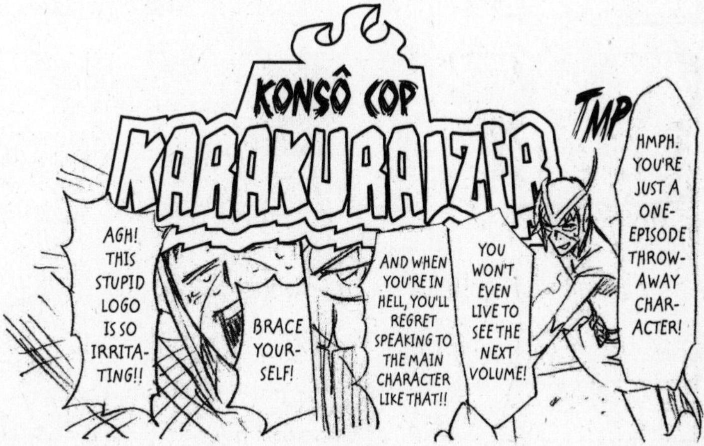
KONSÔ COP
KARAKURAIZER
TMP
HMPH. YOU'RE JUST A ONE-EPISODE THROW-AWAY CHAR-ACTER!
YOU WON'T EVEN LIVE TO SEE THE NEXT VOLUME!
AND WHEN YOU'RE IN HELL, YOU'LL REGRET SPEAKING TO THE MAIN CHARACTER LIKE THAT!!
BRACE YOUR-SELF!
AGH! THIS STUPID LOGO IS SO IRRITA-TING!!

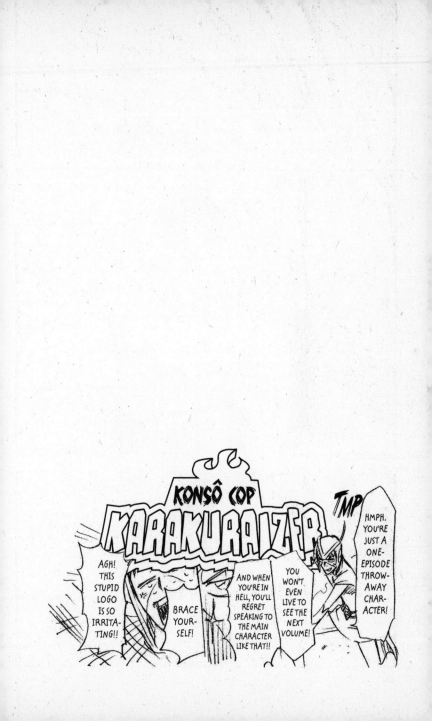

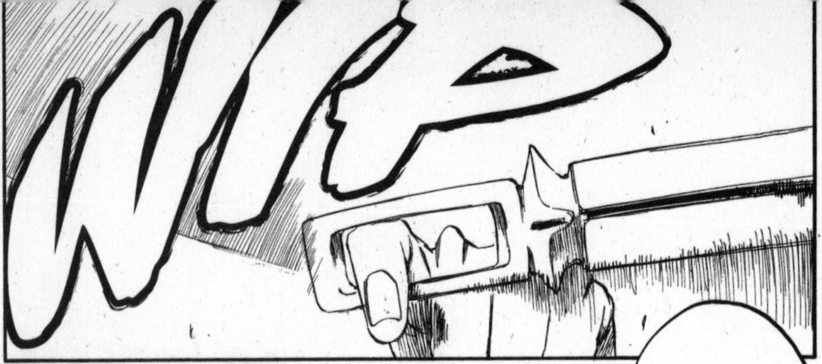
WIP

258. Seeleschneider

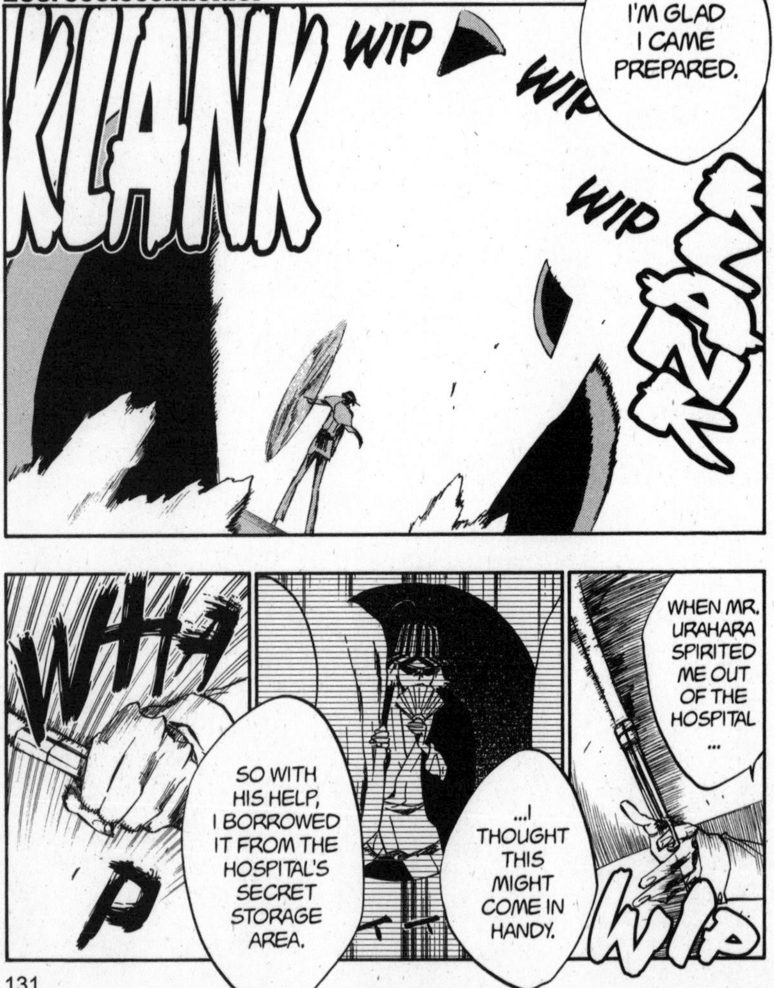
I'M GLAD I CAME PREPARED.
KLANK
WIP
WIP
WIP
WHEN MR. URAHARA SPIRITED ME OUT OF THE HOSPITAL ...
WIP
...I THOUGHT THIS MIGHT COME IN HANDY.
SO WITH HIS HELP, I BORROWED IT FROM THE HOSPITAL'S SECRET STORAGE AREA.

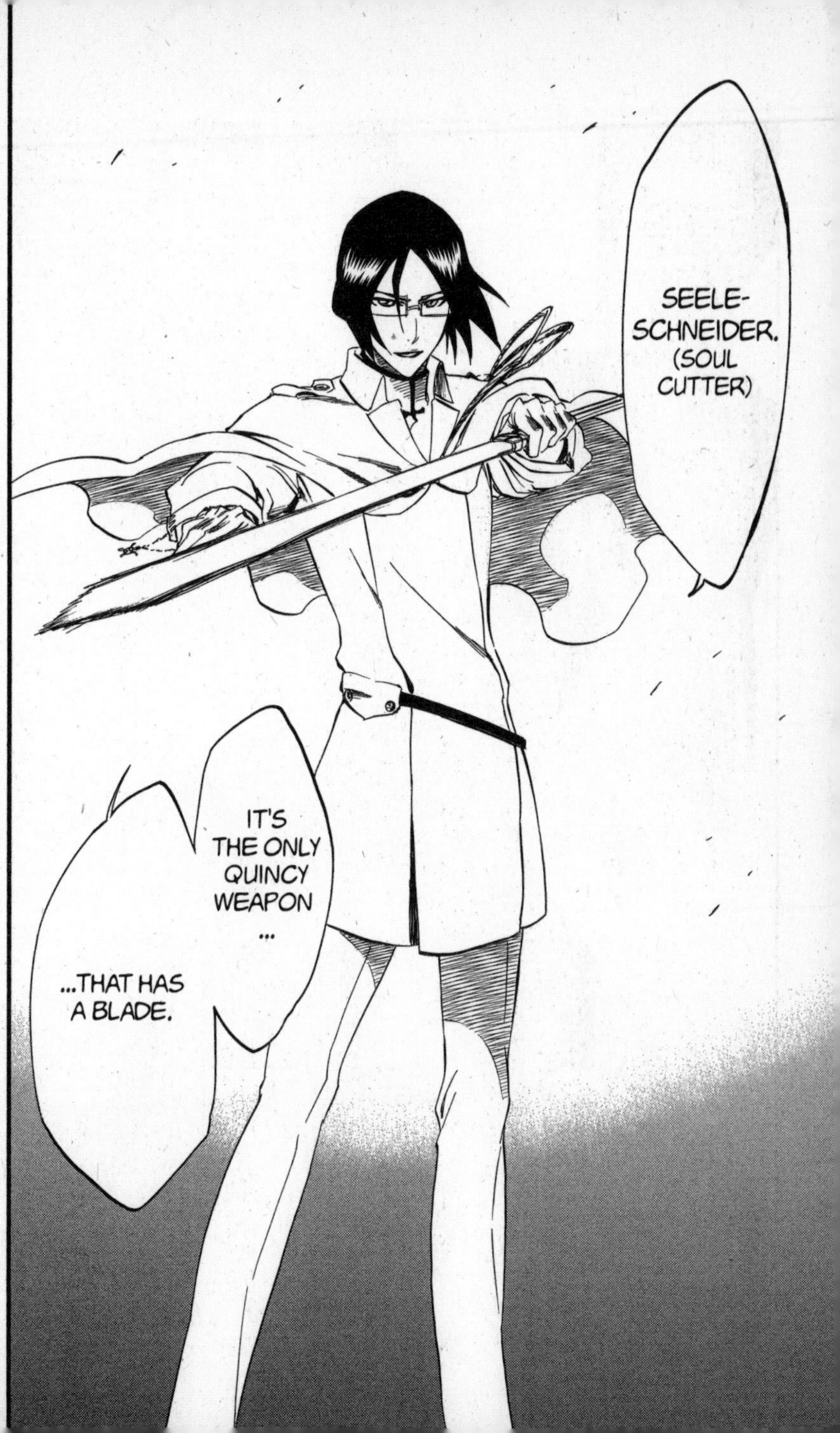
SEELE-SCHNEIDER. (SOUL CUTTER)
IT'S THE ONLY QUINCY WEAPON ...
...THAT HAS A BLADE.

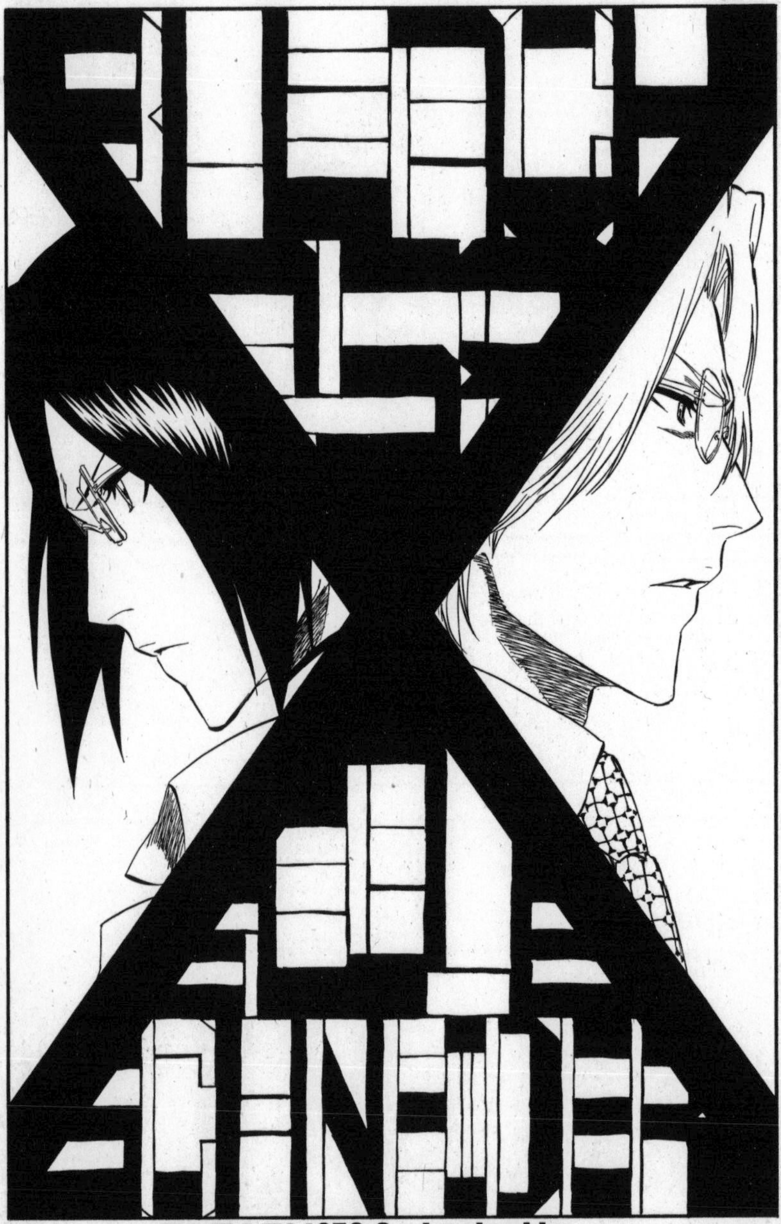

BLEACH 258. Seeleschneider

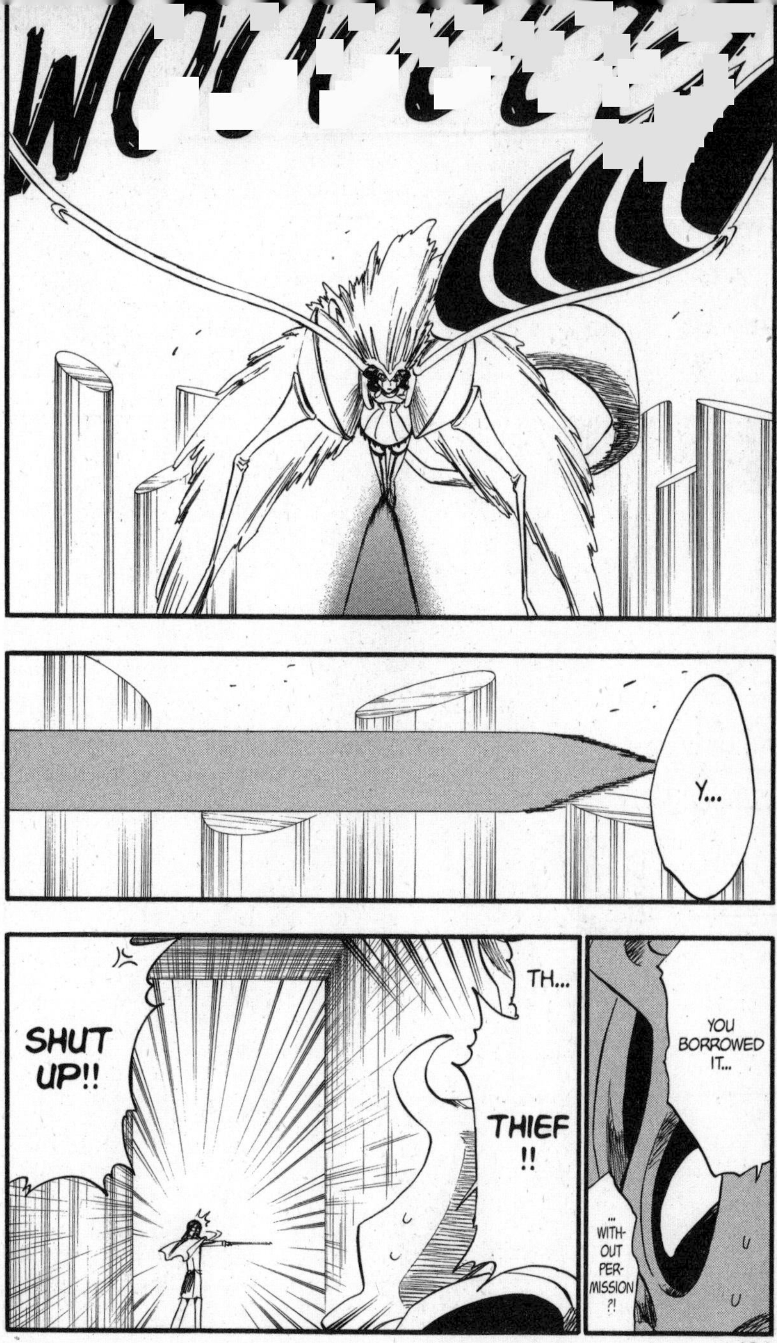
Y...
YOU BORROWED IT...
...WITH-OUT PER-MISSION?!
TH...
THIEF!!
SHUT UP!!

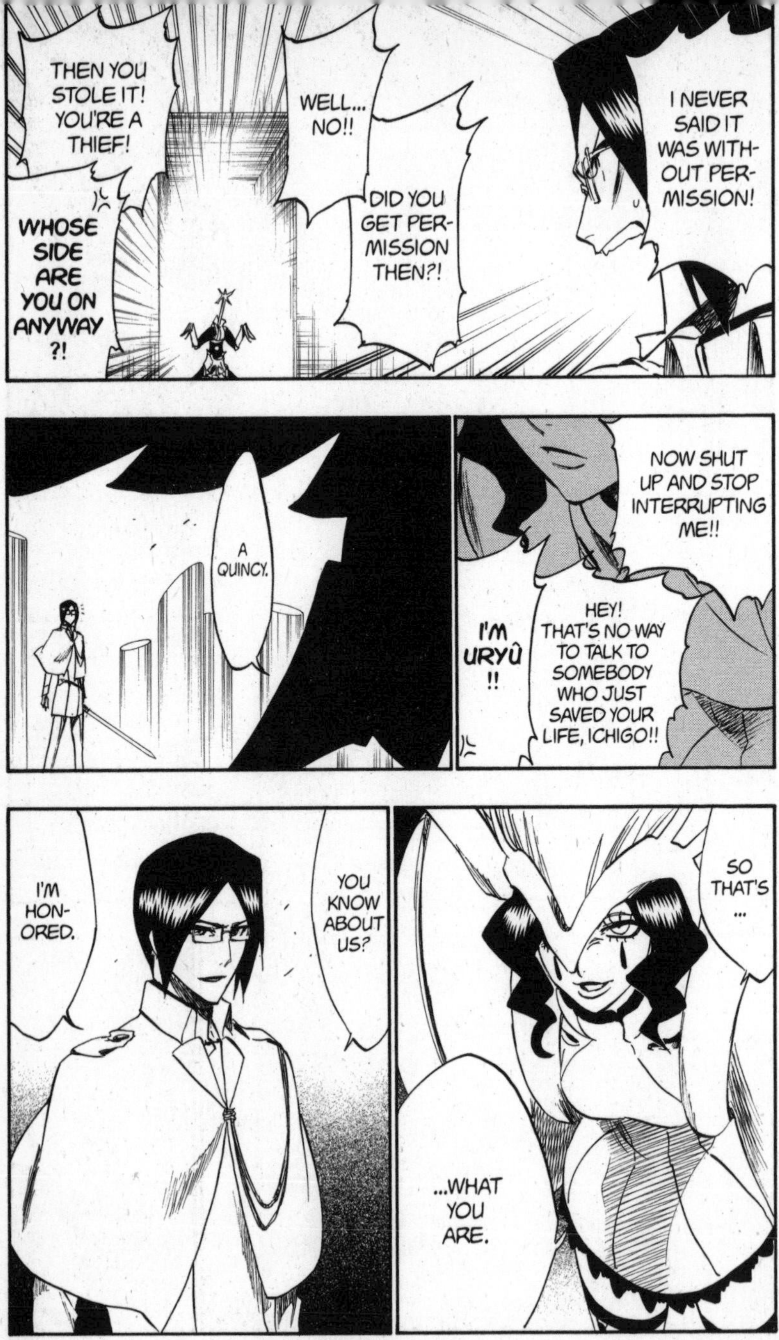
I NEVER SAID IT WAS WITH-OUT PER-MISSION!
DID YOU GET PER-MISSION THEN?!
WELL... NO!!
THEN YOU STOLE IT! YOU'RE A THIEF!
WHOSE SIDE ARE YOU ON ANYWAY ?!
NOW SHUT UP AND STOP INTERRUPTING ME!!
HEY! THAT'S NO WAY TO TALK TO SOMEBODY WHO JUST SAVED YOUR LIFE, ICHIGO!!
I'M URYÛ !!
A QUINCY.
SO THAT'S ...
...WHAT YOU ARE.
YOU KNOW ABOUT US?
I'M HON-ORED.

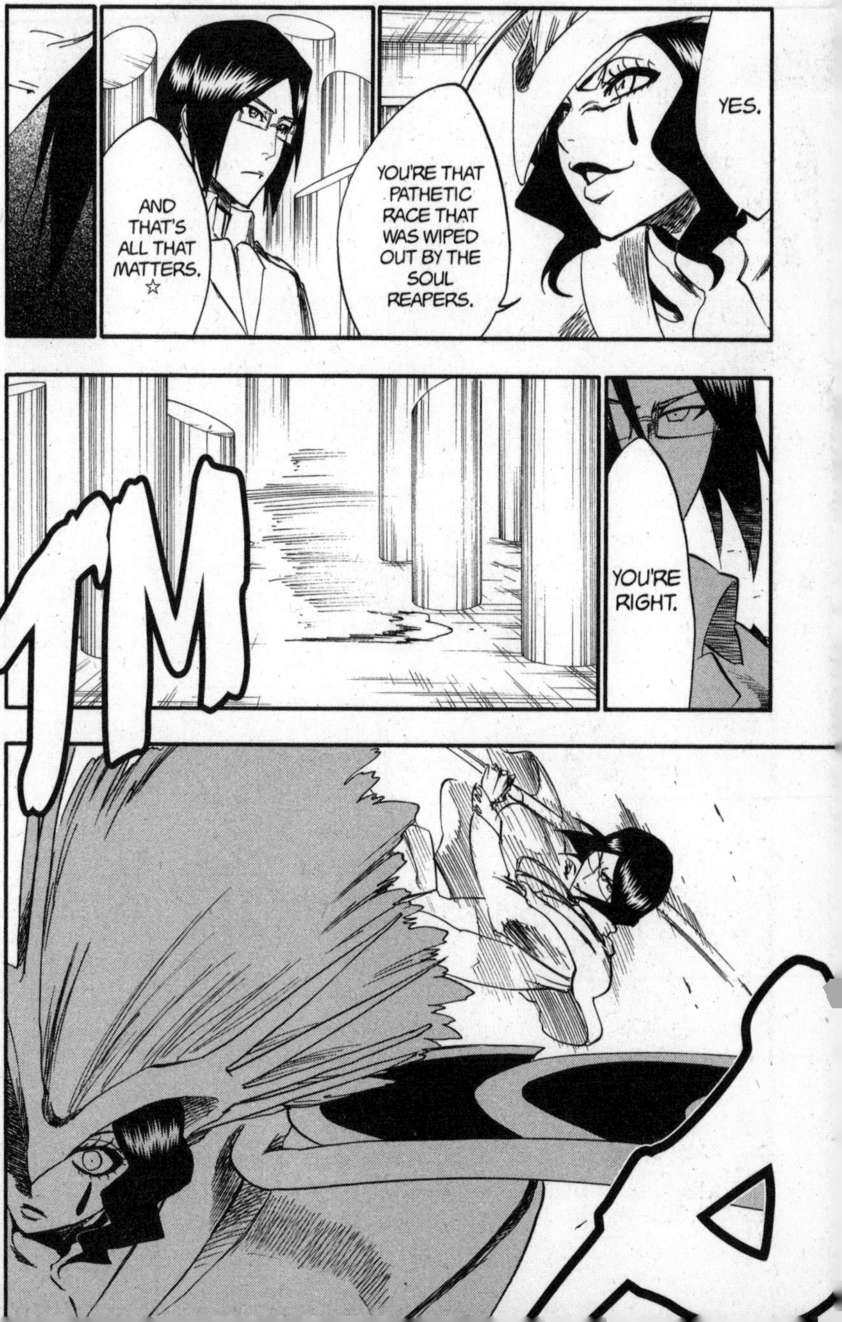
YES.
YOU'RE THAT PATHETIC RACE THAT WAS WIPED OUT BY THE SOUL REAPERS.
AND THAT'S ALL THAT MATTERS. ☆
YOU'RE RIGHT.
TM

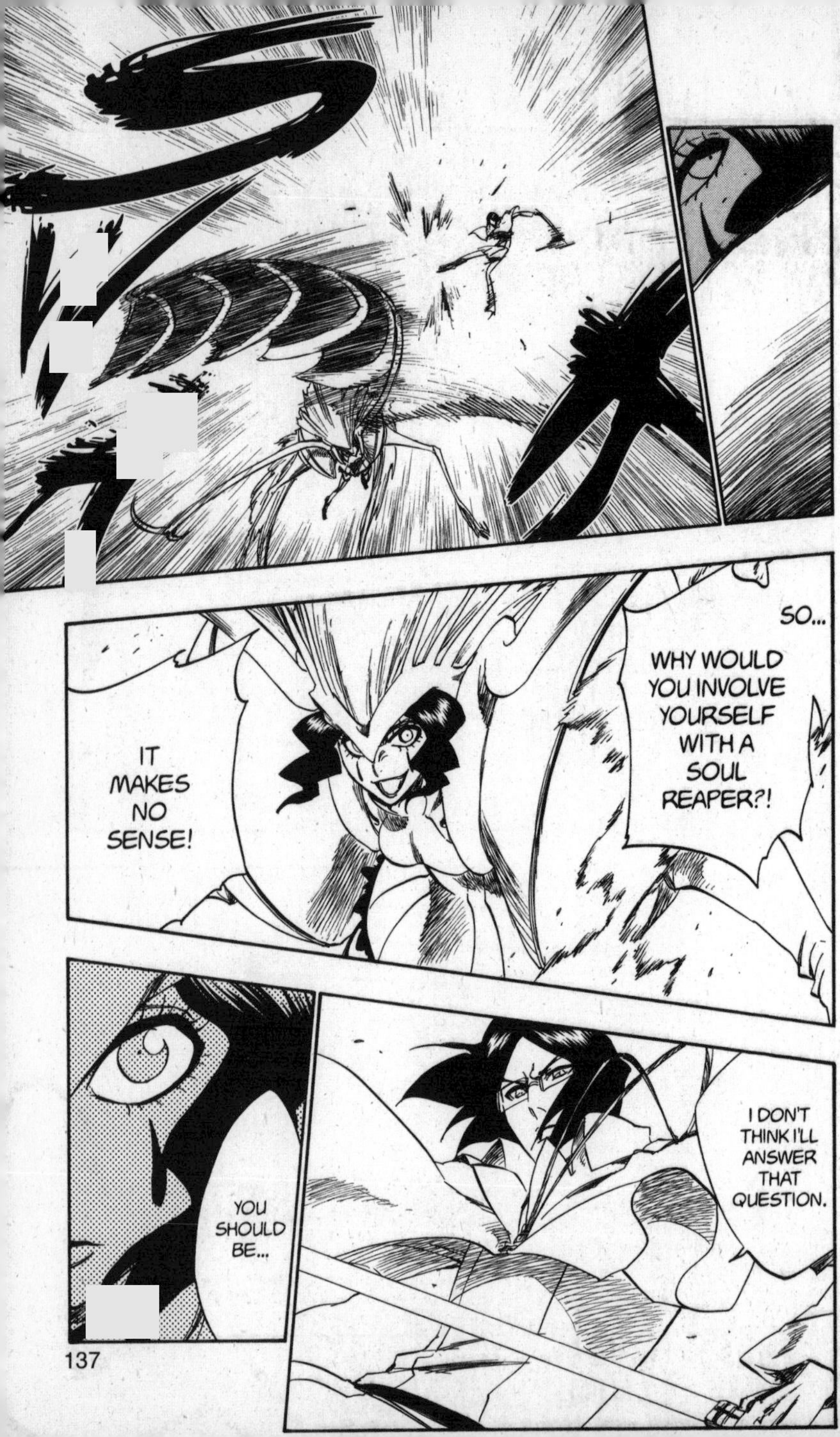
SO...
WHY WOULD YOU INVOLVE YOURSELF WITH A SOUL REAPER?!
IT MAKES NO SENSE!
I DON'T THINK I'LL ANSWER THAT QUESTION.
YOU SHOULD BE...

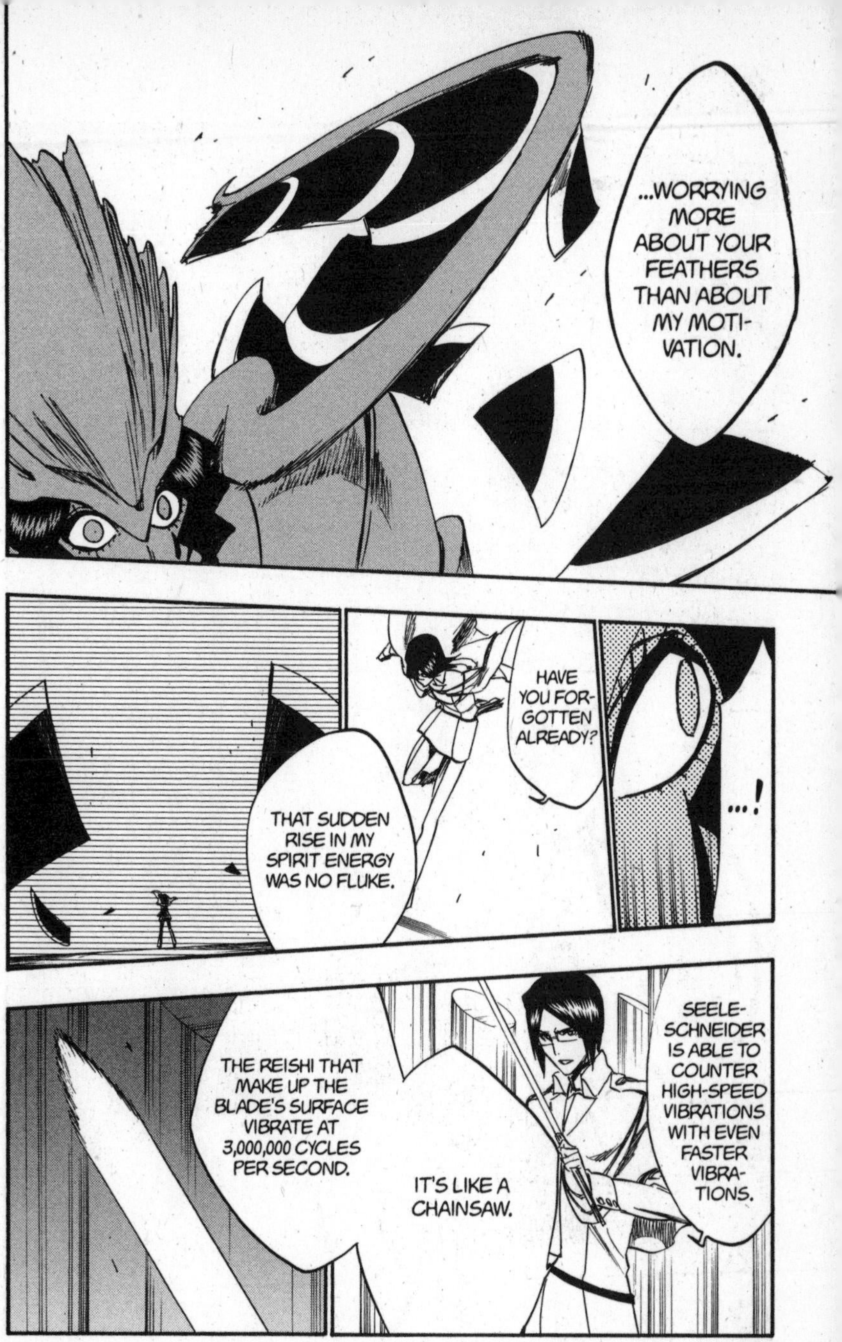
...WORRYING MORE ABOUT YOUR FEATHERS THAN ABOUT MY MOTI-VATION.
...!
HAVE YOU FOR-GOTTEN ALREADY?
THAT SUDDEN RISE IN MY SPIRIT ENERGY WAS NO FLUKE.
SEELE-SCHNEIDER IS ABLE TO COUNTER HIGH-SPEED VIBRATIONS WITH EVEN FASTER VIBRA-TIONS.
THE REISHI THAT MAKE UP THE BLADE'S SURFACE VIBRATE AT 3,000,000 CYCLES PER SECOND.
IT'S LIKE A CHAINSAW.

READ THIS WAY

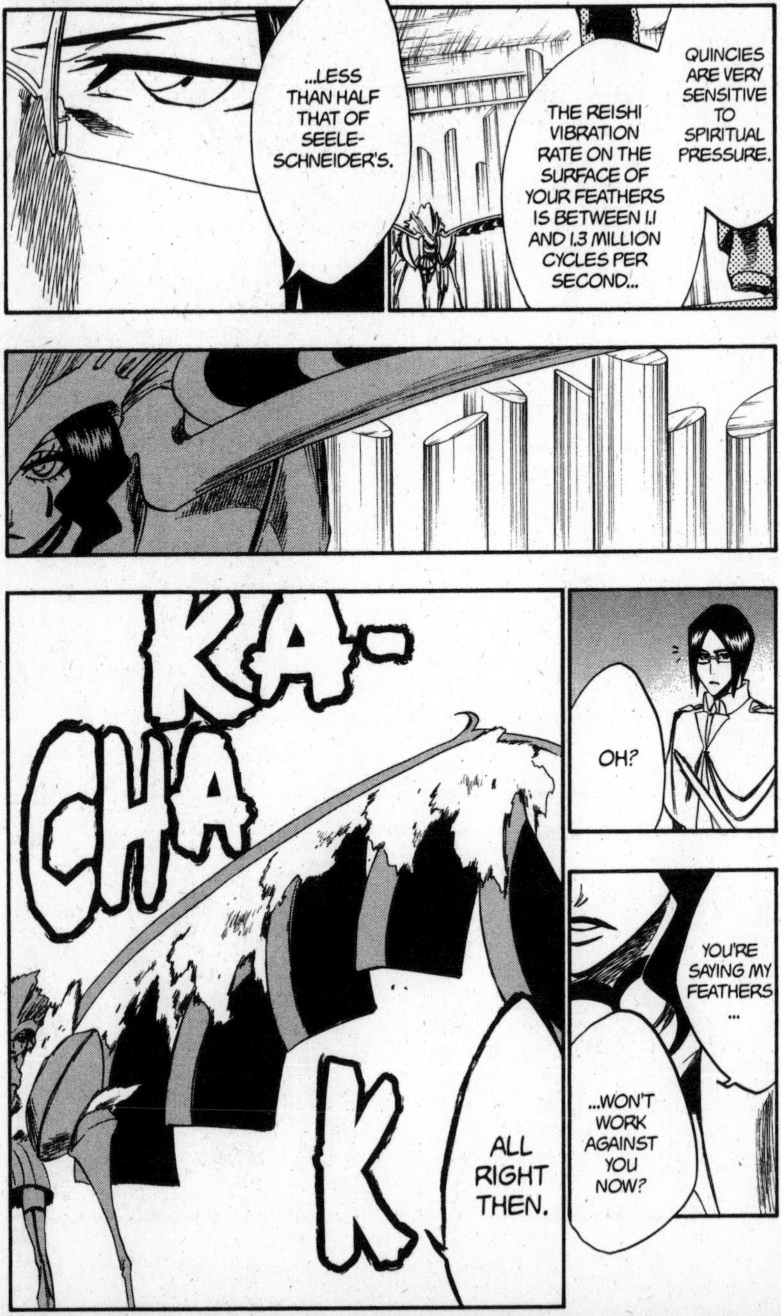
QUINCIES ARE VERY SENSITIVE TO SPIRITUAL PRESSURE.
THE REISHI VIBRATION RATE ON THE SURFACE OF YOUR FEATHERS IS BETWEEN 1.1 AND 1.3 MILLION CYCLES PER SECOND...
...LESS THAN HALF THAT OF SEELE-SCHNEIDER'S.
OH?
YOU'RE SAYING MY FEATHERS...
...WON'T WORK AGAINST YOU NOW?
KA-CHAK
ALL RIGHT THEN.

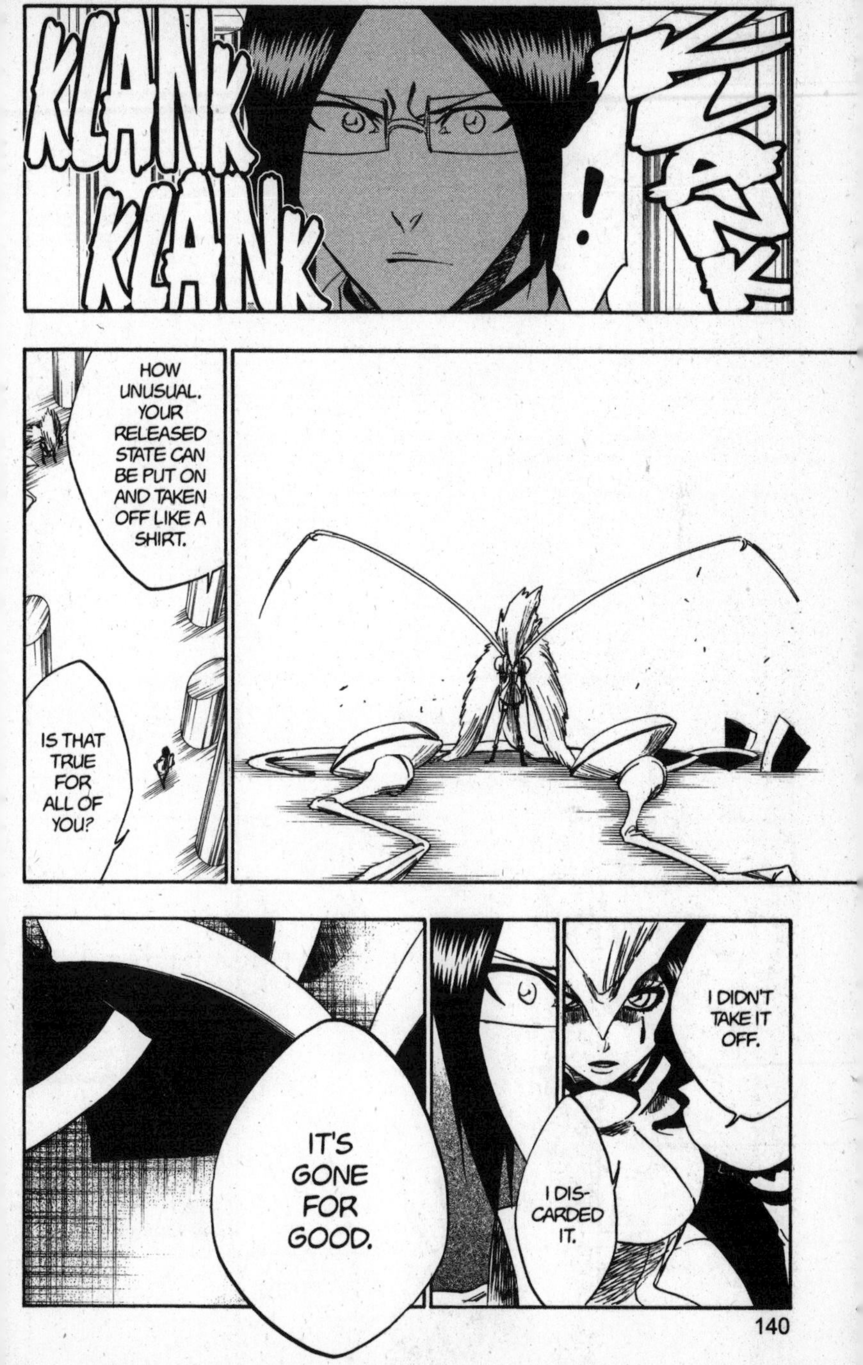
!
KLANK
KLANK
HOW UNUSUAL. YOUR RELEASED STATE CAN BE PUT ON AND TAKEN OFF LIKE A SHIRT.
IS THAT TRUE FOR ALL OF YOU?
I DIDN'T TAKE IT OFF.
I DIS-CARDED IT.
IT'S GONE FOR GOOD.

READ THIS WAY

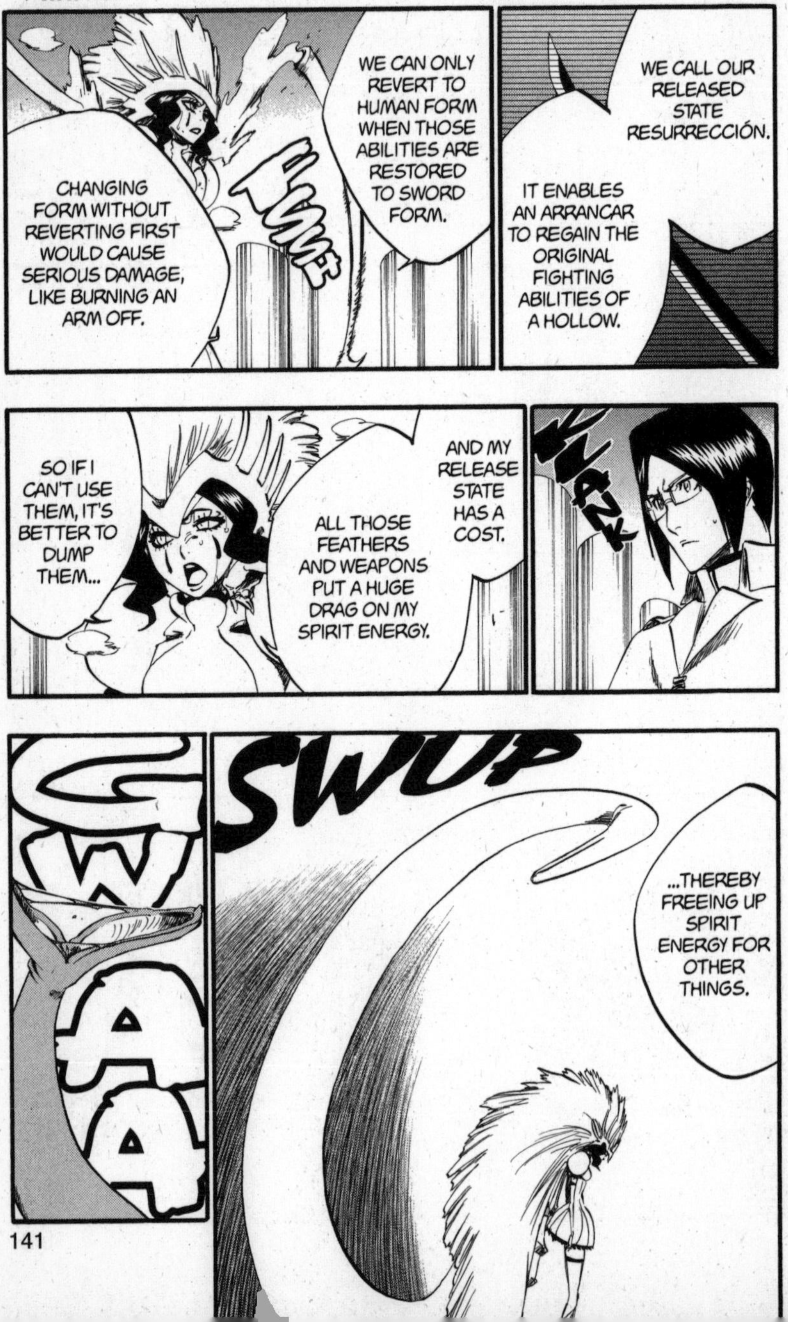
WE CALL OUR RELEASED STATE RESURRECCIÓN.
IT ENABLES AN ARRANCAR TO REGAIN THE ORIGINAL FIGHTING ABILITIES OF A HOLLOW.
WE CAN ONLY REVERT TO HUMAN FORM WHEN THOSE ABILITIES ARE RESTORED TO SWORD FORM.
FLUMP
CHANGING FORM WITHOUT REVERTING FIRST WOULD CAUSE SERIOUS DAMAGE, LIKE BURNING AN ARM OFF.
WHANK
AND MY RELEASE STATE HAS A COST.
ALL THOSE FEATHERS AND WEAPONS PUT A HUGE DRAG ON MY SPIRIT ENERGY.
SO IF I CAN'T USE THEM, IT'S BETTER TO DUMP THEM...
SWUP
...THEREBY FREEING UP SPIRIT ENERGY FOR OTHER THINGS.
GWAA

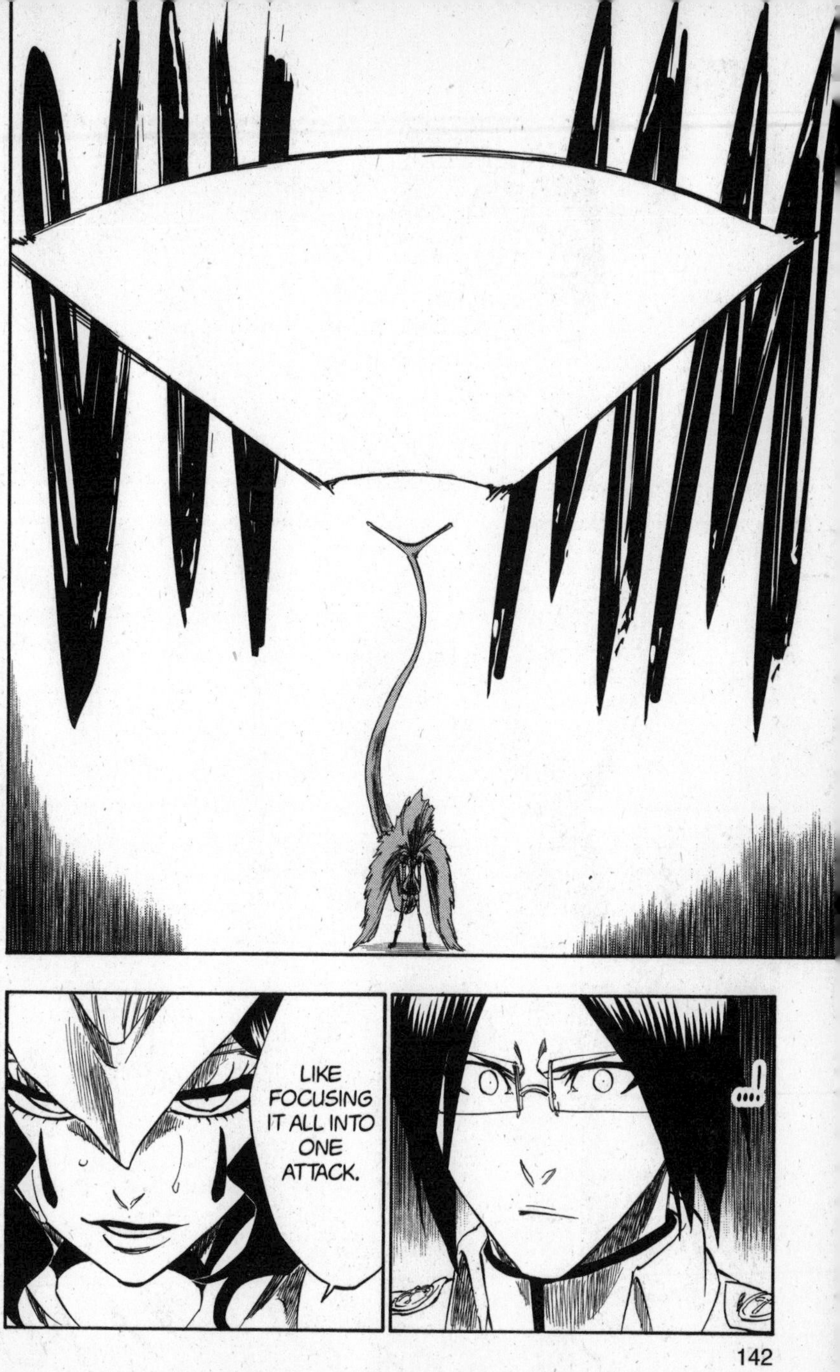
...!
LIKE FOCUSING IT ALL INTO ONE ATTACK.

READ THIS WAY

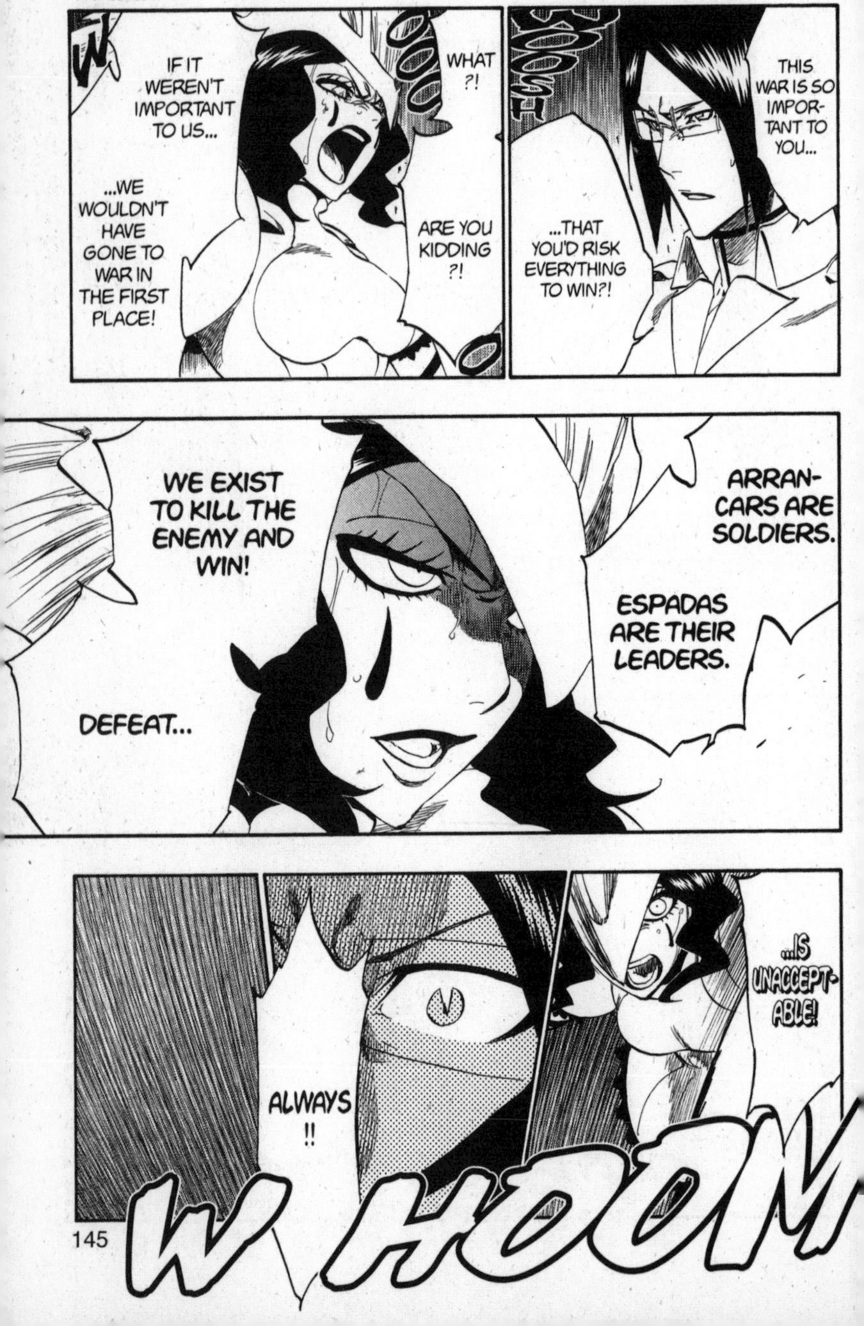

WHOOSH
THIS WAR IS SO IMPORTANT TO YOU...
...THAT YOU'D RISK EVERYTHING TO WIN?!
WHAT?!
ARE YOU KIDDING?!
IF IT WEREN'T IMPORTANT TO US...
...WE WOULDN'T HAVE GONE TO WAR IN THE FIRST PLACE!
ARRANCARS ARE SOLDIERS.
ESPADAS ARE THEIR LEADERS.
WE EXIST TO KILL THE ENEMY AND WIN!
DEFEAT...
...IS UNACCEPTABLE!
ALWAYS!!
WHOOM

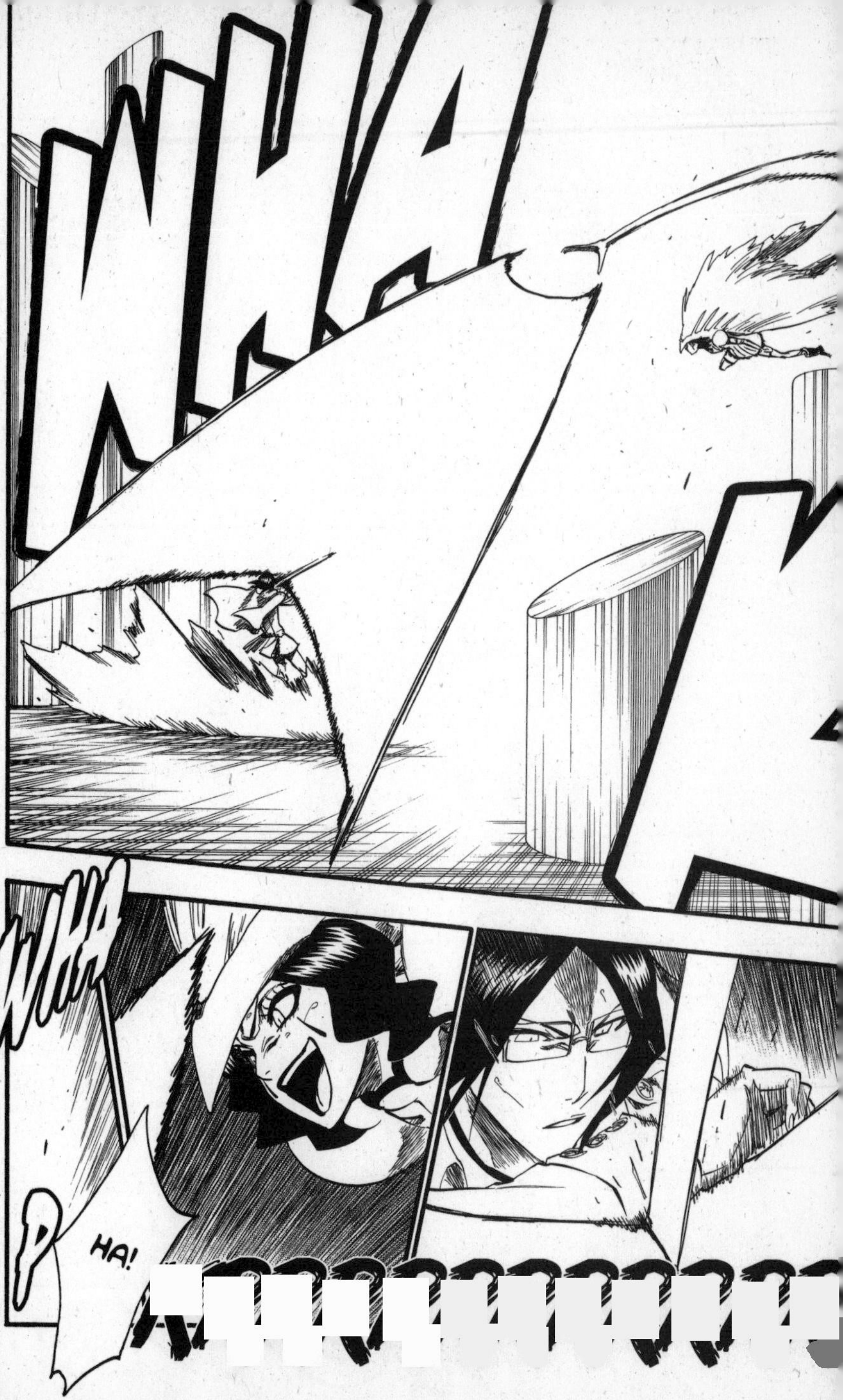
HA!

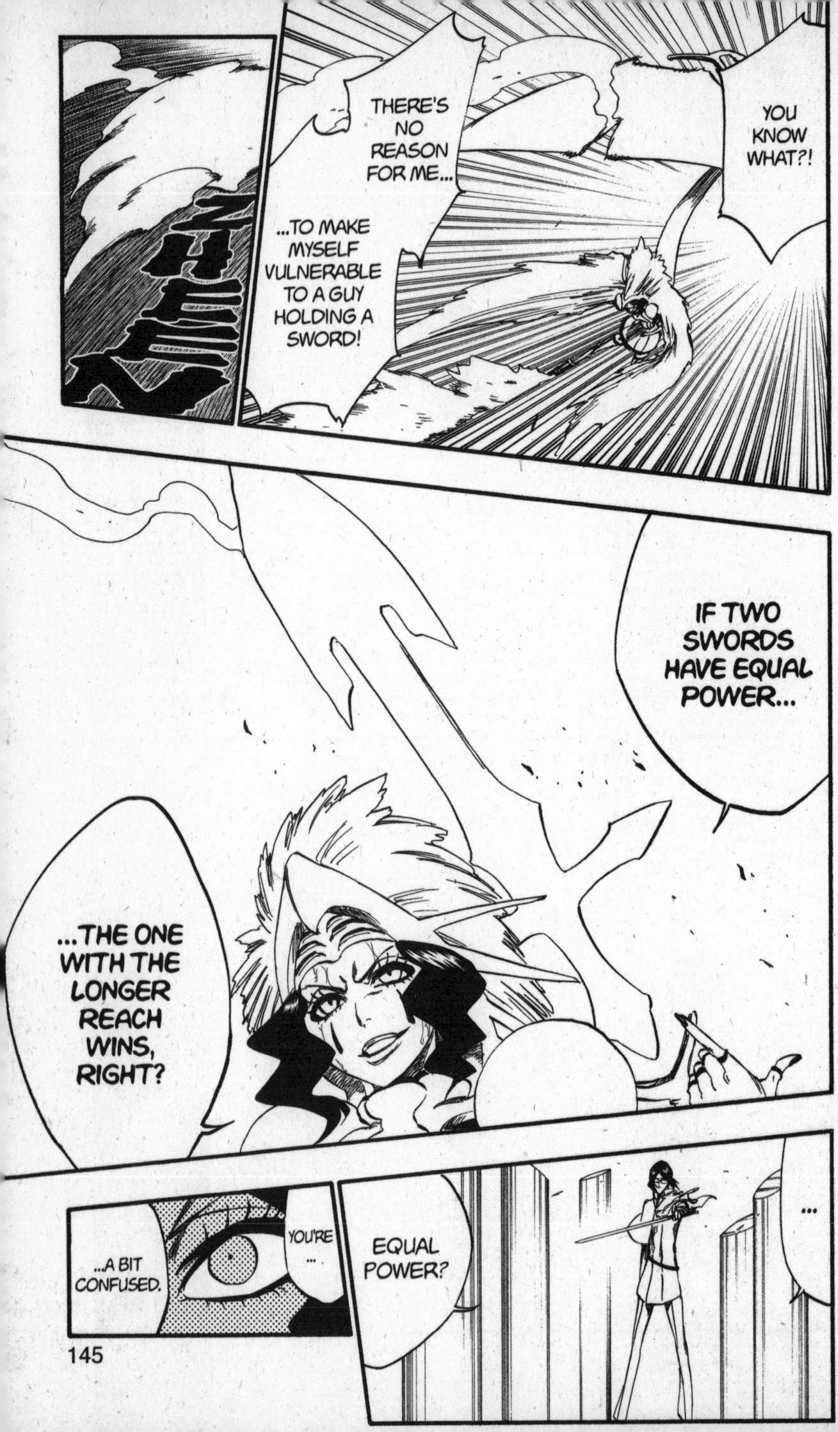

YOU KNOW WHAT?!
THERE'S NO REASON FOR ME...
...TO MAKE MYSELF VULNERABLE TO A GUY HOLDING A SWORD!
IF TWO SWORDS HAVE EQUAL POWER...
...THE ONE WITH THE LONGER REACH WINS, RIGHT?
...
EQUAL POWER?
YOU'RE ...
...A BIT CONFUSED.

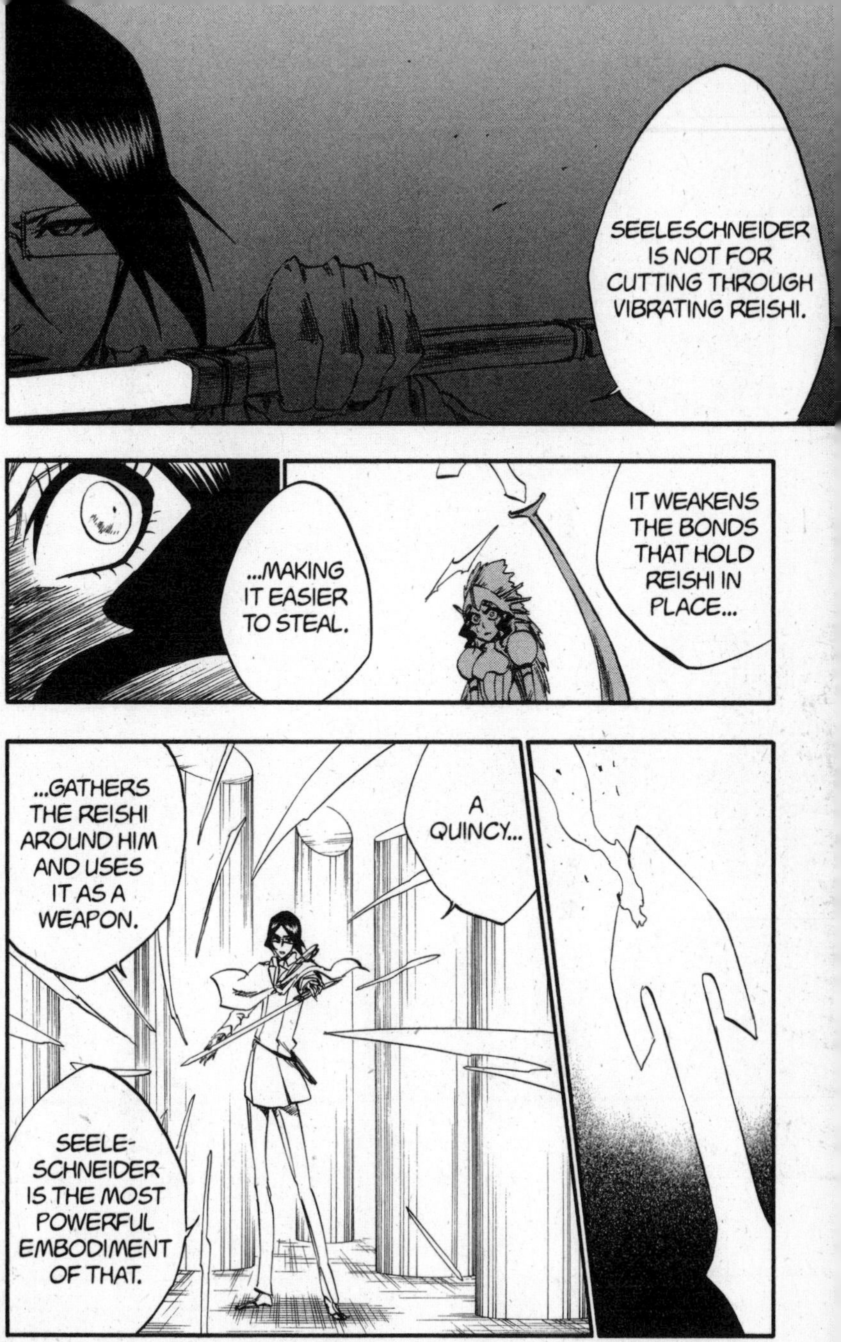
SEELESCHNEIDER IS NOT FOR CUTTING THROUGH VIBRATING REISHI.
IT WEAKENS THE BONDS THAT HOLD REISHI IN PLACE...
...MAKING IT EASIER TO STEAL.
A QUINCY...
...GATHERS THE REISHI AROUND HIM AND USES IT AS A WEAPON.
SEELE-SCHNEIDER IS THE MOST POWERFUL EMBODIMENT OF THAT.

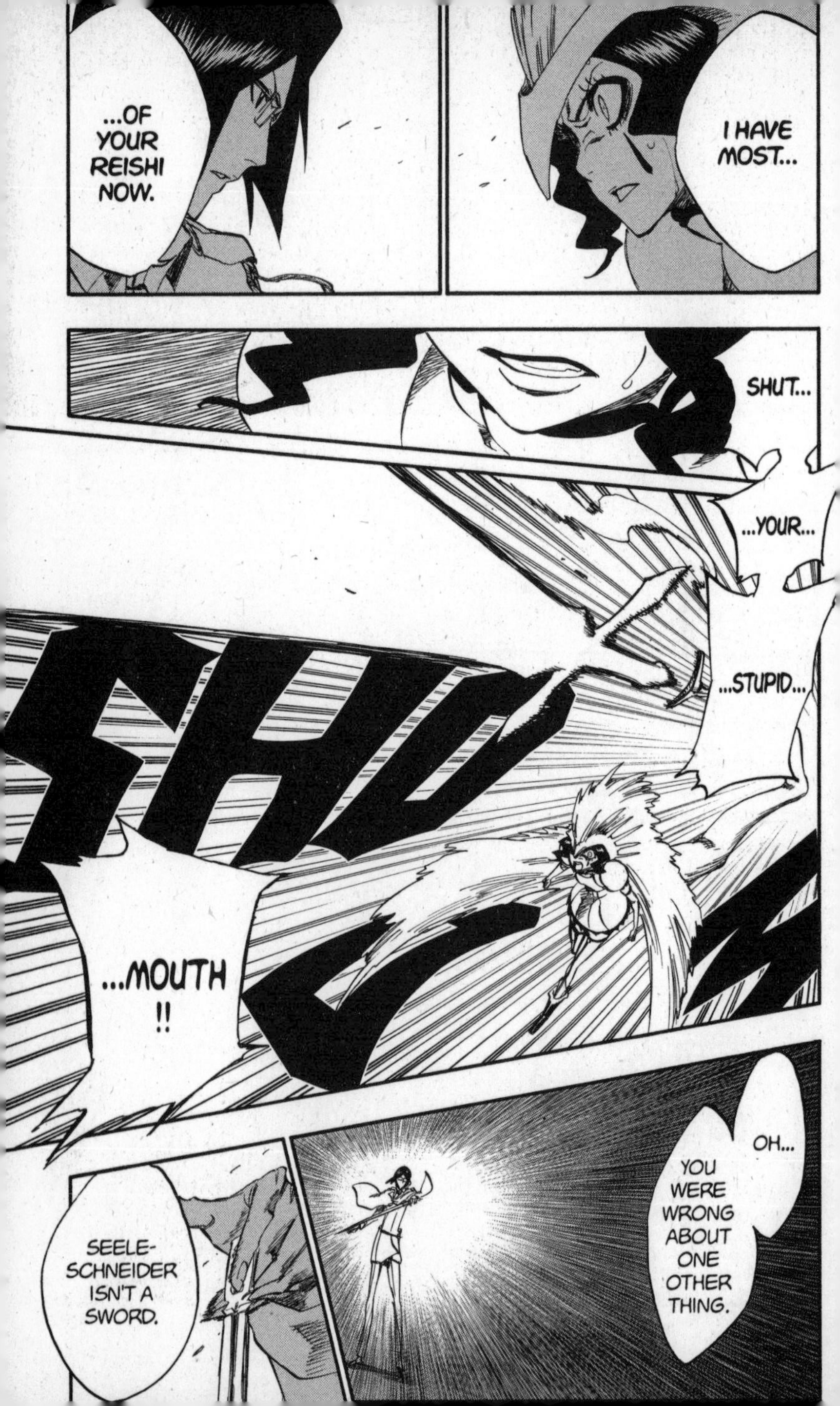
I HAVE MOST...
...OF YOUR REISHI NOW.
SHUT...
...YOUR...
...STUPID...
...MOUTH !!
OH...
YOU WERE WRONG ABOUT ONE OTHER THING.
SEELE-SCHNEIDER ISN'T A SWORD.

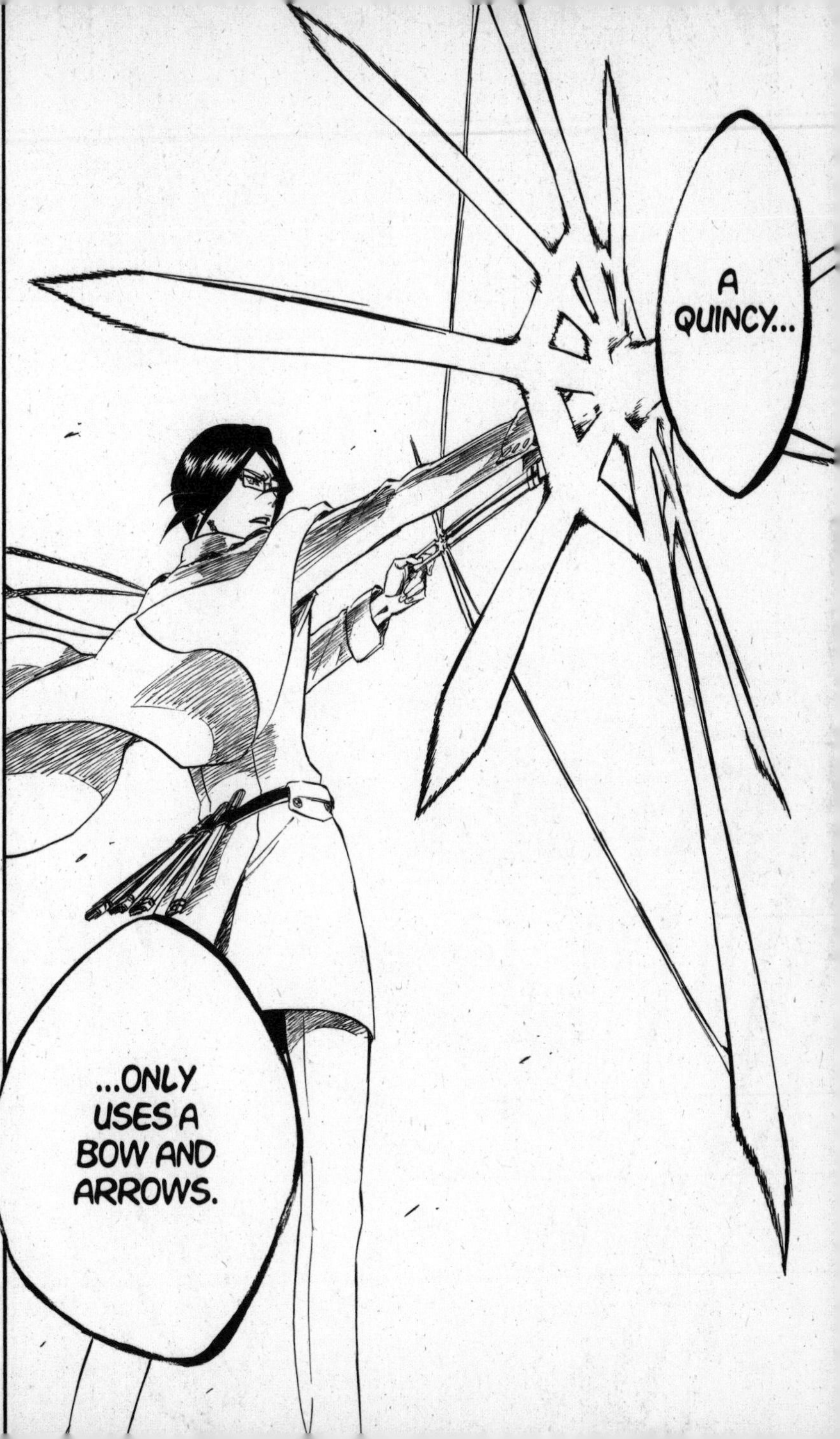
A QUINCY...
...ONLY USES A BOW AND ARROWS.

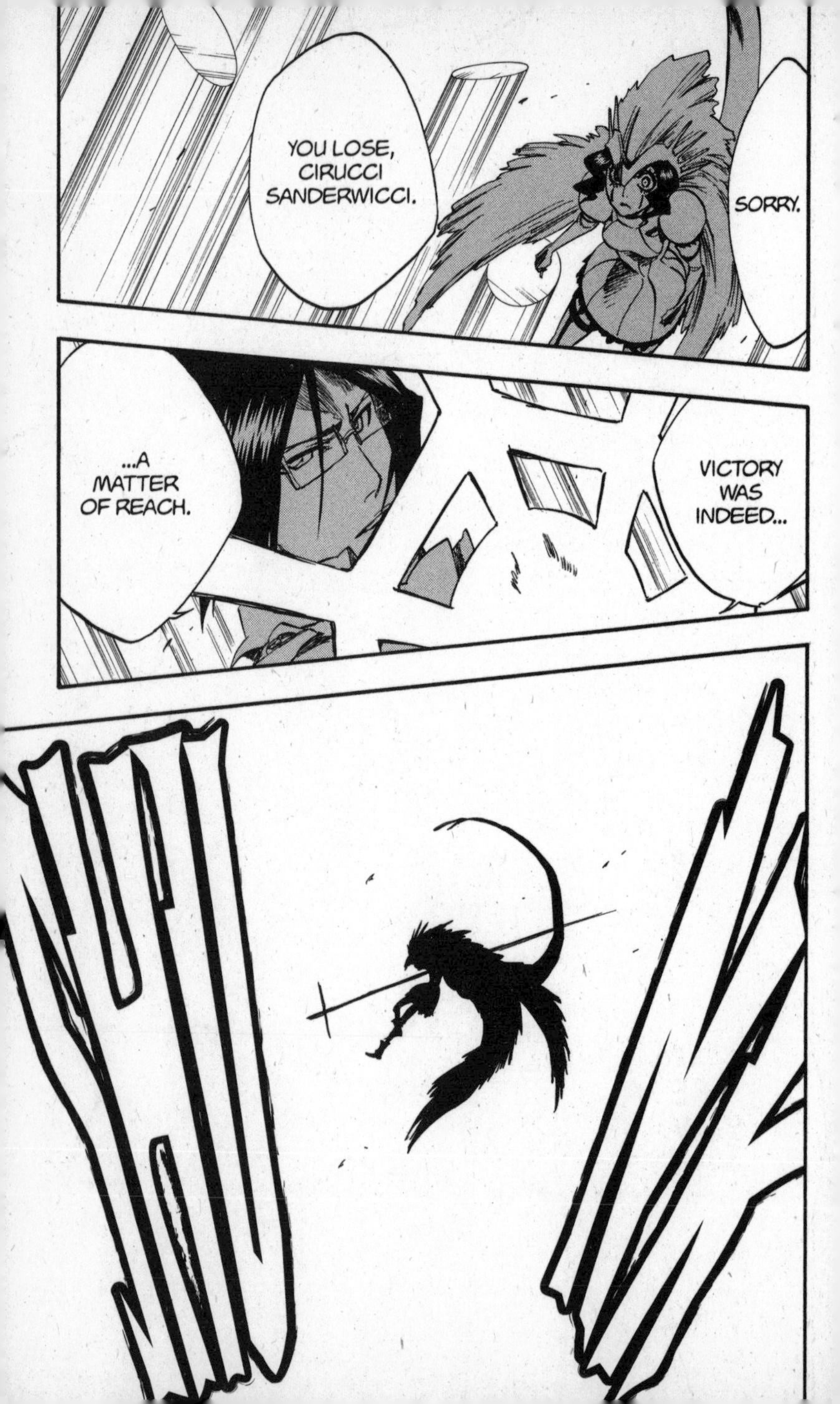
SORRY.
YOU LOSE, CIRUCCI SANDERWICCI.
VICTORY WAS INDEED...
...A MATTER OF REACH.

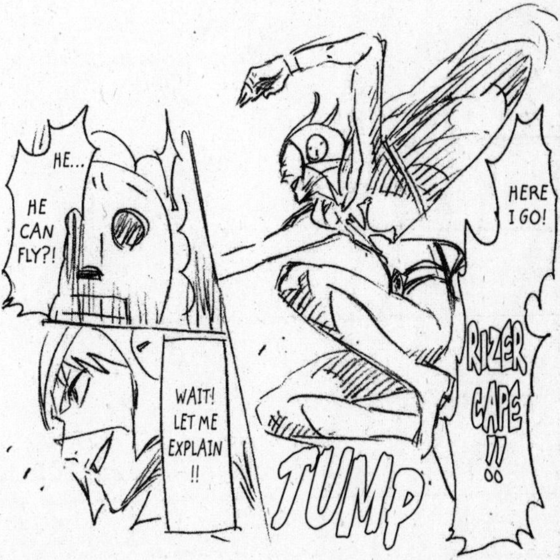
HERE I GO!
RIZER CAPE!!
JUMP
HE...
HE CAN FLY?!
WAIT! LET ME EXPLAIN!!

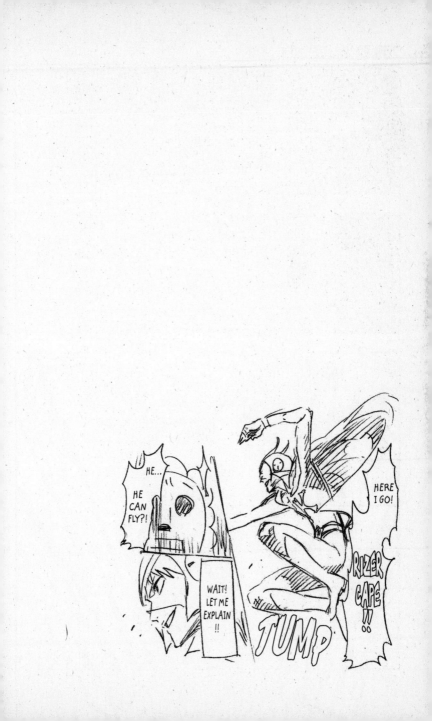

259. Flicker Flames

FWOO
F
WHUP
KLANK

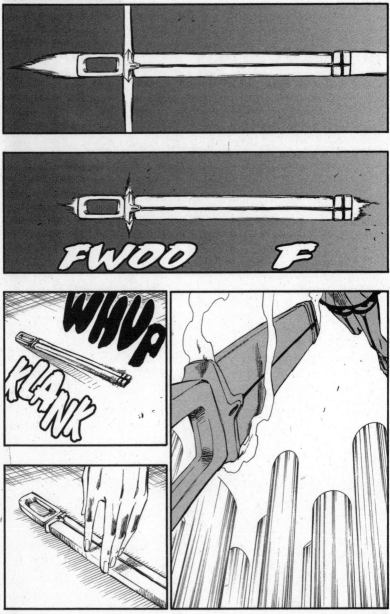

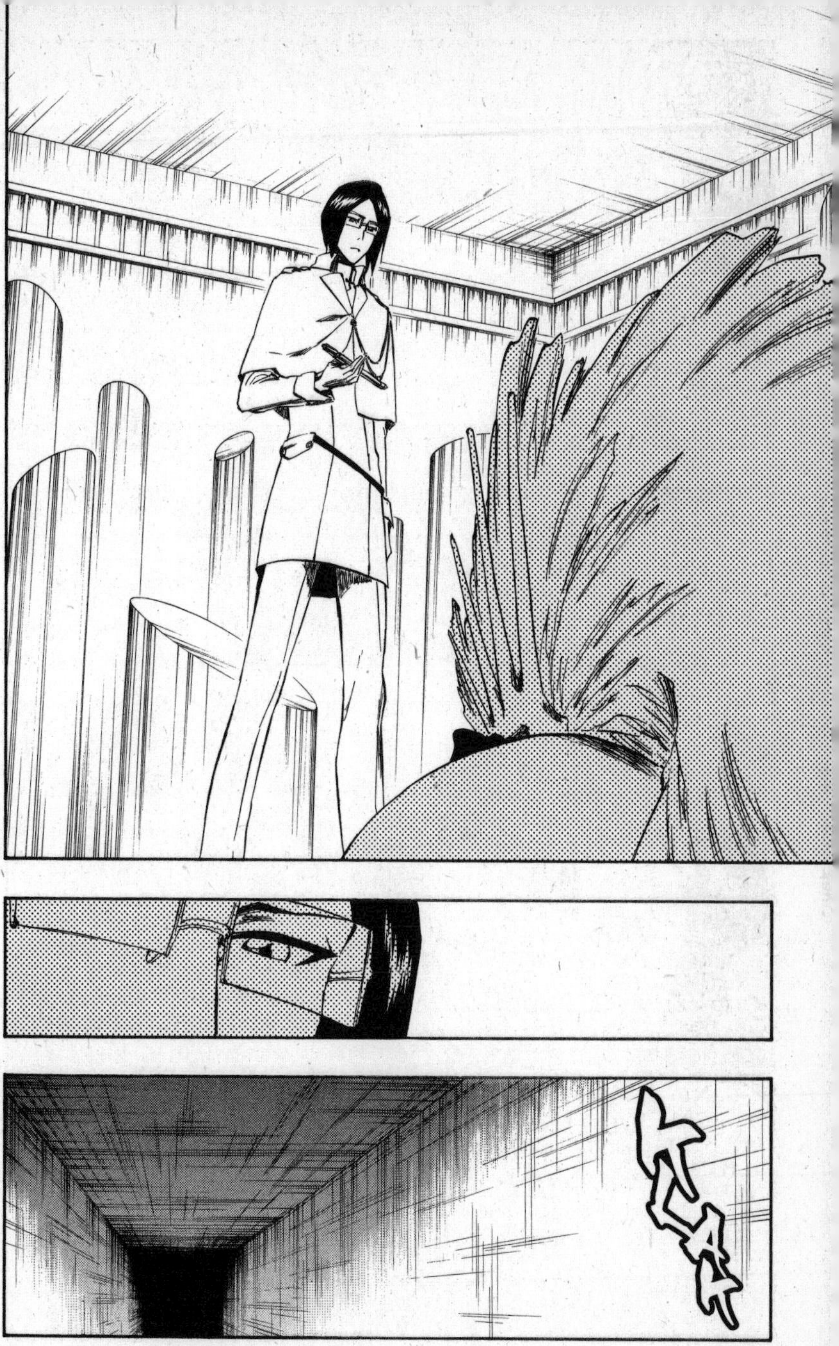
KLAK

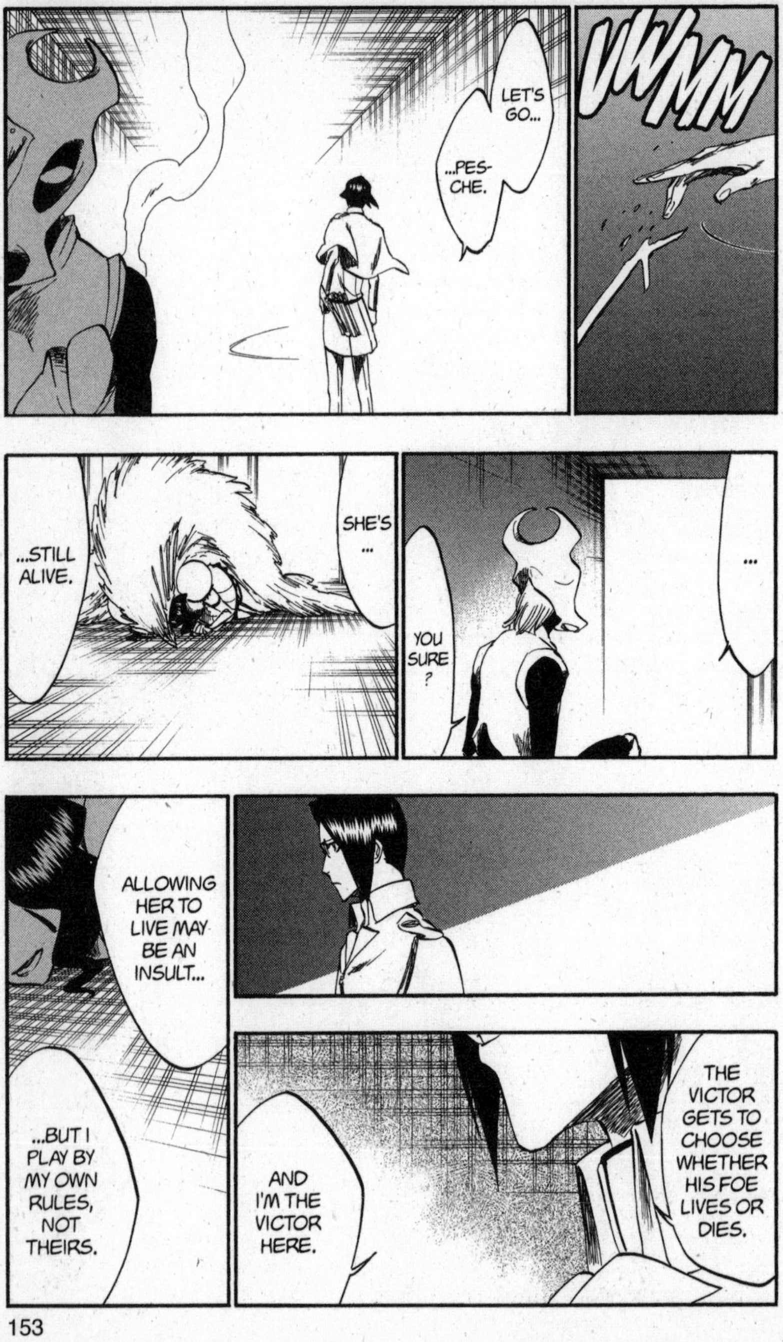
VWMM
LET'S GO...
...PES-CHE.
...
YOU SURE?
SHE'S ...
...STILL ALIVE.
THE VICTOR GETS TO CHOOSE WHETHER HIS FOE LIVES OR DIES.
AND I'M THE VICTOR HERE.
ALLOWING HER TO LIVE MAY BE AN INSULT...
...BUT I PLAY BY MY OWN RULES, NOT THEIRS.

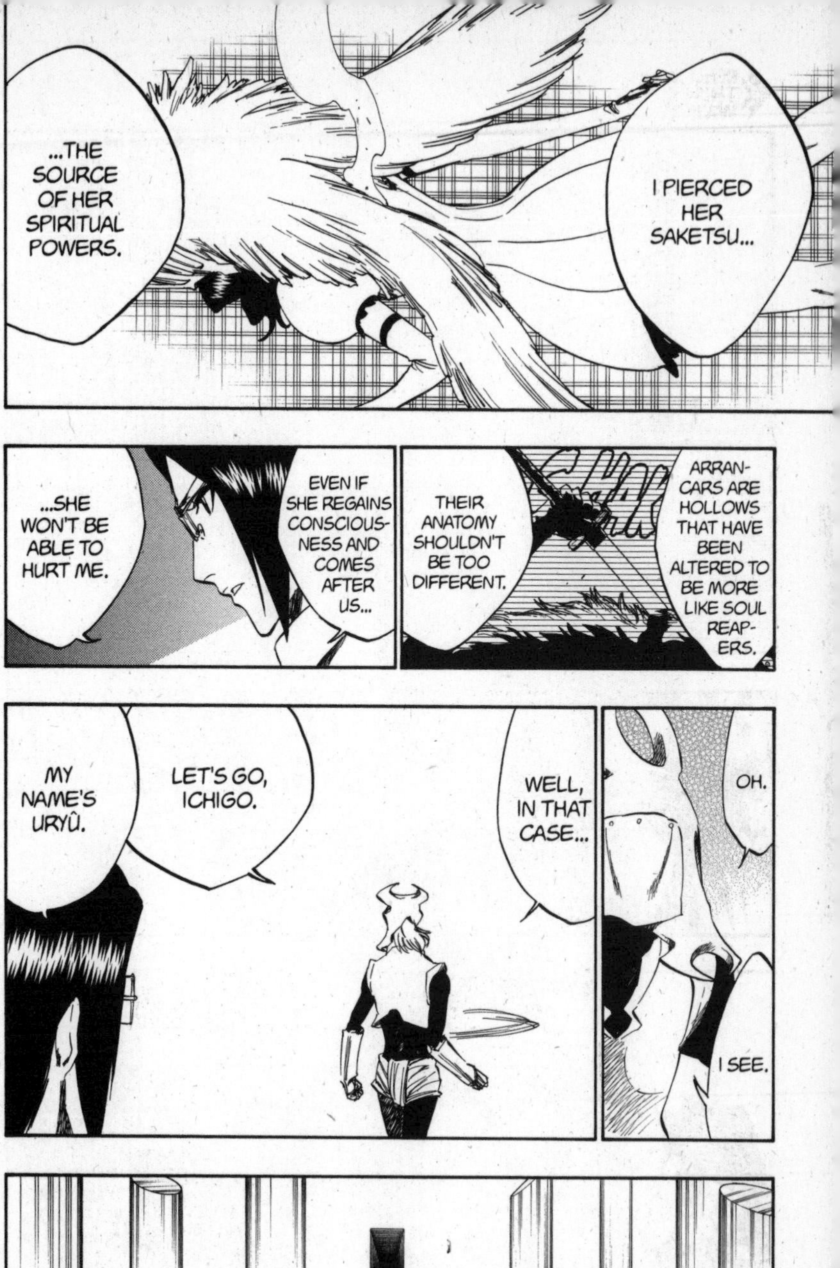
I PIERCED HER SAKETSU...
...THE SOURCE OF HER SPIRITUAL POWERS.
ARRANCARS ARE HOLLOWS THAT HAVE BEEN ALTERED TO BE MORE LIKE SOUL REAPERS.
THEIR ANATOMY SHOULDN'T BE TOO DIFFERENT.
EVEN IF SHE REGAINS CONSCIOUSNESS AND COMES AFTER US...
...SHE WON'T BE ABLE TO HURT ME.
OH.
I SEE.
WELL, IN THAT CASE...
LET'S GO, ICHIGO.
MY NAME'S URYÛ.

READ THIS WAY

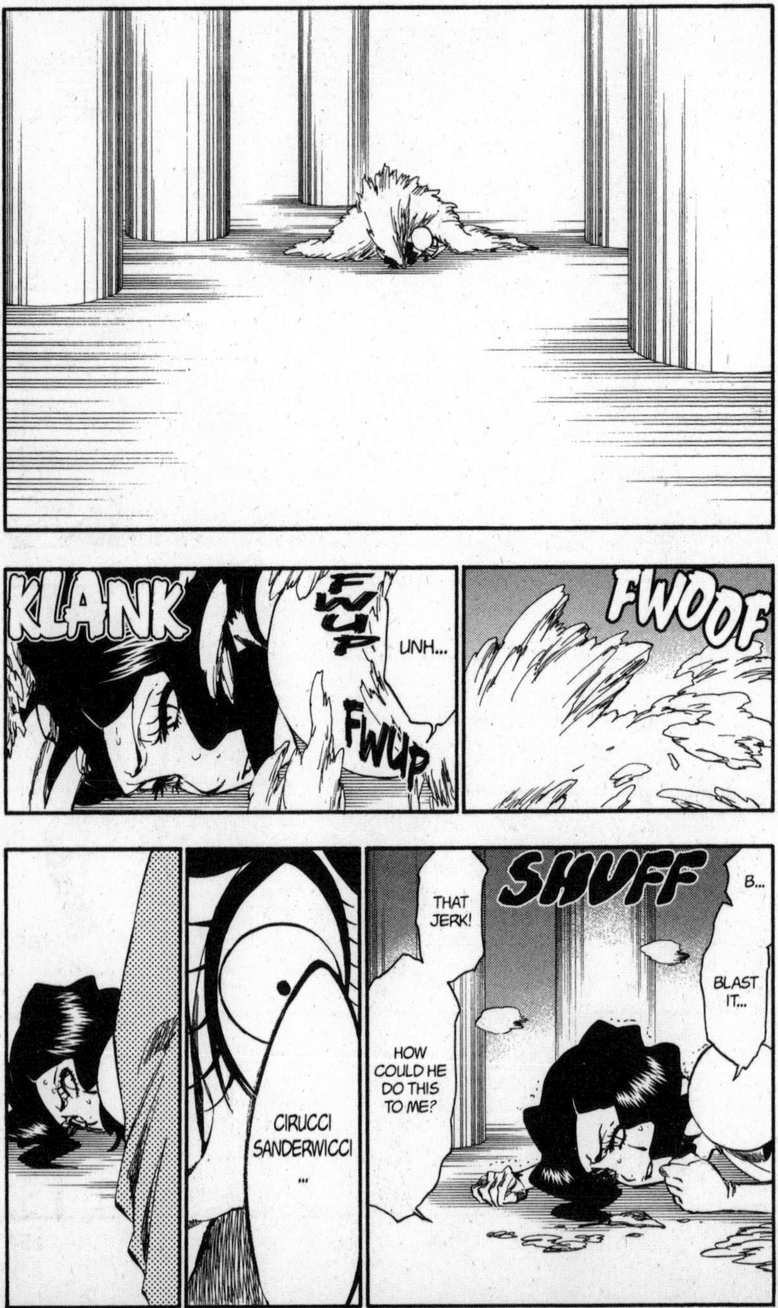
FWOOF
FWUP
KLANK
UNH...
FWUP
B...
SHUFF
THAT JERK!
BLAST IT...
HOW COULD HE DO THIS TO ME?
CIRUCCI SANDERWICCI ...

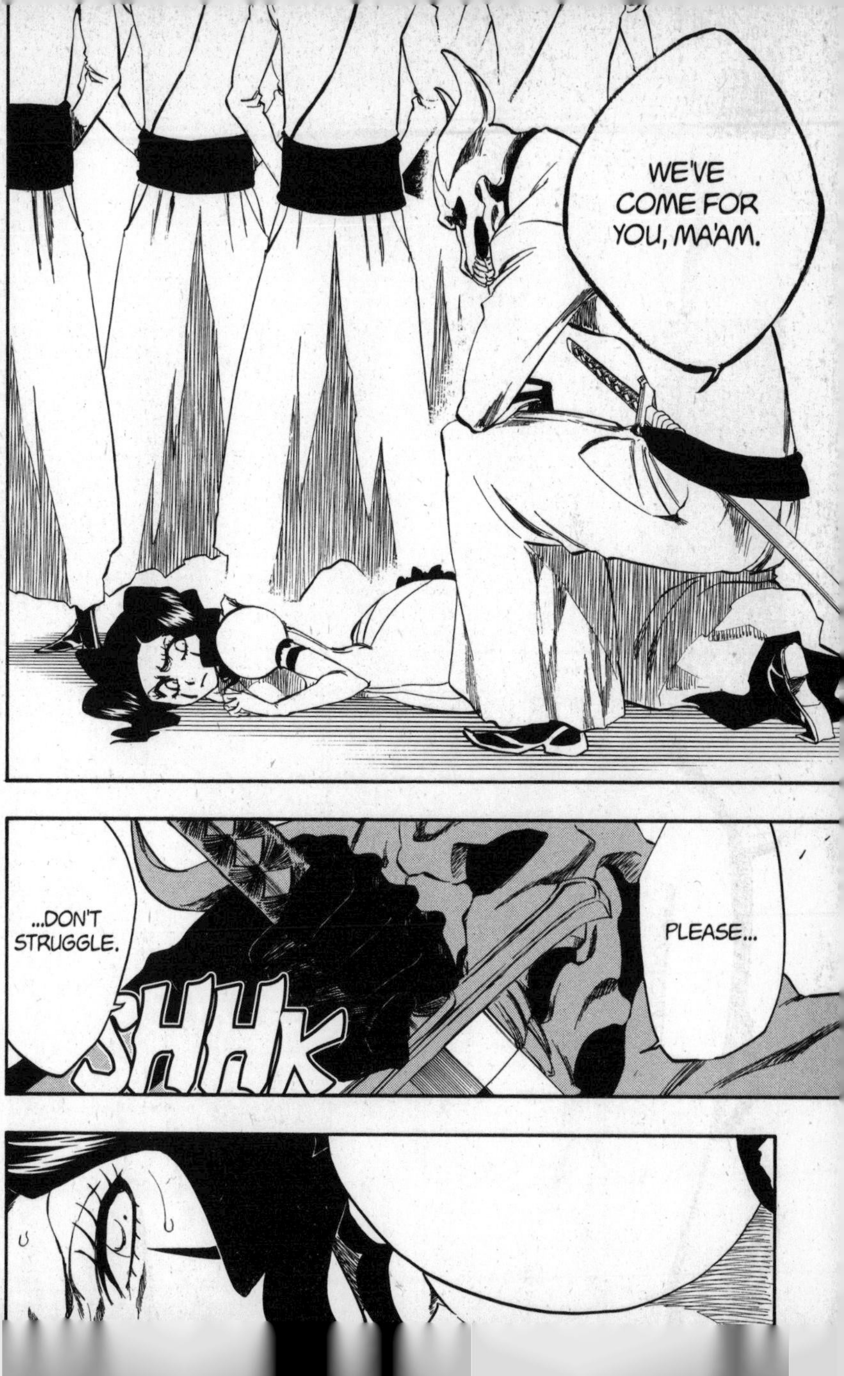
WE'VE COME FOR YOU, MA'AM.
PLEASE...
...DON'T STRUGGLE.
SHHK

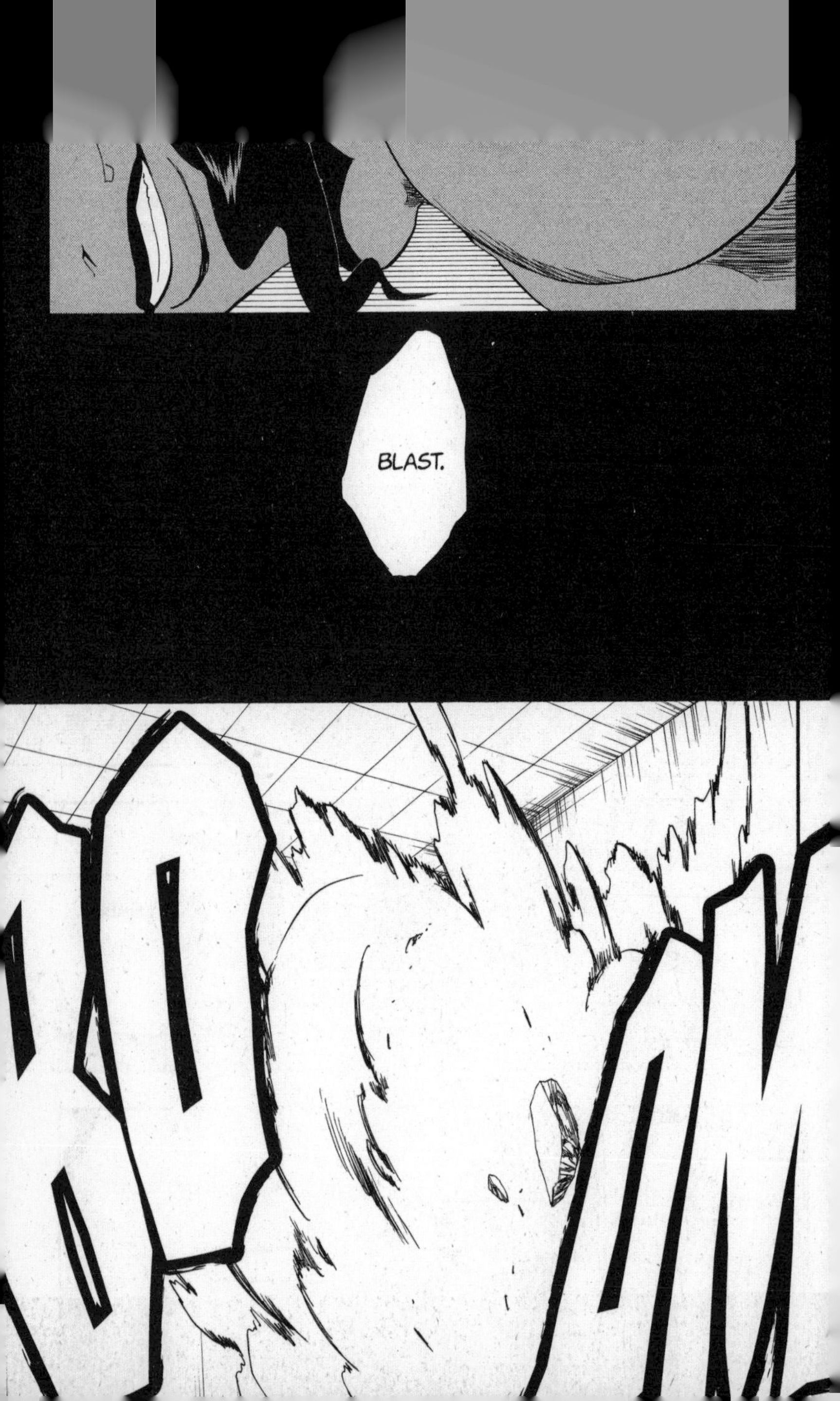
BLAST.

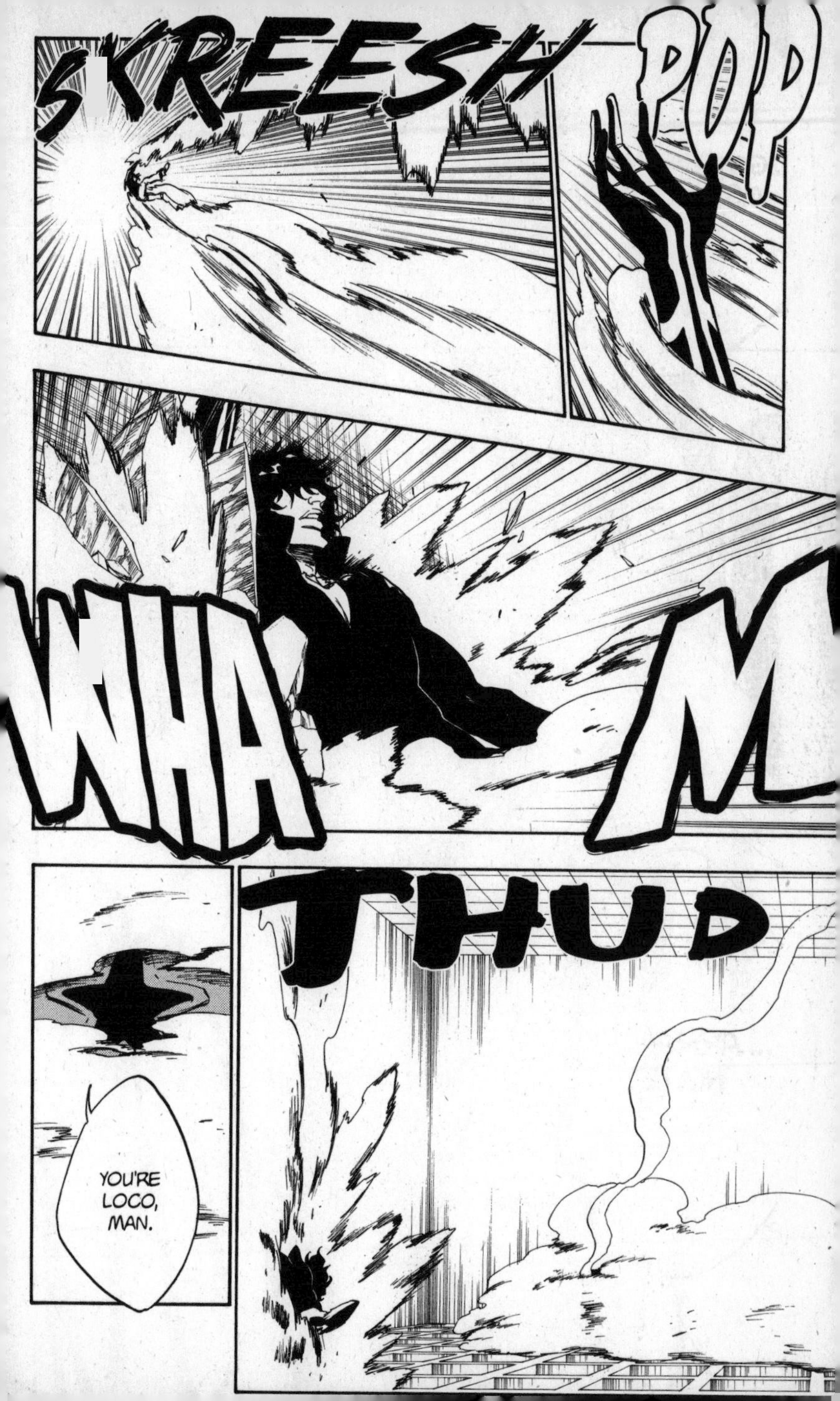
POP
SKREESH
WHAM
THUD
YOU'RE LOCO, MAN.

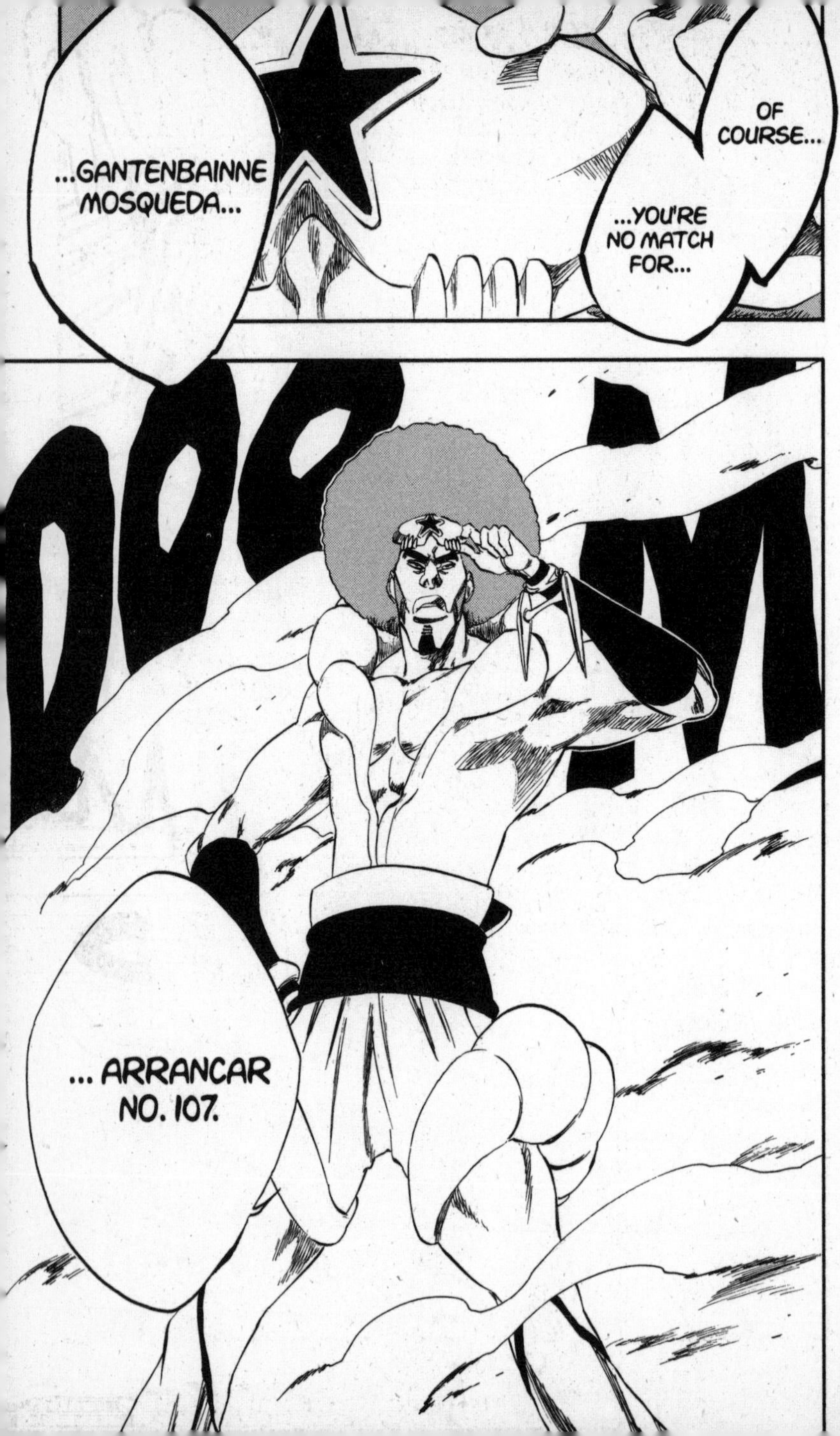
OF COURSE...
...YOU'RE NO MATCH FOR...
...GANTENBAINNE MOSQUEDA...
DOOM
... ARRANCAR NO. 107.

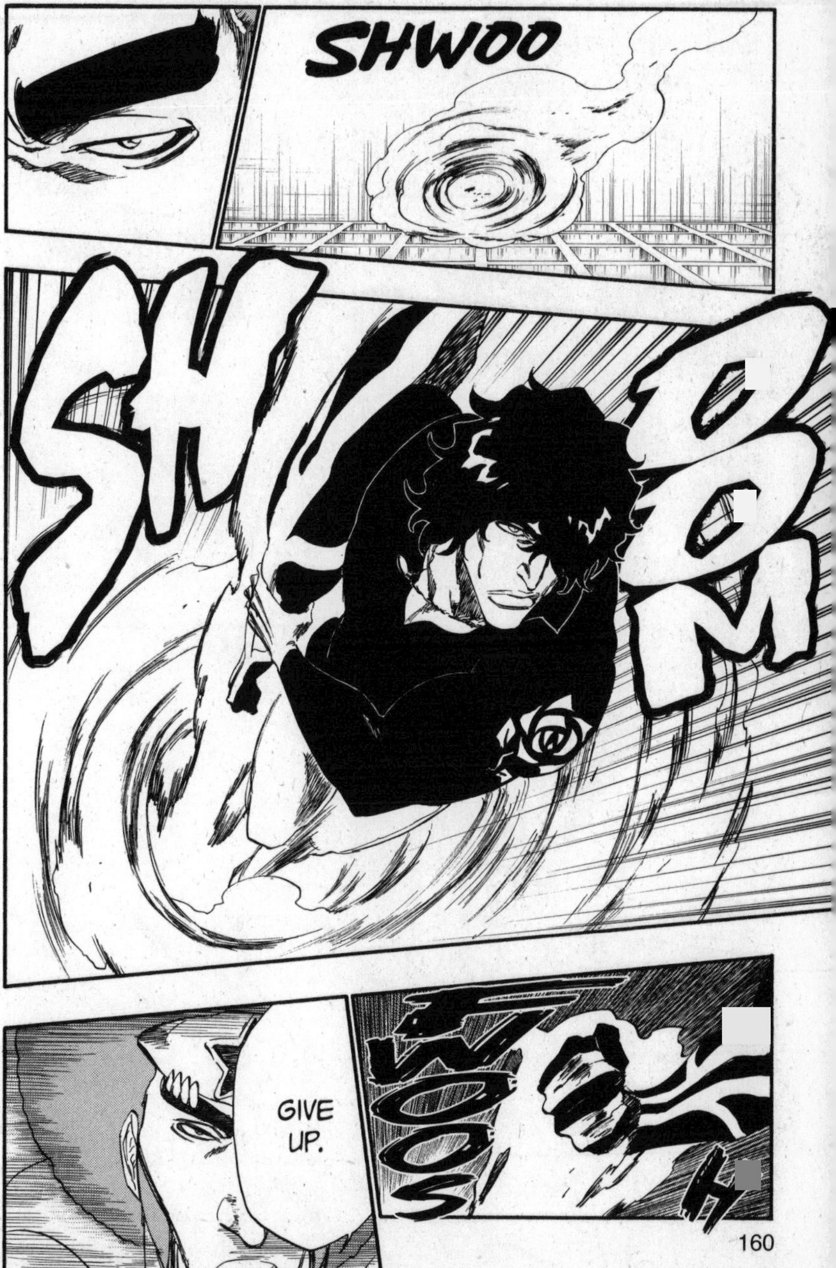
SHWOO
SHOOM
WOOSH
GIVE UP.

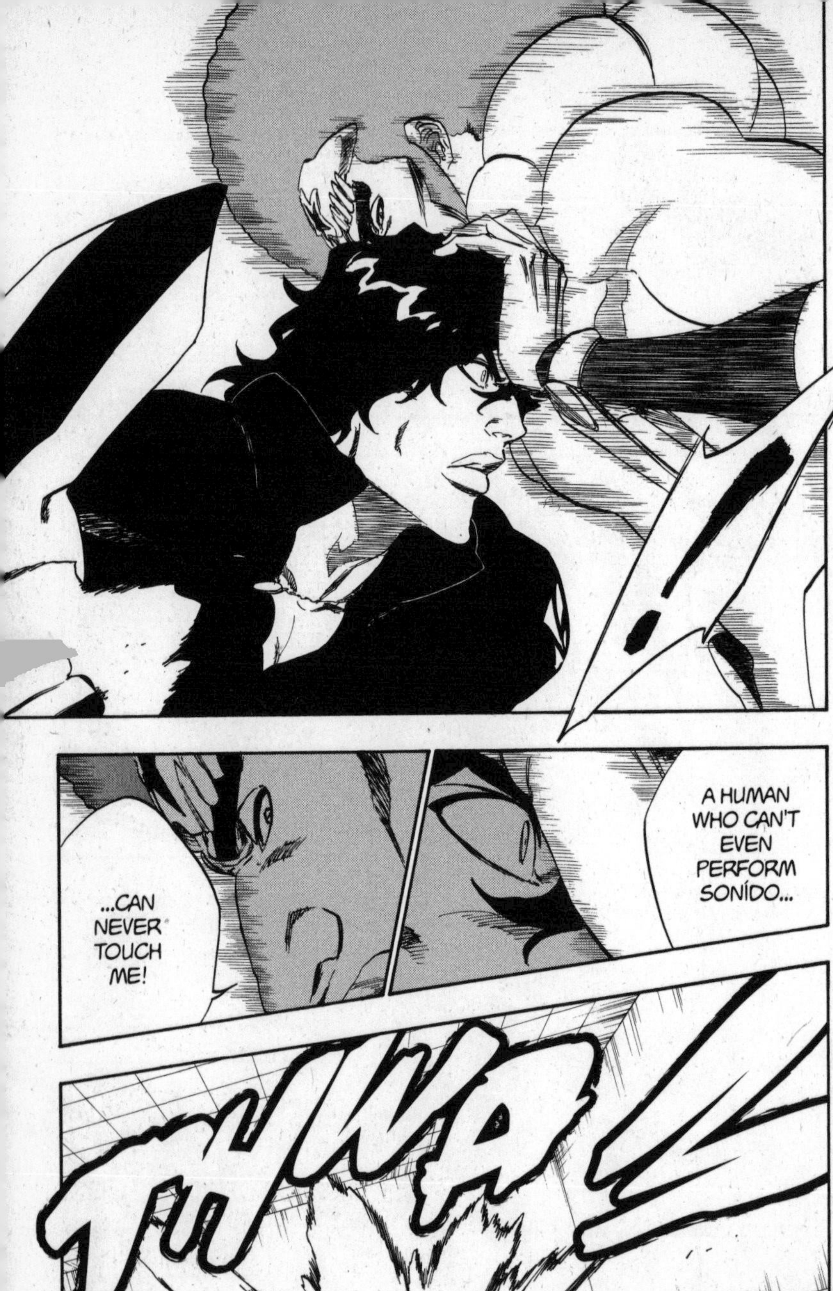
A HUMAN WHO CAN'T EVEN PERFORM SONÍDO...
...CAN NEVER TOUCH ME!

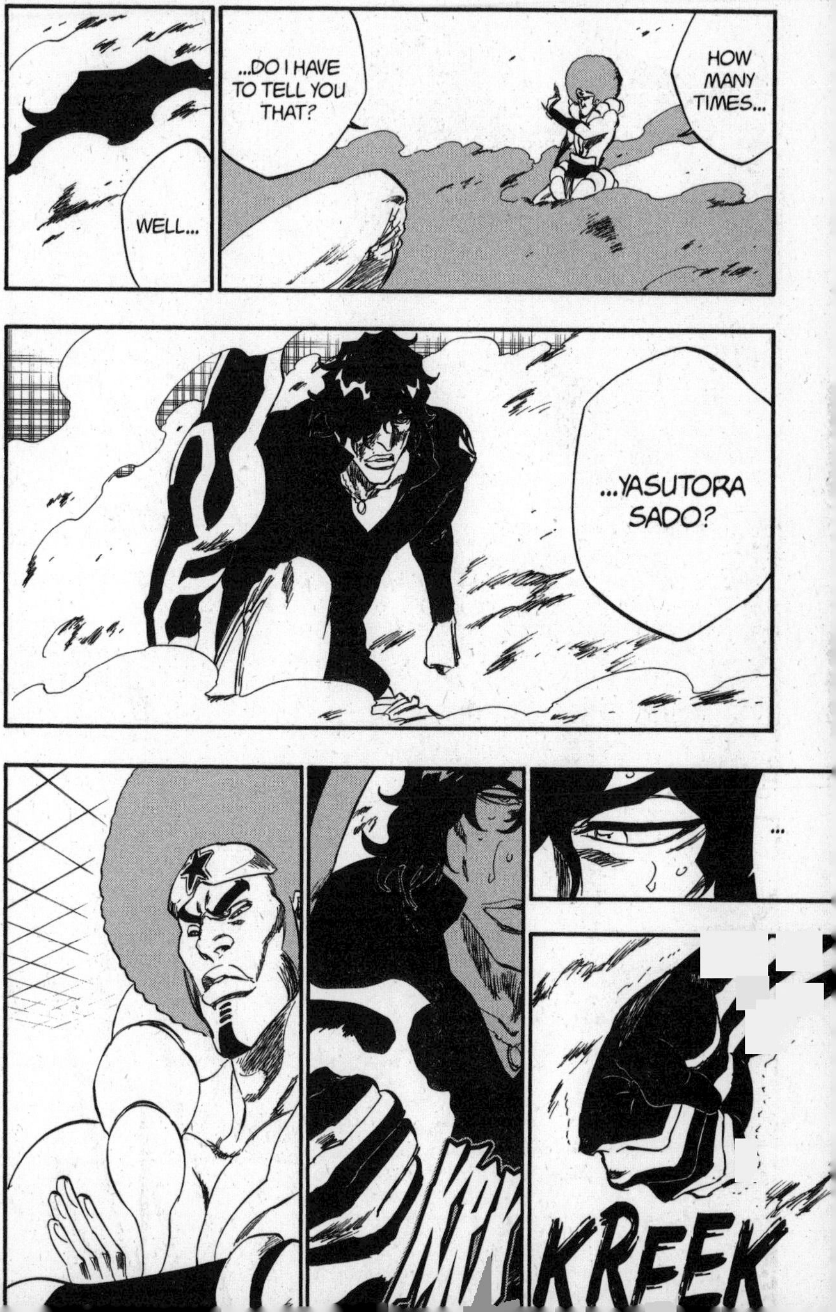
HOW MANY TIMES...
...DO I HAVE TO TELL YOU THAT?
WELL...
...YASUTORA SADO?
...
KREEK

READ THIS WAY

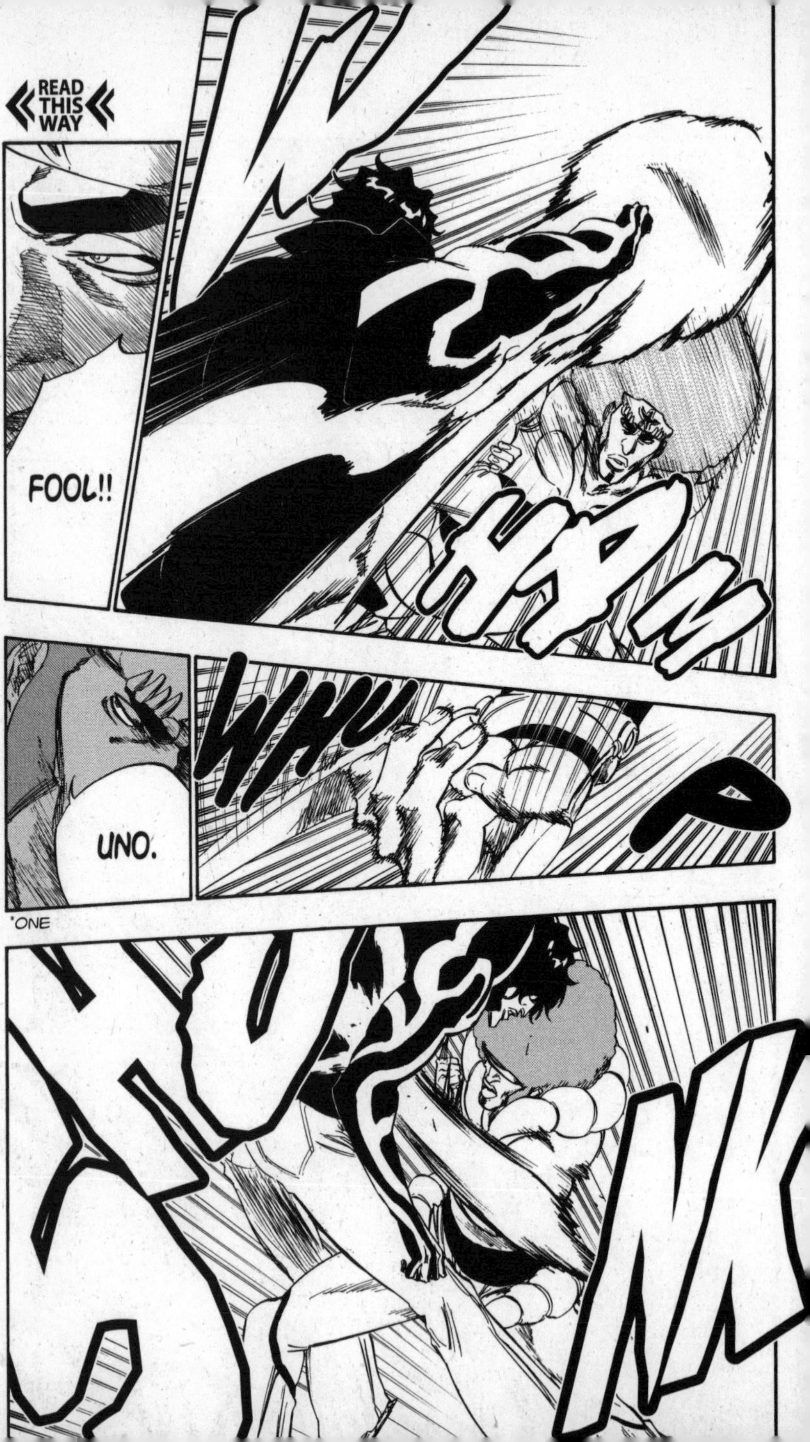
FOOL!!
UNO.
*ONE

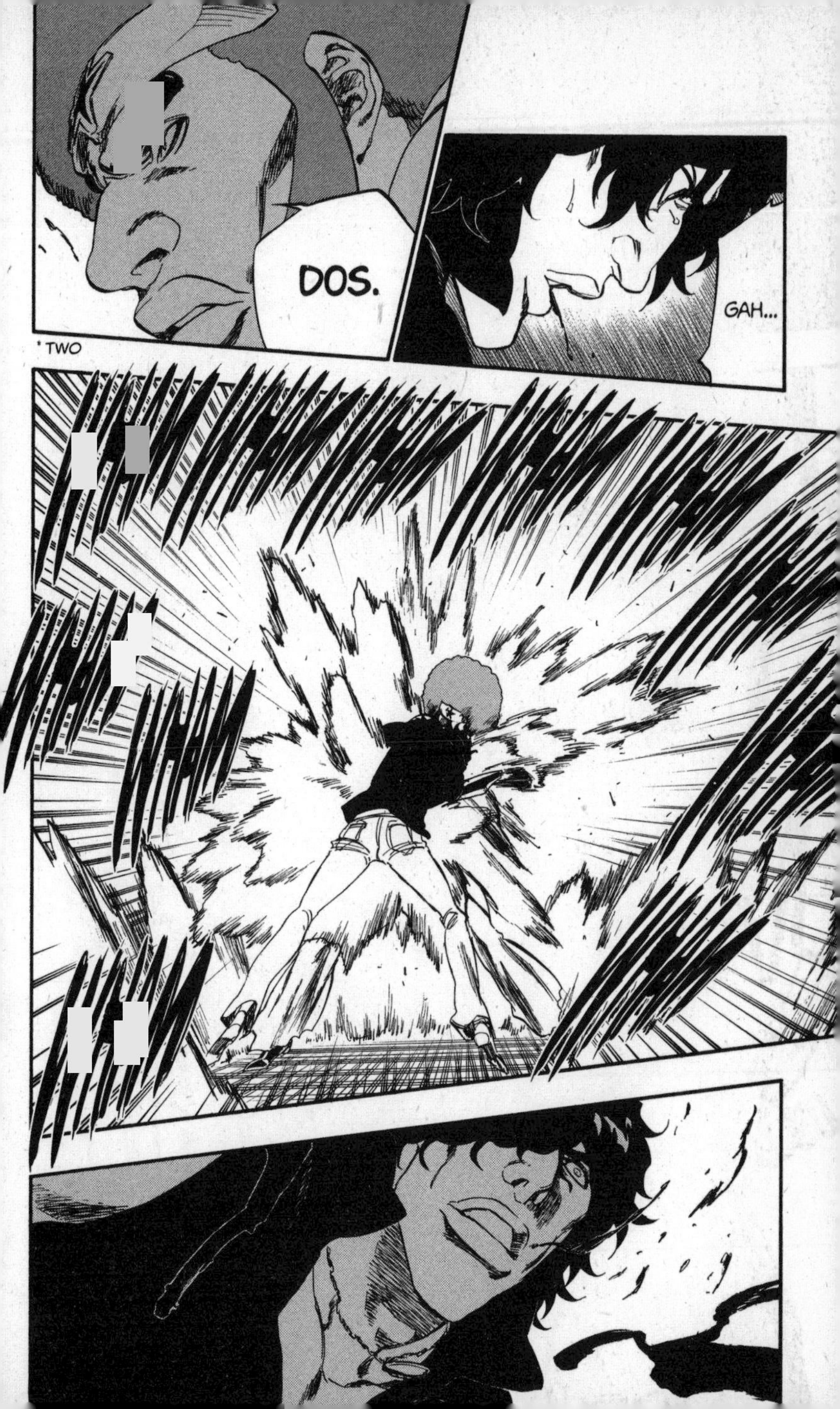
GAH...
DOS.
* TWO

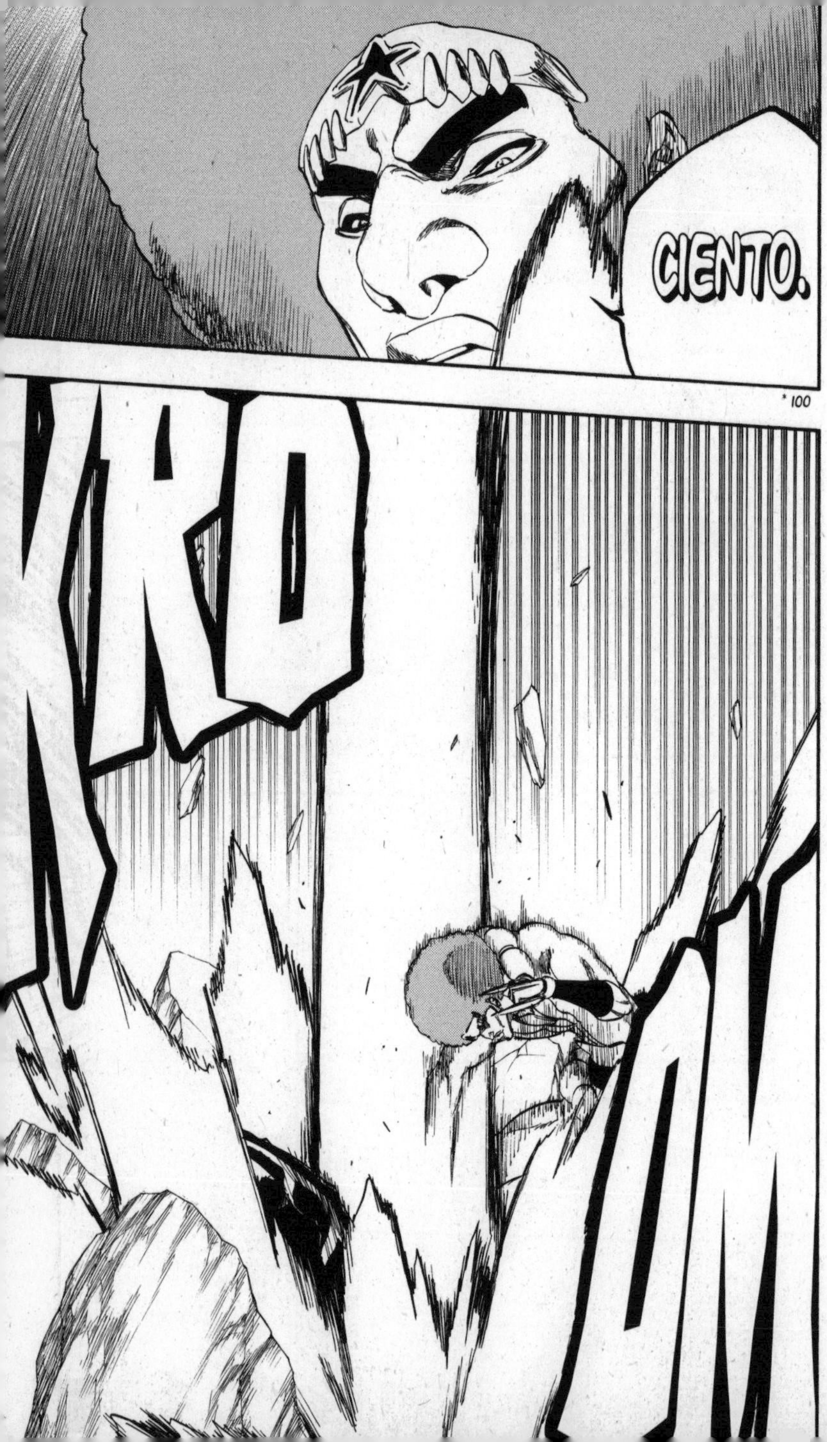
CIENTO.
* 100
KRO
OOM

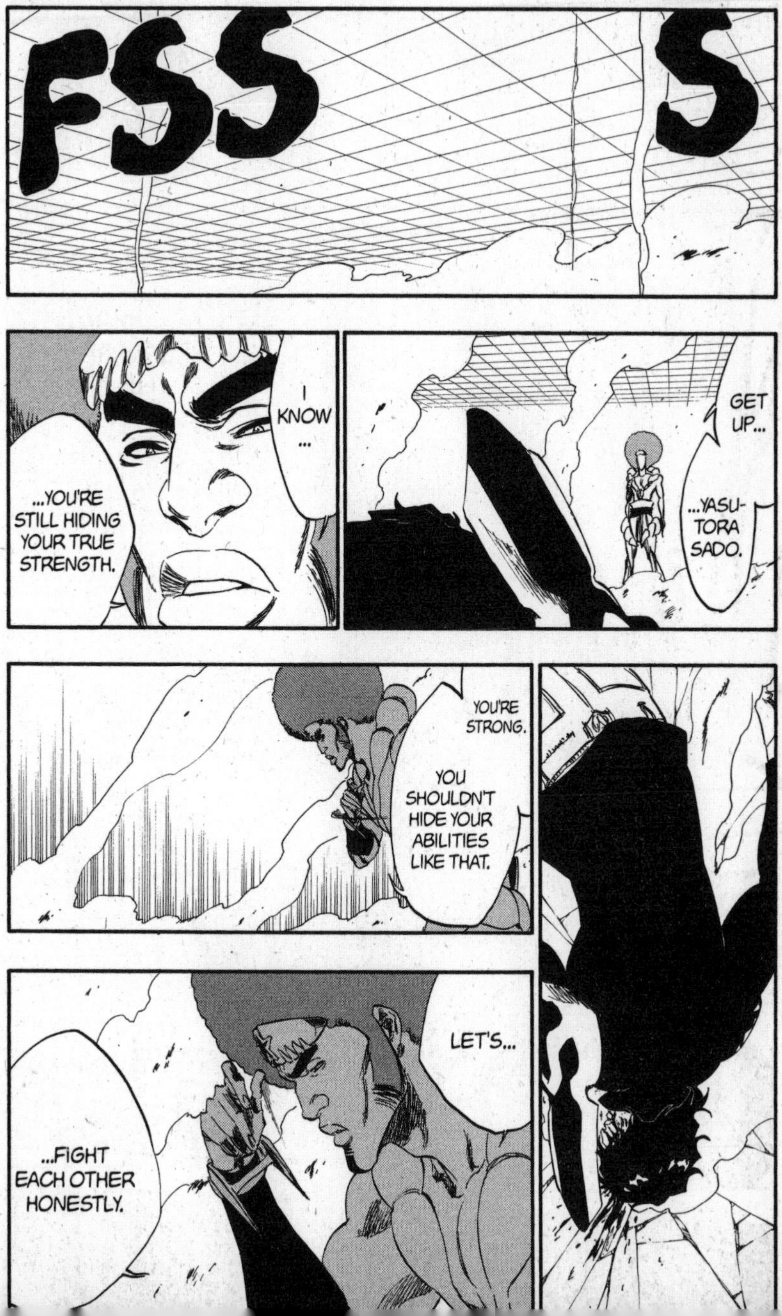
FSS
S
GET UP...
...YASUTORA SADO.
I KNOW ...
...YOU'RE STILL HIDING YOUR TRUE STRENGTH.
YOU'RE STRONG.
YOU SHOULDN'T HIDE YOUR ABILITIES LIKE THAT.
LET'S...
...FIGHT EACH OTHER HONESTLY.

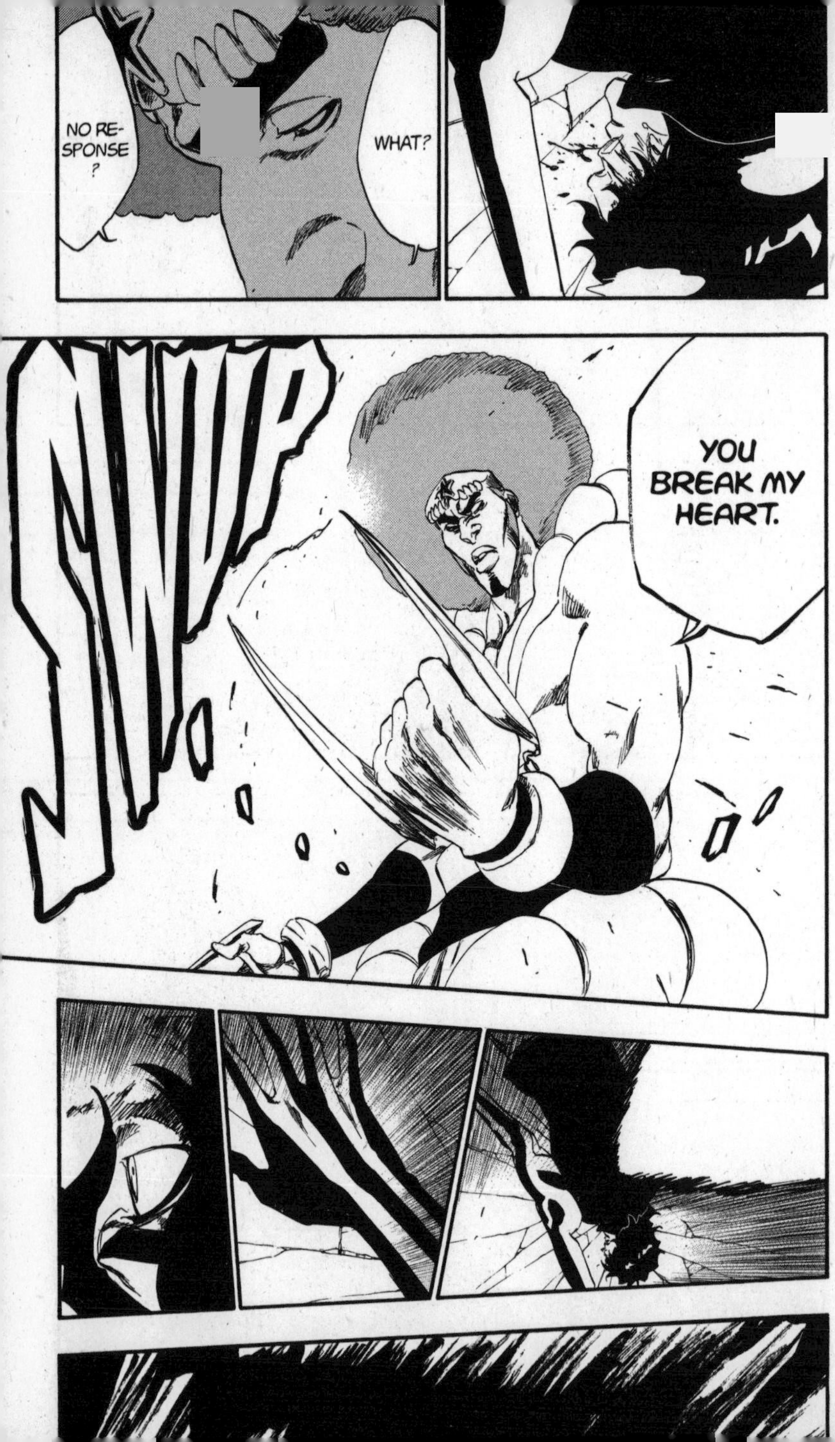

WHAT?
NO RE-SPONSE?
YOU BREAK MY HEART.
SWUP

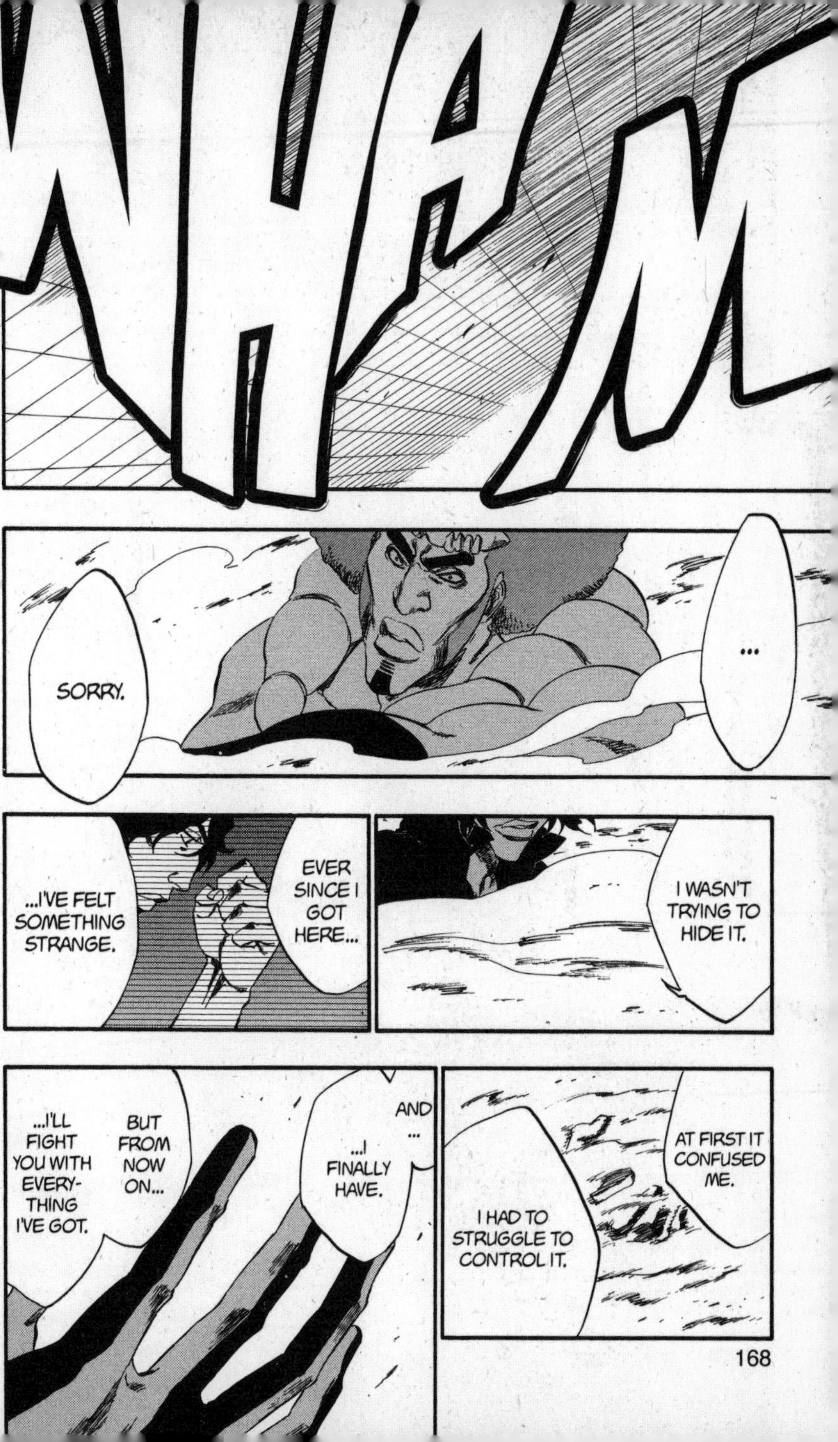
WHAM
...
SORRY.
I WASN'T TRYING TO HIDE IT.
EVER SINCE I GOT HERE...
...I'VE FELT SOMETHING STRANGE.
AT FIRST IT CONFUSED ME.
I HAD TO STRUGGLE TO CONTROL IT.
AND ...
...I FINALLY HAVE.
BUT FROM NOW ON...
...I'LL FIGHT YOU WITH EVERY-THING I'VE GOT.

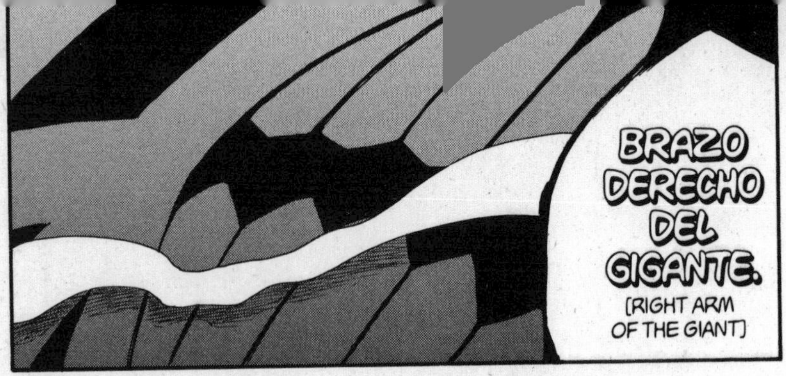
BRAZO DERECHO DEL GIGANTE.
[RIGHT ARM OF THE GIANT]
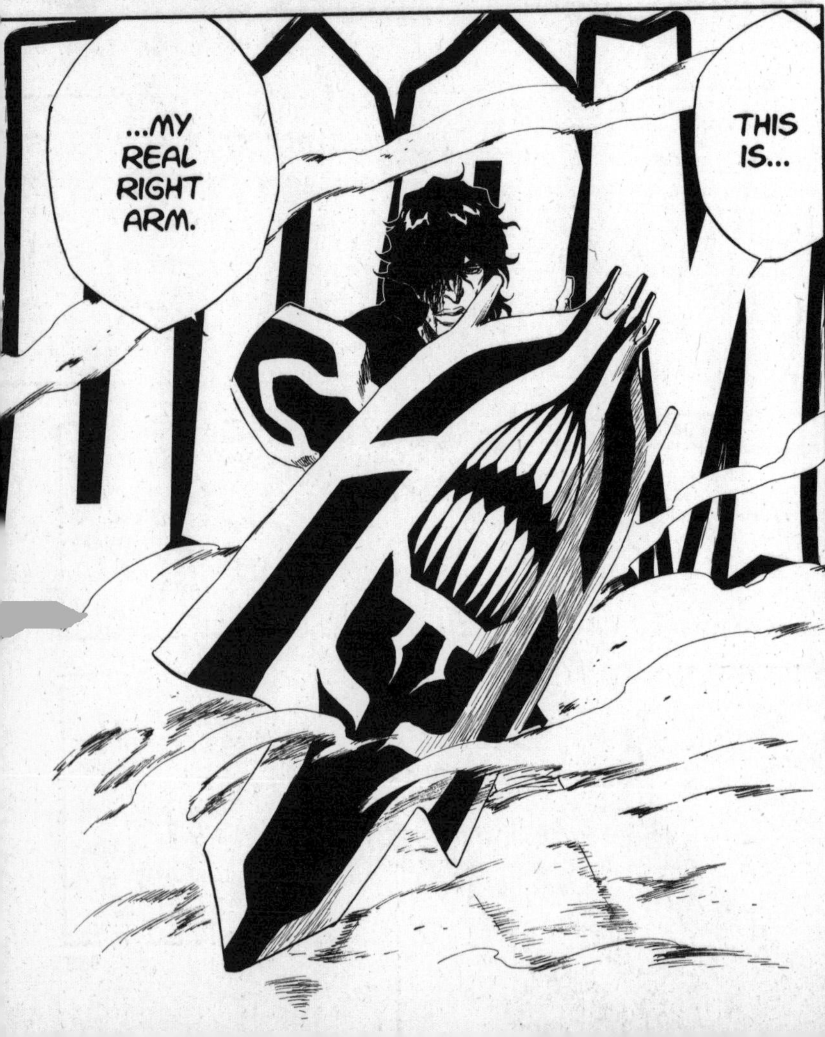
THIS IS...
...MY REAL RIGHT ARM.

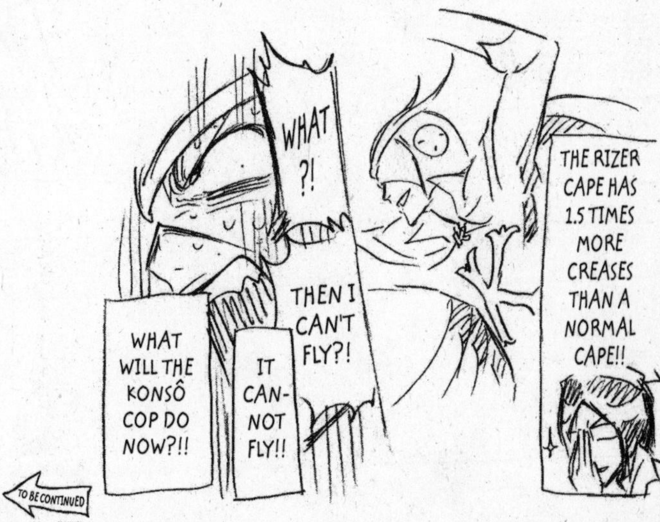
THE RIZER CAPE HAS 1.5 TIMES MORE CREASES THAN A NORMAL CAPE!!
WHAT ?!
THEN I CAN'T FLY?!
IT CAN-NOT FLY!!
WHAT WILL THE KONSÔ COP DO NOW?!!
TO BE CONTINUED

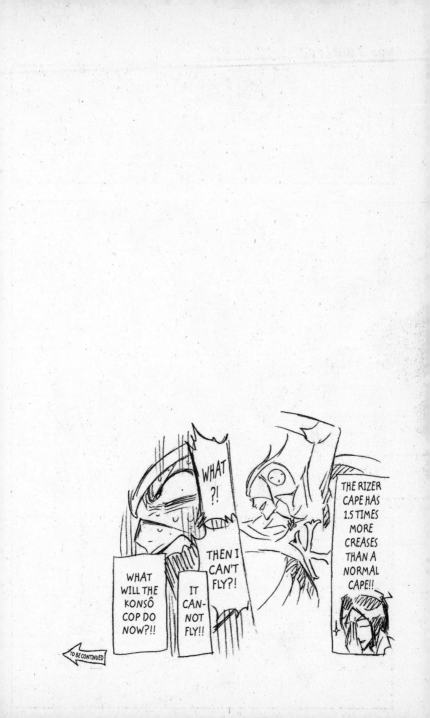

260. RIGHT ARM OF THE GIANT2

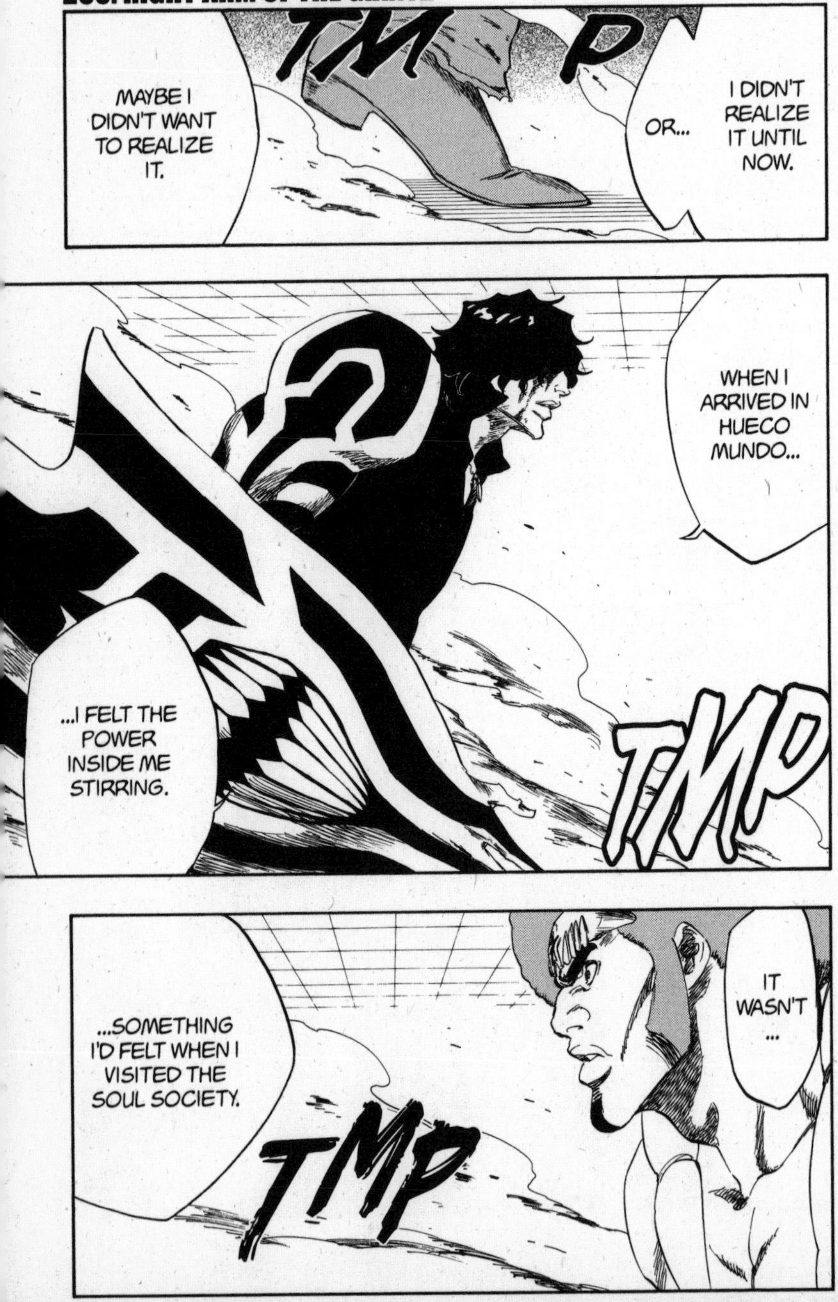
I DIDN'T REALIZE IT UNTIL NOW.
OR...
TMP
MAYBE I DIDN'T WANT TO REALIZE IT.
WHEN I ARRIVED IN HUECO MUNDO...
TMP
...I FELT THE POWER INSIDE ME STIRRING.
IT WASN'T ...
...SOMETHING I'D FELT WHEN I VISITED THE SOUL SOCIETY.
TMP

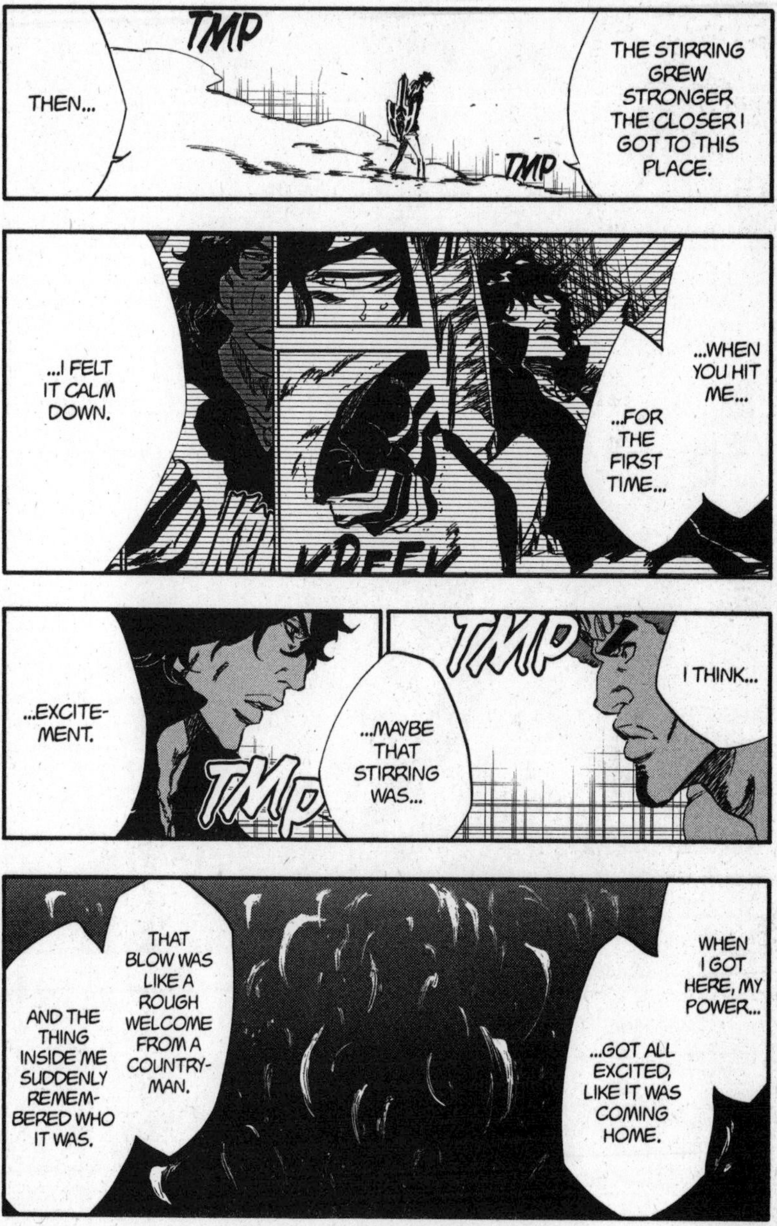
THE STIRRING GREW STRONGER THE CLOSER I GOT TO THIS PLACE.
TMP
TMP
THEN...
...WHEN YOU HIT ME...
...FOR THE FIRST TIME...
...I FELT IT CALM DOWN.
I THINK...
TMP
...MAYBE THAT STIRRING WAS...
TMP
...EXCITE-MENT.
WHEN I GOT HERE, MY POWER...
...GOT ALL EXCITED, LIKE IT WAS COMING HOME.
THAT BLOW WAS LIKE A ROUGH WELCOME FROM A COUNTRY-MAN.
AND THE THING INSIDE ME SUDDENLY REMEM-BERED WHO IT WAS.

READ THIS WAY

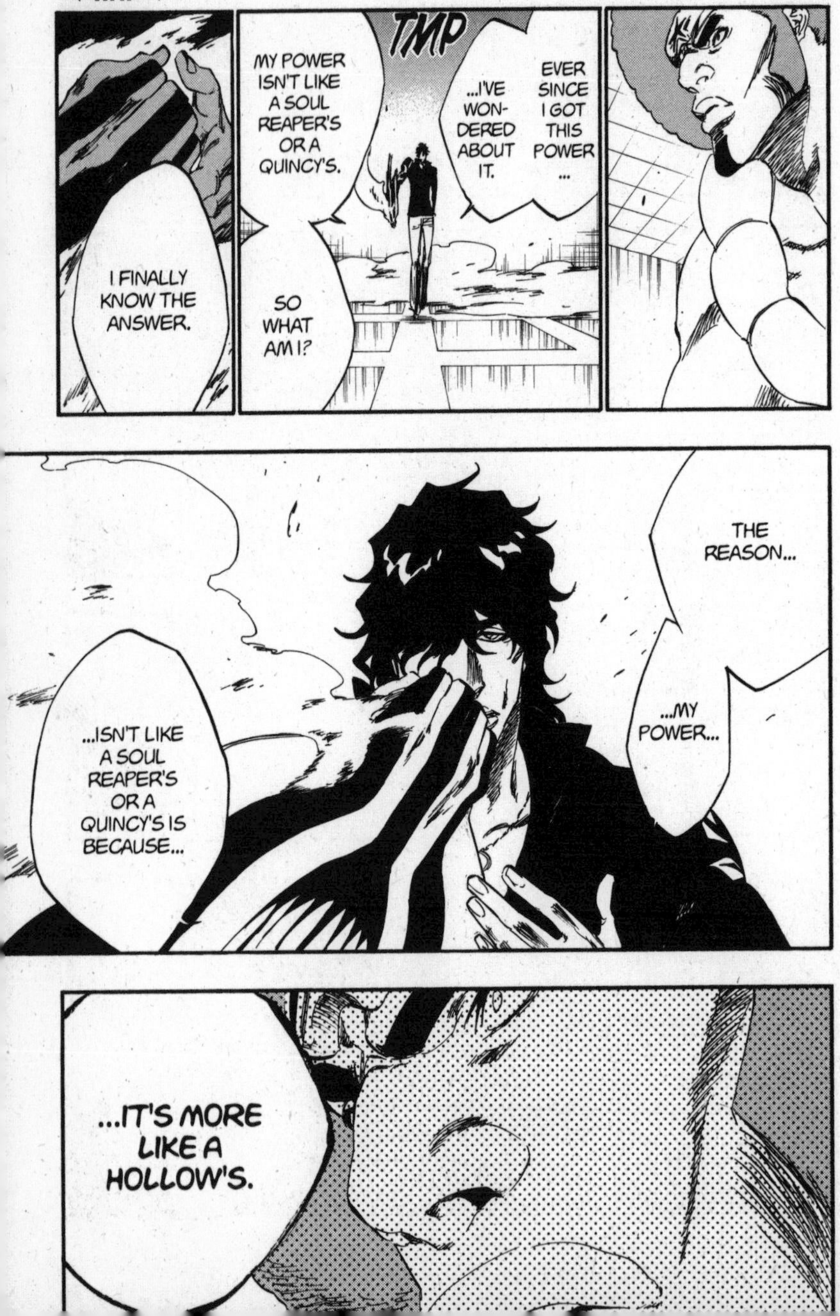
EVER SINCE I GOT THIS POWER...
...I'VE WONDERED ABOUT IT.
TMP
MY POWER ISN'T LIKE A SOUL REAPER'S OR A QUINCY'S.
SO WHAT AM I?
I FINALLY KNOW THE ANSWER.
THE REASON...
...MY POWER...
...ISN'T LIKE A SOUL REAPER'S OR A QUINCY'S IS BECAUSE...
...IT'S MORE LIKE A HOLLOW'S.

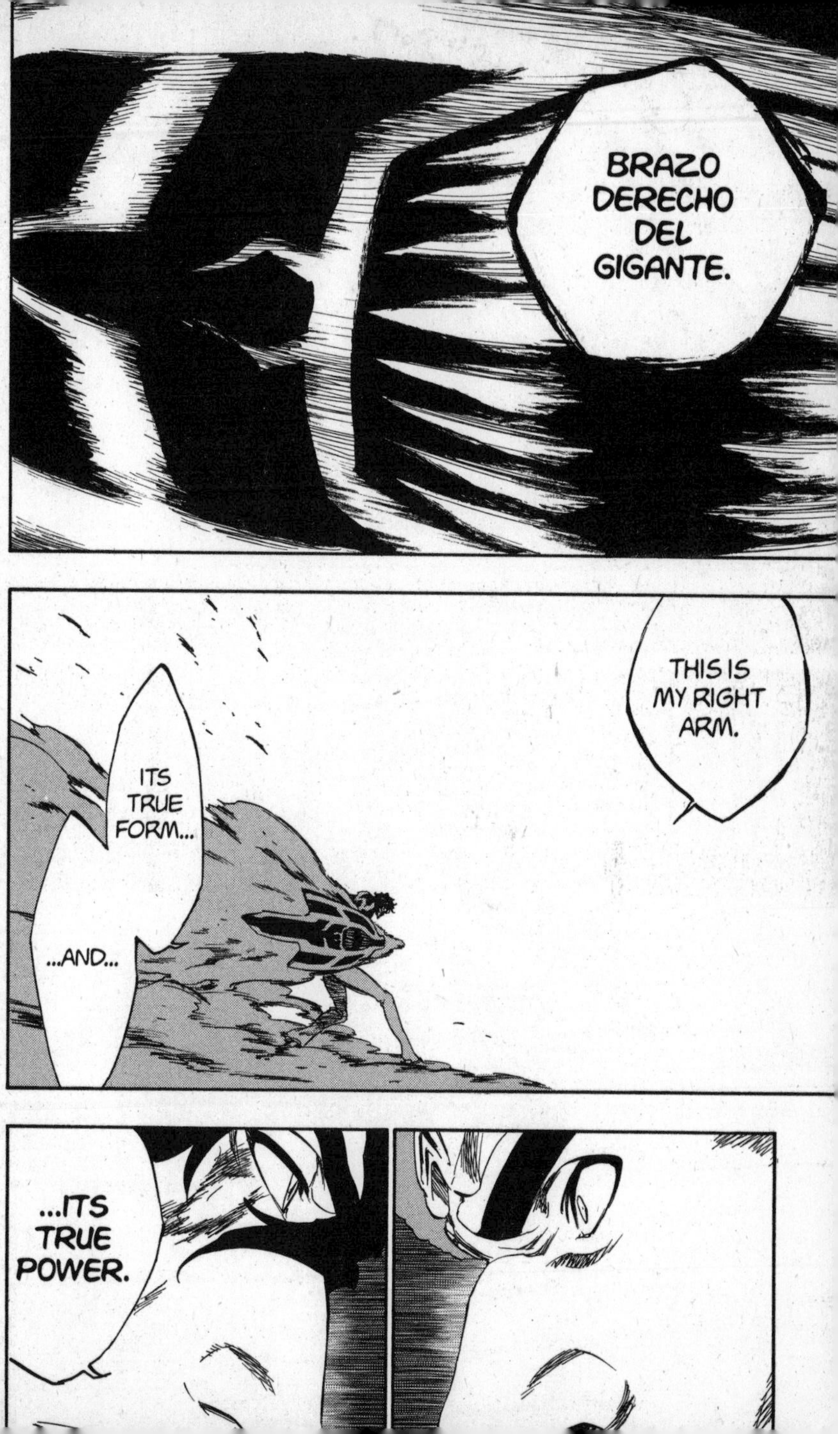
BRAZO DERECHO DEL GIGANTE.
THIS IS MY RIGHT ARM.
ITS TRUE FORM...
...AND...
...ITS TRUE POWER.

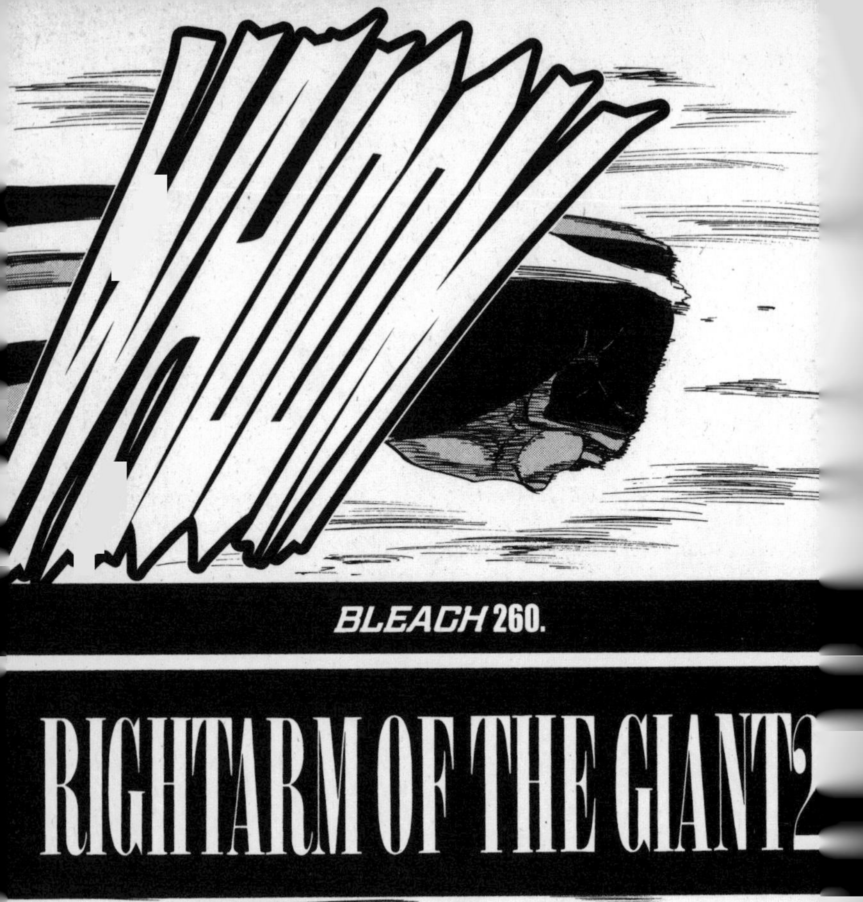

BLEACH 260.

RIGHTARM OF THE GIANT2

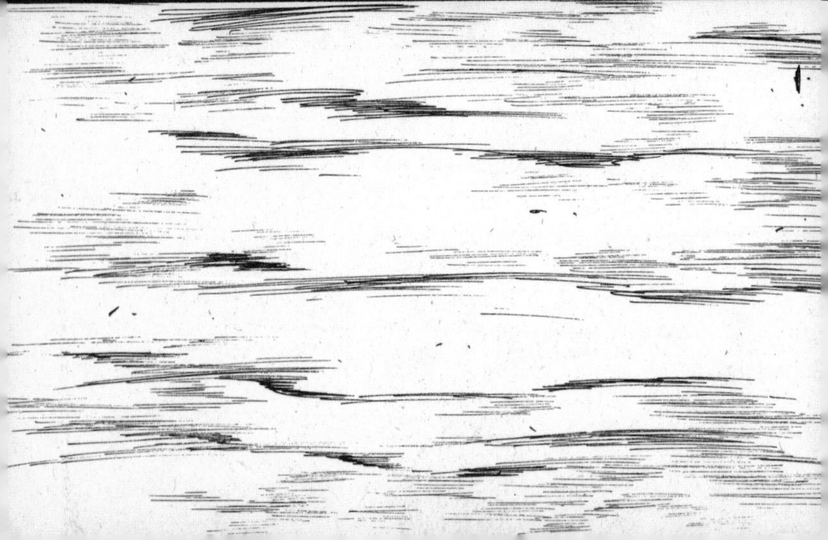

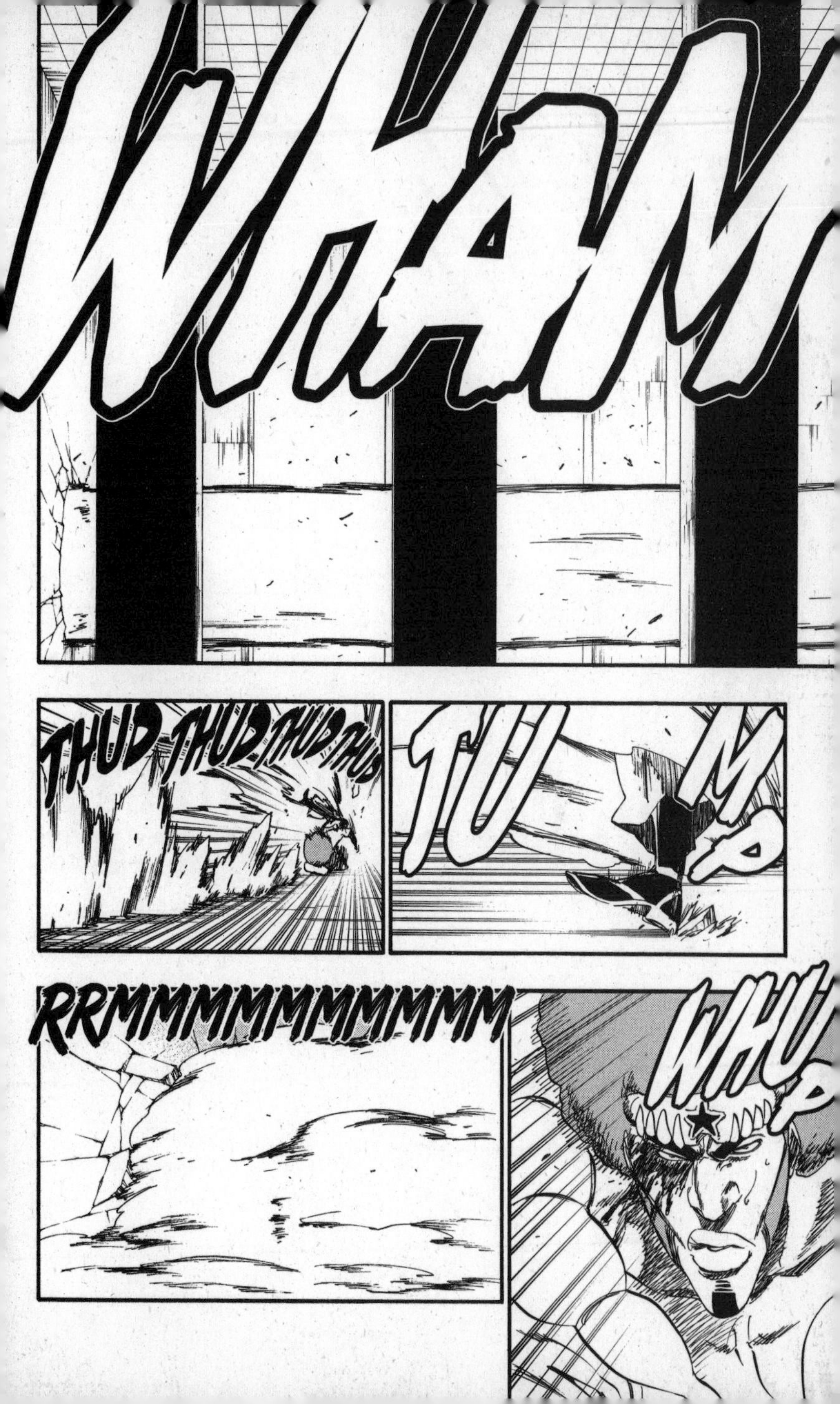
WHAM
TUMP
THUD THUD THUD THUD
WHUP
RRMMMMMMMMMMM

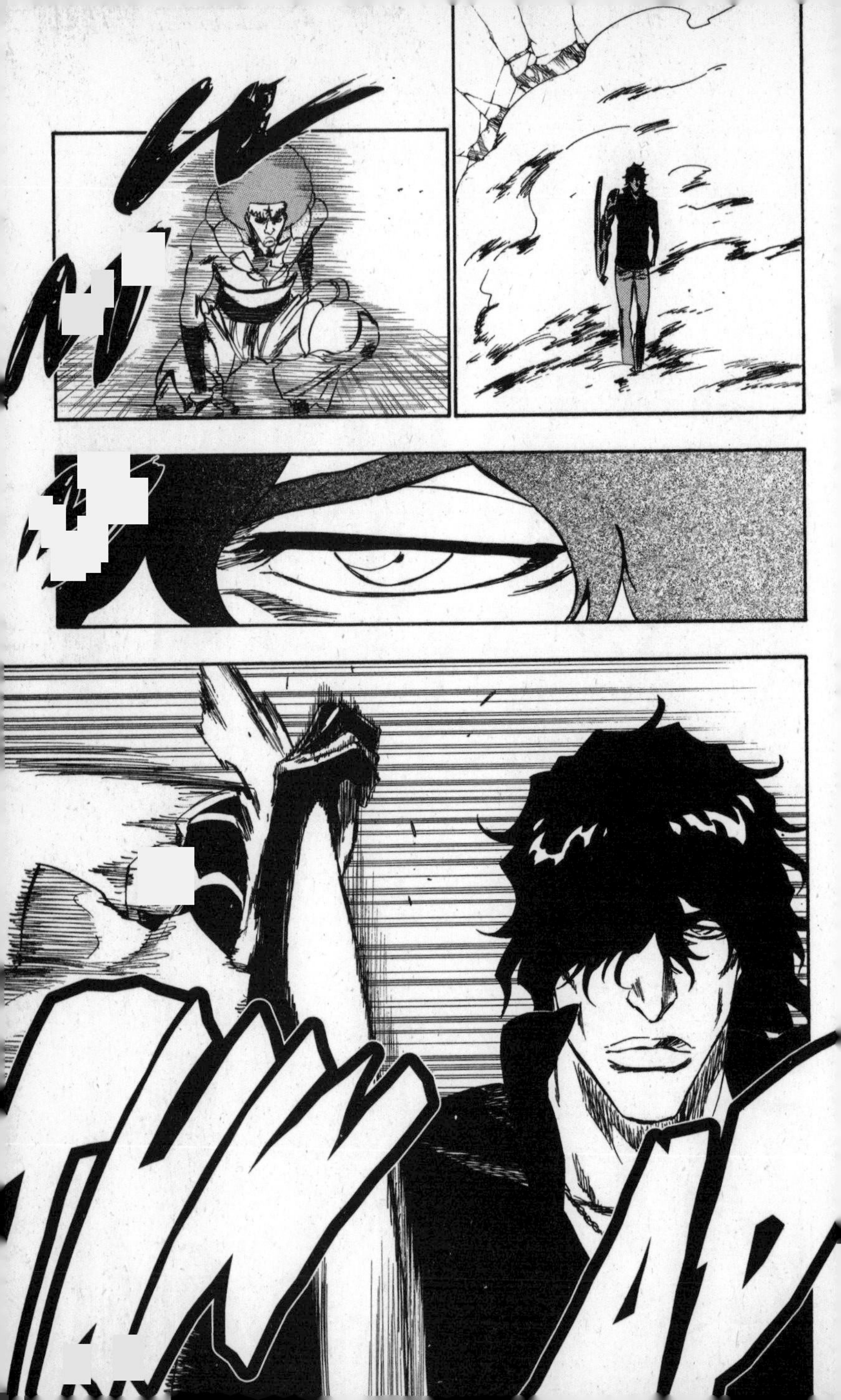

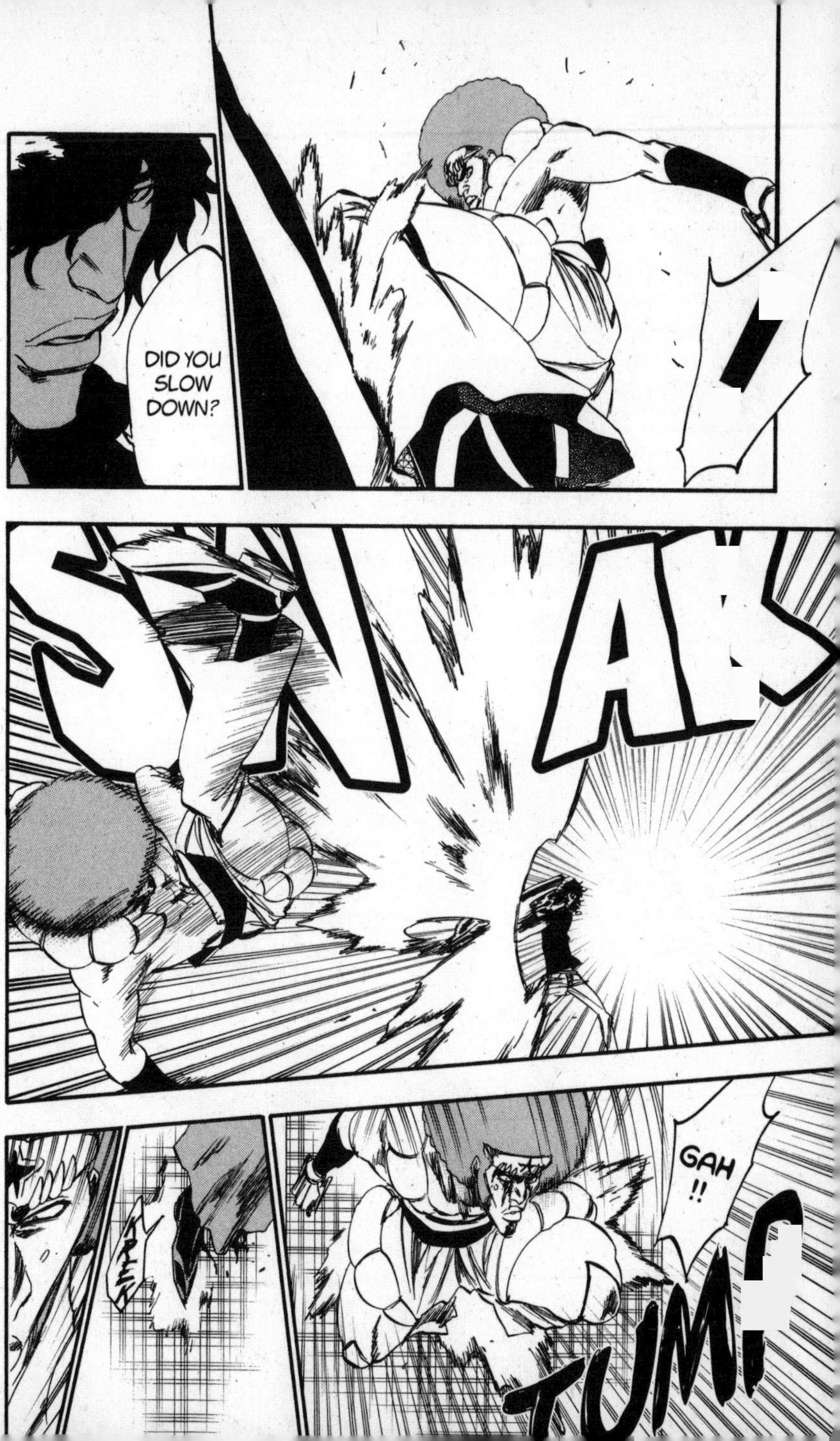
DID YOU SLOW DOWN?
GAH !!
TUM
KREK

READ THIS WAY

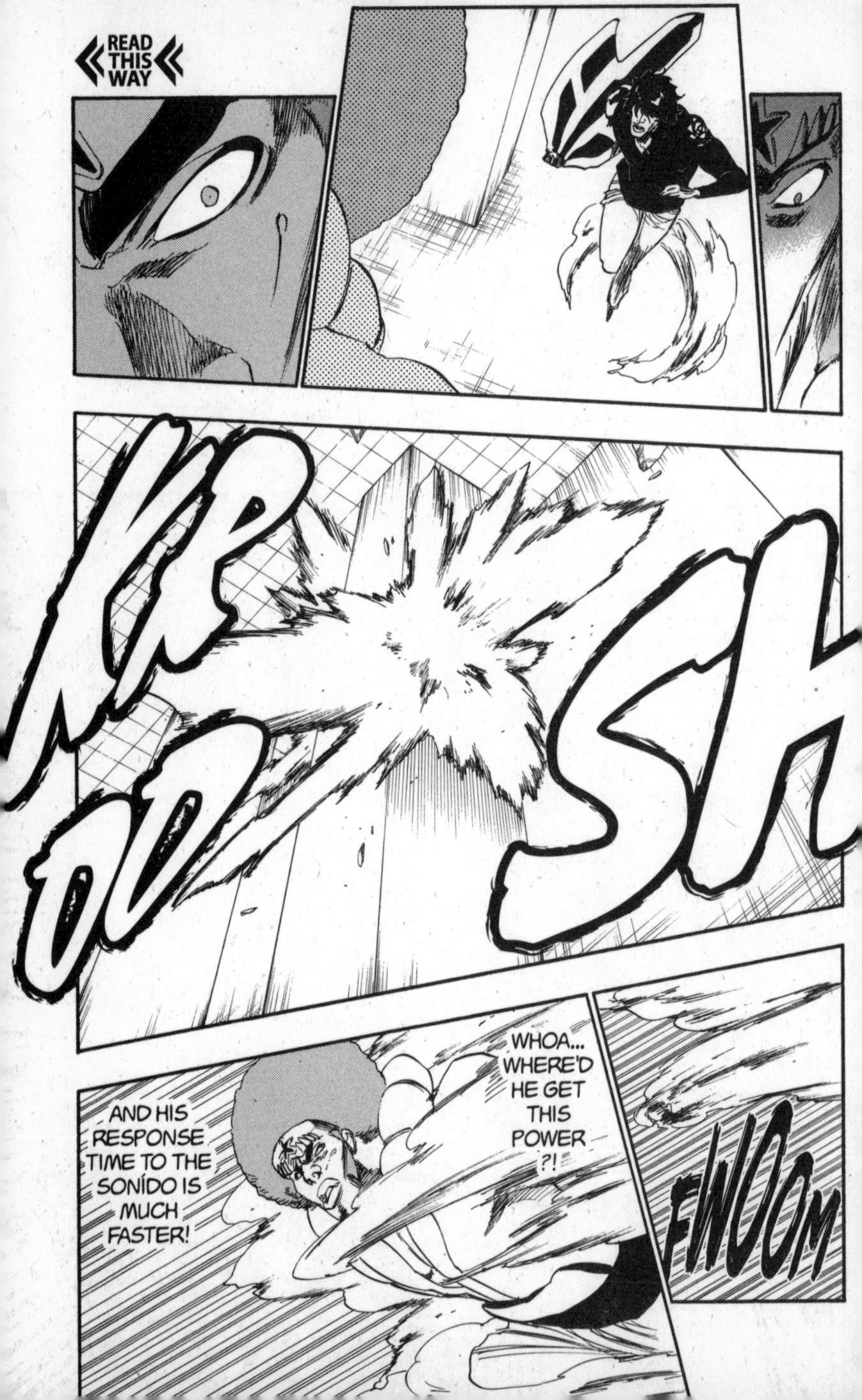
FWOOM
WHOA... WHERE'D HE GET THIS POWER ?!
AND HIS RESPONSE TIME TO THE SONÍDO IS MUCH FASTER!

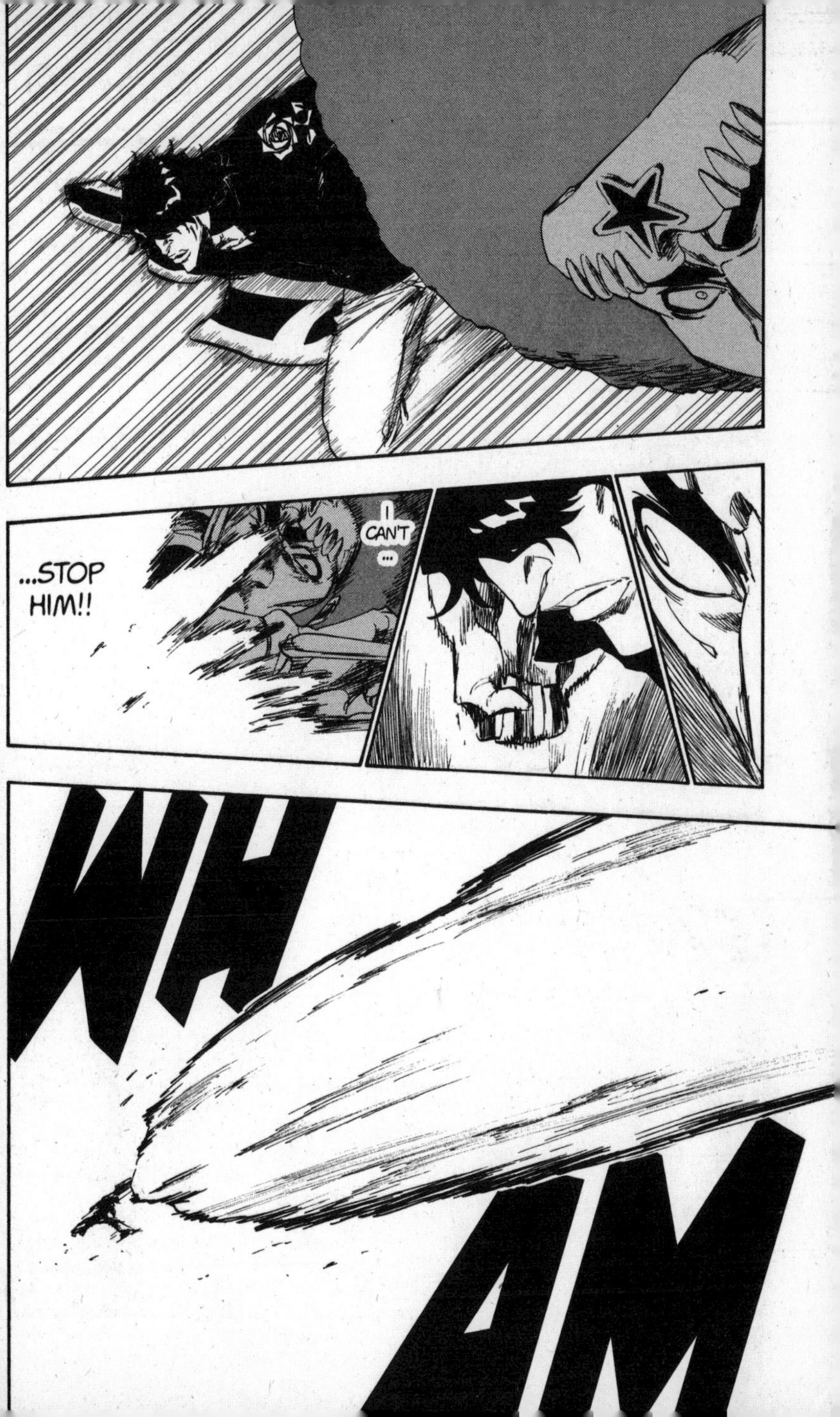
I CAN'T ...
...STOP HIM!!
WHAM

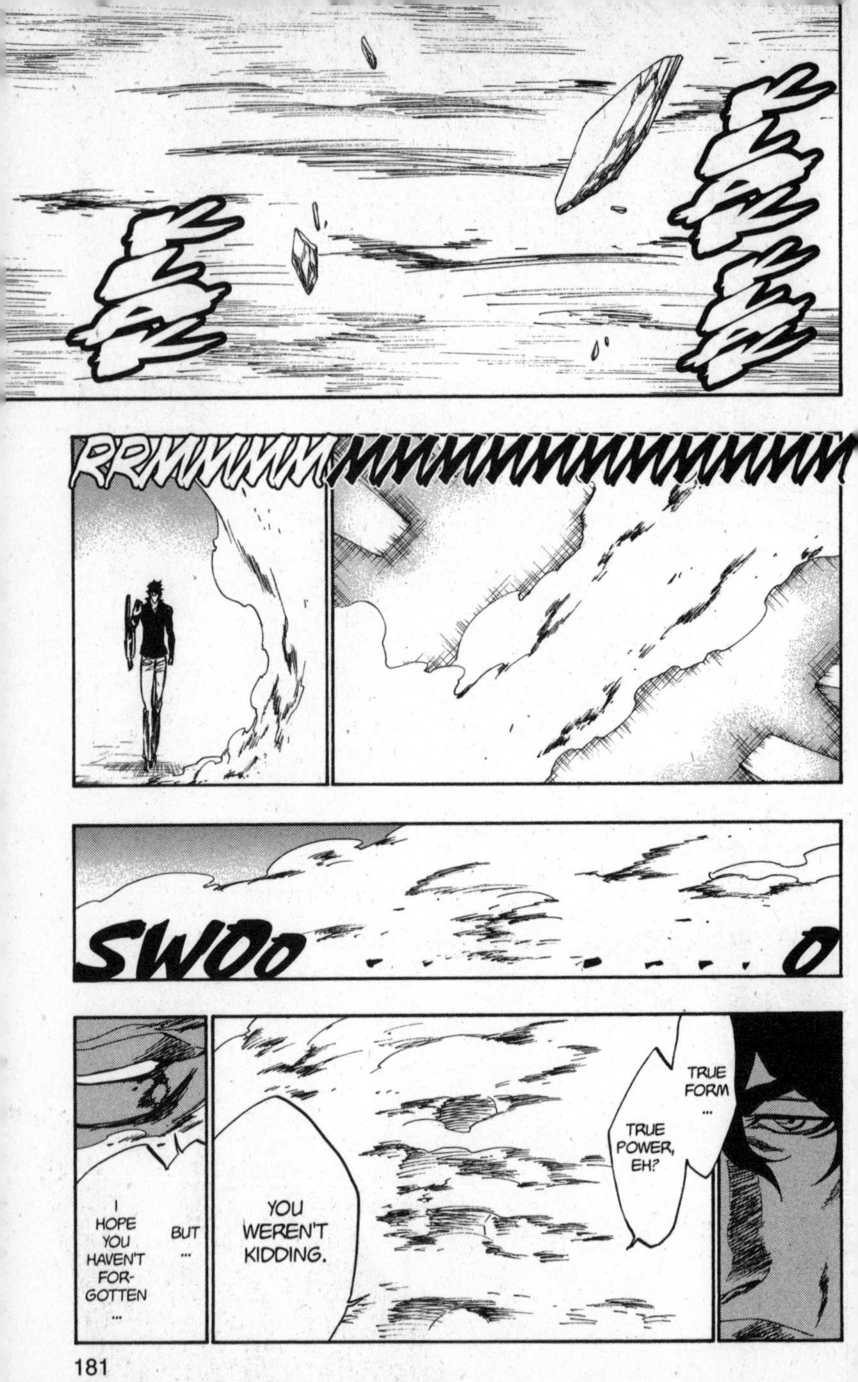
RRMMMMMMMMMMMMMMMMMMMMMMMMMM
SWOO.......O
TRUE FORM...
TRUE POWER, EH?
YOU WEREN'T KIDDING.
BUT...
I HOPE YOU HAVEN'T FOR-GOTTEN...

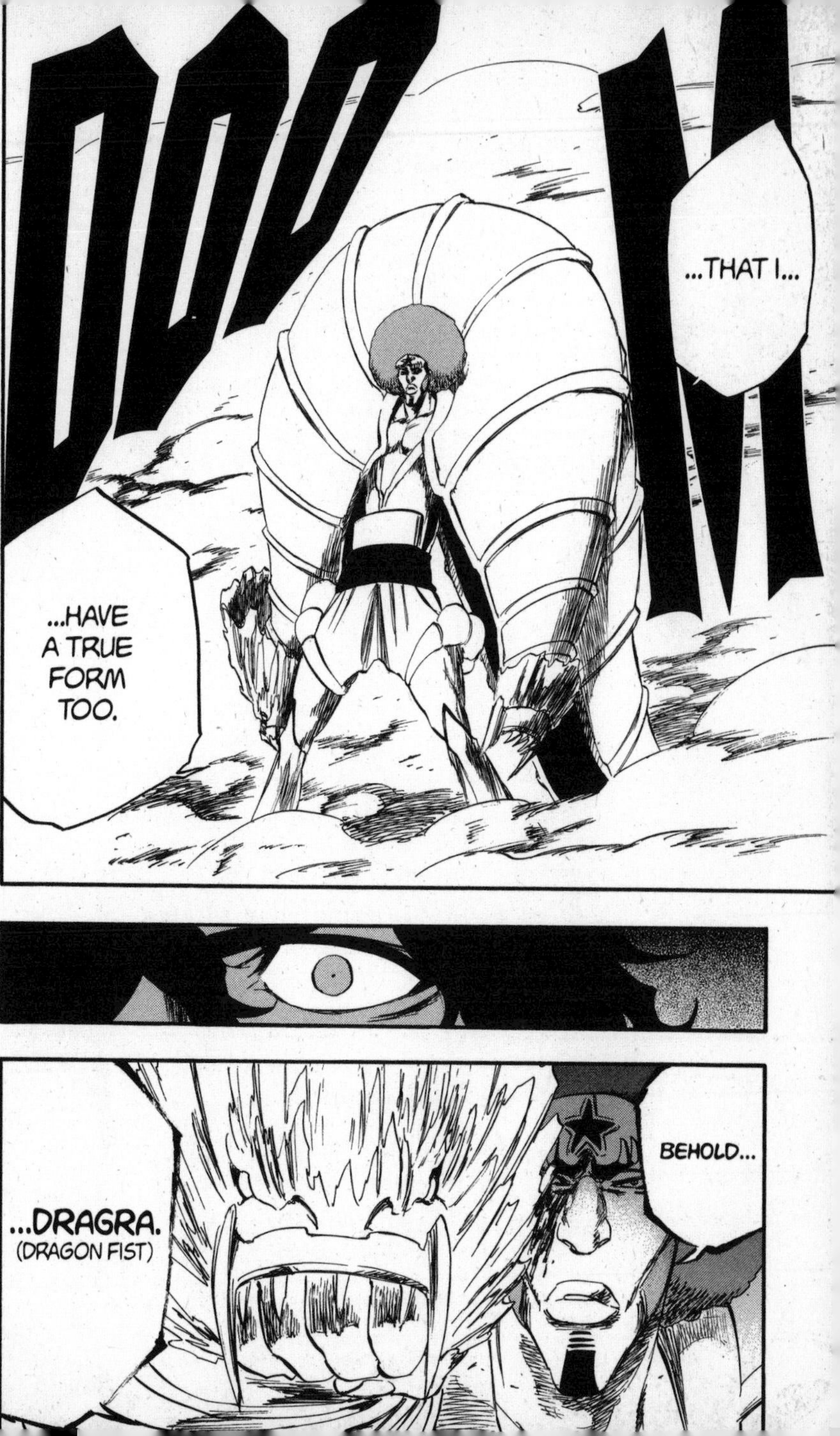
...THAT I...
...HAVE A TRUE FORM TOO.
BEHOLD...
...DRAGRA.
(DRAGON FIST)

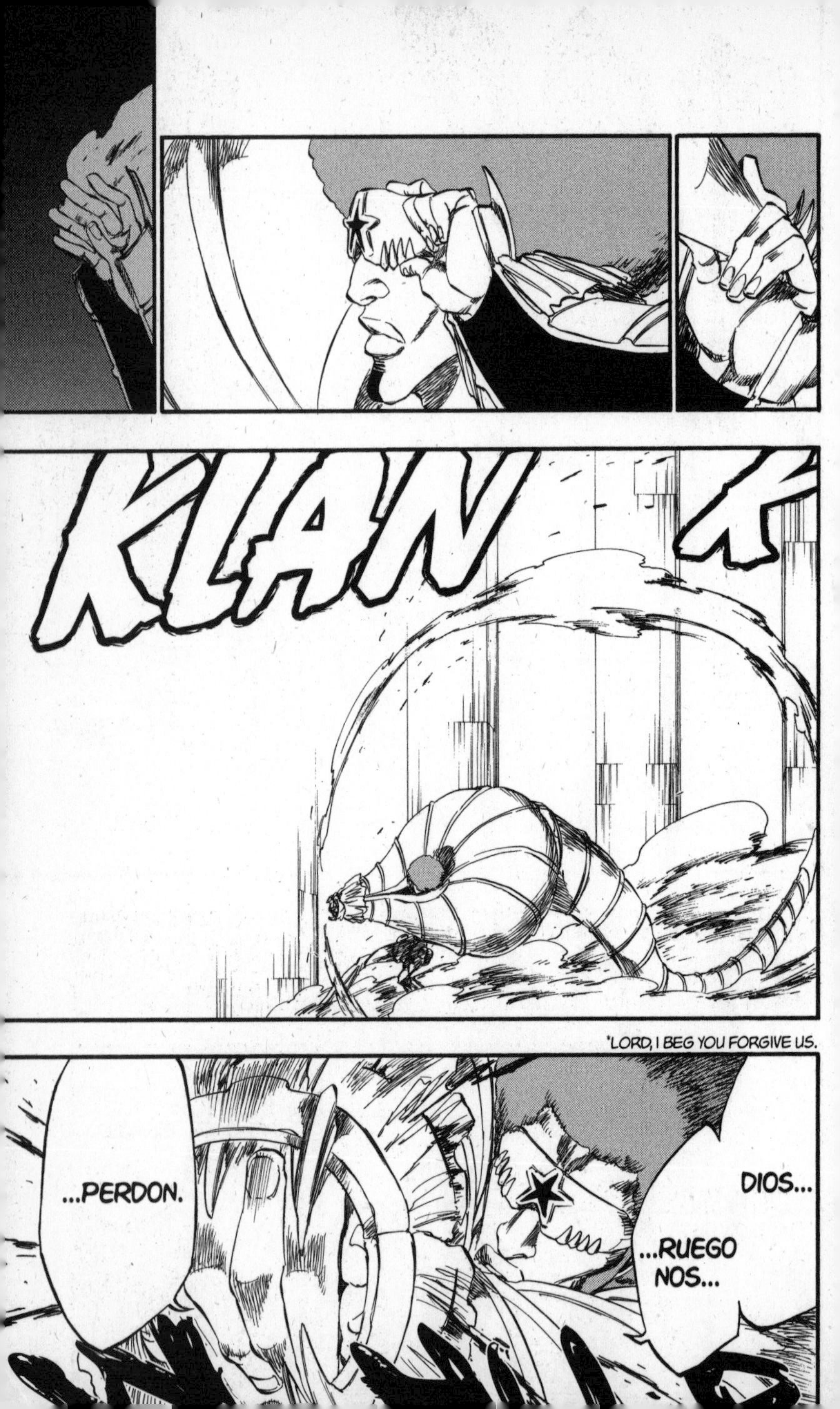
KLAN
DIOS...
...RUEGO NOS...
...PERDON.
*LORD, I BEG YOU FORGIVE US.

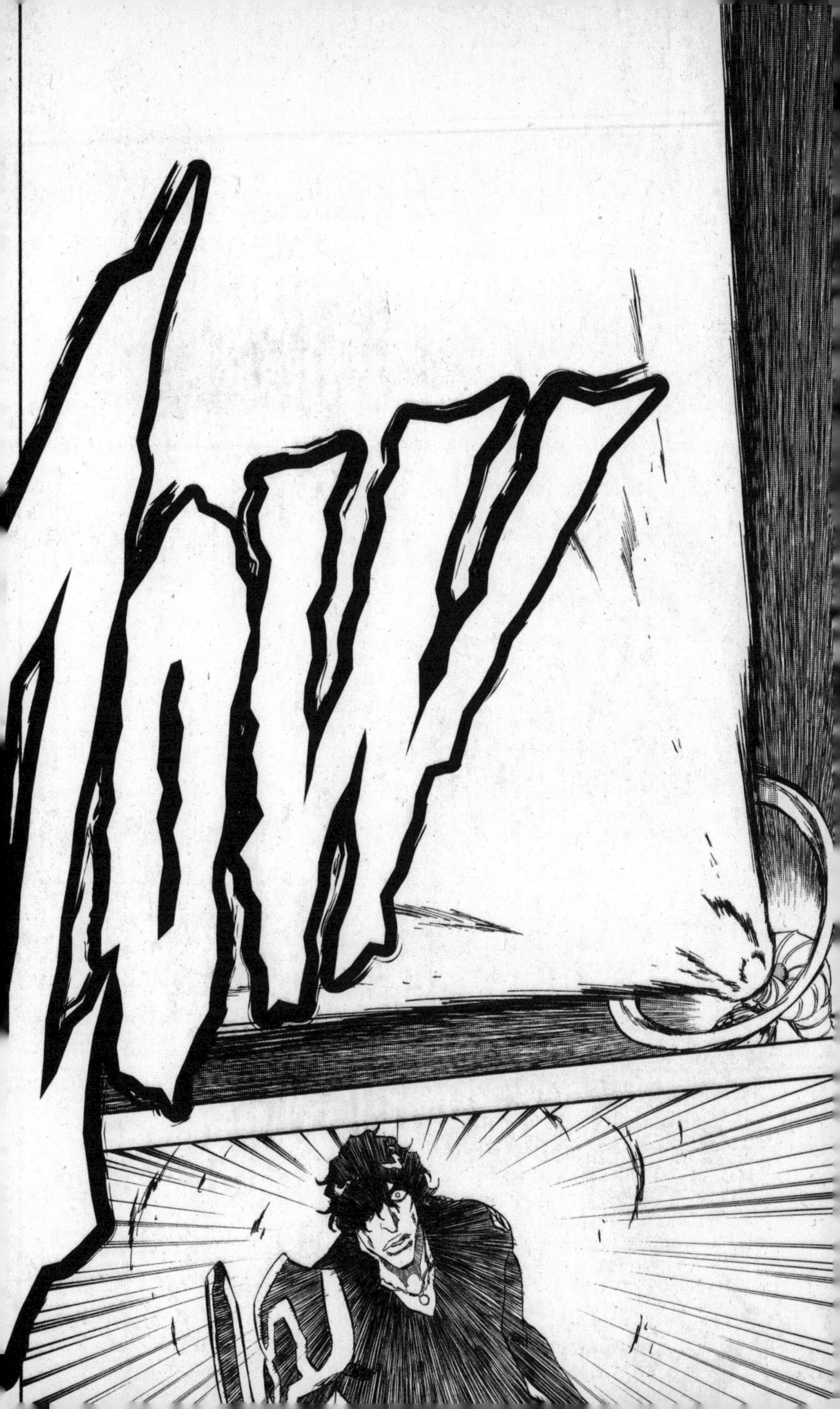

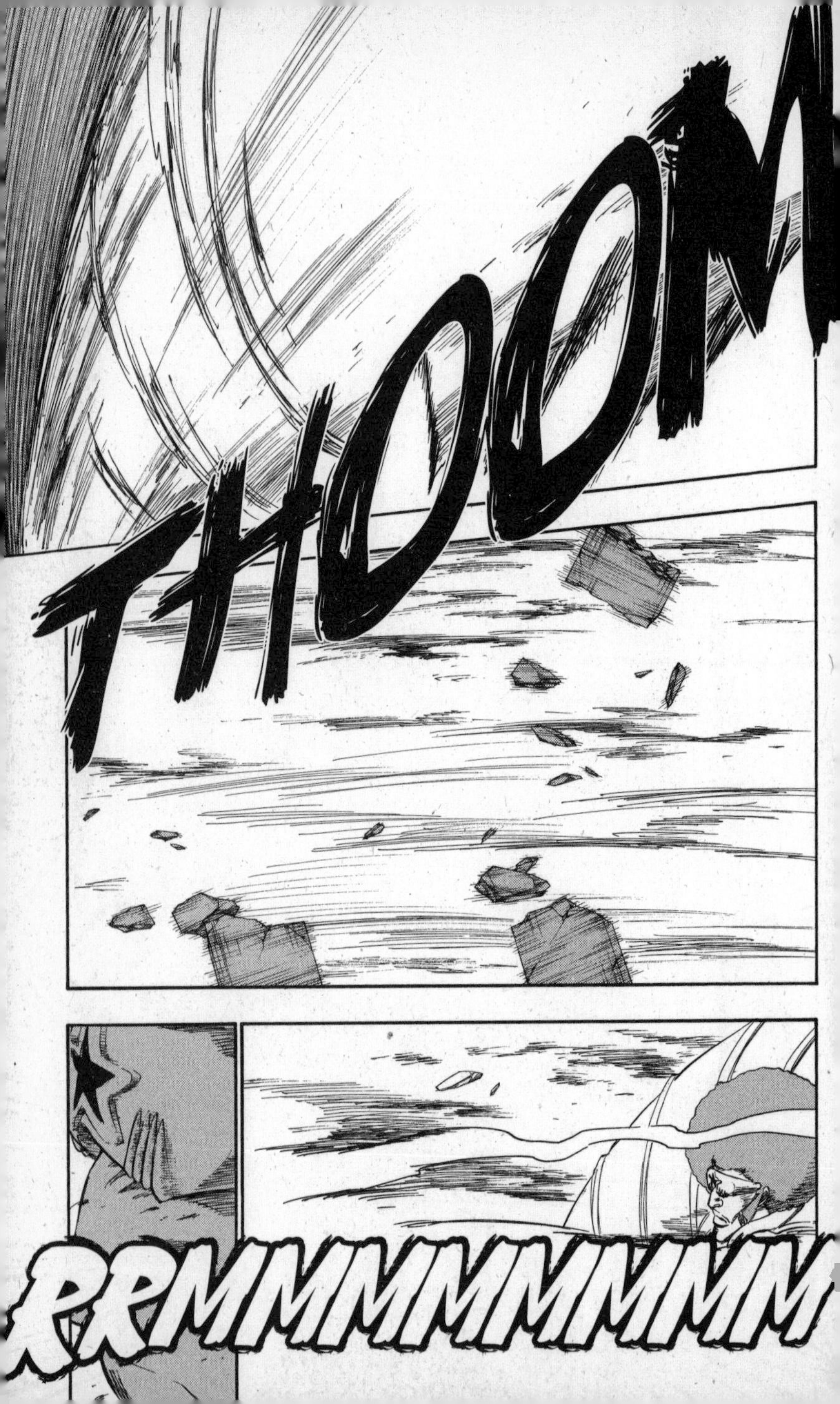
THOOM
RRMMMMMMMM

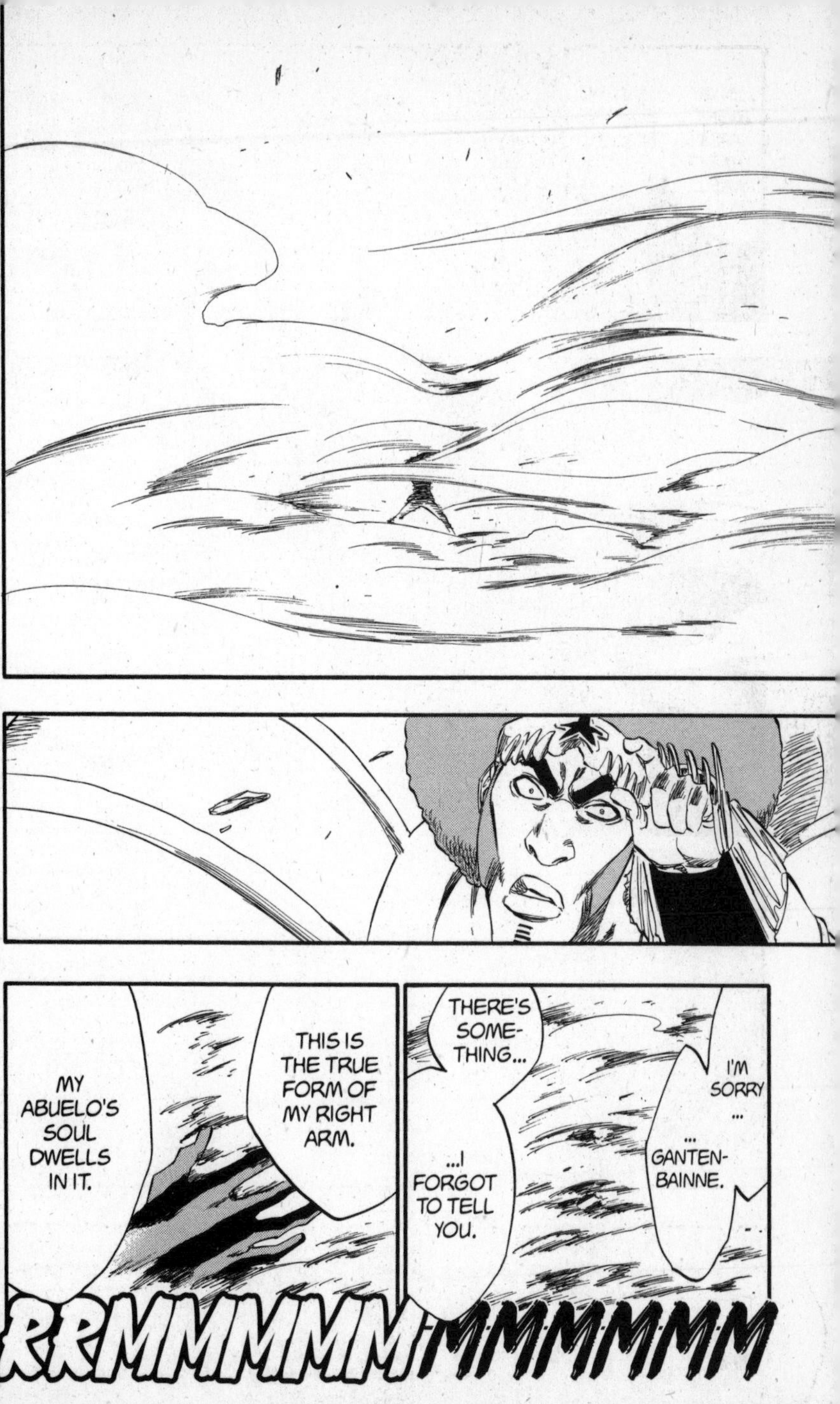
I'M SORRY ... ... GANTEN-BAINNE.
THERE'S SOME-THING...
...I FORGOT TO TELL YOU.
THIS IS THE TRUE FORM OF MY RIGHT ARM.
MY ABUELO'S SOUL DWELLS IN IT.
RRMMMMMMMMMMMMMM

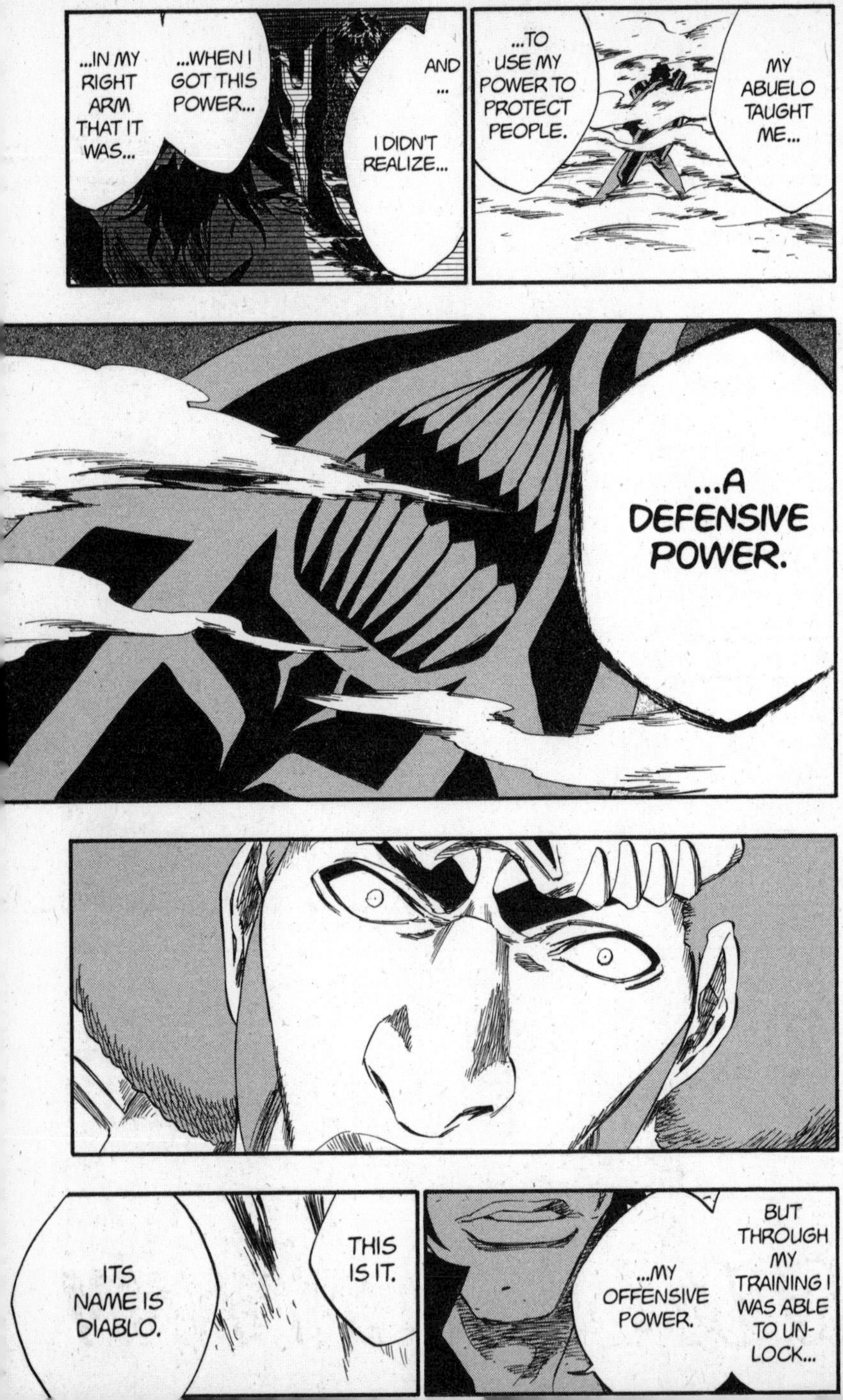
MY ABUELO TAUGHT ME...
...TO USE MY POWER TO PROTECT PEOPLE.
AND ...
I DIDN'T REALIZE...
...WHEN I GOT THIS POWER...
...IN MY RIGHT ARM THAT IT WAS...
...A DEFENSIVE POWER.
BUT THROUGH MY TRAINING I WAS ABLE TO UN-LOCK...
...MY OFFENSIVE POWER.
THIS IS IT.
ITS NAME IS DIABLO.

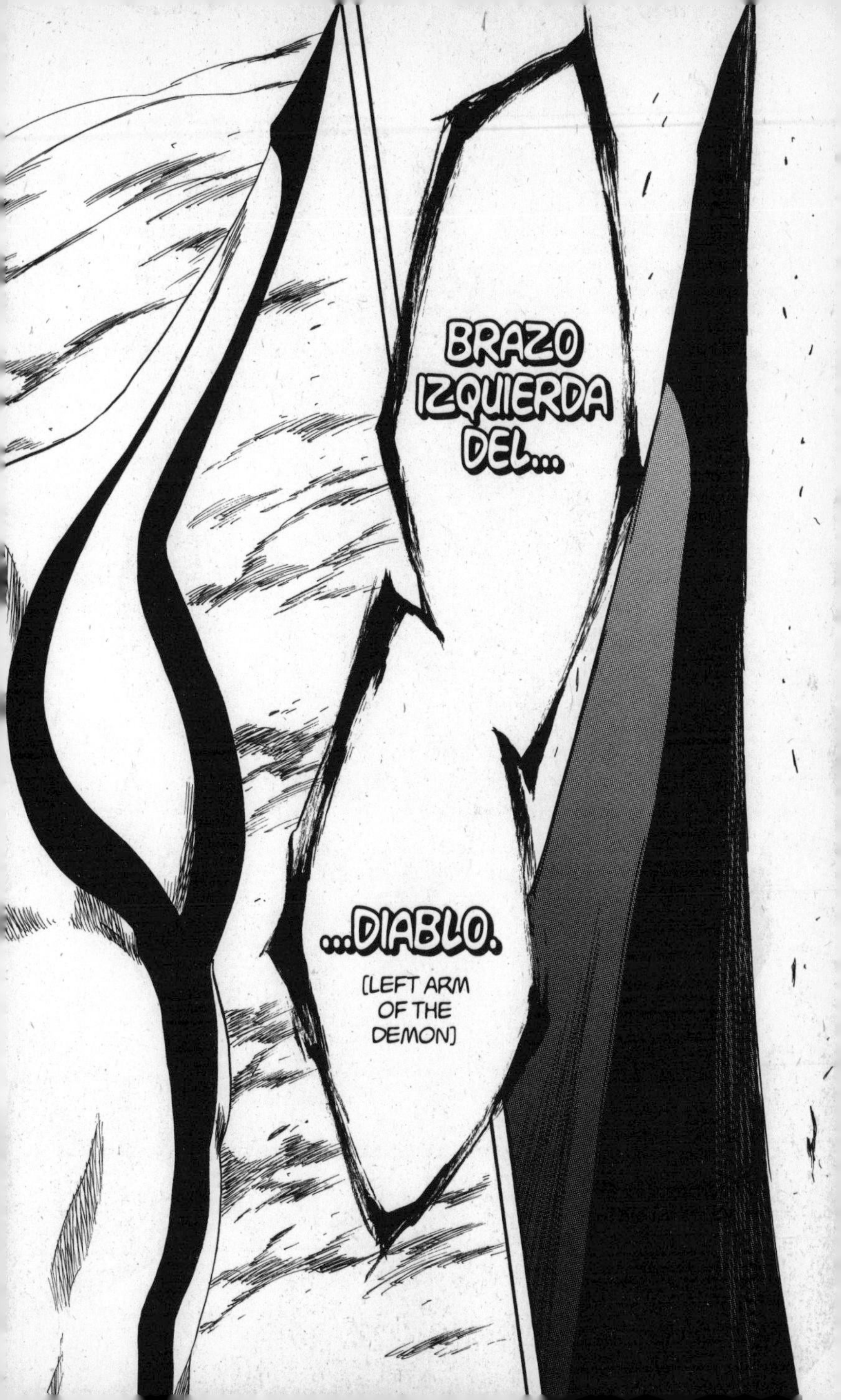
BRAZO IZQUIERDA DEL...
...DIABLO.
[LEFT ARM OF THE DEMON]

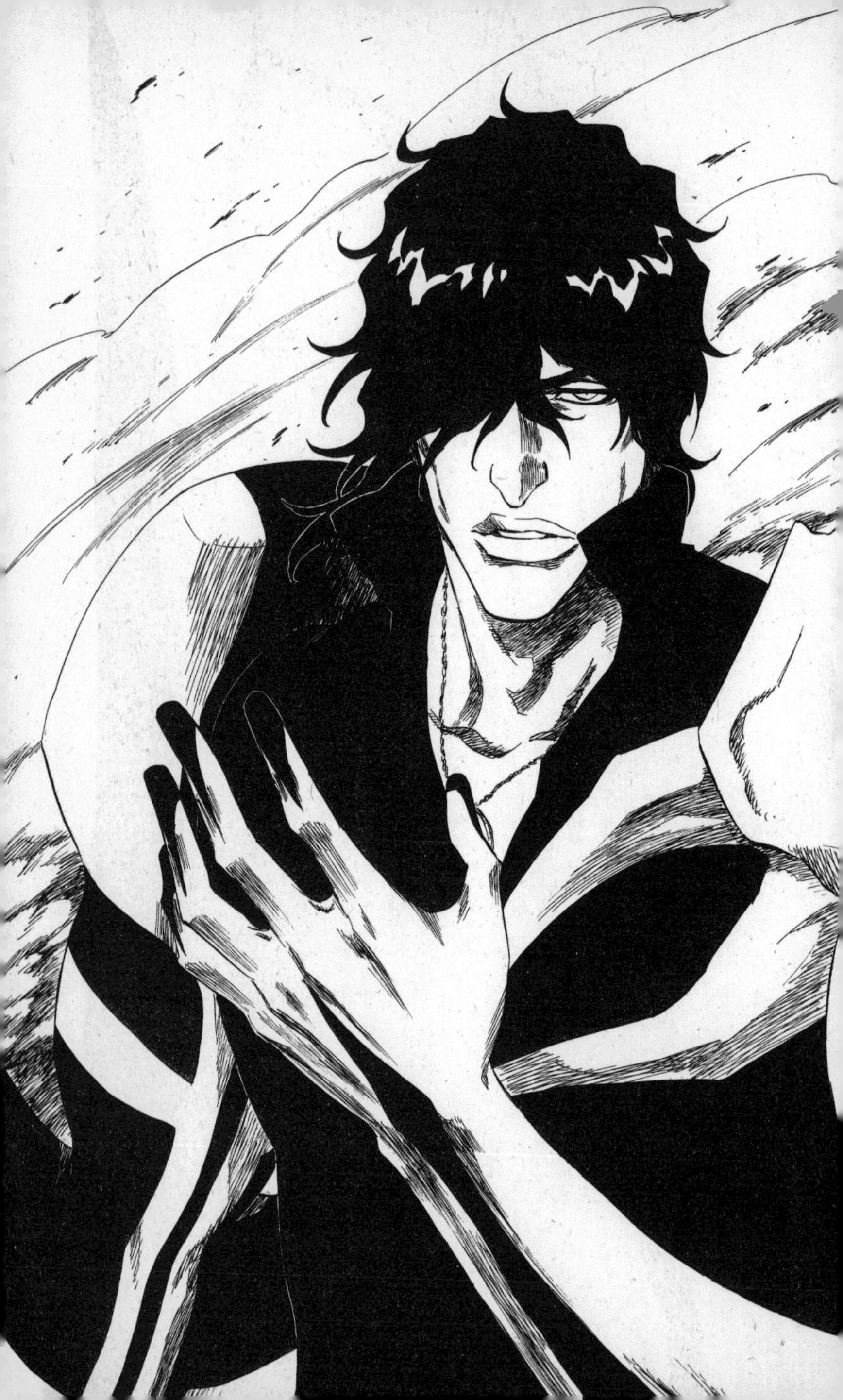

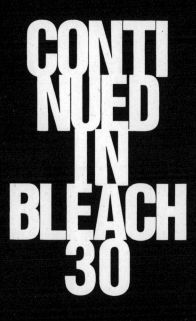

CONTINUED IN BLEACH 30

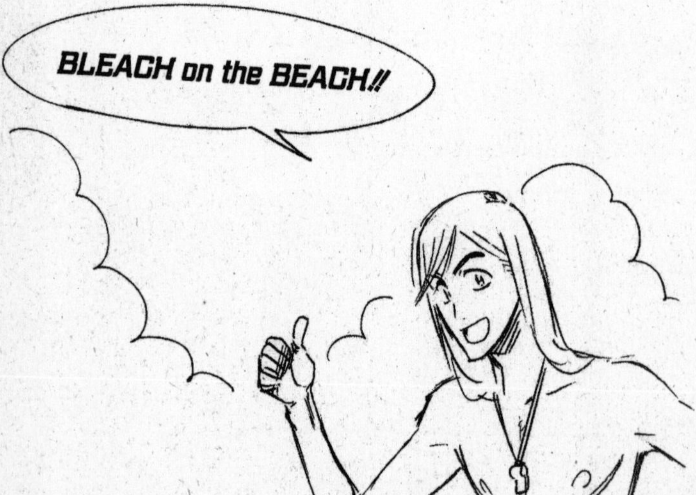
BLEACH on the BEACH!!

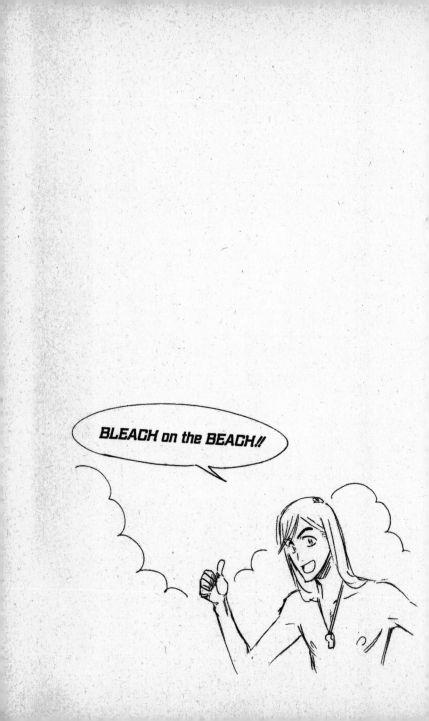

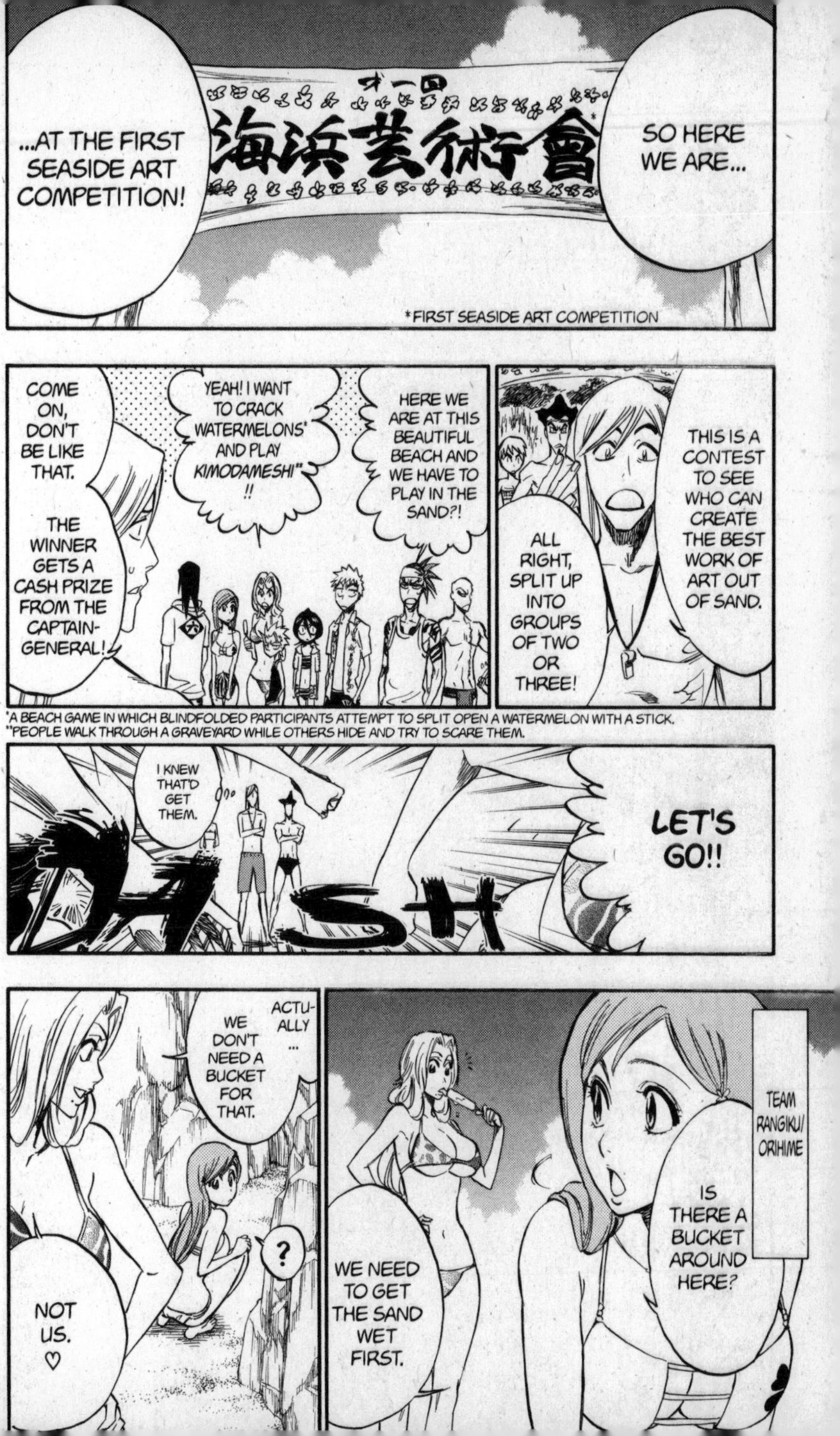
SO HERE WE ARE...
第一回
海浜芸術會*
...AT THE FIRST SEASIDE ART COMPETITION!
*FIRST SEASIDE ART COMPETITION
THIS IS A CONTEST TO SEE WHO CAN CREATE THE BEST WORK OF ART OUT OF SAND.
ALL RIGHT, SPLIT UP INTO GROUPS OF TWO OR THREE!
HERE WE ARE AT THIS BEAUTIFUL BEACH AND WE HAVE TO PLAY IN THE SAND?!
YEAH! I WANT TO CRACK WATERMELONS* AND PLAY *KIMODAMESHI*** !!
COME ON, DON'T BE LIKE THAT.
THE WINNER GETS A CASH PRIZE FROM THE CAPTAIN-GENERAL!
LET'S GO!!
I KNEW THAT'D GET THEM.
DASH
TEAM RANGIKU/ORIHIME
IS THERE A BUCKET AROUND HERE?
WE NEED TO GET THE SAND WET FIRST.
ACTUALLY...
WE DON'T NEED A BUCKET FOR THAT.
?
NOT US. ♡

*A BEACH GAME IN WHICH BLINDFOLDED PARTICIPANTS ATTEMPT TO SPLIT OPEN A WATERMELON WITH A STICK.
**PEOPLE WALK THROUGH A GRAVEYARD WHILE OTHERS HIDE AND TRY TO SCARE THEM.

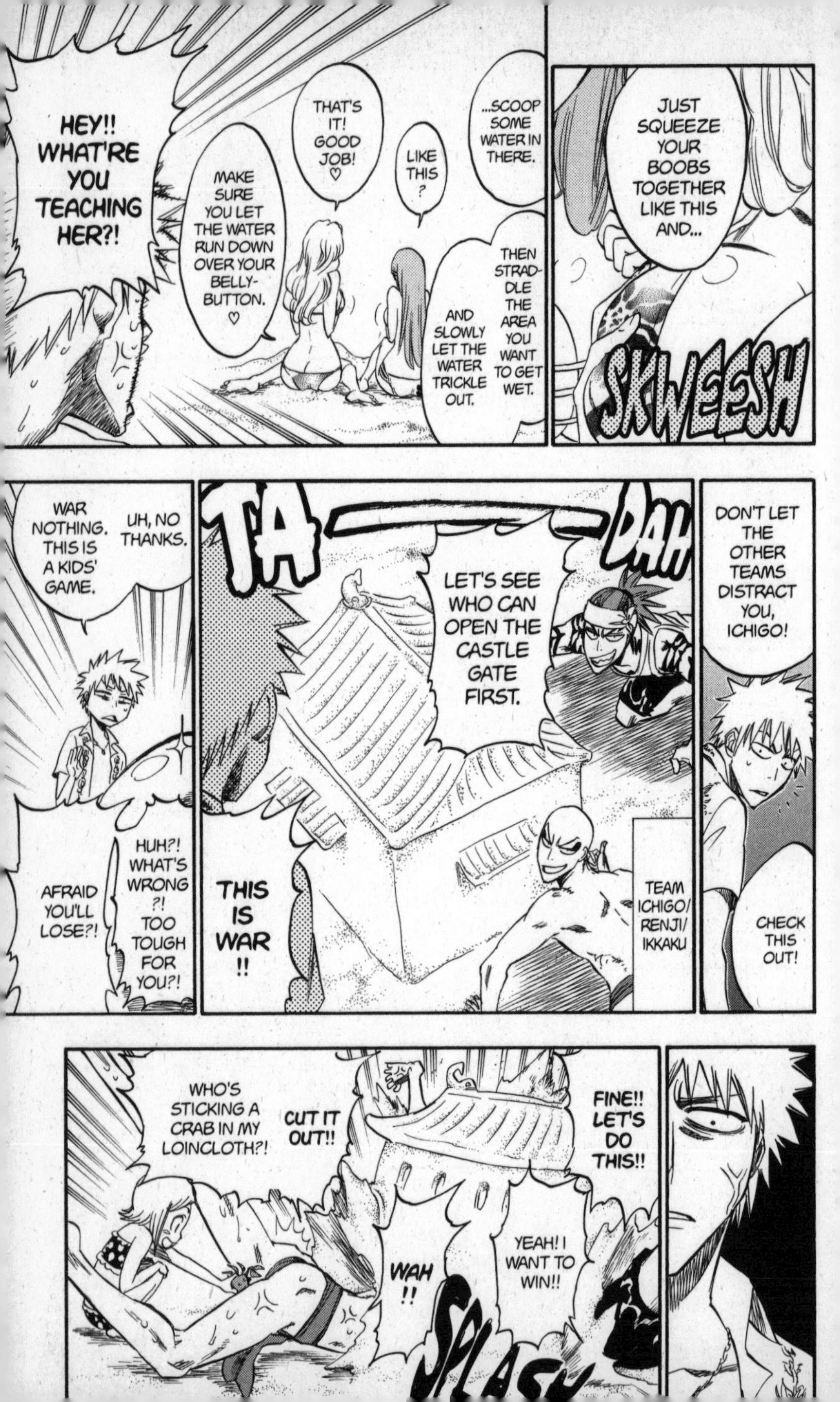
JUST SQUEEZE YOUR BOOBS TOGETHER LIKE THIS AND...
SKWEESH
...SCOOP SOME WATER IN THERE.
THEN STRADDLE THE AREA YOU WANT TO GET WET.
AND SLOWLY LET THE WATER TRICKLE OUT.
LIKE THIS?
THAT'S IT! GOOD JOB! ♡
MAKE SURE YOU LET THE WATER RUN DOWN OVER YOUR BELLY-BUTTON. ♡
HEY!! WHAT'RE YOU TEACHING HER?!
DON'T LET THE OTHER TEAMS DISTRACT YOU, ICHIGO!
CHECK THIS OUT!
TA—DAH
LET'S SEE WHO CAN OPEN THE CASTLE GATE FIRST.
TEAM ICHIGO/RENJI/IKKAKU
THIS IS WAR!!
HUH?! WHAT'S WRONG?! TOO TOUGH FOR YOU?!
AFRAID YOU'LL LOSE?!
UH, NO THANKS.
WAR NOTHING. THIS IS A KIDS' GAME.
FINE!! LET'S DO THIS!!
YEAH! I WANT TO WIN!!
CUT IT OUT!!
WHO'S STICKING A CRAB IN MY LOINCLOTH?!
WAH!!
SPLASH

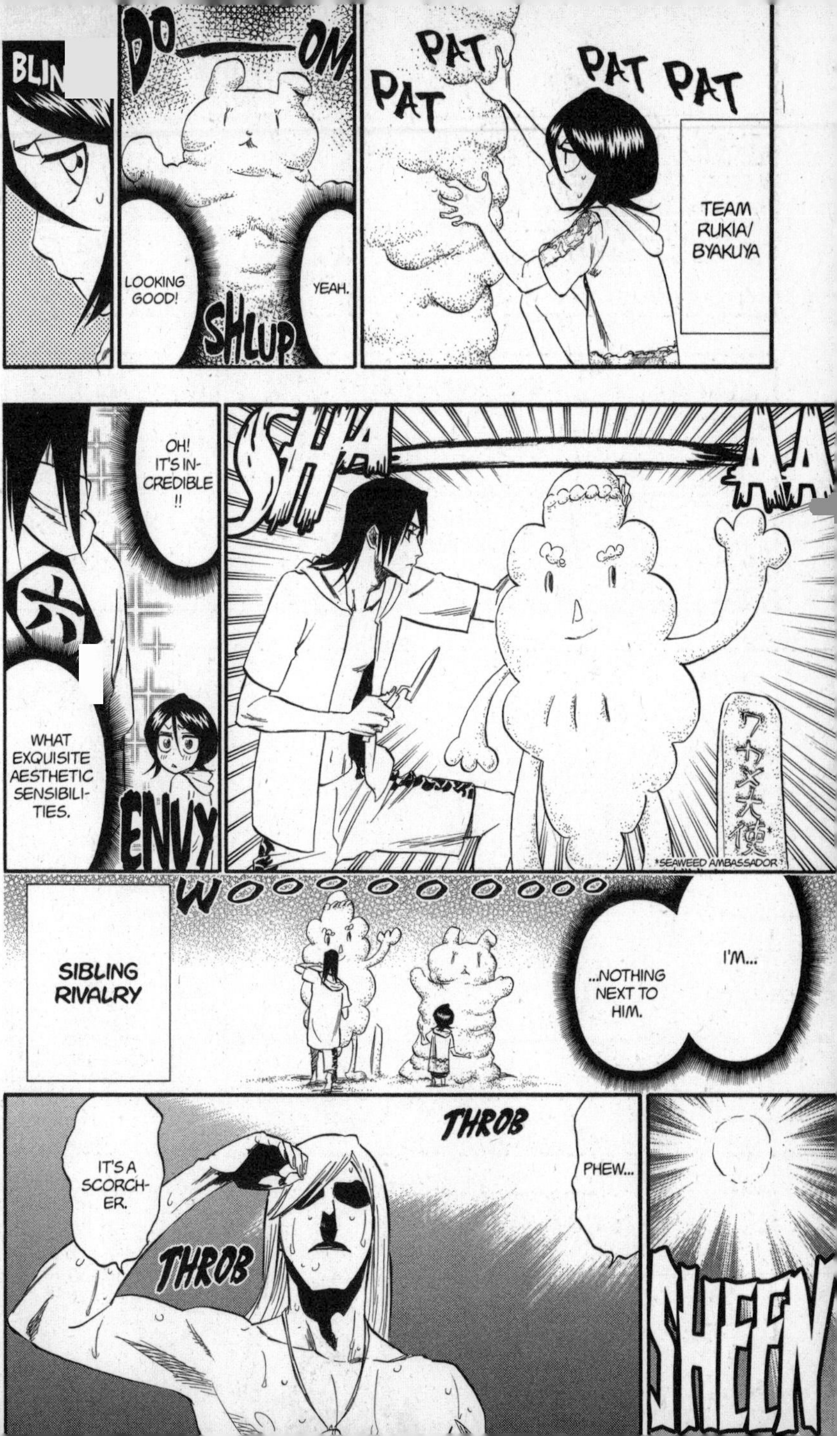
PAT PAT
PAT
PAT PAT
TEAM RUKIA/ BYAKUYA
DO—OM
YEAH.
LOOKING GOOD!
SHLUP
BLIN
SHA—AA
ワカメ大使*
*SEAWEED AMBASSADOR
OH! IT'S IN-CREDIBLE !!
WHAT EXQUISITE AESTHETIC SENSIBILI-TIES.
ENVY
I'M...
...NOTHING NEXT TO HIM.
WOOOOOOOOOO
SIBLING RIVALRY
SHEEN
PHEW...
THROB
IT'S A SCORCH-ER.
THROB

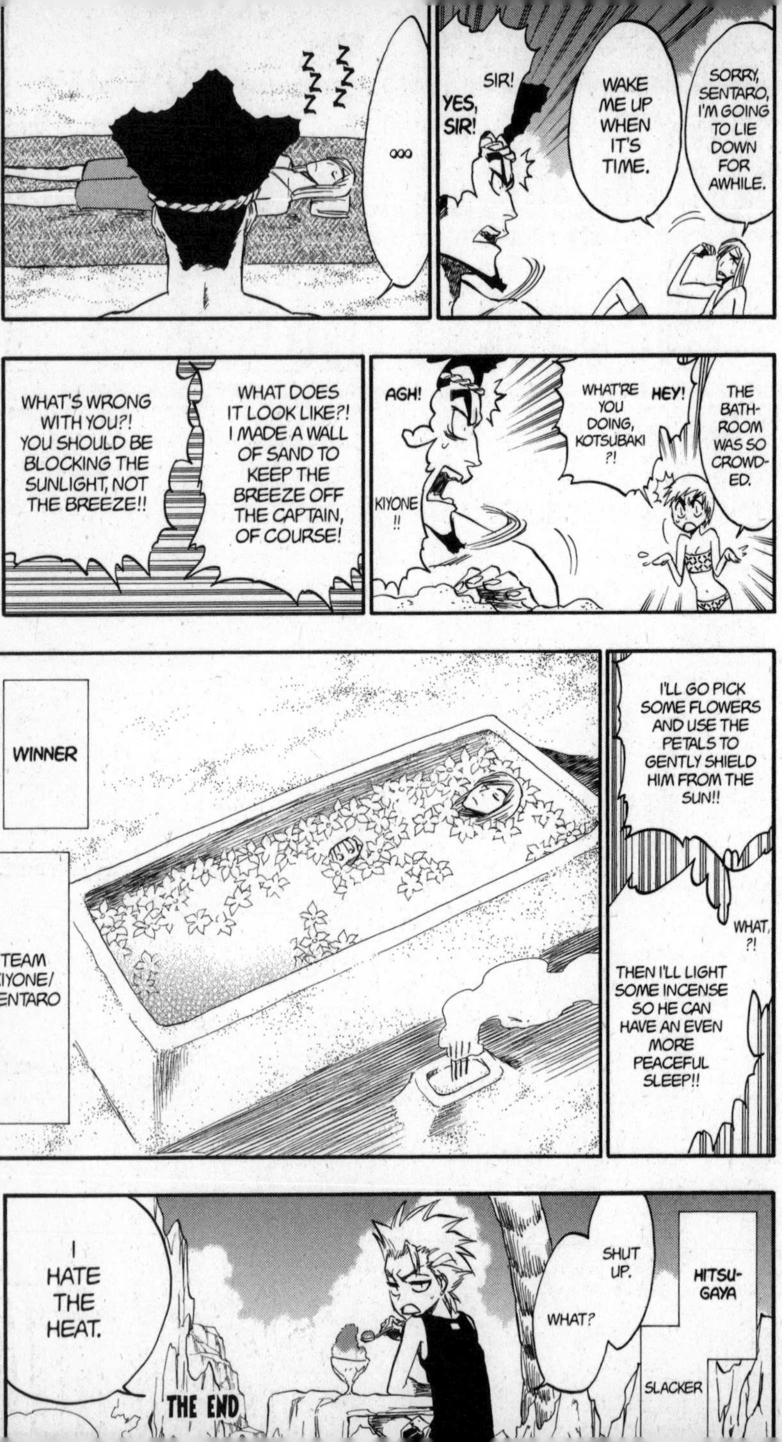
SORRY, SENTARO, I'M GOING TO LIE DOWN FOR AWHILE.
WAKE ME UP WHEN IT'S TIME.
SIR!
YES, SIR!
...
ZZZ
ZZZ
THE BATHROOM WAS SO CROWDED.
HEY!
WHAT'RE YOU DOING, KOTSUBAKI?!
AGH!
KIYONE!!
WHAT DOES IT LOOK LIKE?! I MADE A WALL OF SAND TO KEEP THE BREEZE OFF THE CAPTAIN, OF COURSE!
WHAT'S WRONG WITH YOU?! YOU SHOULD BE BLOCKING THE SUNLIGHT, NOT THE BREEZE!!
I'LL GO PICK SOME FLOWERS AND USE THE PETALS TO GENTLY SHIELD HIM FROM THE SUN!!
WHAT?!
THEN I'LL LIGHT SOME INCENSE SO HE CAN HAVE AN EVEN MORE PEACEFUL SLEEP!!
WINNER
TEAM KIYONE/SENTARO
HITSUGAYA
SLACKER
SHUT UP.
WHAT?
I HATE THE HEAT.
THE END

CONCEPT SKETCHES FOR THE BLEACH TV SHOW

"BOSQUE DE LOS MENOS"

HESE ARE DESIGN CONCEPTS FOR THE "FOREST OF MENOS" STORY ARC OF E *BLEACH* ANIME SERIES. I WASN'T ABLE TO INCLUDE ASHIDO IN THE MANGA BECAUSE OF TIMING ISSUES, SO I'M GLAD I GET TO INTRODUCE HIM HERE.

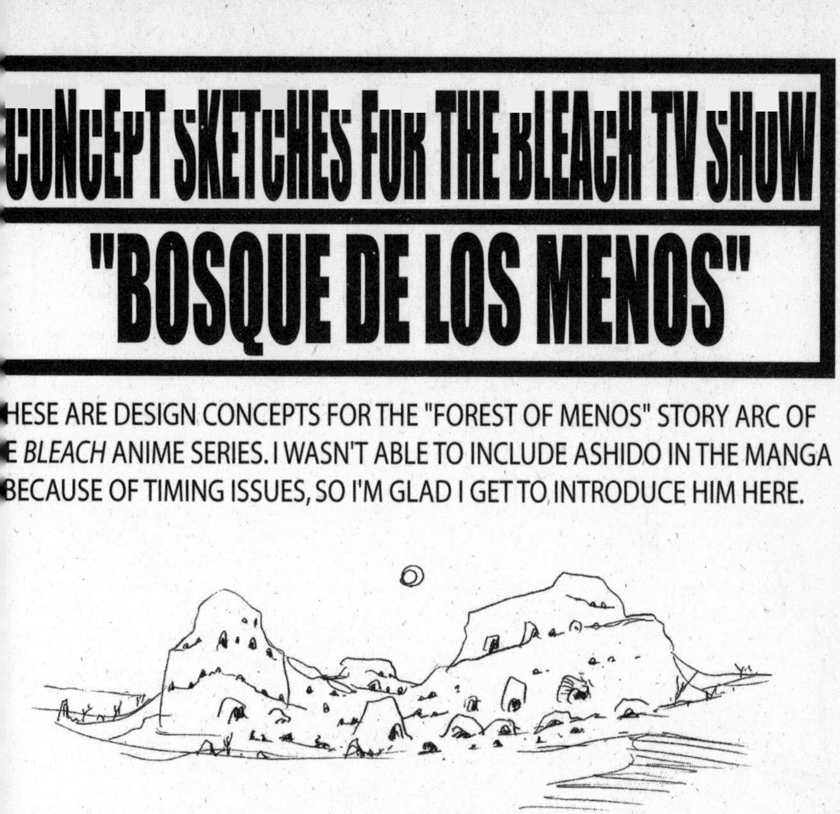

THE ADJUCHAS' DEN - SURFACE

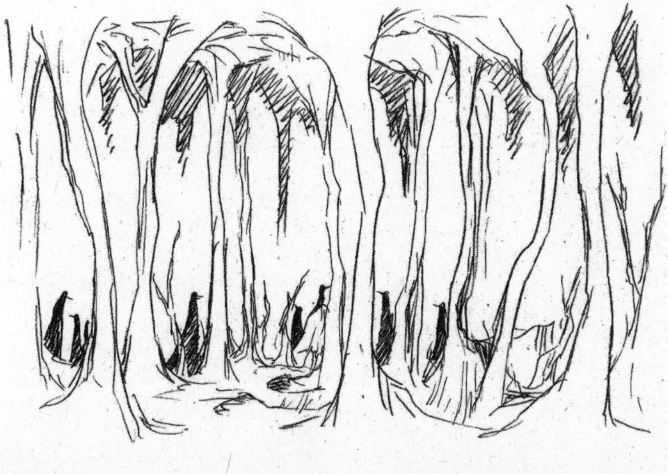

FOREST OF MENOS

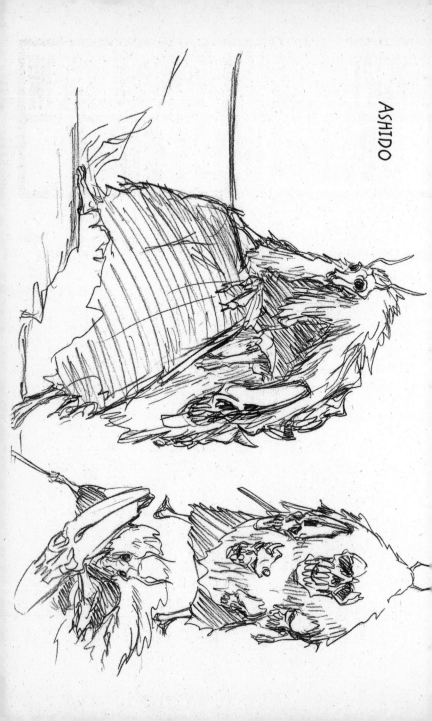

ASHIDO

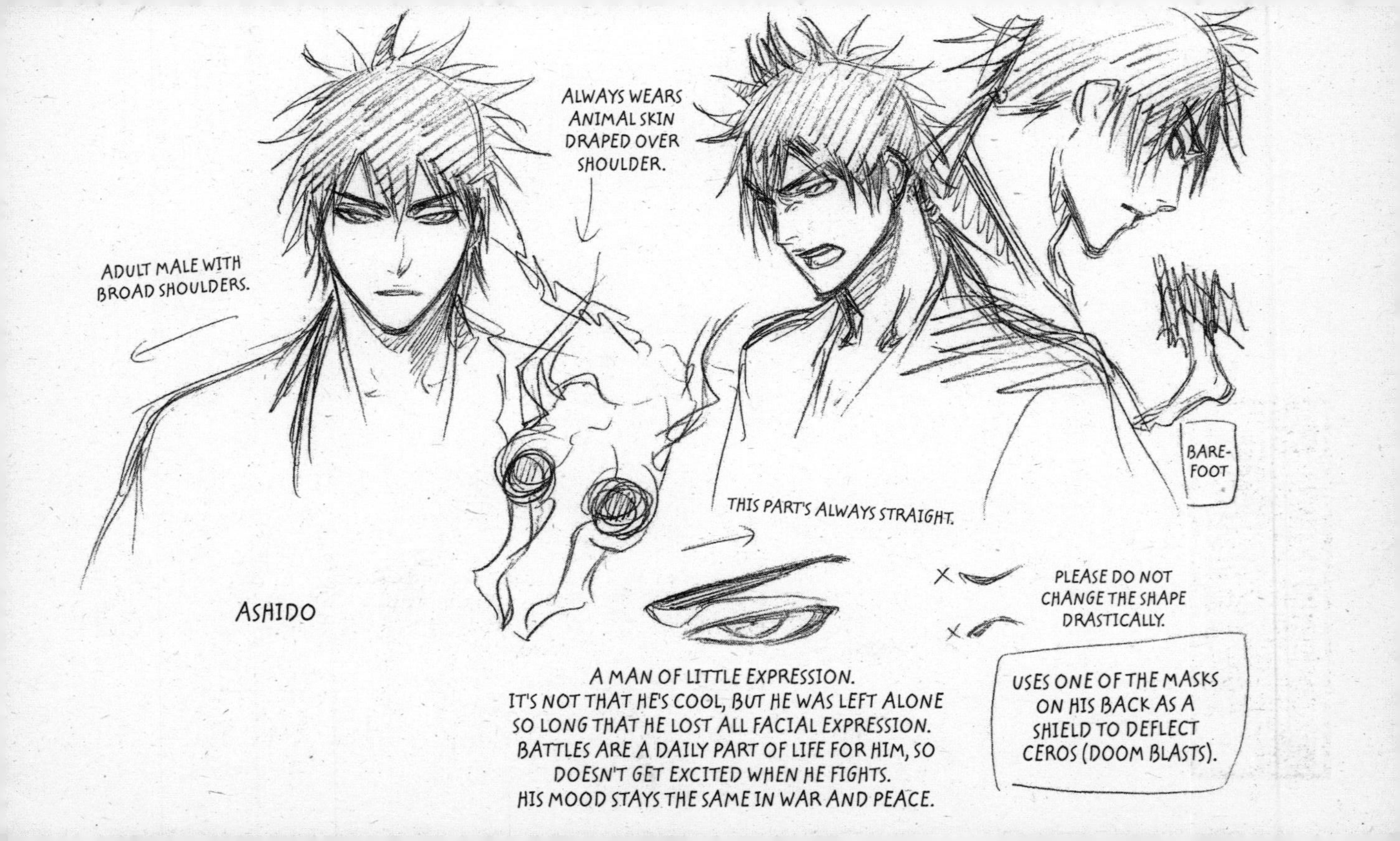
ASHIDO
ADULT MALE WITH BROAD SHOULDERS.
ALWAYS WEARS ANIMAL SKIN DRAPED OVER SHOULDER.
THIS PART'S ALWAYS STRAIGHT.
BARE-FOOT
PLEASE DO NOT CHANGE THE SHAPE DRASTICALLY.
USES ONE OF THE MASKS ON HIS BACK AS A SHIELD TO DEFLECT CEROS (DOOM BLASTS).
A MAN OF LITTLE EXPRESSION.
IT'S NOT THAT HE'S COOL, BUT HE WAS LEFT ALONE SO LONG THAT HE LOST ALL FACIAL EXPRESSION.
BATTLES ARE A DAILY PART OF LIFE FOR HIM, SO DOESN'T GET EXCITED WHEN HE FIGHTS.
HIS MOOD STAYS THE SAME IN WAR AND PEACE.

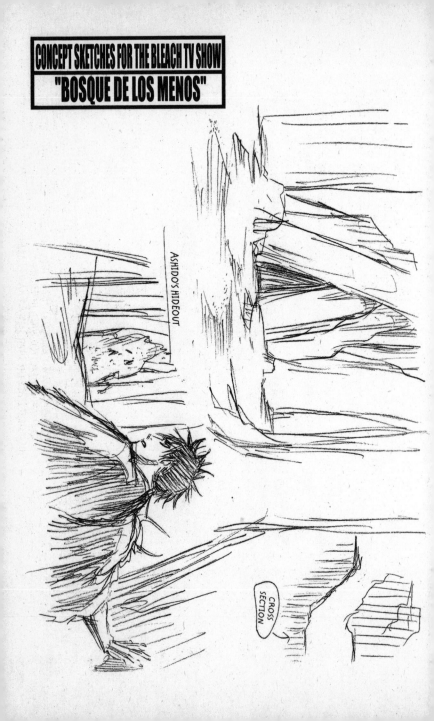

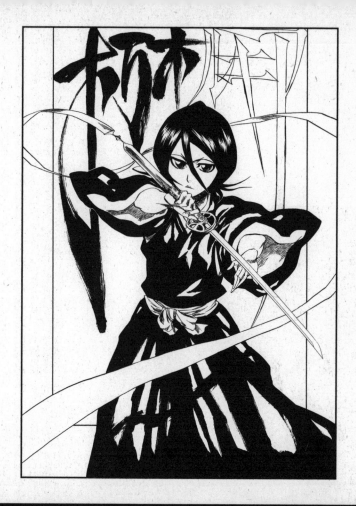

No one thought breaking into Hueco Mundo would be easy, but the challenges Ichigo and the rest of the rescue team face are more than just physical. Will the heroes make it to Aizen's fortress with their souls intact?!

Read it first in SHONEN JUMP magazine!

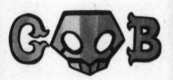

A *profile book* will be coming out at the same time as this volume. It's a collection of funny stories set in the Soul Society that ran in a *Jump*-related game magazine for a little over two years. But that just wasn't enough pages, so we created a real *Monthly Seireitei Bulletin* [v26 p.128]. It's filled with all kinds of features like "Go! Thirteen Court Guard Companies!" and "Okay, Seireitei Men." You'll find new comments from me in every feature. It was a lot of fun to do and I think you'll really enjoy reading it. Please pick up a copy.

-Tite Kubo

BLEACH is author Tite Kubo's second title. Kubo made his debut with ZOMBIEPOWDER., a four-volume series for WEEKLY SHONEN JUMP. To date, BLEACH has been translated into numerous languages and has also inspired an animated TV series that began airing in the U.S. in 2006. Beginning its serialization in 2001, BLEACH is still a mainstay in the pages of WEEKLY SHONEN JUMP. In 2005, BLEACH was awarded the prestigious Shogakukan Manga Award in the *shonen* (boys) category.

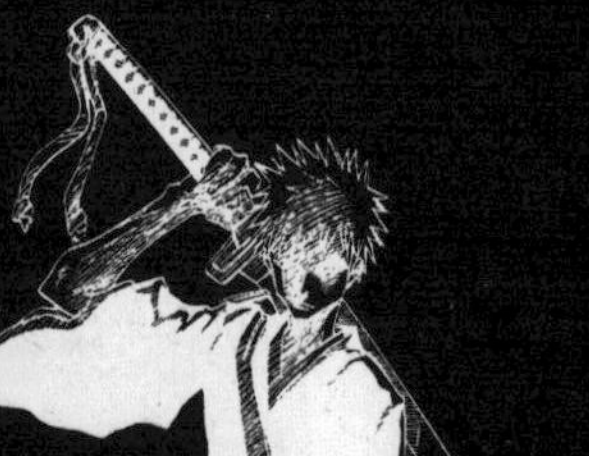

BLEACH
Vol. 29: THE SLASHING OPERA
SHONEN JUMP Manga Edition

This volume contains material that was originally published in English
in SHONEN JUMP #80-83. Artwork in the magazine may have been
altered slightly from what is presented in this volume.

STORY AND ART BY
TITE KUBO

English Adaptation/Lance Caselman
Translation/Joe Yamazaki
Touch-Up Art & Lettering/Mark McMurray
Design/Sean Lee
Editor/Pancha Diaz

VP, Production/Alvin Lu
VP, Publishing Licensing/Rika Inouye
VP, Sales & Product Marketing/Gonzalo Ferreyra
VP, Creative/Linda Espinosa
Publisher/Hyoe Narita

Published by VIZ Media, LLC
P.O. Box 77010
San Francisco, CA 94107

10 9 8 7 6 5 4 3 2 1
First printing, December 2009

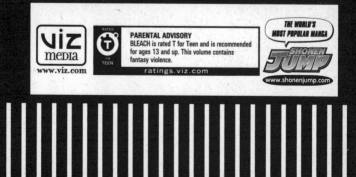

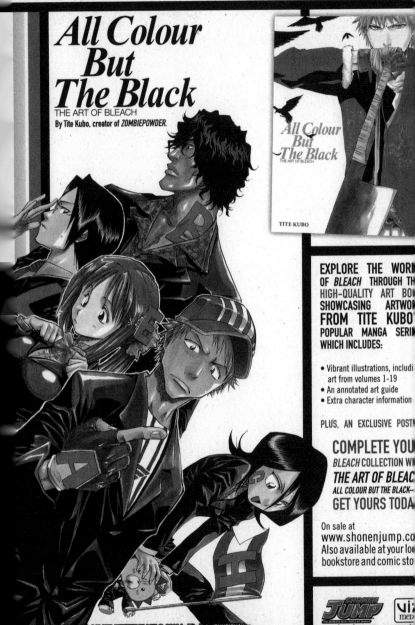

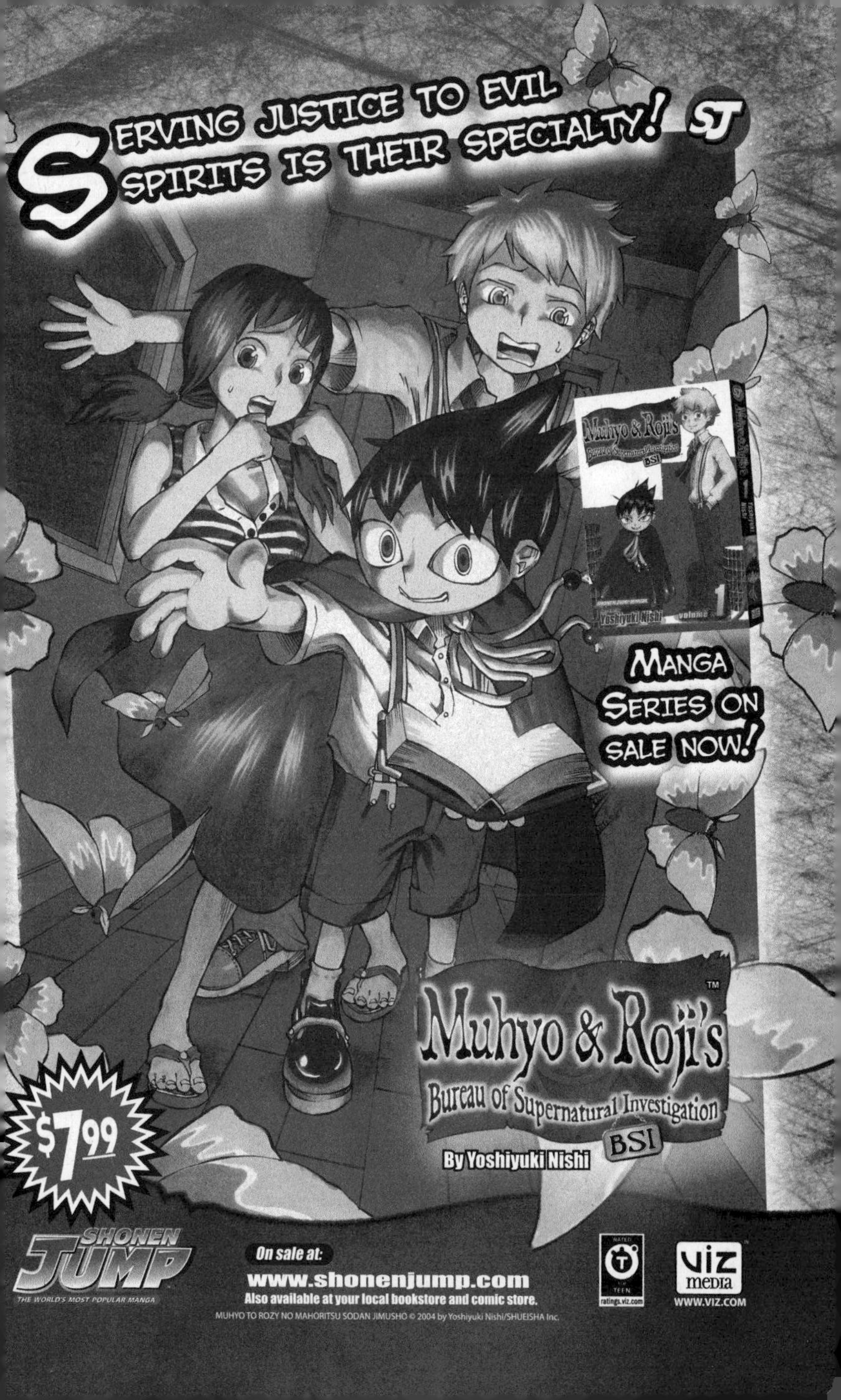
SERVING JUSTICE TO EVIL SPIRITS IS THEIR SPECIALTY!
SJ
MANGA SERIES ON SALE NOW!
Muhyo & Roji's
Bureau of Supernatural Investigation
BSI
By Yoshiyuki Nishi
$7.99
SHONEN JUMP
THE WORLD'S MOST POPULAR MANGA
On sale at:
www.shonenjump.com
Also available at your local bookstore and comic store.
MUHYO TO ROZY NO MAHORITSU SODAN JIMUSHO © 2004 by Yoshiyuki Nishi/SHUEISHA Inc.
ratings.viz.com
viz media
WWW.VIZ.COM

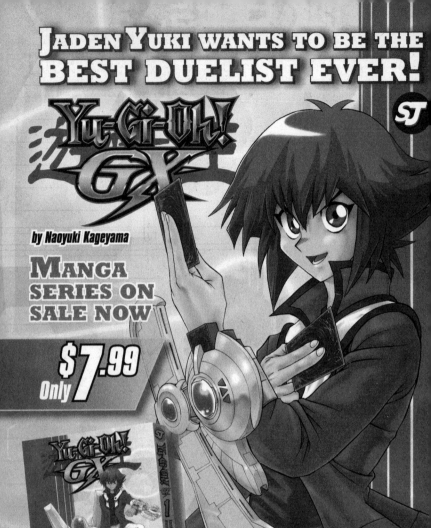

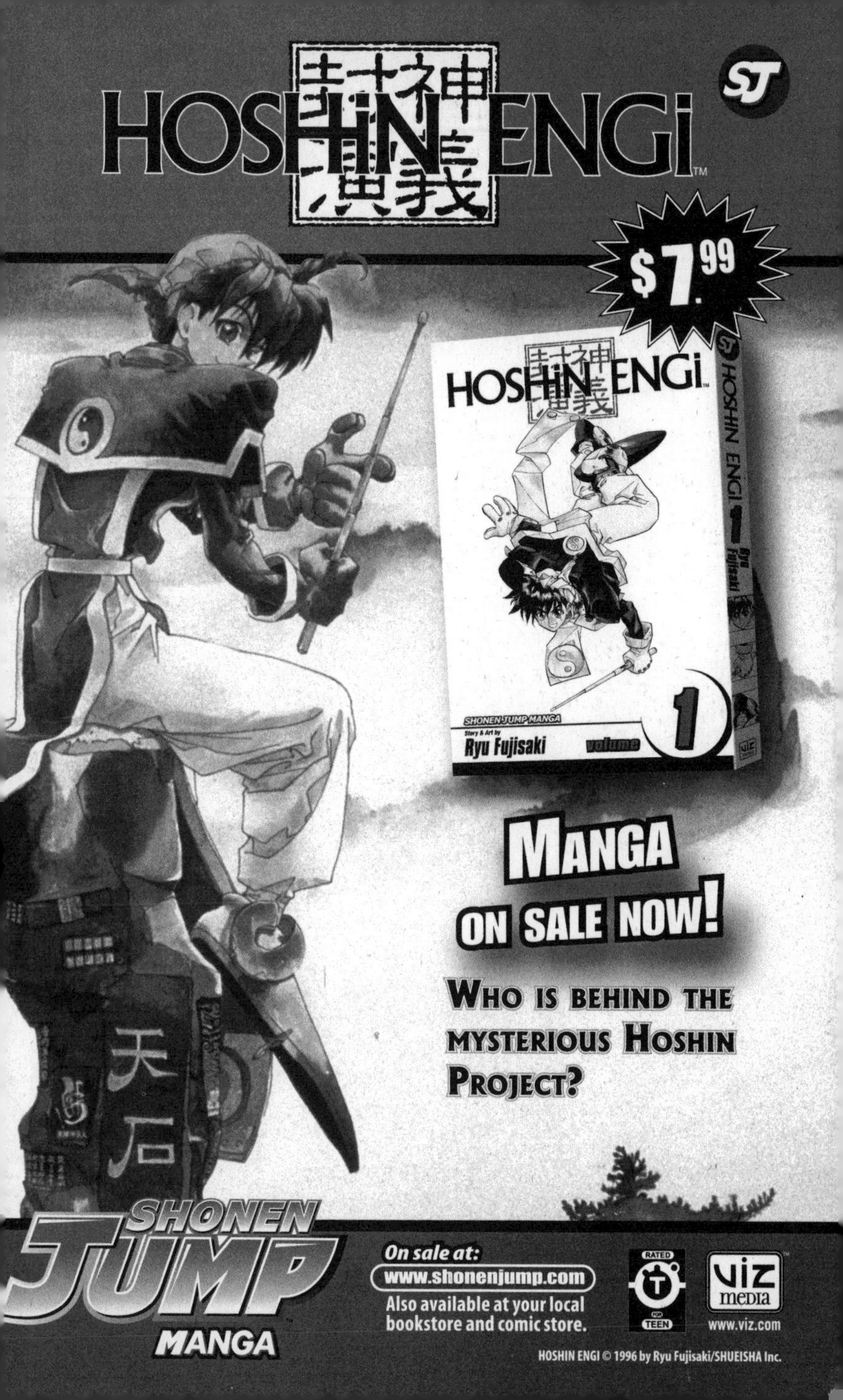

HOSHIN ENGI™
SJ
$7.99
HOSHIN ENGI™
SHONEN JUMP MANGA
Story & Art by
Ryu Fujisaki
volume 1
MANGA
ON SALE NOW!
WHO IS BEHIND THE MYSTERIOUS HOSHIN PROJECT?
SHONEN JUMP MANGA
On sale at:
www.shonenjump.com
Also available at your local bookstore and comic store.
RATED T TEEN
VIZ MEDIA
www.viz.com
HOSHIN ENGI © 1996 by Ryu Fujisaki/SHUEISHA Inc.

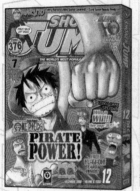
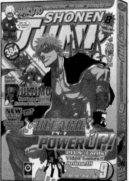
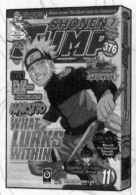

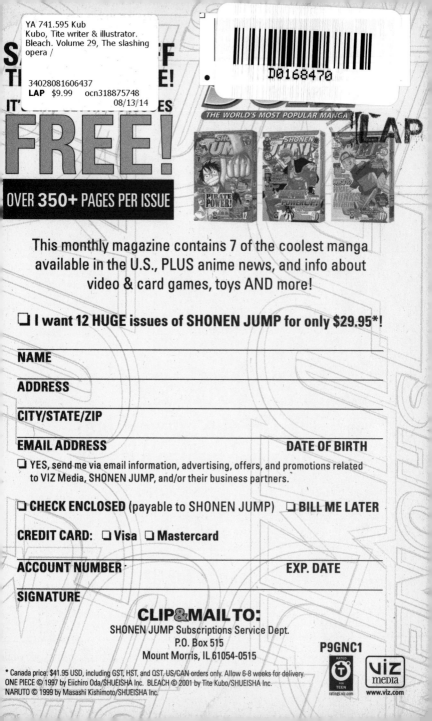